Masks of Empire

Masks of Empire

Edited by
ACHIN VANAIK

Tulika Books

Published by **Tulika Books**
44 (first floor), Shahpur Jat, New Delhi 110 049, India
www.tulikabooks.in

First published in India 2007

ISBN: 978-81-89487-22-5

For sale in India and South Asia only

Designed by Ram Rahman

Contents

Preface

The Transnational Institute (TNI), founded in the early 1970s and based in Amsterdam, was uniquely placed to initiate and carry out this book project, and all the contributors are in one way or the other associated with it. The TNI is both a research body devoted to addressing various developmental problems of the South and their linkages to practices and perspectives of the countries and institutions of the North; and (perhaps uniquely) a long-standing international fellowship of scholars–activists from the South and North bound by a shared commitment to a 'radical necessity' – the struggle for a qualitatively more humane and just world order.

The fellows, associates, researchers and friends of TNI all have their individual areas of expertise and concerns, ranging from issues of water conflicts to the iniquities of the World Trade Organization, from the dangers of nuclear weaponization to promoting solidarities with the anti-invasion and anti-Occupation movements of Iraq and the search for a just resolution of the Israel–Palestine conflict. Given its intrinsic character, the central themes of this book meshed naturally with the ongoing preoccupations of the respective contributors and the TNI. What is more, almost all the chapters were subjected to collective discussion and argument, often fierce, the result being that there were substantial revisions in response to criticisms of style and content. Again, it was felt that this was another important way to utilize the advantages of a group like the TNI, to make this volume a genuinely collective work and not just a collection of disparate essays simply brought together by the editor.

First of all, grateful thanks must be expressed to all those who have written for this volume. They took time off from their busy schedules and commitments not just to write and rewrite, but in most cases to attend repeated rounds of discussions that took place in Amsterdam, The Netherlands and Montevideo, Uruguay, where initial drafts were subjected to much argumentative scrutiny. Apart from the contributors, mention must be made of those whose contributions to these discussions were invaluable, and of others without whose organizational skills this project would never have got off the ground, let alone reached fruition. To Praful Bidwai, Thomas E. Reifer, Daniel Chavez and Laura Corradi de Portillo, many, many thanks.

A special acknowledgement must go to two others. Fiona Dove, Director of the Transnational Institute (TNI), was the real nurturer of this book project. She perceived immediately that the theme of this study fitted naturally into both the political commitments of TNI and into existing preoccupations and expertise of so many of the TNI family of fellows, associates and friends. She then proceeded to exercise her own formidable powers of organization and persuasion to make sure the project was realized. Indispensable to this was also the role of Wilbert van der Zeijden, who took charge of much of the administrative and coordinating responsibilities essential to bringing out this book. All this was in addition to the deep involvement of both in discussions and criticisms which led to an improved final product. Last but not the least, a very special thanks to 'Wilbert's sister', Marjoleine van der Zeijden, who was really the guiding spirit behind all our endeavours. We hope she approves of what we have done.

The South Asian edition of this book would not have been possible without Anil Chaudhury, Director of Popular Education and Action Centre (PEACE). His long-standing commitment to supporting all kinds of progressive works and causes, beyond his own work with its already overburdening responsibilities, has inspired many others and earned him much appreciation, even if this has not been articulated as often as it should.

ACHIN VANAIK

Foreword

Tariq Ali

The Transnational Institute's self-description as a collective of scholars–activists is fully vindicated by the essays in this timely reader, skilfully edited by Achin Vanaik. It comes at a time when there is much talk of the decline of US power, of imperial overreaching, of Iraq as a twenty-first century Vietnam, of the rise of China, and so on.

Only those blinded by factional prejudice can fail to see the disaster that is post-Occupation Iraq. And, as a few of us argued at the time, the occupation of Afghanistan was bound to lead to a resistance of some sort. That, too, has now happened and the NATO occupation forces are under daily attack. One can add to this the debacle in Lebanon, where the United States-backed Israeli assault on that country, designed to transform it into a protectorate on the Jordanian model, failed to achieve its aim due exclusively to the resistance mounted by Hezbollah.

These setbacks will have differential impacts on the countries that launched the wars and occupations, but what do they tell us about the decline of US power? Very little. The notion that these failures, on their own, will lead a meek and chastened Empire to slink away from its role in the world is pure illusion.

We already knew that whenever the West sends in ground troops to occupy a country, it becomes vulnerable to resistance forces. Vietnam, in the last century, was the defeat that rankled the most in Washington and put a stop to imperial adventures for a while. Even after that politico-military defeat, the United States emerged triumphant – it built an alliance with China and helped the Soviet Union to implode. Vietnam itself is today occupied by global corporations.

What of the US economy? That it is structurally weak is recognized even by its partisans, but even an economic crisis does not mean the automatic end of the Empire. In an interview with the *Manchester Guardian* in 1931, the exiled Soviet leader Leon Trotsky explained how in 1928 he had told his comrades in Moscow that even though the economic crisis in the United States was deepening,

> there is no justification whatsoever for the attempt to conclude from this that the hegemony of North America will be restricted or weakened. Such a conclusion can lead only to the grossest strategic errors. Just the contrary is the case. In the period of crisis the hegemony of the United States will operate more completely, more openly and more ruthlessly than in the period of boom. . . .

In today's globalized world this is even more so. True that China is the new workshop of the world. Income distribution is more unequal than that of the United States. It does not have to bother with workers' rights since there are no trade unions worth the name. True that by 2010 the Chinese economy will be double the size of the German (currently ranked third in the world) and will soon probably overtake Japan. But this will not automatically lead to inter-imperial contradictions. First, because China is not an imperial power. Second, because its economy is, till now, heavily dependent on the US market. Third, because even the most effective detective agencies have yet to discover a Chinese foreign policy, apart from the crudest self-interest. In September 2006, the Chinese ambassador to Zambia sought to mimic his US equivalents by publicly denouncing a Presidential candidate who had dared attack Chinese investment practices in his country.

The political challenge to the United States' hegemony, embryonic and rudimentary but necessary, is emerging in South America. The victories of Chávez in Venezuela and Morales in Bolivia have been helped by the human capital of teachers and doctors produced in Cuba. But even here, it would be foolish to exaggerate. This is the beginning of something different, but it is too early to predict how far it will or can go. If Lula's Brazil had moved in a similar direction the whole continent could have been mobilized, but the Brazilian turned out to be a tropical version of Tony Blair.

Where the Empire has suffered a serious blow is in its ideological pretensions. All talk of 'humanitarian' wars has now been seen for what it is – a mask designed to make the new imperial offensive more palatable. Guantánamo and the renditions with full European Union collaboration have shown us the world as it is. Yesterday's 'heroes' Adam Michnik and Václav Havel support US policies even more blindly than their predecessors supported the Soviet Union (Imre Nagy and Alexander Dubcek, to name but two, did resist the Soviet Union). The Eastern European states have now become Washington's willing satellites, vying with each other to be helpful. Humanitarian torture, we must understand, is qualitatively different from authoritarian torture. The Geneva Convention should be altered accordingly.

The widespread use of torture by the West has undoubtedly shocked some of its citizens. Hence the global impact of the torture photographs that too might have remained hidden had not a US network decided to air them, six months later. The Taguba inquiry also confirmed independent reports that US soldiers had raped women prisoners. Some of them were forced to bare their breasts for the camera. The women prisoners sent messages to the Resistance pleading with them to bomb and destroy the prison and obliterate their shame and suffering. Amal Kadham Swadi, an Iraqi woman lawyer who had been given permission in November 2003 to visit a US military base in Baghdad, told *The Guardian*:

> She was the only woman who would talk about her case. She was crying. She told us she had been raped. Several American soldiers had raped her. She had tried to fight them off, and they had hurt her arm. She showed us the stitches. She told us, 'We have daughters and husbands. For God's sake don't tell anyone about this.'

There is another memento from the Occupation – a photograph of a US soldier having sex with an Iraqi woman. War as pornography. This is imperial rule at its most raw and we have seen it before. It has had better moments. And it certainly could be better occupied. For a start it might heed the prudent words of an Iraqi prisoner: 'We need electricity in our homes, not up the arse.'

Intellectual amnesia is widespread. It is convenient to forget the past. What else can explain the genuine surprise that was evinced by so many people when the torture was made public? One does not expect most people to remember the Inquisition or the ordeal by fire or the heresy-hunters of Christianity who tortured and killed Cathars and Albigensians or, later, the majestic polemic by Voltaire against the cruelty of torture. But what about the last century? Have the citizens of the North forgotten what happened in South America, Asia and Africa less than fifty years ago? The former US President Clinton had to apologize publicly to the people of Central America for the horrors inflicted on them by the security services of their own countries, trained, armed and backed by those of the United States. When they know that dead Iraqi bodies are not even counted, why the surprise that the live ones are mistreated? And now that we have been told that 'US lawyers said that torture laws could be violated' (front-page headline, *Financial Times,* Tuesday, 8 June 2004) and 'legal statutes against torture could not override Mr Bush's inherent powers', it is pointless to pretend that the fun-loving GIs were indulging in some spontaneous fun. Orders had come from above. The model was to be a mixture of Gaza and Guantánamo. The soldiers were wrong to obey orders, but who will punish their leaders?

I was in Egypt and Lebanon when news of the torture broke. I did not meet a single person (not even among Europeans and North Americans who work there) who was surprised. In the post-colonial world, the echoes of history have never ceased to resonate. And the tortures in Iraq revived memories of Aden and Algeria, Vietnam and Ireland, and, yes, Palestine. In Vietnam the atrocities were daily and unremitting. Some officers wore necklaces that consisted of the ears of tortured Vietnamese prisoners. The Sinn Fein leader, Gerry Adams, who in his official reincarnation as a statesman became a regular visitor to the Clinton White House and No. 10 Downing Street, nonetheless felt obliged to recall how he and other 'terrorists' were tortured and photographed in a British colonial prison in Ireland during the 1970s:

> Some were stripped naked and had black hessian bags placed over their heads. These bags kept out all light and extended down over the head to shoulders. . . . They were beaten with batons and fists on the testicles and kidneys and kicked between the legs. . . . Arms were twisted, fingers were twisted, ribs were pummelled, objects were shoved up the anus, they were burned with matches and treated to games of Russian roulette. . . . (*The Guardian*, 5 June 2004: 26)

The Palestinian peace activist Mustafa Barghouti wrote of what is still happening in Israeli prisons:

> The pictures of American soldiers torturing prisoners at the Abu Ghraib prison in Iraq have shocked the world. To the Palestinian people however, these photographs of hooded or naked figures come as no surprise. For the tens of thousands of Palestinians who have served time in Israeli prisons, the pictures only bring back memories of their own torture. Despite all the evidence to the contrary, including the death or maiming of numerous Palestinian prisoners, Israel continues to deny that torture is used in its prisons. Over 7000 Palestinian prisoners currently remain in Israeli prisons, many of them held without charge or trial. Most will have suffered some degree of torture before their release. It is shocking to recognize that around 650,000 Palestinians have spent time in Israeli custody since 1967, most of them adult males. This means that almost every second Palestinian adult male has been imprisoned.

One reason for the collective memory loss in the West could be the result of a superiority complex. We won. We defeated the 'Evil Empire'. We are the best. Our culture, our civilization is infinitely more advanced than anything else. If this is the common sense of the epoch as far as Western citizens are concerned, then the shock waves created by the torture revelations at Abu Ghraib become more explicable. One of the features of domination is that those at home or abroad who do not identify with it are categorized as the enemy. It has always been thus. Long live dissidence.

Introduction

Achin Vanaik

> 'I am ready,' said the emperor. 'Does not my suit fit me marvellously?' Then he turned once more to the looking-glass, that people should think he admired his garments. . . . The emperor marched in the procession under the beautiful canopy, and all who saw him in the street and out of the windows exclaimed: 'Indeed, the emperor's new suit is incomparable! What a long train he has! How well it fits him!'. . . 'But he has nothing on at all,' said a little child at last. 'Good heavens! Listen to the voice of an innocent child,' said the father, and one whispered to the other what the child had said. 'But he has nothing on at all,' cried at last the whole people.
>
> Hans Christian Andersen, *The Emperor's New Clothes*

The United States today is militarily by far the most powerful country in the world. Who can doubt this? It should not surprise anyone that its leading elites seek to sustain, extend and strengthen the United States' political dominance. The major lines of division within the elites are on how to go about doing this. Indeed, the terms of discourse have now shifted so dramatically that the language of Empire and Empire-building have become respectable, and worthy of a hearing in the mainstream media in the United States. Even in Europe there is a greater willingness than in the decades past to talk of the 'benevolence of Empire', or of the United States as the 'benevolent' imperial power, and of how the expansion of this empire can now be understood as the precondition for the 'expansion of freedom'. An additional consequence of the emergence of this new political discourse is a much greater willingness to favourably reassess previous imperialisms such as the Pax Britannica, with a view to providing historical insights and advice on the constitution of a Pax Americana. Niall Ferguson's recent works (Ferguson 2004) are but one striking example of this turn towards a modern 'White Man's Burden' – the claim that British imperialism was (and by analogy US imperial behaviour is) primarily of benefit to its supposed victims, to the colonized rather than to the colonizers. The former were the real beneficiaries, the liberated, rather than the exploited or the oppressed!

But if such rightwing effervescence is to be expected in today's intellectual climate, perhaps more disturbing is how liberal intellectuals like John L.

Gaddis and Paul Kennedy are now willing to lend legitimacy and an attentive ear to such views (Gaddis 2004; Kennedy 2004). If liberals justified US foreign policy behaviour as a necessary 'defensive posture' to 'contain' the threat of Communism and the USSR during the Cold War, today the blatantly offensive character of US foreign policy behaviour can no longer be disguised. It is, therefore, in greater need than ever before of the legitimizing discourses that many North American and European intellectuals of the right and 'liberal' centre seem eager to provide. One possible overarching discourse – of 'expanding freedom' through imperial behaviour – is unable to quite fit the bill. A range of such legitimizing discourses is required partly because global domination necessitates not just one all-encompassing discourse but several separate discourses to justify US actions in different parts of the world having their distinctive political contexts, that is, where there exist variant alliance arrangements and rationales for US presence.

This book, therefore, aims to delineate, analyse and evaluate these discourses to expose their role in the United State's empire project. At the same time although the components of the legitimizing discourses may differ, they remain a part of an over-all package – of one overarching imperial project. These discourses have their separate dynamics and highlight different 'dangers' and 'concerns' to the United States. Yet, they also have their areas of overlap and reinforcement which need to be uncovered. Such overlaps mean that the United States can and does shift from the use of one discourse to another. For example, justifications for the invasion of Iraq have shifted from 'weapons of mass destruction' to 'regime change' to 'fighting terrorism', and Washington has continued to justify the Occupation via periodic slippages between, and combinations of, the latter two themes, all 'in the name of democracy'. The objective here is to reveal the origins, nature and purposes of these ideological constructions and political discourses, as well as the consequences of their application in particular geographical contexts. It should be clear that this is a project to dissect the 'software' of US empire-building. The book is not primarily about the hardware or military foundations of empire-building nor does it aim to be a narrative about the conduct and course of US foreign policy.

The thematic structure of the book then is as follows: Since the end of the Cold War, in place of the one overarching ideological banner of the Cold War-era of 'defending the free world' against the Communist threat, there have emerged six ideological banners which, to greater or lesser extent, serve the interests of US empire-building. The book is structured around these six banners of empire-building: (i) the Global War on Terror (GWOT); (ii) Weapons of Mass Destruction in the 'wrong hands'; (iii) Failed States; (iv) the necessity and justice of external and forcible Humanitarian Intervention; (v) Regime Change in the name of democracy; and (vi) the War on Narcotics.

The domains in which consent is to be elicited through use of these banners are threefold. This is, primarily, the domestic population of the United States itself. Then, there are the elites, governments and general public of the target areas of US imperial activity, be these Central and West Asia (the Middle East) or the countries of Upper Amazonia. There is, finally, the rest of the world comprised of countries that might be allies, neutral or critics of the United States, but whose governments and publics also need to be persuaded of the righteousness of US policies. None of these six banners are purely functional for the purposes of empire-building. They all refer to concerns that actually predate the end of the Cold War, though it is after the collapse of the Soviet Union that most got elevated in importance, through a calculated US projection, and achieved a much stronger public and international resonance. Besides, they all represent genuine problems and dangers, regardless of how discourses about them are manipulated, that need to be addressed in their own right. That is why the extent to which each banner is functional for empire also varies. Some are more useful than others, even when their political and geographical terrains of application are separated and do not overlap.

Keeping all this in mind, each of the chapters on these six themes are broadly united by their common concern: (a) to identify the origins or emergence of the particular legitimizing discourse or ideological banner; (b) to examine its character and composition; (c) to point out the purposes or aims that lie behind the unfolding of the banner; (d) to evaluate how effective the use of the banner has actually been; (e) to highlight the falsity of the banner or the dishonesties, deceits and hypocrisies that have guided or lain behind its use; and (f) to suggest how one should morally and practically address the particular problems, be they terrorism, violation of universal human rights, proliferation of weapons of mass destruction or the issue of opium–heroin and cocaine production, distribution and use.

These six chapter presentations – the section on the ideological banners – are preceded by three other chapter contributions. Empires are always constructed for purposes of accumulating power and wealth for some, even if there may be many who seek to justify empire in the name of prosperity for all. There is, then, always an economics of empire. The US imperial project today, unlike the ones of the capitalist past, is an informal one. It is not a formal colonization project of establishing long term direct foreign rule, but one of ensuring an indirect domination and an enduring and significant influence on local elites and their governments. How is this to be achieved? The organization of consent comes in three types. There is active consent which is the best of all where local elites and the middle classes and even sections of the population lower down are persuaded to believe that such indirect domination or 'influence' is good because they have come to share the values that the hegemonizer claims to uphold, be these the fight against terrorism, the assurance of democracy, or the promise of prosperity. The second form of consent is passive. But this is essentially resignation in the face of a dominant power rather than an enthusiastic embrace of its proclaimed values and promises, and, therefore, carries the potential of being politically unstable for empire.

The third form is bought consent – not just the promise of prosperity for collaborating groups, but also the institutionalized realization of such benefits. And if the price for such prosperity is rising inequality for some and deprivation for substantial others – so be it. This is where the current neoliberal economic globalization and the US imperial project converge. They are the two sides of the same coin as US political expansion also aims to expand neoliberalism. An expanding neoliberalism (as economic doctrine and policy direction) promotes and helps stabilize the project of securing US political hegemony globally, through the recruitment of cohort groups materially benefiting from such expansion. This means that even this survey essentially of the software of empire, finds it necessary to precede its dissection of legitimizing discourses by an initial overview of the character of the current global economy, its distinctive characteristics and the roles played by US capital, economically and financially, and by its dominant classes through and besides the US government. This initial overview is followed by two other chapters that examine the ideological preconditions that underlie both the global ascendance of neoliberalism as the economic and social 'common sense' of our times, and the role played by the belief in American exceptionalism.

The ascendance of neoliberalism was ideologically not a happenstance. To begin with, it was systematically prepared for by the United States and the United Kingdom from the late 1970s, but has since spread its influence worldwide. This is the story par excellence of the organization of consent, of creating 'hegemony', one that merits study even, indeed especially, for its opponents. This chapter also carries forward the preceding discussion of the economics of empire by uncovering the institutional and ideological foundations that have led to neoliberal practices themselves. Moreover, the six legitimizing discourses of the US right and centre, after the end of the Cold War, benefited from the rightward shift in the intellectual–political climate from the late 1970s onwards, that is, during the rise of neoliberalism in economic, social and political thought. This came about through a deliberately constructed and systematic intellectual–institutional process in the United States, the West and even more widely in the world. Empire-promoting doctrines since the end of the Cold War have also emerged through some of these established mechanisms and structures of the fast rising and increasingly hegemonic right.

'Americanism' or 'American Exceptionalism' is the belief in the special worth and mission of the US globally. It is the belief that the United States is the best model of a modern and humane society which others should seek to substantially emulate – really the best that a modern capitalist democracy has to offer (though some aspects from the European experience can also be imbibed) – and furthermore, that the United States must take on the responsibility of helping other countries and societies to move in this direction. Empire then is a misnomer. The United States is merely the leading power in a global project to bring prosperity and dignity to all. It is a lumbering giant. It needs sympathetic but also critical friends. It makes mistakes. It even abuses at times its enormous power. But who can doubt its fundamentally good intentions or the importance and validity of its global project? There is no way, then, that this US imperial project can be undermined intellectually and politically without attacking the self-deluding and self-serving character of this belief in the uniqueness of the United States. The fact that the United States might consider itself exceptional is not exceptional, however, for many countries or societies have their own versions of exceptionalism. But their exceptionalisms reside in their past and how it makes them inimitable. It cannot be exported. American exceptionalism is different because it also claims to be imitable universally, indeed it insists on the necessity and desirability of being emulated. It is the emblem of 'modernity' without parallel, and the United States has the responsibility, nay the duty, to use its immense power to share this vision and its construction with all who wish to be truly 'modern'. Hence the innate connection of 'Americanism' to the United States' current empire-building project.

In the survey of chapters that follows the aim is not so much to provide a comprehensive summary as to provide to present a window of sorts, an enticing glimpse into some of the furniture in the larger room of ideas and arguments presented by each contributor.

Economics of Empire: Neoliberal Globalization and the US

Amidst the hype about the emergence of a 'new economy' centred on the revolutionizing impact of information and communication technologies (ICT), and on the widening benefits of globalization, Walden Bello provides a reasoned and balanced corrective. The Northern economies have shaped the character of the world economy and the 'golden age' (1950–1975) had higher average growth rates and far more equitable distribution of benefits to the general public than the present era of neoliberal globalization. Indeed, Bello argues that this very pattern of globalization, characterized more by the incredible financialization of the world economy than by the transnationalization of production, is basically a response to the structural crisis of capitalism after the golden age.

This is a crisis of overaccumulation, that is, of overproduction and excess capacities relative to demand in the North, of too much capital and too few investment opportunities. The overall result was declining profit rates and, therefore, the search for another way to continue the incessant pursuit of profits. This is, after all, the engine that drives capitalism. It explains why neoliberal globalization is what it is – investing hopes in ICT to create new areas of massive and continuous investment and product expansion; the shift from productive to financial activities as a way of making profits; the extension of capital to other territories; and the commercialization of hitherto public spheres of life, such as health and education, public utilities and transport, pensions and social security measures. If it was not for China's extraordinary growth over the last two and a half decades, absorbing huge amounts of investment at home and from abroad, and churning out goods for a debt-based consumption boom in the United States (still the locomotive of the global economy), the world would have been in even a greater mess.

Nevertheless, according to Bello, all that has happened is a postponing of a time of greater reckoning as the crisis of overaccumulation remains. Compared to the golden age of 'stable cooperation', the era of neoliberal globalization is one of 'unstable competition'. Earlier, tensions between the major European allies and the United States were much less. The United States was the accepted hegemon in a world order where the pie was growing fast enough for others to grow relatively faster than the United States itself. But, from 1980 onwards, with a slowly growing world pie, the United States is much more concerned to corner as much of the benefits relative to other major capitalist powers. If this is one source of growing tension, another has been the devastating impact of neoliberal structural adjustment programmes in the South, promoting ever greater inequalities and further impoverishment. The constitutionalization of neoliberalism through the World Trade Organization, International Monetary Fund and the World Bank is getting stalled.

If the Clinton administration at least sought to sustain some degree of multilateral cooperation on the world scale, for both economic and political purposes, even while seeking competitive advantages for US capital and strategic dominance for the US state, the administration of Bush Jr. has been much more nakedly partisan towards a certain faction of the US ruling class, namely, the oil companies, steel, agribusiness, and the military–industrial complex. These are sectors more concerned about protecting their existing turfs via government support than with expanding free trade and the market mechanism globally. Furthermore, Bush differs from Clinton in his greater unilateralism and militarism. Here, the goals of enhancing both US economic and strategic power remain, but the former gets subordinated to the latter. While the invasions of Afghanistan and Iraq are partly motivated by the need of the United States to secure control over energy sources, the political–imperial behaviour here and elsewhere is motivated as much, if not more, by its need to assert itself, to send an 'exemplary' message that it will not hesitate to use all means necessary (including military) to secure its 'vital interests': either accept US domination or face the consequences of resistance, big or small!

Bello's central point is that this greater belligerence is not the expression of a greater strength but of a greater weakness reflected in the deepening problems of the world economy and of the US economy in particular; a massive overextension of US military power; a growing political and ideological disillusionment that is progressively undermining the credibility of the United States as the presumed force to bring about positive change worldwide.

Neoliberal 'Common Sense'

No rightward shift in economic thinking can hope to establish itself as the dominant 'common sense' if it is not accompanied by a rightward shift in political and social thought. That is why the rise of neoliberalism in the United States and the United Kingdom necessarily has an impact on the thinking and behaviour of their policy-making and policy-shaping elites, with respect to both domestic politics and foreign affairs. In tracing the rise and spread of neoliberalism in the United States, it is just this general paradigm shift that Susan George talks about; this is as much a shift in moral attitudes, positions and concerns as in anything else.

Neoliberalism is a marriage of the most conservative interpretation of neoclassical economic doctrines with the Austrian school of libertarian political-legal thought best embodied in the work of Friedrich von Hayek. Neoclassical economics recognizes 'market failure'. The most rightwing current within the neoclassical stream insists, however, that 'government failure' is so much more serious, and that better market failure than government intervention. Hence the advocacy of the minimalist state. But the minimalist state also draws its defence from the libertarian–contractualist political philosophy of theorists like Robert Nozick and von Hayek. There is no such thing as 'society', they declare, only individuals. Notions about collectivities having common needs and goals, or pursuing a common conception of good life, are extremely dangerous. The freedom of individuals must be paramount, anchored firmly in property rights that must be protected legally. This freedom must take precedence over all illusory claims to promoting social welfare, justice and equality.

This is a vision of liberal democracy in which a conservative liberalism (the most restrictive conception of the individual) is considered far more important than a fulsome democracy (the search for greater collective empowerment of ordinary people). George seeks to reveal how, in some three decades, this has become the dominant vision of social organization. Recently, much has been made about the emergence of neoconservatives. George reminds us, however, that they are but a subset of neoliberals, and that the similarities among them are ultimately more important than the differences. That neoliberals only aim to roll back the state is incorrect. They also aim to roll forward the state in other domains, most notably in regard to domestic surveillance and defence preparations. Withdrawing the state worldwide from the economy goes hand in hand with promoting the power of the US state worldwide, precisely to constitutionalize and stabilize neoliberal globalization. George points out that the same institutions and connections in the United States that have promoted the ideology of neoliberalism have also promoted the ideology of empire.

At the heart of this chapter, then, is a remarkable exposé of the institutional network that made possible the victory of rightwing ideas. It is, in fact, more a galaxy than a network that has as its sun, the key funding institutions (extremely wealthy private, rightwing family foundations) that support a host of orbiting bodies from think tanks to university departments, to single-issue development centres, to organizations working at the grassroots, to publications, electronic media channels, individual intellectuals and activists. Over the last 30 years or more, these funders have put in over a billion dollars into the pores of civil society in the United States, with profound effects at both the popular and policy-making levels.

What the political right has achieved, says George, is something that the genuinely liberal centre and the political left can learn from. They must draw the necessary lessons for their own task, to carry out their own form of what the great Italian thinker, Antonio Gramsci, called 'the long march through the institutions', to establish another kind of intellectual and moral hegemony that unequivocally rejects neoliberalism and empire.

American Exceptionalism

Mike Marqusee starts off by alerting us to the US government's National Security Strategy (NSS) paper of 2002, which declared that there was now only a 'single sustainable model' for the world, that the United States represents the vanguard of progress worldwide. American exceptionalism (AE) has always insisted that the United States has a mission, that it is the one country whose pursuit of its 'national interest' is, at one and the same time, the pursuit of a cosmopolitan universal interest! AE has, of course, historical roots, as well as a range of component themes that amalgamate in flexible ways, all of which the author seeks to investigate. To what extent and in what ways has the United States been 'exceptional'? If it really is 'exceptional', then how does it deviate from the supposedly general law of development? Unlike in other cases, US nationalism elevated national identity to the status of an ideology – Americanism. Other nations *have* ideologies, America *is* one itself! And since this ideology is supposed to express the best elements of Enlightenment universalism and rationalism – 'freedom, individualism, opportunity, the rule of law' – America could simply not be or have an Empire, formal or informal.

This is the mystification that Marqusee dispels. America as a mission or an ideal meant that from the beginning it was to be seen not as a fixed territorial entity but as a 'great social experiment', whose own expansion was natural and benevolent, bringing 'freedom' and 'progress' to those whom it embraced. Indeed, that is how its history of expansionist wars against Mexico, Spain and the indigenous Indian population has always been written. The Monroe Doctrine of 1823 was not to be seen as an expression of the US desire for hemispheric dominance but as its adoption of the generous role of 'protector' against possible European depredations. That is to say, the United States has long been an 'empire in denial'. For a certain period from the 1890s onwards, as the United States began to acquire territories in the Pacific, outside the continental landmass, elite opinion talked for the first time of the United States becoming an empire to rival those of Europe, of accepting the 'White Man's Burden', and of bringing civilization to the Philippines. This phase also saw the emergence within the United States of an intellectual and political current that opposed such imperialist behaviour. Ironically, both sides sought sanction for their respective views from the tenets of AE.

Expansion in the Pacific and in the Americas was always compatible with a posture of isolationism, which only meant (in contrast to the 'internationalists') a refusal to involve the United States in the politics of the European powers. Once again, both isolationists and internationalists could call upon AE in their support. The Second World War discredited isolationism, and AE could now be brandished to justify the US mission of exercising moral and political leadership worldwide against the danger of Communism. It was Vietnam, Marqusee says, that shook the general US self-image, as nothing else had ever done. But it did not overturn AE. The rise of the right during Reagan's Presidency, and then the collapse of the USSR, put paid to the prospects of any further self-questioning. Indeed, this retreat from Vietnam-inspired self-doubt gathered momentum, so much so that a new hubris and triumphalism emerged by the beginning of the new millennium. AE was once again alive and well. Through all the political twists and turns – the rise of the New Democrats and then of the Neoconservatives, the post-Cold War interventions in Central America, Africa, the Balkans, West and Central Asia – the empire remains in denial. True, elite discourse is now much more willing to talk of America today as an empire that should recognize itself as being one and behave accordingly. But Marqusee correctly points out that this elite discourse cannot hope to displace the mass public discourse and belief that the United States is not and cannot become an empire.

11 September, however, reinforced the already existing tendencies in the US society towards insularity, chauvinism and xenophobia. It also reinforced already existing expansionist and imperial interpretations of what legitimate 'self-defence' should entail. Not only does the dominant ideology of AE feed such interpretations, it also obscures a realization of what is truly exceptional, or at least, distinctive about US society in comparison with other advanced capitalist democracies. Compared to them, the United States has the worst system of public health care, the highest levels of poverty, and the greatest levels of inequality of income and wealth. AE evades any comparison between, even an interest in comparing, the United States and other advanced capitalist democracies, just as AE prevents a more truthful engagement of Americans with their own history.

Yet, as Marqusee also points out, no other empire has experienced as great a degree of internal dissent, that on occasions rises to very significant policy-changing levels, as the United States. There is much, then, in the history of the United States that gives cause for optimism – rejection, in many circles, of the Cold War, the anti-Vietnam war movement (the greatest anti-imperialist popular movement of modern history), and the black exception to AE (Malcolm X's declaration to blacks that they were not Americans but victims of America). Today, more young Americans are travelling abroad than ever before, developing a greater awareness of how the United States is perceived abroad, while at home there is growing disillusionment with the consequences of the United States' war on Iraq, and its occupation of the country.

Global War on Terrorism

Though a war on terrorism has been announced by the United States on past occasions during the Cold War (when the USSR was designated the main terrorist culprit), it is really after 11 September that the declaration of a global war on terrorism (GWOT) takes centre stage. It becomes the latest and among the most important ideological banners of empire. Using the metaphor of war to combat terrorism only militarizes the solution and paves the way for using one unacceptable form of political violence, that is, terrorism, to deal with another form of terrorism. Indeed, the most dangerous and damaging form has been state terrorism, whose scale has always been enormously greater than that of non-state terrorism. The main reason why state terrorism has never been as strong a focus for public recrimination and anger is that states have had much greater capacities to disguise their terrorism as something else or to justify it in the name of a higher ideal like national security or some other supposedly worthy goal.

I start with an examination of the complexities of the very concept of political terrorism which has prevented the emergence of any universally accepted definition of it. Yet, a working understanding of it, identifying most of its forms and its agents, is easily reachable. Its agents are multiple, from Al Qaeda to the US government. GWOT provides an excellent 'framing device' for the imperial project, for in comparison to the other five ideological banners, it possesses the greatest capacity to mobilize domestic support for the US pursuit of empire abroad. This is not to decry its capacity to win over other governments and publics. Terrorist bombings as in London, Madrid, Bali and elsewhere strengthen the claims of those who would justify GWOT, which in any case is a cover that so many governments, needing to repress their own insurgency movements (Russia, China, India) or to justify their collaboration with the US assaults on Afghanistan and Iraq, find indispensable.

An inevitable corollary of the US-led GWOT has been the demonization of Islam and Muslims. This is unfair. But the temptation to resort to it has proved irresistible. At the heart of the empire project is the requirement that Muslim Central and West Asia be permanently subordinated to US power. For this it is necessary to mobilize maximum support from within the US population and from the publics and governments of the West and Japan. This demonization must be resisted and exposed for its dishonesty and hypocrisy. Along with this is the call for the issue of terrorism to be put into proper perspective. We need to impartially condemn both the 'terrorism of the weak' (non-state actors), and the 'terrorism of the strong' (state actors). Indeed, it is the latter that is our biggest problem. Without developing and strengthening adequate international mechanisms, such as the International Criminal Court, and addressing fairly the actual political contexts in which terrorism occurs, we cannot hope to diminish significantly the occurrence of such terrorism by any or all its agents. Meanwhile, it remains incumbent on us to expose the GWOT for what it primarily is – the most widely and frequently waved banner to hide and justify the US government's imperial ambitions and practices at present.

Weapons of Mass Destruction

Weapons of mass destruction (WMDs), more specifically nuclear weapons, in the 'wrong hands', was first used as an excuse to justify external military intervention by the United States in 2003 when it invaded Iraq. There were no such WMDs and no real evidence that Iraq was preparing them after its secret nuclear programme had been dismantled following the 1991 invasion. Zia Mian shows conclusively how the United States deliberately created and promoted this falsehood and how it systematically manipulated the media to deceive the US public. The point, though, is that there was already a strong predisposition to believe whatever the White House declared, with the media only reinforcing prior prejudices. This suggests a deeper malaise in the US political system, especially as it affects foreign policy behaviour. The 'presidentialization' of the political system both reinforces and expresses a general 'depoliticization', wherein very large sections of the public, unaffected by the availability of alternative information sources, are simply willing to take the US President on trust. For a quite significant part of the public, what he says goes.

Of course, the invasion of Iraq in 2003 was motivated by various strategic calculations, well beyond the specific issue of WMDs. And now that this ideological banner has been unfurled it is not about to be quietly stashed away. Despite the deluge of criticism that the US government has had to face, once it became clear that there were no WMDs in Iraq, Washington is perfectly willing to use the same justification of WMDs in the 'wrong hands' against other deemed enemies. This is what has happened with respect to Iran, which has been singled out for a campaign aimed at politically isolating it in the international community. Again, broader geo-strategic considerations lie behind this pressure that given the conjuncture of conditions could escalate to the level of a US military assault on Iran. This issue features prominently in Mian's analysis. But his exposition also aims to highlight two other key themes.

First, there is the obvious selectivity and hypocrisy with which the US treats the problem of nuclear proliferation, both horizontal and vertical. Since the end of the Cold War, US conservatives have established, as a guiding framework for US foreign policy, the Project for a New American Century or PNAC. The threat of military power must now be exercised as never before to ensure American supremacy globally. The specifically nuclear dimension of the PNAC perspective requires the preparation of new kinds of weapons, such as low-yield tactical and battlefield weapons, alongside the more traditional high-yield ones. The Ballistic Missile Defense (BMD) system and its associated Theatre Missile Defense (TMD) systems are to be constructed to give the United States 'full-spectrum dominance' over the coming decades. There is to be (i) the blurring of lines between nuclear and conventional arms in wartime policy planning, deployments and preparations; (ii) the blurring of the distinction between nuclear weapons and biological/chemical weapons, that is, a shift in doctrine justifying the use and threat of nuclear weapons against non-nuclear opponents suspected of having or preparing biological or chemical weapons; (iii) a selective identification of enemy countries that must on no account be allowed to possess or develop WMDs, even if this requires pre-emptive and preventive military action/war against them. Here, the contrasting perspectives with which the United States has related to North Korea, Iran, Iraq, Israel, India and Pakistan have come in for investigation, not only to highlight the obvious hypocrisies and contradictions, but also to explore the flexibility with which the United States uses this discourse about WMDs in order to pursue its regional–global ambitions.

But the second crucial and distinctive argument that Mian makes is that the United States' belief in the power of the nuclear bomb only comes back to constantly haunt it. The bomb that the United States has wanted to possess to drive fear into others also creates fear within the US power establishment, even of countries lower down in the power scale. From the beginning of 1945, when the United States first acquired this weapon, it has sought to prevent perceived opponents from securing the same, to the point that it has seriously contemplated a nuclear launch against Russia and China in the past, and North Korea and Iran more recently. The United States which has created an 'empire of fear' also finds itself entrapped in its own construct. If we want a sane future – indeed any kind of future – then there is no escape from the necessity of global nuclear disarmament. This can only fully come about if the United States is willing to take the lead in pursuing this.

In the Name of Democracy: Humanitarian Intervention and Regime Change

This ideological cover for direct and forcible intervention can also be described as 'military humanism'. Not all such intervention ends with or aims to unseat existing governments and install another. But it can also, at times, mean precisely such 'regime change'. Of all the 'legitimations of empire', this is among the most useful one for the United States as it is applicable to many parts of the world; also, because of its greater plausibility in areas of most strategic concern for the United States – West and Central Asia – where most regimes are authoritarian and undemocratic. This discourse also has the advantage of being very persuasive for a wider global audience beyond the population of the targetted area, who can be expected to be most resentful of the United States' foreign policy behaviour and the rationales offered for it. This particular ideological banner is probably more effective for winning over a European public, which has historically been socialized to interpret its colonial past in more benign terms than by colonialism's victims. Therefore, it is more willing to accept the idea of a 'democratic mission' for the non-West as the gift of the occident to the rest.

How much continuity and change of structure and sub-themes, of carriers and agents, is there between this discourse of military humanism and the dominant discourse of the Cold War (the 'defence of freedom and democracy' against the evil at that time, namely, Communism)? Can this 'democratic crusade' be as successfully sustained and promoted as was the 'anti-Communist crusade'? Or, is it doomed to be short-lived? If so, why? Since 'defending democracy' meaning 'defending the free world' was the principal banner behind which the US fought the Cold War, it was very important. There were no other equally effective or convincing optional banners. But despite the emergence of new and more banners in the post-Cold War era for advancing US interests, it must be noted that in certain respects the 'democracy banner' has become even more important now. The absence of a Soviet countervailing force means that US imperialism has shifted into a much more offensive mode and, therefore, must have a more 'aggressive' interpretation of the need to 'promote' democracy (not merely 'defend' it) as its pre-eminent disguise for militarism.

There is a difference between the two banners of humanitarian intervention and a democracy promotion that envisages a regime change. Humanitarian intervention is supposed to be a response to a humanitarian crisis and is meant to stop after the crisis is over. Regime change in the name of democracy is necessarily a more long term and drawn out affair. There is, of course, no Chinese wall of separation between the two. The first can easily flow into the second – short term intervention becoming a longer term occupation. Mariano Aguirre's chapter is a powerful defence of international law and the limits it imposes on forcible, that is, military intervention to correct human rights violations. It is also a subtle analysis of the crucial differences between concepts that are often deliberately jumbled together, so as to provide the most flexible set of justifications for unjustifiable state actions.

Humanitarian action should not be confused with humanitarian intervention, or the latter with war operations. Nor should humanitarian action or humanitarian intervention be confused with peacekeeping and peace-enforcing, the special domains of the United Nations. US behaviour since the end of the Cold War has drawn on a discourse which carries out just such distortions. The result has been the delegitimation of the United Nations, the usurpation of its functions by the North Atlantic Treaty Organization (NATO), the self-elevation of the United States to global leadership and the endorsement for its interpretation of international law and the provisions of the UN Charter. Under the pressure of contemporary developments, the United Nations' top bureaucracy has conceded ground to the legally ambiguous notion of the 'right to interfere', interpreting the failure of states who have the 'responsibility to protect' their citizens (that is, to correct severe human rights violations) as tantamount to being 'threats to' or 'breaches of' international peace.

This opens the way for powerful countries like the United States to pressurize the UN Security Council to sanction military interventions under Chapter VII of the UN Charter, when the spirit and letter of the Charter clearly makes national sovereignty paramount and denies forcible intervention, except in the case of genuine self-defence. Not that the United States has bothered too much about securing UN endorsement for its actions. Since the end of the Cold War it has generally preferred to manipulate and suborn the United Nations when possible, and to ignore it when it has somehow resisted such subordination. Aguirre provides illuminating evidence of this in his surveys of humanitarian intervention and 'democracy promotion' in places like Bosnia, Kosovo and Iraq.

Phyllis Bennis makes a similar point. After 11 September, the United States could have, if it had wanted to, propelled the United Nations and international law to a new level of global authority and credibility. No one then would have objected to a proposal to set up a special, global anti-terrorist tribunal backed by an international police force empowered to trace and bring to trial the perpetrators of 11 September. Instead, the United States preferred not to bring in the United Nations, but to give itself a completely free hand to do whatever it wanted to with regard to Afghanistan. The hollowness of US claims about its concern for democracy is revealed in several ways, all coolly exposed by Bennis. Democracy promotion was a subsequent justification for the invasion of Iraq in 2003, preceded by the false claims of the presence of WMDs, and then by the allegations of a nexus between Al Qaeda and the Saddam Hussein regime. Similarly, the 'Coalition of the Willing' rounded up by the United States was no glorious front of democracies. Many of its members had dismal democratic records, witness Pakistan and Uzbekistan. While the likes of Russia, China, India and Turkey were delighted that their own repressive behaviour towards their insurgency movements could now, courtesy the United States, be overlooked internationally, as they too had jumped onto the US war bandwagon.

As for the post-invasion experiences of Afghanistan and Iraq, no one can seriously claim that democracy has been institutionalized, or that this is the concern of the United States as the main occupying force. In Afghanistan, the puppet Karzai government reigns in Kabul on the basis of a tacit acceptance of the rule of different warlords in the rest of the country. Both drug production and even the Taliban are making a comeback. But as long as the government in Kabul holds and obeys the United States, Washington is satisfied. In Iraq, the façade of elections is all that the United States can point to as evidence of establishing democracy. It is a fraudulent claim common to many colonial masters who sometimes have had to set up such elections precisely to more effectively rule a foreign terrain through collaboration with the local elites. The British did this repeatedly in India in the decades before India achieved genuine freedom, and established a real democracy. The reality in Iraq is (a) the establishment of a US puppet regime that will enable the United States to have permanent military bases; (b) the shameful imposition of a basically US drafted Constitution under foreign occupation; (c) the promotion of corporate privatization that most suits US business and state interests; and (d) the activation of a divide-and-rule policy that has created terrible sectarian hostilities, now threatening to become an enduring civil war. So much, then, for the US claim to be promoting democracy!

As for democratization of the Arab world as a whole, who, asks Bennis, is the United States fooling? Its major allies in the region are all authoritarian regimes – Egypt, Jordan, Lebanon, Saudi Arabia and the Gulf monarchies. Worst of all is Israel, further emboldened by US behaviour and policy declarations after 11 September, becoming even more brutally repressive and further expanding its land grab activities in the West Bank. For Bennis, matters are quite clear – the pursuit of empire and the promotion of democracy are utterly incompatible. And who exactly does the United States think it is? Its own model of democracy suffers from serious imperfections. On so many counts it contrasts unfavourably with European models. It is being eroded by the pre- and post-11 September assaults on civil liberties, justified earlier in the name of neoliberal efficiency, now in the name of fighting terrorism. Bennis's account is an honest, hard-hitting, unsparing exposure of the United States and of how it is anything but what it claims to be – the 'beacon of freedom' for the rest of the world.

Failed States

State failure, David Sogge tells us, has many labels – 'weak states', 'fragile states', 'crisis states', 'Countries at Risk of Instability', 'Low-income Countries Under Stress'. But it is a term that panders to Western condescension towards the non-Western nations and betrays a strong sense of superiority. This discourse of state failure emerged really after the end of the Cold War. Before that, the West led by the United States was much more concerned about 'threats' represented by 'strong', enemy states to the world order, which, therefore, needed the benevolent guardianship of the United States and the Atlantic Alliance. In the 1990s, 'state failure' became the primary source of danger. According to some rightwing ideologues what was happening in the Balkans, Asia and Africa reflected an encroaching 'anarchy', a 're-primitivization' of human behaviour, a resurfacing of barbarism and ethnic hostilities inconceivable in the more 'civilized' parts of the world. Left to fester, these places would become hotbeds of terrorism and retrograde forms of development antithetical to the needs of a globalizing economy and to the associated stability provided only by the United States. After 11 September these fears were further accentuated.

While some of the characteristics of a weak state – inadequate provision of vital public services, country-wide lawlessness, difficulties in establishing and giving effect to collectively binding decisions – are clearly recognizable and can fit a very wide array of countries, the more important question is 'failure *for whom*'? Who decides the norms according to which failure is to be judged? And why? The disturbing answer here is that it is invariably powerful countries of the West who decide. For them 'success' is measured by the degree to which other states in the developing world, from the Balkans to Central, West and South Asia to sub-Saharan Africa, to the Caribbean and the Americas, fit the current conjuncture of neoliberal globalization stabilized by US power and authority. Thus, states unwilling to accept the rules laid down by the United States as well as states with valuable raw materials but which are poorly governed, can all be designated as 'failed' or 'failing' states, with the sword of Damocles hanging over them.

'Failed states' are usually identified with sub-Saharan Africa, where internecine strife, often connected to issues of control over scarce or valued material resources (minerals, timber, oil, diamonds, etc.) coveted by Western powers, has been of considerable intensity. This has drawn in the Western powers including the United States, and led to direct or indirect (via the United Nations) forms of military intervention. The United States has generally seen the strategic importance of these regions in terms of the resources they possess, rather than considering them of geopolitical significance. Thus, human rights abuses, whether in Sudan, Rwanda or in the Republic of Congo, have not been taken as realities that compel military interventions by the United States or other Western powers. Geopolitical rather than moral considerations have usually been a much stronger spur to direct military interventions. Moreover, interventions can be indirect as well as direct, partial as well as comprehensive. Direct intervention is one way of 'punishing' recalcitrant states and creating 'friendly' ones. But, at another level, low-intensity warfare against 'undesirables' (be they forces of politicized Islam or other anti-US currents) will do. After all, state failure comes in many degrees and guises and the response to it need not always be regime change, but different forms of 'nation-building', 'state-building' and 'institution-building'.

Yet, those who talk most of the dangers of 'state failure' and its spreading ambit refuse to recognize the reasons for it. For Sogge, there are two crucially important reasons for 'state failure'. First, neoliberal forms of economic globalization demand that states greatly reduce their involvement in the economy, but then bemoan their failure to overcome the negative consequences of neoliberal recipes for growth and development – rising debt, escalating inequalities and greater poverty in much of Africa and elsewhere. Export-oriented primary production as the main source of wealth exclusively for ruling elites reinforces a disregard for balanced and widespread domestic development. Unmotivated and independent studies, says Sogge, show clearly that the two main sources for state breakdown and instability are rising socio-economic inequalities (not just poverty) and the criminalization and informal 'privatization' of state apparatuses, now suborned to the pursuit of powerful sectional interests. Nor is the legacy of the Cold War – the damage caused by the superpowers' conflict through proxies in much of Africa, for example – properly taken into account. Pushing forward 'democratic change' via the 'shell of elections' is no answer, especially when these states are accountable not to their publics but 'upwards' and 'outwards' to foreign powers and external agencies via structural adjustment programmes, debt repayments and pressures to meet World Bank requirements for 'good governance'.

The second reason is that Western powers led by the United States demand that states everywhere conform to what they believe are the conditions for sustaining international peace and stability. This is a misleading label that really means the acceptance of the hegemonic global supervision carried out by the United States in conjunction with willing allies in Europe, Asia and elsewhere. States not willing to abide by these 'rules' risk being designated as 'failed' states or, even worse, as 'rogue' states.

Unless the efforts at further neoliberal globalization and empire are thwarted, there will be a growing trend towards the emergence of more militarized protectorates for shorter or longer periods of time. The big power interventions, whether under UN missions or separately that have taken place since 1990 in Cambodia, Haiti, Sierra Leone, Kosovo, East Timor, Bosnia–Herzegovina, Afghanistan and Iraq, should serve as a salutary reminder of what might lie ahead.

War on Narcotics

According to David Bewley–Taylor and Martin Jelsma, the two pillars on which US drug policy has been based are: (a) a moralist 'prohibition above all' approach, and (b) a recognition of how useful the 'war on drugs' can be for legitimizing US military presence and intervention in certain parts of the world. This second aspect was made possible because in the 1970s, President Nixon first used the war metaphor to define US drug policy, and in the 1980s, the United States went on to militarize this policy by creating specially trained armed personnel to carry out counter-narcotics interdiction operations in the Andes. Bewley–Taylor and Jelsma remind us that this 'war on drugs', in effect, bridged an ideological gap in the interregnum between the end of the Cold War and the 'war on terror', by helping to justify US bases, interventions and military operations abroad.

Historically, the United States has always had a preference for supply side approaches to tackle the drug problem. It could externalize blame on outside drug producing countries (opium–heroin and cocaine), even though demand and much profit-making trade originated from within its own shores where Protestant moralism criminalized drug use. Internationally formulated policies and conventions on drugs, both before and after the Second World War, faithfully reflect the US approach. The way in which after 1945 the United States could dictate UN drug policy was an early example of how the United States could shape the structure of international laws, bodies and conventions. The 1961 Single Convention, the 1971 Convention on Psychotropic Substances, and the 1988 Trafficking Convention provided international ground rules that identified which drugs were to be banned and how their trade was to be made illegal.

This international framework policed by the United States through the use of coercive measures made it difficult for national governments to pursue a policy different from that of the United States. Moreover, the United States would link a country's 'good behaviour' on the drugs front to other issues between itself and the country in question. Indeed, the United States has a 'drug certification' procedure whereby the US Congress authorizes the executive to impose sanctions on countries that do not cooperate with US anti-narcotics efforts. This certification mechanism is, understandably, widely resented, especially in Latin America.

The militarization of US drug policy links it to issues of security. This is yet another rationale for having a high military budget. In 1989, one of the main reasons used to justify the US invasion of Panama and the overthrow of one-time ally General Noriega was that he was involved in drug-trafficking. Politically, this militarization of drug policy was clearly useful, but when evaluated by the yardstick of effectivity in curbing drug trade and use within the United States, it was clearly a dismal failure. Interdiction campaigns simply have not affected overall supplies. But despite this, US drug policy has not seen any shift in influence from the Department of Defense to the Department of Health. Plan Colombia and the 'war on drugs' has been too useful an approach for other more political purposes, such as attacking leftwing insurgency groups termed 'narco-guerrillas' in Colombia, putting pressure on leftwing governments from Venezuela to Bolivia, and for justifying the maintenance of US armed presence on the territories of collaborating regimes. The United States has gone ahead to link the 'war on drugs' with the 'war on terror'. This has helped to re-legitimize a militarized approach which was being discredited because it was both expensive and unsuccessful. It has also provided a convenient channel for funds to allied governments and rightwing counter-insurgency groups operating against leftist groups and governments in Latin America. For this there are historical precedents in Indo-China and Nicaragua, where US allies were funded through heroin and cocaine smuggling.

On the other side of the globe, Bewley–Taylor and Jelsma point out how poorly US drug policy has fared in Afghanistan. The Taliban drug control policy of banning and destroying production, backed internationally, was no way to deal with a huge humanitarian problem, given the large numbers of Afghans dependent on poppy production. With the overthrow of the Taliban, the opium economy has again boomed, but its financial beneficiaries are mainly the 'warlord allies' of the United States who helped it overthrow the Taliban regime. Meanwhile the drug business continues to flourish in the North, especially in the United States.

Quite apart from how the 'war on drugs' serves US imperial interests, it remains a serious problem in its own right. Bewley–Taylor and Jelsma reject the US 'zero-tolerance' attitude to drugs. It is in Europe that a serious dissatisfaction with the American approach has grown along with a search for alternative approaches based on principles of 'harm reduction' and 'decriminalization' of the end-user. The authors endorse this change in discourse. Here, the HIV/AIDS crisis has played an important role in promoting the 'harm reduction' approach. Among the great advantages of this approach are that it is humane, practical, morally sensitive, and politically more sensible since it 'de-militarizes' the drugs issue, thereby moving in the direction of depriving the United States of one disguise for empire.

References

Ferguson, Niall (2004), *Colossus: The Price of America's Empire* (New York: Penguin Books).

Gaddis, J.L. (2004), book review of N. Ferguson, *Colossus, New York Times Book Review*, 25 July.

Kennedy, P. (2004), book review of N. Ferguson, *Colossus, New York Review of Books*, 10 June.

The Economics of Empire

The Capitalist Conjuncture

Overaccumulation, Financial Crises and the Retreat from Globalization

Walden Bello

> The real barrier of capitalist production is capital itself. . . . This means – unconditional development of the productive forces – comes continually into conflict with the limited purpose, the self-expansion of existing capital.
>
> Karl Marx, *Capital*

During the annual spring meetings of the World Bank and the International Monetary Fund in April 2006, Sebastian Mallaby, the influential economic columnist of the *Washington Post*, made the following observation:

> A few years ago, anti-globalization rioters were clogging the streets, disrupting meetings of the world's multilateral organizations. Today, something more serious is afoot. The protesters have mercifully vanished, but international institutions are in disarray. Anti-globalization may have lost its voice, but so has globalization. (Mallaby 2006)

Noting that 'trade liberalization has stalled, aid is less coherent than it should be, and the next financial conflagration will be managed by an injured fireman', he concluded that 'the great powers of today are simply not interested in creating a resilient multilateral system' (ibid.).

In fact, globalization has not only 'stalled', as Mallaby puts it; it is going into reverse. And it is not just the key institutions of global economic governance, such as the World Trade Organization (WTO), the World Bank and the International Monetary Fund (IMF) that are in crisis, but also the deeper structures and processes of what was formerly seen as an inevitable pheno-menon. What was seen, by many people on both the left and the right, as the wave of the future – that is, a functionally integrated global economy marked by massive flows of commodities, capital, and labour across borders of weakened nation states and presided over by a 'transnational capitalist class' – has retreated in a chain reaction of economic crises, growing inter-capitalist rivalries, and wars. Only by a stretch of the imagination can the United States under the George W. Bush administration be said to be promoting a 'globalist agenda'.

Globalization was no mirage. But in retrospect, rather than being a new, higher phase of capitalism, it was in fact a reaction to the underlying structural crisis of capitalism, something that was masked in the early 1990s by the collapse of the centralized socialist regimes in Central and Eastern Europe. 15 years on, globalization seems to have been a desperate effort by global capital to escape the stagnation and disequilibria overtaking the global economy in the 1970s and 1980s, rather than the Brave New Phase in the capitalist adventure promised by Margaret Thatcher when she coined her famous slogan TINA – 'There is no alternative' to capitalism. The promise of globalization, like the promise of the New Economy with which it was associated, was largely stillborn.

The crisis of globalization and overaccumulation is one of the three central crises that are currently eroding US hegemony. The other two are the overextension of US military power and the crisis of legitimacy of liberal democracy. All three have been discussed in *Dilemmas of Domination* (Bello 2005). This piece is an effort to extend and deepen the analysis of one of these crises: that of overaccumulation.

End of the Long Boom

The period from 1945 to 1975 was marked by relatively high growth rates as Keynesian policies institutionalized the reinvigoration of capitalism that had been brought on by the state-led war economies during the Second World War. Also known as the Fordist model of production, the post-War capitalist economy involved significant state intervention and regulation, and rested on a class compromise between Big Capital and Big Labour – a compromise that was expressed in relatively high wages that translated into expanding demand that fuelled growth. Most of the newly independent countries also adopted varieties of state-assisted capitalism. The result was what is now seen in retrospect as the 'Long Boom' of the international economy.

To some analysts, this boom was a manifestation of the 'A phase' of the so-called Kondratieff Wave, where growth was triggered partly from the civilian application of technologies developed during the Second World War in key industries such as aviation, metals, and information technology.

The long boom came to an end in the 1970s, and one of its main manifestations was the 'stagflation' or stagnation cum inflation – a phenomenon not supposed to occur in Keynesian economic theory – that overtook the Northern economies, in particular, the US economy. The period of state-supported 'import substitution industrialization' also ran into trouble in the South, with stagnation, inflation, and massive indebtedness combining to reverse trends on the reduction of poverty and inequality.

From the early 1980s on, competition, rather than synergy or complementarity, became the principal aspect of the relations among key Northern economies. The key cause of this development was capitalism's classic crisis of overproduction, overinvestment, and overcapacity, meaning the emergence of too much productive capacity globally relative to global demand, resulting in a decline in the rate of profit. Also contributing to stagnation was the end of the profitable exploitation of the new technologies of the post-Second World War era, leading the international economy to the so-called B phase of the Kondratieff Wave, the main features of which were, as Wallerstein points out:

> the slowdown of growth in production, and probably a decline in per capita world production; a rise in rates of active waged work unemployment; a relative shift of loci in profits, from productive activity to gains from financial manipulations; a rise of state indebtedness; relocation of 'older' industries to lower-wage zones; a rise in military expenditures, whose justification is not really military in nature, but rather countercyclical demand creation; falling real wages in the formal economy; expansion of the informal economy; a decline in low-cost food production; increased 'illegalization' of interzonal migration. (Wallerstein 1996: 28)

Growth in one centre economy became dependent on recession in another, and with the generalized adoption of floating exchange rates after the Nixon administration abandoned the gold–dollar peg in 1971, currency manipulation became a key instrument of competition, with the United States, for instance, seeking to reflate its economy by pushing the revaluation of the Japanese yen. This made Japanese imports to the United States more expensive in dollar terms, and made production in high-wage Japan increasingly non-competitive, forcing the Japanese to shift a significant part of their manufacturing operations to South-east Asia and China.

Monetary manipulation, via the high interest rate regime initiated by Federal Reserve Chief Paul Volcker after his appointment in 1979, while directed at fighting inflation, was also geared strategically at channelling global savings to the United States to fuel economic expansion. One key consequence of this momentous move was the third world debt crisis of the early 1980s, which ended the boom of the economies of the South and led to their resubordination to the Northern capitalist centres. As Carlos Diaz Alejandro put it:

> What could have been a serious but manageable recession has turned into a major development crisis unprecedented since the early 1930's mainly because of the breakdown of international financial markets and an abrupt change in the conditions and rules for international lending. (quoted in Ocampo 2006: 79)

Latin America, for instance, changed from being a net capital importer, enjoying positive net resource transfers of two to three per cent of GDP, into a net capital exporter, haemorrhaging net negative transfers of four to five per cent of GDP (ibid.).

In an effort to regain 'international competitiveness', the United States and Britain, under Ronald Reagan and Margaret Thatcher respectively, adopted neoliberal, free-market policies aimed at ending the Keynesian class compromise, rolling back state participation in and regulation of production, reducing protectionism in trade policies, and ending capital controls. The result was an increase in inequality in the key Northern economies, but without their regaining the high growth rates of the first two decades after the Second World War that neoliberal economists had hoped for.

The search for profitability amidst stagnation pushed the United States and the other centre economies, via the World Bank and the IMF, to resubordinate the economies of the South through pro-market, structural adjustment policies. The dismantling of developmental states in much of the South deepened and consolidated the comprehensive crisis of the developing world that was ushered in by Volcker's high interest rate regime.

The trend toward global stagnation was striking. Angus Maddison's statistical work – regarded as the most reliable – shows that the annual rate of growth of global GDP fell from 4.9 per cent in 1950–1973 to 3 per cent in 1973–1989, a drop of 39 per cent (cited in Crotty 2002: 25). The United Nations confirmed this trend, estimating that world GDP grew at an annual rate of 5.4 per cent in the 1960s, 4.1 per cent in the 1970s, 3 per cent in the 1980s, and 2.3 per cent in the 1990s (ibid.).

Clinton and the Globalist Project

The reign of the Democratic Party led by Bill Clinton appeared to portend a break with this pattern of low and erratic growth. The US economy moved into an eight-year boom that many interpreted as a sign that it had become a 'New Economy' impermeable to the cycle of boom-and-bust. The administration embraced globalization as its 'Grand Strategy', that is, as its fundamental foreign policy posture towards the world. The accelerated integration of production and markets, based on a faith in the efficacy of minimally regulated markets, was felt to play to the strengths of US corporations. As the director of intelligence of the National Security Council saw it:

> The United States can benefit immensely from this shift because we are well placed to thrive in a globalized political economy. Indeed, a globalized society of market states plays into and enhances American strengths to such a degree that it worries some states that the United States will become so dominant that no other state will be able to catch up to it. (ibid.: 145)

The dominant position of the United States allowed the liberal faction of the US capitalist class to act as a leading edge of a transnational ruling elite in the process of formation – a transnational elite alliance that could act to promote the comprehensive interest of the international capitalist class. It appeared to demonstrate this capacity when it pursued the strong dollar policy, one that was meant to revive the economies of Japan and Germany, even if this was not in the short-term interest of many US corporations that had to compete against cheaper Japanese and German products. Thriving markets in Japan and Europe, however, were ultimately beneficial for US capital in terms of providing healthy, expanding export markets, and this is what the Clintonites had as a strategic aim (Brenner 2002: 127–33).

The Clinton conjuncture is captured by Stephen Gill when he calls attention to the emergence of a 'neoliberal historical bloc that practices a politics of supremacy within and across nations' (Gill 2003: 120). Gill calls this a politics of supremacy instead of hegemony because this historical bloc was able to gain only a fragile legitimacy for the globalist project. Thus, while neoliberal globalization brought about 'a growth in the structural power of capital, its contradictory consequences mean that neoliberalism has failed to gain more than temporary dominance in our societies' (ibid.).

Achieving hegemony and not simply supremacy was, nevertheless, a major concern, and a major thrust of the Clinton administration was geared towards institutionalizing the emerging neoliberal global order, that is, to make its functioning independent of the coercive power of the hegemon. Its crowning achievement in this area was the founding of the WTO in 1995. A product of eight years of negotiations, but one conducted principally between the United States and the European Union, the WTO was the most ambitious effort to codify trade rules, in order to consolidate a free trade regime globally that responded to corporate profitability. The WTO was the key project of what Gill called the 'New Constitutionalism', that is, the 'legalization' of neoliberal principles in order to make a relapse into the old protectionism very difficult, if not impossible (ibid.: 131–35).

Meanwhile, the IMF sought the dismantling of capital controls worldwide by making capital account liberalization one of its articles of association. The IMF and the WTO, along with the World Bank, were seen by the transnational class alliance as the key pillars of the system of global governance of the neoliberal global order, and at the Singapore Ministerial of the WTO in 1996, the challenge of the future was defined by the three agencies as the achievement of 'coherence', that is, the technocratic integration of their policies and their co-management of the global economy in the direction of freer and freer capital and commodity markets.

Finance Capital and its Contradictions

The transnationalization of production via the outsourcing of different phases of the production process was expected to be the central dynamic of the era of globalization. But, in fact, the dominant dynamic of global capitalism during the Clinton period – one that was the source of its strength as well as its Achilles heel – was not the movement of productive capital, but the gyrations of finance capital.

The centrality of finance capital owed itself to the declining profitability of industry brought about by the crisis of overproduction. By 1997, profits in US industry had stopped growing. Financial speculation, or what one might conceptualize as the squeezing of value from already created value, became the most dynamic source of profitability. The 'financialization' of global capital that drove the Clinton period's eight-year boom had several key dimensions:

- Elimination of restrictions dating back to the 1930s that had created a Chinese wall between investment banking and commercial banking in the United States opened up a new era of rapid consolidation in the US financial sector.

- The creation of a whole host of new financial instruments such as derivatives which monetized and traded risk in the exchange of a whole range of commodities. The 1990s ushered in a 'world where practically anything can be traded, from weather predictions to broadband Internet connections to forecasts involving the housing market' (Berenson 2006: 44). Enron exemplified the firm that detached itself from producing and trading on any one commodity to trading and profiting on risk in a large number of unrelated commodities.
- The creation of massive consumer credit to fuel consumption, with much of the source of this capital coming from foreign investors. While stimulating the economy in the short-run, this created a dangerous gap between the consumers' debt and their income, opening up the possibility of consumer collapse or default that would carry away both consumers and their creditors – a possibility that was a constant preoccupation of the IMF (Rajan 2005).
- The salient role of the stock market in driving growth, a phenomenon labelled by Robert Brenner as 'stock market Keynesianism'. Stock market activity drove, in particular, the so-called technology sector, creating a condition of 'virtual capitalism' whose dynamics were based on the expectation of future profitability rather than on current performance, which was the iron rule in the 'real economy'. The workings of virtual capitalism were exemplified by the rapid rise in stock values of Internet firms such as Amazon.com, which by 2001 had not yet turned a profit. Once future profitability rather than actual performance became the driving force of investment decisions, Wall Street operations became indistinguishable from high-stakes gambling in Las Vegas, leading some observers to coin the term 'casino capitalism'.
- The elimination of capital controls among economies, to enable speculative capital to move quickly to take advantage of differentials in value of currencies, stocks, and other financial instruments resulted in the emergence of a truly unified global capital market, whose operations were, owing to the advances in information technology, carried out in 'real time'. Special targets of capital account liberalization in the 1990s by the IMF and the US Treasury Department were the Asian economies, which Northern finance capital was eager to enter in order to get its share of their seemingly endless growth.

Yet, even before the decade was over, the contradictions of global financial capital had caught up with it.

Perhaps most dramatic was the bursting of the Wall Street bubble in 2000–2001, which ended the speculation that the United States had developed a recession-proof 'New Economy'. The dizzying rise in market capitalization of non-financial corporations, from $4.8 trillion in 1994 to $15.6 trillion in the first months of 2000, represented what Brenner calls an 'absurd disconnect between the rise of paper wealth and the growth of actual output, and particularly of profits, in the underlying economy' (Brenner 2002: 192). But the law of gravity was not to be defied. With the profitability of the financial sector dependent on the actual profitability of the manufacturing and industrial sectors, stock prices had to fall back to their real values. An astounding $7 trillion in investor wealth was wiped out in the collapse of 2001–2002. This massive loss of paper wealth represented the rude reassertion of the reality of a global economy crippled by overcapacity, overproduction, and lack of profitability. With the mechanism of 'stock market Keynesianism' – that is, reliance on speculative activity in the financial sector to drive growth – 'broken and perhaps beyond repair', the economy plunged into recession in 2001 and 2002, and crawled into an era of weak and jobless growth (Brenner 2003: 20).

Speculative crises marked the deregulation of finance capital in different parts of the world, and one crisis in one market touched off another in another market in an increasingly unified global market. The rush of speculative investors into Mexico forced a real appreciation of the Mexican currency, provoking a massive current account deficit as Mexican exports got more expensive in foreign markets and foreign imports cheaper in Mexico. This triggered a speculative attack on the peso that had investors in panic cashing their pesos for dollars, leading to the devaluation and collapse of the Mexican economy in 1994.

Essentially the same dynamics unfolded in East Asia in 1997. $100 billion in speculative capital flooded into the region between 1994 and 1997, as countries liberalized their capital accounts. Seeking a quick and high return, most of this money went into choice sectors, such as real estate and the stock market, resulting in overinvestment and a chain reaction of economic dislocations. Smelling crisis in the air, hedge funds and other speculators targeted the Thai baht, Korean won, and other currencies, triggering a massive financial panic that led to the drastic devaluation of these currencies and laid low Asia's tiger economies. In a few short weeks in the summer of 1997, some $100 billion rushed out of the Asian economies, leading to a drastic reversal of the sizzling growth that had marked those economies in the preceding decade. In less than a month, some 21 million Indonesians and 1 million Thais found themselves thrust under the poverty line (Chomthongdi 2000: 18, 22).

The Asian financial crisis precipitated the Russian financial crisis in 1998, as well as financial troubles in Brazil and Argentina that contributed to the spectacular unravelling of Argentina's economy in 2001 and 2002, when the economy that had distinguished itself as the most faithful follower of the IMF's prescriptions of trade and financial liberalization found itself forced to declare a default on $100 billion of its $140 billion external debt.

Financial volatility promised to continue in a world, where, despite a chain reaction of speculative crises, there was no serious move to reregulate finance capital's central role in the new global economy. As Robert Rubin,

Clinton's Secretary of the Treasury, asserted in 2003, '[F]uture financial crises are almost surely inevitable, and could be even more severe. The markets are getting bigger, information is moving faster, flows are larger, and trade and capital markets have continued to integrate. . . . It's also important to point out that no one can predict in what area – real estate, emerging markets, or whatever else – the next crises will occur' (Rubin and Weisberg 2003: 296).

Globalization Stalls and Multilateralism Unravels

Paradoxically, while financial integration advanced, the integration of production that would create one borderless world economy marked by weakened states and under the direction of one dominant transnational faction of the international capitalist class stalled. As Hirst and Thompson (1996) demonstrated in their classic work *Globalization in Question,* truly global transnational corporations (TNC) are relatively few, with most continuing to have the bulk of their production and sales in national or regional markets rather than spread out globally. While states in the South were weakened by structural adjustment programmes, states in the North, particularly the United States and the European states, remained significant economic actors tied to advancing the interests not of a putative global capitalist elite but of their national or regional capitalist classes. This was also the case in China, where the power and influence of the Chinese state over economic activities grew rather than diminished with China's integration into the international economy. Rather than globalization or the emergence of one functionally integrated global economy, what was taking place was a process that was pretty much along the lines of what David Held and Anthony McGrew (2002: 40) describe as the 'skeptical' position, that is, while relocation of industrial facilities and outsourcing of services escalated, what was taking place was not the advent of a qualitatively new stage of capitalism, but 'an intensification of linkages between discrete national economies . . . [wherein] internationalization complements rather than displaces the predominantly national organization and regulation of contemporary economic and financial activity, conducted by national or local public and private entities.'

The stalling of the structural processes of globalization at the level of production was accompanied by a deep crisis of legitimacy of the much vaunted multilateral system that was supposed to govern global production, trade, finance, and development.

The IMF, the agency that was supposed to be the lynchpin of the global financial system in the new global order, was undergoing a severe crisis of legitimacy. The Fund never recovered from the Asian financial crisis, when it 'lost its legitimacy and never recovered it', as one former IMF staff member put it.[1] The Fund suffered three devastating hits during the crisis. First, it was seen as being responsible for the policy of eliminating capital controls that many of the governments of East Asia followed in the years preceding the crisis.

The second hit was the widespread perception that the multibillion rescue packages assembled by the IMF for the afflicted countries did not actually go to rescuing the economies, but to paying off foreign creditors and speculative investors. Citibank, for instance, though heavily overexposed in Asia, did not lose a cent in the crisis. These scandalous developments led to strong criticism of the IMF, even from free-market partisans such as George Shultz, Secretary of State under Richard Nixon, who said that the Fund was encouraging 'moral hazard' or risk-free investment and lending and should, therefore, be abolished.

The third blow to the Fund sprang from the results of the stabilization programmes it pushed on the crisis economies. With their wrong-headed emphasis on cutting back on government spending in order to fight the wrong enemy – inflation – these programmes actually accelerated the descent of these economies into recession. In a manner similar to the way Volcker's high interest rate regime impacted on the indebted Latin American countries in the early 1980s, the IMF turned what should have been a manageable crisis into an economic catastrophe. The Asian governments were all the more bitter since the Fund, colluding with the United States, had vetoed, at the height of the crisis, the creation of an 'Asian Monetary Fund' that would have provided loans with relatively loose conditions which would have allowed them to surmount the crisis.

The Fund went from one institutional disaster to another. The Russian financial crisis in 1998 was attributed partly to its policies, as was Argentina's economic collapse in 2002. By 2006, the IMF, according to the Governor of the Bank of England, had 'lost its way' (Woods 2006: 2).

The World Bank, the second pillar of the global multilateral order, was also under assault after a decade of failed reform under Clinton appointee James Wolfensohn, who sought to make the Bank the spearhead of the neoliberal transformation of developing countries. Structural adjustment programmes that it had imposed on over 90 developing countries and post-socialist economies and co-managed with the IMF, resulted most often in more poverty, more inequality, and stagnation. A commission appointed by the US Congress called for devolving the Bank's lending operations to other organizations after finding out that, by the Bank's own assessments, the failure rate for its projects in the poorest countries was 65–70 per cent and 55–60 per cent in all developing societies (Meltzer 2000). The Bank was also accused of abetting corruption in Indonesia and Kenya. And when George Bush appointed Paul Wolfowitz head of the Bank to replace Wolfensohn in 2005, the move led to further erosion of the Bank's multilateral image since Wolfowitz, former deputy secretary of defense, was widely seen as one of the key architects of the war in Iraq and his appointment was regarded as a move to tie the Bank more closely to the United States' strategic policies.

Perhaps the most serious threat to the multilateral order was that posed to the WTO, which had been described by one former director-general as the 'jewel in the crown of multilateralism'.[2] The outlook for the WTO a decade after its founding was much less rosy. A de facto alliance between developing countries resistant to further trade liberalization and civil society networks critical of the subordination of social and environmental concerns to corporate trade, plus increasing competition between the United States and the European Union, triggered the dramatic collapse of the third ministerial of the WTO in Seattle in 1999 and the fifth ministerial in Cancún in 2003. A third collapse in Hong Kong was barely averted in December 2005, but a successful conclusion to the 'Doha Round' in the form of significant trade liberalization in industrial, agricultural, and service trades was getting more and more unlikely in 2006. With its authority fading, the future of the WTO as the main engine of corporate-driven free trade is in doubt, as is the future of neoliberal globalization.

Reflecting the worries of the establishment, *Washington Post* commentator Sebastian Mallaby (2006) laid out a bleak picture for the future of the multilateral system, after the spring 2006 meetings of the World Bank and the IMF:

> The troubles at the IMF, World Bank, and World Trade Organization are paradoxical. It's not that the underlying forces of globalization have gone limp; it's that nobody wants to invest political capital in global institutions. Trade is expanding, and bilateral trade deals sprout like weeds; but governments don't find the multilateral Doha talks to be a congenial setting in which to reduce tariffs. Equally, aid is expanding; but too much of the new money is flowing through uncoordinated bilateral channels rather than through the World Bank. International financial flows continue on a massive scale; but countries don't seem interested in sustaining the IMF in its historical role as the insurer against crises.

Persistence of Overproduction

The chain of crises since the last years of the Clinton era have been, in the view of many analysts, a reassertion of the underlying crisis of overaccumulation and underconsumption that was papered over by the superficial boom in the United States, Asia, and Europe in the first half of the 1990s. On this, there is an interesting convergence between Marxists and the IMF, a point noted by analyst Ho-fung Hung (2006). As Raghuram Rajan (2005), the director of the IMF's research centre, put it recently:

> I see the problem as the world investing too little. The current situation has its roots in a series of crises over the last decade that were caused by excessive investment, such as the Japanese asset bubble, the crises in Emerging Asia and Latin America, and most recently, the IT bubble. Investment has fallen off sharply since, with only very cautious recovery.

Overcapacity was, in fact, a constant feature of the New Economy, even at its height. The crisis was particularly severe in the core industries. In the United States, the computer industry's capacity was rising at 40 per cent annually, far above projected increases in demand. The world auto industry was selling just 74 per cent of the 70.1 million cars it sold each year, creating a profitability crunch for the weakest players, like former giant General Motors, which lost $10.6 billion in 2005 (*NYT* 2006). In steel, excess capacity neared 20 per cent (Crotty 2002: 24). It was estimated, in volume terms, to be an astounding 200 million tons, so that plans by steel producing countries to reduce capacity by 100 million tons by 2005 would still leave 'a sizeable amount of capacity which . . . would not be viable' (USEU 2002). And according to the former General Electric Chairman Jack Welch, 'there was excess capacity in almost every industry' (Shilling 1998: 177). By the turn of the century, the gap between global capacity and sales was, according to *The Economist* (20 February 1999: 15), the largest since the Great Depression.

Globalization and financialization were mechanisms designed to escape the inexorable pressures of overaccumulation and overproduction. *In fact, they worsened it.*

The spur to overcapacity provided by hothouse finance was strikingly evident in the telecommunications industry, where aggressive Wall Street financial intermediaries linked capital-flush investors with capital-hungry techno-entrepreneurs, all three interests united by a naïve faith in a high-tech boom that they expected would go on and on. The supply of capital rather than real demand was driving investment decisions, and the telecom firms 'were soon laying tens of millions of fiber-optic cable across the [United States] and under the oceans' (Brenner 2003: 20). By the spring of 2000, the market capitalization of telecom firms had reached $2.7 trillion, close to 15 per cent of the total for non-financial corporations. The result of this overcapitalization was a 'mountainous glut: the utilization rate of telecom networks hovers today at a disastrously low 2.5–3 per cent, that of undersea cable at just 13 per cent' (ibid.: 21).

Not surprisingly, profits plunged drastically from a peak of $35.2 billion in 1996, the year the industry was deregulated, to $6.1 billion in 1999, and then to minus $5.5 billion in 2000. Once the darlings of Wall Street dealmakers like Salomon Barney Smith and Merrill Lynch, the telecom firms led the way to high profile bankruptcy: Global Crossing, Qwest, and Worldcom.

Overaccumulation and the China Problem

But probably the most serious single factor worsening the global overcapacity and overaccumulation crisis was a development that was one of the main achievements of the globalist project – the integration of China into the international economy.

On the one hand, China's 8–10 per cent growth rate per annum has probably been the principal stimulus of growth in the world economy in the last decade. In the case of Japan, for instance, a decade-long stagnation was broken in 2003 by the country's first sustained recovery, fuelled by exports to slake China's thirst for capital and technology-intensive goods; exports shot up by a record 44 per cent, or $60 billion (*BW* 2004: 50). Indeed, China became the main destination for Asia's exports, accounting for 31 per cent while Japan's share dropped from 20 to 10 per cent. As one account points out, 'In country-by-country profiles, China is now the overwhelming driver of export growth in Taiwan and the Philippines, and the majority buyer of products from Japan, South Korea, Malaysia, and Australia' (*ST* 2004: 12).

On the other hand, China became a central contributor to the crisis of global overcapacity. Even as investment declined sharply in many economies, particularly in Japan and other East Asian economies, in response to the crisis of excess capacity, it increased at a breakneck pace in China (Rajan 2005). Investment in China was not just the obverse of disinvestment elsewhere, although the shutting down of facilities and sloughing off of labor was significant, not only in Japan and the United States but in the countries on China's periphery, like the Philippines, Thailand, and Malaysia. *China was significantly beefing up its industrial capacity and was not simply absorbing capacity eliminated elsewhere.* At the same time, the ability of the Chinese market to absorb its industrial output was limited.

A major actor in overinvestment was transnational capital. Originally, when TNCs moved to China in the late 1980s and 1990s, they saw it as the last frontier, the unlimited market that could endlessly absorb investment and endlessly throw off profitable returns. However, investment, in many cases, turned into excess investment because of China's restrictive rules on trade and investment, which forced transnational corporations to locate most of their production processes in the country, instead of outsourcing only a selected number of them. This is what analysts termed the 'excessive internalization' of production activities by transnational corporations (UN 2003: 45).

By the turn of the millennium, the dream of exploiting a limitless market had vanished. Foreign companies headed for China not so much to sell to millions of newly prosperous Chinese customers as to make China a manufacturing base for global markets, taking advantage of its inexhaustible supply of cheap labour. Typical of companies that found themselves in this quandary was Philips, the Dutch electronics manufacturer. Philips operates 23 factories in China and produces about $5 billion worth of goods, but two-thirds of their production is not consumed in China but exported to other countries (*Feer* 2002: 30).

The other set of actors promoting overcapacity were local governments which invested in and built up key industries. While these efforts are often 'well planned and executed at the local level,' notes analyst Ho-fung Hung (2006), 'the totality of these efforts combined . . . entail anarchic competition among localities, resulting in uncoordinated construction of redundant production capacity and infrastructure.'

The result is that idle capacity in such key sectors as steel, automobile, cement, aluminium, and real estate has been soaring since the mid-1990s, with estimates that over 75 per cent of China's industries are currently plagued by overcapacity, and that fixed asset investments in industries already experiencing overinvestment accounts for 40–50 per cent of China's GDP growth in 2005 (ibid.). The State Development and Reform Commission projects that automobile production will more than double what the market can absorb by 2010 (ibid.). The impact on profitability is not to be underestimated if we are to believe government statistics – at the end of 2005, the average annual profit growth rate of all major enterprises had plunged by half, and the total deficit of losing enterprises had increased sharply by 57.6 per cent (ibid.).

Excess capacity could have been overcome had the Chinese government focused on expanding people's purchasing power via a policy of income and asset redistribution. Doing so would have meant a slower process of growth but a more stable one. China's authorities, however, chose a strategy of dominating world markets by exploiting the country's cheap labour. Although China's population is 1.3 billion, 700 million people – or over half – live in the countryside, earning an average of just $285 a year, serving as an almost inexhaustible source of cheap labour. Because of this reserve army of rural poor, manufacturers, both foreign and local, have been able to keep wages down. The negative social and economic impacts of this strategy are well described by Ho-fung Hung (ibid.):

> [U]nder the post-Tiananmen consensus among the ruling elite, the Communist Party single-mindedly pursues rapid economic growth without directing much attention to the alleviation of social polarization. Class, urban-rural, and inter-regional inequalities expanded hand in hand with the economic miracle. Poverty spreads and intensifies in the rural inland area and the old bastions of state industry are besieged by extensive unemployment. The peasants-turned-workers in the coastal boom towns are not doing much better. Owing to the colossal size of the pool of surplus labor and the 'despotic factory regime' under the auspices of the party-state, industrial wage growth amid China's economic miracle is dismal in comparison with the growth of manufacturing wage in other East Asian NICs during their miraculous moment. During the most explosive phase of takeoff, South Korea and Taiwan remained modestly equalitarian societies. . . . In contrast, China's gini-coefficient has ascended from 0.33 in 1980 to more than 0.45 today. The pattern of income distribution in China's development is more reminiscent of the Latin American experiences than the East Asian ones, so much so that some begin to forewarn of the 'Latin Americanization of China'.

Aside from being potentially destabilizing politically, this wealth concentration in a few hands and the relative immiseration of the vast majority 'impedes the growth of consumption relative to the phenomenal economic expansion and great leap of investment' (ibid.). This means, among other things, an exacerbation of the crisis of overproduction in that a significant amount of China's industrial production is dumped on global markets constrained by slow growth.

The Global Macroeconomic Picture Today

The accumulation of crises rooted in persistent overproduction culminated in the stock market collapse, recession, and weak recovery cum jobless growth of the US economy in the first term of the G.W. Bush administration.

In the last few years, the global economy has been marked by underinvestment in most key economic regions apart from China and by persistent tendencies toward stagnation. Weak growth has marked most other regions, notably Europe, which grew annually by 1.45 per cent in the last few years. It is increasingly marked by a circular relationship: on the one hand, China's growth has increasingly depended on the ability of US consumers to continue their debt financed spending spree to absorb much of the output of China's production brought about by excessive investment; on the other hand, this relationship in turn depends on a massive financial reality – the dependence of US consumption on China's lending the US private and public sectors billions of dollars from the reserves it accumulated from its yawning trade surplus with the United States. Parenthetically, this relationship is ironic, since, notwithstanding its opportunistic alliance with China in the 'war on terror', the Bush administration identified China as a 'strategic competitor' in its 2002 National Security Strategy Paper.

Reflecting the worries of the IMF about global overproduction, a Fund official called attention to the 'excessive dependence of global growth on unsustainable processes in the United States and to a lesser extent in China'... (Rajan 2005). He noted: 'Perhaps the central concern has to be about consumption growth in the United States, which has been holding up the world economy' (ibid.). Consumption-led growth, which led to a current account deficit of 6.25 per cent of the United State's GDP and 1.5 per cent of the world GDP, was sustained mainly by the United States' ability to pull in 70 per cent of all global capital flows, much of it from China, as noted above (ibid.). It was helped by tax cuts for the rich and massive deficit spending that led to the evaporation of the federal budget surplus accumulated during the Clinton years. Much of the deficit spending went to defence expenditures, resulting in defence-related production accounting for 14 per cent of GDP growth in 2003, though it represented only about 4 per cent of the GDP of the United States.

'Growing global imbalances' was the IMF's euphemism for the chain reaction of overproduction, underinvestment, and reliance of global growth on volatile financial flows sustaining consumer expenditure in the United States. The disruption of these flows coupled with higher energy prices, it warned, posed the possibility that it would 'slow abruptly, taking away a major support from world growth before other supports are in place' (ibid.).

End of the Long Wave?

Consumption-driven growth – the volatile driver of the tepid growth of the so-called 'Goldilocks' economy – was, in the view of the Fund, unsustainable. So was overinvestment in China. These two factors were conditioned by a third: to many observers, the resumption of stagnation and listless growth were not only manifestations of a medium-term structural crisis, but also underlined the broader, degenerative long-term trend referred to earlier that had begun in the late 1970s – the B phase or downward trend of the Kondratieff Wave. The crisis of overproduction was both a cause and an effect of the exhaustion of the profitable exploitation of technologies that had been the driver of growth in the immediate post-Second World War era.

Contrary to forecasts by analysts who saw information technology as the core of a long-wave upswing in the first decade of the twenty-first century, the productivity gains from information and communications technology have been disappointing and certainly are insufficient to propel an upswing. Following David Gordon, Philip O'Hara (2003: 496) has argued that the much vaunted information revolution of the 1980s and 1990s – the so-called driver of the New Economy – was actually a 'pale imitation of a major technological revolution compared with the applications of electricity, the automobile, the airplane, chemicals, telephone, radio, television, sanitation, and plumbing in previous phases of capitalist development.'

The jobless growth of the recent 'recovery' under Bush, in which productivity gains have come not from new applications of information and communications technology, but from the shedding of labour, would seem to support this claim. The contradictory trends of the last few years may be the prelude to deflation, a deeper recession, and perhaps, even a depression, as the world enters the tail end of the current, long wave of capitalist expansion.

Bush and the Retreat from Globalization

The Bush administration's foreign economic policies must be seen partly as a response to the inability of globalization to surmount the crisis of overaccumulation and long wave-related exhaustion plaguing the United States and the global economy. Indeed, it is a retreat from globalization conceived as a project of functional integration of the global economy across national borders, led by a transnational capitalist elite, and governed by multilateral institutions that 'constitutionalize' neoliberal, pro-corporate economic principles.

But this retreat from globalization takes place within a broader, momentous shift in Washington's Grand Strategy owing to a reconfiguration of the ruling bloc brought about by the Bush II ascendancy. The key elements of the Bush II paradigm appear to be the following:

- Unlike the Clinton administration and even the Bush senior administration, the Bush II people have aggressively put the interests of US corporations ahead of the common interest of the global capitalist class, even if severe disharmony is the outcome. Their project is the unilateral assertion of the power of the US elite, rather than the construction of a system of shared power within a US-led global elite that was the thrust of the Clinton globalist project.
- Bush's political economy is very wary of a process of globalization that is not managed by the US government, and seeks to ensure that the process does not dilute the economic power of the United States. After all, a truly free market might victimize key US corporations, compromising US economic interests. Thus, despite its free market rhetoric, this is a group that is very protectionist when it comes to trade, investment, and the management of government contracts. It seems that the motto of the Bushites is protectionism for the United States and free trade for the rest of the world.
- The Bush approach towards the developing world increasingly resorts to

naked force to impose radical structural adjustment or free-market policies, not content to leave the task to financial coercion by the IMF, World Bank, and the private banks. Iraq and Afghanistan are experiments in this enterprise of militarized economic adjustment. Moreover, although this ominous trend began before Bush, there is under his administration an intensification of 'accumulation by dispossession', as David Harvey (2003: 1–42) calls the latest stage in the privatization of the commons. Through mechanisms like the imposition of 'patent rights' via the WTO's Trade Related Intellectual Property Rights (TRIPs) Agreement, US corporations seek to privatize the fund of commonly shared knowledge and technology passed down through the generations of farming communities in the South, by restricting the use of genetically modified seeds developed at the end point of this communal process. TRIPs also allow corporations to restrict the natural processes of the communal diffusion of knowledge, thus making industrialization by imitation – the traditional route to industrialization – all but impossible.

- The Bush inner circle is strongly sceptical about multilateralism. They fear it because although multilateralism may promote the interests of the global capitalist class in general, it may, in many instances, contradict particular US corporate interests. The administration's growing ambivalence towards the WTO stems from the fact that the United States has lost a number of rulings there – rulings that have hurt US capital – while not bringing about the expected openings for US exports in both Northern and developing country markets.
- For the Bush people, politics is key, not only in the sense of using state power to repay political favours to corporate interests, but, even more importantly in the sense that for them, *strategic power is the ultimate modality of power.* The neoconservatives and nationalists that command enormous power in the administration, see economic power as a means to achieve strategic power. Economic arrangements, like trade deals and the WTO, are judged less by their adherence to free trade, than by the extent to which they contribute to the strategic power of the United States. Given their emphasis on strategic power, the Bush elite has put the emphasis on disciplining the South via military force, instead of relying only or mainly on IMF and World Bank-imposed structural adjustment programmes. While economic and related factors, such as control of oil are certainly important in accounting for the US invasion of Iraq, they are not primary: the US expedition was meant mainly as an 'exemplary war' whose purposes reached far into the future, to teach countries of the South the costs of defying the United States, and to warn potential rivals like China not to even think of challenging Washington militarily (Harvey 2003: 1–42).
- While the Bush administration is dedicated to advancing the interests of US capital as a whole, it is especially tied to the interests of what might

be called the 'Hard Economy'. This is in sharp contrast to the Clinton administration, which was closely tied, via Treasury Secretary Robert Rubin, to Wall Street, the most internationalist section of the US capitalist class. The interests closest to Bush are either tied to government leaders by direct business links, as is the case with the oil industry (Bush and Cheney count as its special sons); those interests that can only subsist with massive subsidies from the government, like the steel industry and agribusiness; or those which often operate outside the free market and depend instead on secure government contracts that run on 'cost-plus' arrangements. The third kind of firms make up the powerful 'military industrial complex' that is really the most powerful bloc among corporate lobbyists in Washington today.

Not surprisingly, since many of the interests supporting Bush are not subject to the market, they regard the free market and free trade as no more than rhetorical weapons to be deployed against external competitors and not to be taken seriously as an operating principle.

Key Economic Policy Thrusts

If the foregoing forms the fundamental perspective of the Bush administration, then the following prominent elements of recent US economic policy make sense:

Achieving Control over Middle East and Central Asian Energy Resources

While this did not exhaust the war aims of the Bush administration in invading Iraq, it was certainly high on the list. Partly this is aimed at potential European competitors. But perhaps the more strategic goal was to pre-empt the region's resources in order to control access to them by energy poor China, which, as noted earlier, is identified as a strategic competitor in the 2002 National Security Strategy Paper, notwithstanding its serving as an ally in the war on terror (Wood 2003: 145).

Aggressive Protectionism in Trade and Investment

The Bush administration has, in fact, not hesitated to destabilize the multilateral trading order to protect its own corporate interests. In addition to pushing for massive farm subsidies and raising steel tariffs , it defied the Doha Declaration that health should take priority over intellectual property claims. Responding to its powerful pharmaceutical lobby, the administration sought to limit the easing of patent controls to just three diseases. Since the Doha ministerial, in fact, Washington has put less energy into making the WTO a success. It prefers to pour its efforts into bilateral or multilateral trade deals, such as the Free Trade Area of the Americas (FTAA) or the Central America Free Trade Agreement (CAFTA). Indeed the term 'free trade agreements' is a misnomer since these are actually preferential trade deals designed to severely disadvantage parties outside the agreement like the European Union.

Incorporating Strategic Considerations into Trade Agreements

Former US Trade Representative Robert Zoellick stated explicitly that

> countries that seek free-trade agreements with the United States must pass muster on more than trade and economic criteria in order to be eligible. At a minimum, these countries must cooperate with the United States on its foreign policy and national security goals, as part of 13 criteria that will guide the US selection of potential FTA partners.

New Zealand, a government committed to free trade, has nevertheless not been offered a free trade deal because it has a policy that prevents visits of nuclear weapons carrying ships.[3]

Manipulation of the Dollar's Value

To shift the costs of economic crises to rivals among the centre economies and regain competitiveness for the US economy, the manipulation of the dollar's value has been a key economic policy thrust. The 25 per cent fall in the value of the dollar relative to the euro within a relatively short period of time in 2002–2003 was not the result of market forces but of conscious policy. While the Bush administration issued denials that this was a beggar-thy-neighbor policy, the US business press saw it for what it was: an effort to revive the US economy at the expense of the European Union and other centre economies, to counter the stagnationist pressures of the crisis of overaccumulation. With a falling dollar, US products could be competitively priced vis-à-vis foreign products in the US market as well as in foreign markets. The Bush policy was a reversal of the Clinton administration's strong dollar policy, and a return to the weak dollar policy of another nationalistic administration, the Reagan presidency.

Aggressive Manipulation of Multilateral Agencies and a Renewed Reliance on Bilateral Aid

While instrumental employment of a multilateral agency may not be too easy to achieve in the WTO owing to the strength of the European Union, it can be done more readily at the World Bank and the IMF, where US dominance is more effectively institutionalized. Despite support for the proposal from many European governments, the US Treasury recently torpedoed the IMF management's proposal for a Sovereign Debt Restructuring Mechanism (SDRM) to enable developing countries to restructure their debt, while giving them a measure of protection from creditors. Already a very weak mechanism from the point of view of developing countries, the SDRM was vetoed by the US Treasury in the interest of US banks.[4]

In another example of intensifying conflict between the European Union and Washington over the use of the IMF, the United States prevented the Fund from exerting significant pressure on Argentina when the latter threatened to unilaterally devalue its $100 billion private debt that was owed mainly to European bondholders, on grounds that it opposed a bail out of the latter.

Even before Paul Wolfowitz was appointed head of the World Bank in 2005, the Bush administration was already moving to make the World Bank a more pliable instrument of its bilateral aid and development initiatives, including the radical privatization effort known as the Private Sector Development (PSD). Nancy Alexander's account (2002) of how this came about is instructive:

> Initially, most of the Bank's Board of Directors opposed the PSD Strategy's proposal to launch a third generation of adjustment focused on investment and to privatize services, especially health, education, and water. Gradually, outright opposition dissipated as Board members described the hard, uncompromising, 'you're with us or against us' attitude of US officials. The PSD Strategy, which was finally approved by the Board on February 26, 2002, calls for a radical transformation of the form and functions of the World Bank group in order to promote the private sector. The Bank is now promoting investor rights while, at the same time, liberalizing and privatizing services, especially in low-income countries where regulatory regimes are generally weak to non-existent.

Perhaps even more important, the US lassoed the World Bank and the IMF to provide public finance for its so-called reconstruction efforts in both Afghanistan and Iraq. This is using international taxpayers' money to stabilize economies devastated by US wars. The World Bank, in particular, is not only being harnessed to provide money but to implement a blueprint of radical privatization in close cooperation with consultants and agencies of the US government. This trend is likely to intensify with Paul Wolfowitz heading the World Bank.

Instead of multilateral aid, bilateral aid in the form of grants has become the main conduit of US aid policy. Bilateral grant aid, Bush's foreign policy people argue, is more effectively controlled and thus tailored for one's purposes. 'Grants can be tied more effectively to performance in a way that longer-term loans simply cannot. You have to keep delivering the service or you don't get the grant,' said John Taylor, undersecretary of the Treasury.[5]

The most ambitious new bilateral aid programme unveiled by the administration was the Millennium Challenge Account (MCA), which called for a $5 billion increase in US aid, in addition to the average of $10 billion now regularly appropriated. To qualify for aid under the new programme and for aid to continue flowing once a country qualifies, it has to get passing grades on 16 criteria that include trade policy, 'days needed to start a business', inflation, budget deficit, control of corruption, rule of law, civil liberties, and immunization rate (Soederberg 2004: 295). The World Bank would provide assessments of the eligibility of countries for aid, as would conservative private NGOs like Freedom House and the Heritage Foundation. The aid process itself would be conducted like a business venture, as the State Department makes clear:

> [T]he MCA will use time-limited, business-like contracts that represent a commitment between the US and the developing country to meet agreed performance benchmarks. Developing countries will set their own priorities and

> identify their own greatest hurdles to development. They will do so by engaging their citizens, businesses, and governments in an open debate, which will result in a proposal for MCA funding. This proposal will include objectives, a plan and timetable for achieving them, benchmarks for assessing progress and how results will be sustained at the end of the contract, delineation of the responsibilities of the MCA and the MCA country, the role of civil society, business and other donors, and a plan for ensuring financial accountability for funds used. The MCA will review the proposal, consulting with the MCA country. The Board will approve all contracts. (quoted in Soederberg 2004: 295)

The aim of this radical rightwing transformation of the aid policy is not just to accelerate market reform but, equally, to push political reform along narrow US-preferred lines (ibid.).

Passing the Burden of Adjustment to Environmental Crisis on to Centre Economies and Developing Countries

While some of the Bush people do not believe there is an environmental crisis, others know that the current rate of global greenhouse emissions is unsustainable. However, they want others – specifically the European Union and Japan – to bear the brunt of adjustment, since not signing would mean not only exempting environmentally inefficient US industry from the costs of adjustment, but hobbling other economies with even greater costs. Raw economic realpolitik, not fundamentalist blindness, lies at the root of Washington's decision not to sign the Kyoto Protocol on Climate Change.

Conclusion

Overaccumulation or overproduction has been the spectre that has hovered over the global economy since the 1970s. Neoliberal adjustment via structural adjustment and other contractionary programmes merely worsened the crisis in the 1980s. Globalization and financialization during the Clinton period appeared to be a successful response in the 1990s as the central capitalist economy, the United States, embarked on an eight-year-long boom. However, they merely added to contradictory pressures that broke out in a chain reaction of financial crises from the mid-1990s onwards that culminated in the recession that inaugurated the Bush administration in 2001.

A major casualty of these developments has been the phenomenon of globalization. At the structural level, the much vaunted relocation of industrial facilities, outsourcing of services, and decline in trade barriers have not resulted in a functionally integrated global economy, where nation states and their institutions cease to be the central determinants of economic affairs. At the 'superstructural' level, the system of multilateral institutions that was supposed to govern and manage the system has been unravelling.

Over the last few years, as a reaction to the overinvestment in the 1980s and 1990s, underinvestment has been the trend in most key economies. Growth has depended mainly on sustained consumer spending in the United States to absorb China's massive production, with US demand being sustained by the flow of global savings from China and other key capitalist countries. This circular relationship is unfolding amidst a momentous change in the paradigm of the US elite that can only, in the long run, worsen the crisis of overaccumulation.

Washington is currently dominated by a faction of the US ruling class that is intent on increasing the strategic power and hegemony of the United States. The exercise of force, particularly against dissident forces in the South, is the main currency of this administration. In terms of meeting the global crisis of overaccumulation, the strategy of this faction has not been the Clintonite strategy of coordinated transnational response among allied capitalist elites, but of forcing the burden of adjustment onto other centre economies while competing with them to exploit the developing word more intensely via new innovations in 'primitive accumulation' such as TRIPs. The conflicts between the European Union and the United States over agriculture in the WTO, over adherence to the Kyoto Protocol, over the debt problem of developing countries, over the value of the US dollar, and over the policies of the IMF are manifestations of growing inter-capitalist and inter-imperialist competition. Added to policy conflicts such as differences over Iraq, these conflicts spell an end to the politico-economic Transatlantic Alliance which had sustained the hegemony of the western capitalist bloc since the end of the Second World War.

A question of profound importance is how the US–China relationship will develop. Washington today has a grudging détente with China owing to the necessity of enlisting China as an ally in the War against Terror. But probably less compelling as a rationale for alliance to an elite that values the strategic supremacy of the United States above all, is the current economic dependence of the US on China's lending and its turning out of commodities to meet US consumer demand. With strong pressures from within its ranks and from the Pentagon to act towards China as a strategic enemy, the future of the grand economic bargain between the two key pillars of the capitalist global economy hangs in the balance.

The global economy being held hostage to geopolitics on the part of two political leaderships that value the accumulation of strategic power above all is not the future that corporate-driven globalization was supposed to deliver.

Notes

1 Dennis De Tray, Comments at Luncheon sponsored by the Carnegie Endowment for International Peace, Washington, DC, 21 April 2006.
2 The description is that of Mike Moore.
3 This *IUSI* (2003) article summarizes an 8 May 2003 speech by Zoellick.
4 For the sharpening conflicts between the US Treasury Department and IMF officials over unilateralist moves of the United States, see Bullard (2002).
5 See, among other accounts, Bello (2005: 170–73).

References

Alexander, Nancy (2002), 'The US on the World Stage: Reshaping Development, Finance, and Trade Initiatives,' Citizens' Network on Essential Services, Washington DC, October.

Bello, Walden (2005), *Dilemmas of Domination: The Unmaking of the American Empire* (New York: Metropolitan Books).
Berenson, Alex (2006), 'The Other Legacy of Enron', *The New York Times,* Week in Review, 29 May.
Brenner, Robert (2002), *The Boom and the Bubble* (New York: Verso).
——— (2003), 'Towards the Precipice', *London Review of Books,* 6 February.
Bullard, Nicola (2002), 'The Puppet Master Shows His Hand', *Focus on Trade*, April, http://focusweb.prg/popups/articleswindow.php?id=41.
BW, Business Week (2004), 'Riding China's Coattails', 1 March.
Chomthongdi, Jacques Chai (2000), 'The IMF's Asian Legacy', in *Prague 2000: Why We Need to Decommission the IMF and the World Bank* (Bangkok: Focus on the Global South).
Crotty, James (2002), 'Why There is Chronic Excess Capacity', *Challenge*, November–December.
FEER, Far Eastern Economic Review (2002), 'Burying the Competition', 17 October.
Gill, Stephen (2003), *Power and Resistance in the New World Order* (Basingstoke: Palgrave Macmillan).
Harvey, David (2003), 'The New Imperialism: Accumulation by Dispossession', in Leo Panitch and Colin Leys (eds), *The New Imperial Challenge: Socialist Register, 2003* (New York: Monthly Review).
Held, David and Anthony McGrew (2002), *Globalization/Anti-Globalization* (Cambridge: Polity Press).
Hirst, Paul and Grahame Thompson (1996), *Globalization in Question: The International Economy and the Possibilities of Governance* (Cambridge: Polity Press).
Ho-fung Hung (2006), 'Rise of China and the Global Overaccumulation Crisis', paper presented at the Global Division of the Annual Meeting of the Society for the Study of Social Problems, 10–12 August, Montreal, Canada.
IUST, Inside US Trade (2003), 'Zoellick Says FTA Candidates Must Support US Foreign Policy', 16 May.
Mallaby, Sebastian (2006), 'Why Globalization has Stalled', *The Washington Post*, 24 April.
Meltzer, A.H. (2000), 'International Finance Institutions Reform: Report of the International Financial Institutions Advisory Commission', Report to US Congress, Washington DC, March.
NYT, *The New York Times* (2006), 'Chief named for Troubled GM Unit', 31 May, C1.
Ocampo, José Antonio (2006), 'Latin America and the World Economy in the Long Twentieth Century', in Jomo K.S. (ed.), *The Great Divergence: Hegemony, Uneven Development, and Global Inequality* (New York: Oxford University Press).
O'Hara, Philip Anthony (2003), 'Recent Changes to the IMF, WTO, and SPD: Emerging Global Mode of Regulation in Social Structures of Accumulation for Long Wave Upswing?', *Review of International Political Economy,* Vol. 10, No. 3, August.
Rajan, Raghuram (2005), 'Global Imbalances: An Assessment', International Monetary Fund, Washington DC, October, http://www.imf.org/external/np/speeches/2005/102505.
Rubin, Robert and Jacob Weisberg (2003), *In an Uncertain World: Tough Choices from Wall Street to Washington* (New York: Random House).
Shilling, A. Gary (1998), *Deflation* (Short Hills NJ: Lakeview).
Soerderberg, Susanne (2004), 'American Empire and "Excluded States": The Millennium Challenge Account and the Shift to Preemptive Development', *Third World Quarterly*, Vol. 25, No. 2.
ST, Straits Times (2004), 'China the Locomotive', 23 February.
UN, United Nations (2003), *World Investment Report 2003* (New York: United Nations).
USEU, US Mission to the European Union (2002), 'OECD Nations Pledge Reduction in Global Steel Capacity', 8 February, http://www.useu.be/Categories/Trade/Feb0802SteelReductionsOECD.html.
Wallerstein, Immanuel (1996), *After Liberalism* (New York: New Press).
Wood, Ellen Meiksins (2003), *The Empire of Capital* (Delhi: LeftWord Books).
Woods, Ngaire (2006), 'The Globalizers in Search of a Future: Four Reasons Why The IMF and World Bank Must Change and Four Ways They Can', *Center for Global Development Brief,* April.

The Ideological Preconditions

Manufacturing 'Common Sense'

or Cultural Hegemony for Beginners

Susan George

> One of the most important characteristics of any group that is developing towards dominance is its struggle to assimilate and to conquer 'ideologically' the traditional intellectuals, but this assimilation and conquest is made quicker and more efficacious the more the group in question succeeds in elaborating its own organic intellectuals.
>
> Antonio Gramsci

The market solution is always preferable to state regulation. Private enterprise surpasses the public sector on criteria of efficiency, quality, availability and price. Free trade will ultimately serve the entire population of any country better than protectionism. It is normal and desirable that health care and education be profit-making activities. Higher defence spending and tax cuts for the rich will guarantee security and prosperity. Inequality is inbuilt in any society, and is probably genetic, if not racial. If people are poor, they have only themselves to blame. Hard work will always be rewarded.

A free society cannot exist in the absence of market freedom; it follows that capitalism and democracy are mutually supportive. The United States, by virtue of its history, its ideals and its superior democratic system, should use its economic and military might to intervene in the affairs of the rest of the world. Such interventions will rid us of undesirable and disruptive elements in the international community, and will, ultimately, prove to be for the good of all.

The majority of US citizens, it now seems, would agree with most or all of these statements.

They have not been encouraged to ask such basic questions as – 'What is an economy for?' If the economy siphons ever-greater wealth from working people to the already wealthy, rather than satisfying the needs of every individual in a given population, regardless of his or her station in life, this is assumed to be the natural order of things. Nor have they been encouraged to examine the place of their country in the international order, much less understand the rights, the interests and the place of others.

Why have such beliefs and such attitudes, which one can lump together under the headings of 'neoliberal' or 'neoconservative' doctrine, triumphed over the past quarter century, not just in the United States, but throughout the English speaking world and well beyond? Does this trend reflect a natural evolution and simple acquiescence to reality, or, are deeper and more explicit forces at work?

This chapter will attempt to answer these questions briefly and examine the nature of the ideology-makers and shakers, and their 'long march through the institutions', in the words of the path-breaking Italian Marxist thinker Antonio Gramsci. Gramsci brought to light the concept of cultural hegemony, the capacity of a given class to occupy the ideological high ground. The neoliberal elite of the United States (and now of Europe and most other places on the planet) has indeed marched through and penetrated both our public and private institutions one after another, so that they now enjoy a virtual monopoly over ordinary peoples' minds.

Their success reflects a long-term strategy that progressives have barely noticed, much less counteracted. An activist and wealthy minority has consciously put this strategy into play, carefully cultivating its advantage from seedlings planted in the 1940s and 1950s. We shall trace the progress of this ideological transformation, particularly in the United States, from its philosophical origins to its full fruition in our own time, identifying the major actors, their motivations and their methods.

Neoliberalism's Ideological Roots

Peter Mandelson, an intimate friend and advisor to Tony Blair is, with Anthony Giddens, the inventor of the 'Third Way'. He is now European Commissioner for Trade, and remains a powerful figure in the Labour Party. Thus, it may come as a surprise that in June 2002, he declared before an audience, including the cream of British Labour and various visiting luminaries like Bill Clinton: 'We are all Thatcherites now.'[1]

Mandelson surely deserves praise for his forthrightness. The reasoning behind his unexpected statement goes like this: in April 2002, Lionel Jospin, the socialist candidate for the French presidency, suffered a humiliating defeat, coming in third, and reducing the run-off vote to a choice between the right (Chirac) and the far right (Le Pen). That same year, various other European social-democratic leaders were similarly knocked off their pedestals. George Bush had already defeated Clinton's natural successor, Al Gore.

It does not seem to have occurred to Mandelson that such defeats might have been protest votes against the rightward shift of these purportedly progressive governments. He concluded, rather, that the electorate was clamouring for 'reform', along the lines of those Margaret Thatcher had earlier forced upon a reluctant Britain; including wholesale privatization of public services and 'flexibility' for markets in goods, services, capital and, especially, labour. The United States, under Bill Clinton, had already perfected such a programme with particular success in reducing welfare rolls while increasing the prison population.

Third Way ideology rests on the proposition that one can do nothing against market forces, nor should one even want to. Capitalist globalization is simply a fact, not a problem in need of a solution; nor is it a state of affairs to be criticized, much less overthrown. Since market forces cannot be countered and will prevail, intelligent people and social-democratic politicians can only accept the reality, and echo Saint Margaret's battle cry: 'TINA: There Is No Alternative'.

What is 'Thatcherism', then, and who are the 'Thatcherites' – including the 'Reaganites', the 'Bushites', etc. – if all Peter's friends have now joined their ranks? What is the content of their doctrine, and what lies behind their ideology? Why has this doctrine become mainstream worldwide, not just among the followers of the traditional or extreme rightwing but inside the US Democratic Party, and among European social democrats as well? These are changes crying out for an explanation.

Nearly everyone now knows the answer to the first question. Thatcherism is the doctrine that tells us to put our faith in market freedom, monetarist economics, high defence spending, privatization of public services, tax cuts for the higher brackets, curbs on trade unions, general opposition to the welfare state, general friendliness towards the corporate sector and, as the now defunct European Constitution repeatedly stated, 'free and undistorted competition'.

The concept of Thatcherism requires, however, a bit more archaeological digging to uncover its foundations. Margaret Thatcher did not emerge fully armed from the head of Zeus, and she herself was not, strictly speaking, a Thatcherite, but a 'Hayekian'. The story goes that one day in the House of Commons, she retrieved a book from her briefcase, thumped it vigorously and announced to the assembled MPs: '*This is what we believe*'. The book in question was Friedrich von Hayek's *The Constitution of Liberty* (1978).

Hayek was an Austrian economist, jurist and philosopher with an astonishing output. He had observed the beginnings of National Socialism in Austria and exiled himself to England as early as 1932, where he taught at the London School of Economics, until his departure for the University of Chicago, where he was to enjoy a long and highly influential career. Since he wrote some two dozen books, innumerable articles and influenced generations of students, I can attempt only the briefest and most inadequate summary of his thought and action here.

According to the generally received wisdom among economic historians, Hayek lost the great theoretical battle against John Maynard Keynes in the 1930s. Consequently, Keynesian economic policies were to dominate not just theory, but also practice, over the next several decades, beginning with F.D. Roosevelt's determined government interventions during the Great Depression. Following this intellectual defeat, Hayek virtually ceased to write on the economics subjects that would win him a belated Nobel Prize in 1974.[2]

Instead of economics papers, he began producing an abundance of political articles, and gained fame in 1944 with *The Road to Serfdom*, still a classic among neoliberals. Thomas Sowell, a black rightwing Fellow of the Hoover Institution at Stanford says that 'Hayek was the central pioneering figure in changing the course of thought in the 20th century.'[3] Progressives had always thought it was Keynes!

In *The Road to Serfdom*, Hayek develops the following argument:

> In any large system, knowledge is by nature fragmented and widely dispersed; it depends in particular on too many factors and too many actors for any central authority ever to become omniscient enough to plan a national economy. Any State intervention in the economy will be arbitrary, pernicious and tend necessarily towards tyranny. One must have confidence in the market, as order will emerge spontaneously from the expression of millions of individual preferences.

Adam Smith had been the first to make this point in *The Wealth of Nations*. Recall the famous quote pointing out that we do not expect to get our dinners thanks to the benevolence of the butcher, the baker and the brewer, but from their selfish pursuit of their own interests. Individual self-interest is a better guide to satisfying human wants, than any kind of economic planning or interference by a centralized authority, no matter how benign and well-intentioned. Prices will give us all the information we need concerning what the public desires. The government has no business deciding in the place of the public.

Hayek stresses the importance of law in a free society, but only in so far as *negative* law is concerned. The role of the law is restricted to stating what is forbidden. It should not give anyone the positive power to carry out any interventionist action. Freedom consists in the absence of coercion; to be free is not to depend on anyone else's will, including the will of the legislator, except when the legislator decrees that certain acts are illegal. Pursuing Hayek's theory to its logical conclusion, one can better understand Ms Thatcher's meaning when she exclaimed, '*There is no such thing as society*'.

This is also how Hayek sees his ideal world – not as a society in which people have common interests, common goals and seek to attain the common good; but, rather, as a collection of atomized individuals, all choosing what they consider best for themselves, subject to no constraining framework, except for a small body of legally prohibited actions.

The human consequences of this doctrine are immediately apparent. The doctrine of negative freedom says, for example, 'I can eat, you can eat' because no law forbids it, and thus we are free to eat. It says nothing whatever about the actual presence of food on the table, which alone could make the 'right' to eat effective. Positive law (and progressive politics) says that, contrary to Hayek's assertions, the 'freedom' to eat is both meaningless and worthless, without practical, concrete access to food. The task of government and the purpose of society is to create a framework within which everyone has the *power* to eat, not merely the theoretical possibility. In this light, the entire body of human rights law can be seen as a kind of anti-Hayekian manifesto.[4]

Lest one give the wrong impression, it is important to say that Hayek was not some sort of moral monster. He saw his philosophy as entirely compatible with a state which would ensure that everyone had sufficient food, shelter and clothing, so as not to perish from hunger or exposure. He did not accept, however, that a government might, say, tax rich people in order to provide schools and hospitals for poor people. It is not the state's business to decide that one group should pay so that another group can enjoy certain benefits. According to Hayek, social justice is a pernicious illusion. One should stand against redistributive measures (the hallmark of the welfare state) because they are bound to be purely arbitrary, and whatever is arbitrary eventually and inevitably leads to tyranny – the 'serfdom' of his most famous title.

Hayek's reasoning has influenced generations of neoliberals, never more so than today. The solidity of his doctrine depends, however, on a conflation of several different concepts of freedom, which Western, particularly Anglo-Saxon, philosophy has tried to keep separate for at least three centuries. The first of these is the concept of political freedom, which is the basis of democracy as it allows citizens to be actively involved in deciding how society and government are to be organized. Second come intellectual and religious freedoms and freedom of expression (including freedom of the press) which are necessary corollaries to political freedom. These freedoms allow everyone to think, state opinions and worship freely, so long as these expressions do not impinge upon the freedom of others and, thereby, harm society.[5] A third category of freedom, usually defined as personal or individual freedom, underlies the right to hold property, and concerns the protection of the family and the right to one's private life.

Most thinkers consider that a fourth category, economic freedom, is of a different nature from political, intellectual or personal freedom. This distinction is one which Hayekians (or Thatcherites) refuse to make. They believe that an individual's right to dispose of his or her income and property is inviolable and that no public or private authority, including the state, has the right to interfere.

Here we arrive at the core of the ideological opposition between progressives and neoliberals (or neoconservatives). The former believe that democratic governance and the survival of society itself depend on limits imposed on economic freedom. Only the 'sovereign' can determine those limits (most thinkers from Hobbes onwards gave this role to the state), which could be benevolent, popular and democratic, or authoritarian, coercive, and even tyrannical. This is why Constitutions issuing from the American and French Revolutions onwards have made clear that the *people* are sovereign. Ideally, popular sovereignty arbitrates between conflicting interests, in order to arrive at the common good. In any case, the people must be free to choose the nature of the state under which they will live.

In practice, the balance struck will be that of the social forces present at a given moment: Marx was the foremost and most radical exponent of this theory. If the sovereign is neither the state nor the people, but the *market*, then society and government will be organized in such a way that economic freedom overrides all the others. Society will eventually be reduced to an aggregate of unlinked individuals, or, if one prefers, 'consumers'. Little by little, the erosion and eventual breakdown of social cohesion will make life scarcely worth living, even for the rich.[6]

Peter Mandelson and those who are 'all Thatcherites now' have thus chosen a slippery slope – far more slippery than the one Hayek saw leading from state intervention in the economy, to political tyranny and 'serfdom'. They have taken the path that leads to the concentration of rights in the hands of the only people actually able to enjoy their 'freedom', which is to say the minority of the rich, who are, thereby, also the powerful. Their 'right' to eat (or to own a yacht) is not just a theoretical possibility, but also a practical one. In a system of negative law, wealth necessarily equals power – the power to express one's own desires, to command others, to prevail. Perhaps some neo-Thatcherites, who listened to Mandelson at the Labour-fest in 2002, were unaware of this shift due to a combination of intellectual laziness and naked self-interest.

This concept of society and of law is the adversary that progressives must fight. As the great nineteenth-century reformer and French Dominican priest Henri Lacordaire declared, 'Between the strong and the weak, between the rich and the poor, between the master and the slave, it is freedom that oppresses and the law that frees' (Fifty-second Conférence de Notre-Dame, 1848). Market freedom does, indeed, oppress the weak, and the task of progressives is to strive for a framework of positive law, at both the national and the international levels, ensuring respect for the rights and the dignity of all human beings.

Who Are the Neoliberals? The Neoconservatives? What's the Difference? Who Cares?

As Butch Cassidy and Sundance Kid said, as they were pursued by a mysterious posse, 'Who are these guys anyway?' The answer, as regards neoliberals and neoconservatives, requires a bit of historical grounding, and is not a simple one. It could involve endless distinctions, which will not be attempted here. But the 'who cares?' question is easily answered: the whole world does, or should, care because no part of the globe has been left untouched by the doctrines that these people champion. The tale of how they gained the power to put their beliefs into practice is the main concern of this chapter. Their broad domestic agenda visibly and demonstrably creates inequalities, and serves the needs of the better-off. Elites everywhere have enthusiastically seized upon these policies made in the US. Their foreign affairs agenda continues to cause untold suffering, and to place dangerous people in positions of great influence.

Is Hayek's philosophy relevant to global, as opposed to national, politics and ideology? Definitely so; if only because the doctrine of market supremacy he advocated has gone global; it lies at the very heart of what is now called neoliberal globalization. International institutions, working hand in hand with the US Treasury department, are busy applying privatization, market-friendly, and state-weakening policies across the globe. They are trying everywhere to reduce citizenship to consumerhood, with sweeping disregard for human rights.

Does Hayek's philosophy suffice to illuminate entirely the latest phase in US and world history? Definitely not: it does not explain the propensity to war, to armed intervention, to ever increasing defence budgets that are also a hallmark of the neoliberal/neoconservative elites in power. Some wits have pointed out that these policies constitute the US version of socialism, requiring a strong interventionist state, and heavy public spending in certain well-defined and limited areas. Naturally, market supremacy and expansionist interventionism go together – no analysis of past or present imperialism has ever failed to note the point.

The strong US state now also plays its designated role in imposing market law on unwilling victims. In a recent example, one of the first acts of Paul Bremer, the imperial governor of Iraq, was to abrogate the existing investment code and instate a new one, entirely favourable to mostly American business interests. Hayek himself would have rejected the notion that one state should intervene in the affairs of another, in order to 'export democracy'.

When we ask, 'who are these guys anyway?', we encounter various terminological problems. In the United States, to be 'liberal' means to be, at least, mildly progressive. Democrats are thought, rightly or wrongly, to be more 'liberal' than Republicans, and the right pretends to be victimized by the 'liberal media'. This is probably why the designation 'neoliberal' is not in such common usage in the United States as it is in Europe and elsewhere – it is simply too confusing. Beyond US borders, 'neoliberal' unequivocally designates people who are Hayekian in their political views – although, just to confuse the picture even further, some of the latter would call themselves 'libertarians'.

Whatever the name, those guys seek to reduce taxes and state intervention and to rescind legislation providing citizens with social benefits, protective labour laws, or assistance in the case of unemployment, illness and other personal mishaps. Private companies should, in their view, replace any remaining public services, and private schools and health care facilities are preferable to public ones.

In the area of foreign policy, they tend to support US foreign interventionist policies, including military ones (although the American isolationist tradition is still alive); they are in favour of NATO and give the United Nations short shrift. They also defend the 'Washington Consensus', although not necessarily the international financial institutions which impose it on countries of the South and the East (about which more later).

In the United States, neoconservatives defend all of the above, but they are also extremely preoccupied by what can be called 'body politics'. Who can have sex with whom, at what age, under what conditions and with what education regarding reproduction and sexually transmitted diseases; the rights of women to control their own bodies and reproductive organs; what civil rights, if any, should apply to people whose sexuality is considered deviant – all these are grist to the neocon mill. They are extremely sensitive to issues of racial equality as well, and have never digested the achievements of the civil rights and the women's movements during the 1960s and 1970s.

So the neocons are on a cultural, moralistic and usually religious trip, as well as a political one; for many of them the two indeed are inseparable. A great many 'born-again Christians' fall into this category, one that includes Bush himself. Their action is blurring ever further the separation between Church and State (evident, for example, in the concerted efforts to teach creationism, or its more presentable replacement, 'intelligent design' in the public schools). Perhaps 70 million Americans would include themselves in this category and they make up the ground troops of many neocon organizations.[7]

Plenty of outstanding neocons used to be leftists, dabbling in Trotskyism or communism; their intellectuals wrote in publications like the *Partisan Review* and they all knew each other. Many were Jewish radicals. As Norman Podhoretz, a neocon 'Godfather' figure, has remarked, criticizing the critics of the Iraq war:

> At first the framers and early spreaders of this defamatory charge [that a cabal of Jewish officials in the first George W. Bush administration had promoted the interests not of the United States but of Israel] considered it the better part of prudence to identify the conspirators not as Jews but as 'neoconservatives.' It was a clever tactic, in that Jews did in fact constitute a large proportion of the repentant liberals and leftists who, having some two or three decades earlier broken ranks with the Left and moved rightward, came to be identified as neoconservatives. (Podhoretz 2004)[8]

Historically, the Jewish community, particularly on the East Coast and in New York City, was unswervingly leftwing and voted solidly Democrat. Many now side with Bush and his ilk. As one critic says about Podhoretz himself, he always 'knew just when to jump on the latest liberal-left hobby-horse – and, more importantly, when to jump off' (Raimondo 2000). Many Jews, but also many non-Jews are active in JINSA, the Jewish Institute for National Security Affairs, a think tank supported by 20,000 members and a Board of 55 hawks, which lobbies for higher military budgets, and supports the aims of the Likud. Its basic claim is that there is no difference between the security interests of the United States and those of Israel, that Israeli policies 'bolster' the interests of the United States.

Other recruits to the neocon cause used to be known in the United States as 'Scoop Jackson Democrats'. Senator Jackson, representing the state of Washington, was also called (though perhaps not to his face) the 'Senator from Boeing'; a hawk and defence build-up advocate, who got *The New York Times* to go along with his views.

Some neocons are, thus, in favour of interventionism abroad, but others are not. Traditional US conservatism always opposed the United States's entry into war and becoming involved in what the founding fathers called 'foreign entanglements'. Even the occasional modern Army officer, writing in the pages of the *American Conservative*, has denounced George W. Bush's interventionism and the concept of 'preventive war' (Kwiatowski 2003; 2004). According to Seymour Hersh's account (2006) of the US plan to intervene in Iran, several high-ranking officers have threatened to resign if a bombing campaign, especially a nuclear one, is launched.

The new right in the United States pulls together many strands: political and economic, religious and secular, outward and inward looking, Republican and Democrat. Generalizations are hazardous; perhaps one can still attempt a modest one. Although the categories clearly overlap and the vocabulary differs from one side of the Atlantic to the other (and from there to the rest of the world); all neocons are neoliberals, but all neoliberals are not neocons. Further than this one dare not tread.

Foreign Affairs

Most of the ideological energy of the US promoters of neoliberalism has been devoted to anchoring their social and economic doctrine in national institutions, and in the minds of the media and the general public, so as to ensure that it becomes a universally accepted, indeed moral, philosophy. It is important to note that the same institutions that have promoted neoliberalism in the United States have invariably promoted US state power, especially its military power abroad, and the country's right to do as it pleases on the world scene. For neoliberals, the civilian state should be weak, deferring to market forces; the military one should be strong and defer to no one.

Even before the advent of the new right, the United States was notorious for refusing to sign international agreements. It has never signed the major ILO conventions for the protection of workers, and has refused the Kyoto Protocol on grounds that it would be detrimental to the US economy. In the dispute (United States *et al.* v. the European Union) concerning Genetically Modified Organisms (GMO), the World Trade Organization's Dispute Resolution Body has delivered an initial judgement against the six European countries that imposed bans on imports of GMOs. Part of the European defence involved invoking the Precautionary Principle and the Biosafety or Cartagena Protocol. The United States retorted that it does not recognize the Precautionary Principle (nor, generally, does the WTO), and that the Protocol does not constitute international law for the excellent reason that the United States has not signed it. Even the Convention on the Rights of the Child remains unratified by only two countries, the United States and Somalia.

The International Criminal Court (ICC) provokes neocon rage, particularly that of Bush's Attorney General (Justice Minister) Alberto Gonzales. The Heritage Foundation has declared that the United States should inform countries that have ratified it that this is a 'hostile act' against the United States, and rejecting it should be a condition for foreign aid. In this context, it is unsurprising that the Bush administration immediately revoked President Clinton's signature of the Rome Statute which created the ICC.

As pointed out earlier, Hayek's philosophy intrinsically rejects positive law and the observance of human rights, whether in the domestic or the international sphere. In the latter, neoliberal policy goes by many names, including 'structural adjustment' or the 'Washington Consensus'; it is put into practice by international institutions like the World Bank and the International Monetary Fund, in virtually perfect harmony with the US government. Together they have subjected at least 100 countries throughout the South and the East to this shock treatment.[9]

The full set of structural adjustment policies includes high interest rates, wholesale privatization of public services, 'export-led growth', and open borders for imports. These policies have had the predictable result of increasing inequalities, both within and between countries. A vast literature exists on these topics, some of it by the present author. No matter how many socio-economic disasters occur as a consequence of neoliberal policies, these policies are unlikely to change under the current US Presidency. An administration which can name Paul Wolfowitz to the Presidency of the World Bank, and John Bolton US ambassador to the United Nations speaks for itself.

President Bush's choice of the prominent neocon Bolton for the United Nations perhaps most blatantly embodied US unilateralist doctrine. Americans are famously indifferent to their country's actions abroad, except when these may involve the loss of US lives. A campaign to defame the United Nations has been going on for decades, including – although this is very marginal – the invention of its ominous 'black helicopters' heading off on unspeakable missions. More serious are the views of rightwingers like Phyllis Schlafly (among other accomplishments, she contributed in important ways to the defeat of the Equal Rights for Women amendment) who delicately called Bolton's nomination a golden opportunity for the United States to say 'bug off' to other nations.

A sampling of Bolton's views:

> There is no such thing as the United Nations. There is an international community that occasionally can be led by the only real power left in the world and that is the US when it suits our interest and we can get others to go along.
>
> [The International Criminal Court] is a product of fuzzy-minded romanticism that is not just naïve but dangerous.
>
> [The UN vote against invading Iraq is] further evidence why nothing should be paid to the UN.
>
> If I were redoing the Security Council, I'd have one permanent member because that's the real reflection of the distribution of power in the world.
>
> It is a big mistake for us to grant any validity to international law even when it may be in our short-term interest to do so; because, over the long term, those who think that international law really means anything are those who want to constrict the US.[10]

Such considerations were enough to goad 59 former US diplomats into action. They jointly addressed a letter to the Chair of the Senate Foreign Relations Committee, Senator Richard Lugar, to point out that 'given [Bolton's] past actions and statements, [he] cannot be an effective promoter of the US national interest at the UN'; they hoped that the Senate would block his appointment. To no avail – Bush used a procedure unknown since the eighteenth century and made a 'recess [of the Senate] appointment'. Bolton thus slipped through the confirmation procedure (*USAT* 2005). However, we had to be replaced by Democrat pressure after the Republican debacle in the mid-2006 Congressional elections.

Neoliberal doctrine also permeates the numerous agreements signed under the auspices of the WTO (agriculture, industrial goods, services, intellectual property, technical barriers to trade, the Dispute Resolution Body, etc.). According to WTO officials themselves, transnational corporations, particularly US ones, actively promoted particular WTO agreements that served their interests.[11] They continue to exert strong pressure via the member states against trade barriers in the South, but erect them when their own industries are challenged, as in the case of the US steel tariffs or agricultural export subsidies.

Although, all the now-developed countries used high tariffs and targeted government spending and subsidies to protect themselves until their industries were strong enough to compete on world markets, they are unwilling to allow the now-developing countries to do the same.

The WTO, like dozens of bilateral or regional trade agreements, acts as a tool for prying open markets on behalf of corporations worldwide. The US Africa Growth and Opportunity Act, for example, will extend trade benefits to African countries (now 37) but only if they practice neoliberal policies, and refrain from engaging in 'any act that undermines US national security and foreign policy interests'. As a result of this Act, passed in 2000, US trade with Africa has increased, yet oil alone represents 87 per cent of total imports from this continent, and the great majority of benefits have flowed to only a few countries (Nigeria, South Africa, Angola, Gabon etc.). Just as with Bank–Fund structural adjustment and Washington Consensus-type conditionality, US trade legislation is designed to further its ideologically-driven, market-oriented objectives.[12]

The Quicksands of Iraq

Before public opinion began to sour, the invasion of Iraq had cemented a huge majority of the US public against any foreigners who dared to oppose Bush. A popular bumper sticker in the United States read 'First Iraq, Then France'. Ms Phyllis Schlafly took pains to criticize the United States' 'so-called European allies', claiming that they 'deserve a prize for impertinence' (Schlafly 2003).

Once involved in Afghanistan and Iraq, the Bush government used many pseudo-legal means for doing exactly as it pleased, with the 'War on Terrorism' serving as a convenient fig leaf. Thus, in a series of memos, White House counsel (now Attorney General) Alberto Gonzales, argued that the provisions of the Geneva Convention were 'obsolete'; that terrorism had made them 'quaint'. In 2002, he declared that Afghan prisoners, in particular, were not covered by the Geneva Convention.[13] Gonzales' then Assistant Attorney General (since rewarded with an appointment to the 9th Circuit Court of Appeals) concluded that all interrogation methods were legitimate, except for those 'specifically intended' to produce severe pain equivalent to that of 'serious physical injury, such as organ failure, impairment of bodily functions or even death'. Any method that falls short of causing such pain does not qualify as torture, and may be used, according to these authorities, on prisoners in Guantánamo and/or in the Abu Ghraib prison (see PFAW 2005).

Neoliberal defence policy always rested on the bedrock of anti-communism, high levels of armaments and the tried-and-true imperial strategies of resource capture. Iraq is only the most recent example. Now that communism has disappeared as a geopolitical force, neoliberalism has been able to penetrate every region of the globe in which it takes the slightest interest. Whenever necessary, the United States invents new security concepts, such as preventive war, rogue states in need of discipline, justification of any action in the name of the war on terrorism and so on. (Other contributors to this book deal with these aspects.)

Since the end of communism, the most successful US initiative in the creation and dissemination of a bellicose ideology in foreign affairs surely belongs to the Project for a New American Century (PNAC). Created in 1997, by some two dozen neocon policy experts with broad experience in government, the PNAC set out to directly shape the United States' place in the world. Its statement of principles is clear in this regard:

> [We need] a military that is strong and ready to meet both present and future challenges; a foreign policy that boldly and purposefully promotes American principles abroad; and national leadership that accepts the United States' global responsibilities . . . America has a vital role in maintaining peace and security in Europe, Asia, and the Middle East. If we shirk our responsibilities, we invite challenges to our fundamental interests. . . . It is important to shape circumstances before crises emerge, and to meet threats before they become dire. The history of the past century should have taught us to embrace the cause of American leadership.

A more effective and articulate apology for intervention would be hard to conceive. To accomplish the goals thus set by the PNAC, a nation must be proactive and daring. Thus, on 20 September 2001, a mere nine days after the attack on the World Trade Center, PNAC leaders wrote to President Bush, exhorting him to punish Saddam Hussein. Their logic may appear tortured, even crazy, but their intentions were clear:

> It may be that the Iraqi government provided assistance in some form to the recent attack on the United States. But even if evidence does not link Iraq directly to the attack, any strategy aiming at the eradication of terrorism and its sponsors must include a determined effort to remove Saddam Hussein from power in Iraq. Failure to undertake such an effort will constitute an early and perhaps decisive surrender in the war on international terrorism.

This passage is more than curious. On the one hand, the PNAC's membership is a hotbed of foreign policy experts. On the other, opinion is unanimous that the terrorist acts perpetrated on 11 September had an undeniably Islamic, which is to say religious, dimension. Why, then, go after one of the very few Muslim countries where the state was entirely secular, with a nationalist Ba'athist party in charge? Osama bin Laden and Saddam Hussein would have had about as much in common as the Pope and a sect of Holy Rollers. Furthermore, as PNAC experts must surely have known, there were no 'weapons of mass destruction' in Iraq.

The PNAC's obsession with Iraq was not, however, unprecedented. Paul Wolfowitz, one of its co-founders, had already recommended attacking Iraq in his 'Defense Planning Guidance' paper of 1992. About a year after its establishment, 17 PNAC founders had also written to Congressional leaders Representative Newt Gingrich and Senator Trent Lott, begging them to act decisively in the 'absence of Presidential leadership'. And what should these elected representatives aim for, given that President Clinton was not leading the nation as it deserved to be led? 'US policy should have as its explicit goal removing Saddam Hussein's regime from power and establishing a peaceful and democratic Iraq in its place'. This missive was signed by (among others) John Bolton, Francis Fukuyama, Richard Perle, Donald Rumsfeld, Paul Wolfowitz and Robert Zoellick (PNAC 1998).

Is the PNAC influential? Plenty of its people were or still are in high government positions and many more intervene regularly in the media and other opinion-shaping circuits. In September 2000, the PNAC called for 'Rebuilding America's Defenses' and set the benchmark for a proper Pentagon budget at 3.8 per cent of the GNP. When, shortly afterwards, Bush took office, he pushed the defence budget up to $379 billion, exactly 3.8 per cent of the GNP. In this same document, the PNAC signatories admitted that their goals would be difficult to realize 'absent some catastrophic catalytic event – like a new Pearl Harbor', a role which 11 September perfectly fulfilled (PNAC 2000).

As the 9/11 Commission Staff Report stated, between April and September 2001, the Federal Aviation Agency received 52 reports concerning possible attacks against the United States. One might have thought such a number of threats was sufficient for some action to be taken, even though massive bureaucratic failure remained a distinct possibility. One might further argue that, by their own admission, the PNAC saw the need for, perhaps even welcomed, Al Qaeda's daring and 'catastrophic catalytic' attack against the United States. The PNAC also stated the need for permanent military bases in Iraq; Condoleezza Rice, who is not a PNAC member, later assured the Congress that US engagement in the Middle East was no less than a 'generational commitment'.

One could thus easily draw the conclusion that the PNAC is indeed influential; that it has acted as a kind of back-up or shadow government, setting targets for the nation and contributing to achieving them.

The Neocon Galaxy

We shall now examine the systematic dissemination of neoliberal economic and social policies inside the United States. These policies have affected not only the lives of the US people, but have also exercised a dire influence well beyond its borders.

The first thing to notice about the neoliberal hijacking of economic and social thought is that progressive social forces, even moderate ones, inside or outside the United States, failed to notice it in time. A quiet revolution was taking place under their noses, but they did not even smell a rat, much less pay it serious attention. The right was able to go about its business unobserved and unchecked.

Here we meet once more Friedrich von Hayek, by 1950 a professor at the University of Chicago, where he had gathered around him a small coterie of devoted followers, who came to be known as the Chicago School and, more ominously in Chile and elsewhere, as the Chicago Boys. Even earlier, in 1947, with the help of the young Milton Friedman, he had already founded the Mont Pelerin Society, a secretive community of true-believer, neoliberal economists of which Margaret Thatcher is still a member.

Despite slow beginnings, these embryonic institutions have endured and played an important, if largely occult, role at home and abroad. Between 1985 and 2002, Mont Pelerin received over $500,000 from various conservative foundations and has recruited top drawer, neoliberal thinkers – now over 500 members from 40 countries. Its best-known past presidents, apart from Hayek and Friedman, are Nobel Prize Laureates George Stigler, James Buchanan and Gary Becker.

One member of the Chicago circle, Richard Weaver, had titled his 1948 book *Ideas Have Consequences*. How right he was! Rightwing family foundations took that statement seriously and put, what we now call 'neoliberal' or 'neocon' theory and practice, on the national and international agenda. They used their money strategically and their 'freedom to choose', to quote the title of one of Milton Friedman's books. They bought and paid for a cadre of scholars and a network of academic and non-academic think tanks. They created, in fact, virtually *ex nihilo*, an entire ideological climate under which we live today, as dangerous in its own way as global warming is for the physical world.

Progressives, doubtless sure of the force and rightness of their own ideas, were unconscionably slow to recognize the threat; they scarcely deigned to even argue, until the culture wars had already been won by the neocons, at least in the United States. One of the earliest progressive critiques of neoliberal ideology is a thoroughly researched analysis by James Allen Smith (1991) – appearing fully a decade after Ronald Reagan first occupied the White House, and had already overseen the translation of many neocon proposals into legislation. A much shorter piece by Jon Wiener (1990) had appeared a year earlier in the weekly magazine *The Nation*, but for far too long, the people, the planners and the institutions behind Reaganism and Thatcherism attracted scant attention.

A few other contributions to the literature emerged during the 1990s, including one by the present author that appeared in 1997 in *Le Monde Diplomatique* and *Dissent* (George 1997a; 1997b). These attempted not only to trace the history of the right's successful intellectual paradigm shift, but also to point out to potential progressive donors the folly of supporting projects but not ideas such as those produced by the Transnational Institute (TNI) and other like-minded institutions. Such efforts elicited little response, especially in the quarters that mattered:

> Today, few would deny that we live under the virtually undisputed rule of the market-dominated, ultra-competitive, globalized society with its cortege of manifold iniquities and everyday violence. Have we got the hegemony we deserve? I think we have, and by 'we', I mean the progressive movement, or what's left of it . . . the 'war of ideas' has been tragically neglected by the side of the angels. Many public and private institutions that genuinely believe they are working for a more equitable world have in fact actively contributed to the triumph of neo-liberalism or have passively allowed this triumph to occur. . . . [But] if we recognize that a market-dominated, iniquitous world is neither natural nor inevitable, then it should be possible to build a counter-project for a different kind of world. . . . The now-dominant economic doctrine did not descend from heaven. It has, rather, been carefully nurtured over decades, through thought, action and propaganda, bought and paid for by a closely knit fraternity. . . (George 1997b)

The buying and paying were always crucial. In his book, James Allen Smith introduces the key dramatis personae who shaped and still shape the neocon movement. He describes the institutions in which they and their descendants work and the intricate money machine that funds them. He shows how these founding fathers (few mothers make an appearance) departed from the US empirical tradition in the social sciences and journalism, to place their message in an overtly ideological framework.

They also developed formidable communications and Public Relations skills, understanding that mainstream print and audio–visual journalists would use their work in the name of 'balance', as well as out of laziness. The stock-in-trade of any number of neocon outfits includes the preparation of myriad press briefings, communiqués and ready-to-use commentaries, and a supply of articulate experts to appear on talk shows and news networks like CNN on a broad range of subjects. The left has nothing like the machinery, the money, the communications savvy and the personnel, the neocons can mobilize. This is one way the latter have shifted the 'balance' further and further to the right.

Irving Kristol, often considered (along with Norman Podhoretz) the godfather of US neoconservatism, identified the target as the 'New Class', which according to him was not only hostile to the private sector, but had successfully taken over the bastions of ideas – the universities, the think tanks and foundations that acted as 'idea legitimisers'. Kristol's answer to what he saw as 'liberal' (in the US, moderately left sense of the word) ideological hegemony was to build the right's own rival institutions, supported by philanthropy from corporations and conservative foundations. Kristol's aim of creating a network of neocon institutions and scholars was explicit from the outset; his strategy focused on the capacity to influence national policy debates, inside and outside Washington.

What began as a network is now more like a galaxy. As far as one can judge from the outside, the cohesion between the various nodes in the network – funders, think tanks, universities, single-issue policy development centres, organizations working at the grassroots level, publications, individual intellectuals and activists – is remarkable. The best way to study them, one that cannot be attempted here, would be to find an enormous piece of blank paper and write on it the names of all the donors and recipients. One would include all the relevant sub-categories (for instance, individual scholars in specific research centres in particular universities, all three of which are receiving grants) and draw the connecting lines between them. Similar lines in colours might represent not money but affinities (between organizations, publications, and so on that work together, for instance). The most lines leading to a node would give some idea of the power, reach and influence of each actor.

One could then make a reasonably accurate map of the galaxy, locating the individual 'stars', the 'suns' around which the most 'planets' orbit; the 'moons' that in turn orbit those planets, and so on. Such a process would also illustrate Gramsci's concept of a 'long march through the institutions' towards a new cultural hegemony. In the past quarter-century, these actors have brought about genuine ideological climate change, although many of them falsely continue to pretend that the media, the universities and other institutions are still dominated by 'liberals', an appellation which remains their code-word for 'leftists'.

At the heart of our map of the galaxy, we would find the funders, because without them, the rest of the infrastructure would collapse. They have been quick to seize upon the importance of ideas, and to embrace enthusiastically the 'Irving Kristol programme' of building alternative rightwing institutions capable of changing the national policy debate. The most important neoconservative foundations are Bradley, Olin, Smith–Richardson, Charles Koch and Scaife–Mellon (the last comprising four separate foundations based on the same family steel fortune). Some smaller foundations pursue identical goals, including Eli Lilly, JM, Earhart, Castle Rock, and David Koch. The so-called 'four sisters' – Bradley, Olin, Smith–Richardson and Scaife – often join forces in funding the same recipients. Large or small, all these foundations are intensely aware that together they are 'building a movement'. Corporate donors tend to follow their lead.

How do these foundations use their money strategically to 'build a movement'? The short answer is that they do everything that progressives refuse to do. Neocon donors give large, predictable long-term grants. Some of their grantees have received support for decades. Recipients know they can undertake long-term work; that their funders are prepared to wait for their ideological pay-off. Rightwing foundations fund individual scholars lavishly, and give extremely generous operating support to neocon institutions, not limited merely to overheads. They identify the future stars and nurture their grantees. As the President of the

Bradley Foundation said about his funding policy and scholarship programme for younger conservative scholars, 'It's like building a wine collection.'

In marked and tragic contrast, few progressive donors are prepared to contribute anything at all to the production and dissemination of ideas. The few that are willing, rarely feel comfortable making grants to individual scholars. At most, they may fund 'projects' which the individual scholars may be able to define, but they will be also required to manage and coordinate, rather than doing their own research, thinking and writing full-time. Left-leaning donors are also generally unwilling to exceed a three-year commitment (often renewing grants only from one year to the next), and routinely limit operational expenditures to 'project overheads' of about ten per cent maximum. They almost never support institutions per se, no matter how good their track record.

Furthermore, economic incentives built into foundation practice are counterproductive for the spread of progressive ideas. Personnel employed by donor organizations must of necessity justify their own tenure, so they must make work for their grantees, that they can then discuss, criticize and evaluate. The donors are not simply going to hand over money, even to people and organizations who have proven their capacity to spend it well, if only because such an approach would take about five minutes. Consequently, institutions and individuals hoping to gain or renew their standing with donors must spend inordinate amounts of time filling in forms, answering questionnaires and courting their 'benefactors', when they should be sticking to their 'core business' of producing and disseminating ideas.

One former programme manager with one of the largest, mainstream US foundations has explained (requesting anonymity) that the foundation he worked for had no overall institutional policy, nor did it set Foundation-wide goals. Each programme director was able to build their own unit without regard to what any of the others were doing. The capacity to fund progressive work, therefore, depends greatly on the individual preferences and politics of programme directors. The large, potentially progressive, or at least even-handed Foundations, are also, he says, extremely susceptible to criticism. They tend to stampede into 'safer' areas at the slightest warning (which neoliberals will always be happy to provide) in order to avoid anything smacking of controversy. Under the circumstances, it is amazing that any left scholarship gets done at all; that any progressive ideas ever reach the public or the policy agenda.

In other words, whether they realize it or not, progressive, or potentially progressive, donors frequently do everything in their considerable power to limit, if not halt entirely, the production and diffusion of progressive analysis, proposals and action. They make it difficult for good individual scholars and institutions to survive, whereas the funding strategy of the right allows reactionary ones to prosper and endure.[14] As the right gains ground, with its media and communications professionals shifting the 'balance' further and further in the neocon direction, progressive thought begins to seem truly eccentric, beyond the pale and grows ever more marginalized.

The Brightest Stars in the Galaxy

Although it is impossible here to examine in detail all the neocon financial powerhouses, it is useful to underline the importance of one or two, beginning with the Bradley Foundation. The Bradley brothers of Milwaukee, Wisconsin, were members of the ultra-right John Birch Society from its inception in the 1950s. They made their money in high-tech, precision-guided machinery, paid women less than men to operate the same machines (their women workers won a lawsuit against them in 1966), and sold out to the military–industrial giant Rockwell in 1985 for $1.65 billion. Their foundation suddenly became one of the largest in the United States.

Bradley found its new director, Michael Joyce, in another neocon organization, the Olin Foundation (this one founded on chemical and munitions money, about which more in a moment). The influential *Atlantic Monthly* quickly named Joyce one of the three people most responsible for the success of the US conservative movement. Joyce also founded the Philanthropy Roundtable, a collection of about 600 smaller right-leaning donors, who contribute thousands rather than millions, but whose collective cash allows Joyce to use their funds strategically as well. The Roundtable generally gives neocons an additional $2.5 million or so yearly for grants. In 2004, Bradley's Annual Report celebrated '20 years of strategic philanthropy' totalling $527 million. It still has more than $700 million in assets.[15]

Recruit and Reward

Bradley exemplifies the 'support individual scholars' philosophy, not just through its scholarship programmes or its regular grants to established authors and research centres, but also through four handsome yearly awards of $250,000 each for 'outstanding intellectual achievement'. One recent winner is Ward Connerly, the head of the American Civil Rights Institute. Connerly, who is black, successfully led the California ballot initiative ('proposition 209') to end affirmative action in the State's colleges and universities. Affirmative action, the practice of giving preference to racial minorities, sometimes at the risk of excluding better qualified white candidates, is dismissed by the prize winner, who says 'Race has no place in American life or law.' He calls for 'colour-blind' policies with no goals set for purposes of 'diversity', an approach that suits the wealthy white majority perfectly.

Although some disgruntled white candidates have taken successful legal action against the academic authorities for excluding them, affirmative action has been, on the whole, a tool to reduce somewhat the United States' ever present and endemic racism. Only when public primary and secondary schools in poorer neighbourhoods allow minority students a reasonable degree of scholarly attainment can affirmative action ensure that at least some poorer young people of colour can jump the hurdles.

The other $250,000 Bradley laureates are Charles Krauthammer, who received a MD from Harvard University, before turning to journalism. Now a syndicated conservative columnist writing on foreign affairs in *The Washington Post* and a frequent commentator on Rupert Murdoch's Fox News, Krauthammer (2001) has said of the United States' foreign policy: 'We run a uniquely benign imperium.' George Will, another conservative syndicated columnist, has also won the Bradley award for outstanding intellectual achievement, as has Thomas Sowell, a black economist who did his doctoral work at the University of Chicago and is now 'Rose and Milton Friedman Senior Fellow' at the Hoover Institution, a venerable conservative think tank situated at Stanford, also generously funded by the neocons.

Charles Murray, whose home base is the American Enterprise Institute (founded in 1943, consistently supported by the four sisters and other rightwing foundations) has received since 1988 at least 19 grants, all but one from Bradley, for a startling total of nearly $2.8 million. Murray's two best-known works are *Losing Ground: American Social Policy 1950–1980* (1985), which attempts to demonstrate that welfare actually causes poverty; and *Bell Curve: Intelligence and Class Structure in American Life*, co-authored with Herrnstein (1994), whose thesis is that blacks have inherently (hereditarily) lower mental ability than whites. Both these books caused great controversy, but the point was that they became best-sellers, were discussed and argued over on radio and television, and that Murray became an 'expert authority' on these questions.

The 'Sisters' have also given unstinting support to Dinesh D'Souza, a still youngish neocon of Indian origin, who first made his mark as a militant anti-affirmative action student at Dartmouth. He now fights against social welfare and feminism as well, and like Ward Connerly, rejects the notion that institutional racism can exist in the United States. In foreign affairs, he denies the existence of US imperialism and believes in strict, laissez-faire economics. Dinesh D'Souza appears so often on current events and commentary programmes that his adversaries sometimes refer to him as 'Distort D'Newsa'. He has, nonetheless, received over $1.5 million in 21 separate grants from the Bradley, Scaife and Olin Foundations, and routinely receives $10,000 for a speech at corporate venues. Other well-known recipients of smaller sums from the Sisters include Samuel Huntington and Francis Fukuyama.

The Olin Foundation, which closed its doors in September 2005 after half a century and $370 million worth of grants, was particularly precocious in supporting rightwing institutions and individuals. Its director has said: 'We invested at the top of society . . . in Washington think tanks and the best universities. The idea is this would have a much larger impact because they were influential places.'

As early as 1988, the Foundation's annual report showed grants of $55 million to underwrite university programmes 'intended to strengthen the economic, political and cultural institutions upon which . . . private enterprise is based.' Olin president William Simon was a power in the Reagan administration and he convinced corporations to stop 'financing their own destruction'. 'Why', asked Simon, 'should businessmen be financing left-wing intellectuals and institutions which espouse the exact opposite of what they believe in?'[16] He encouraged them to join the neoliberal funding bandwagon.

The Olin Foundation grants to selected conservative scholars include the hefty $3.6 million awarded to Allan Bloom to head the University of Chicago's John M. Olin Center for Inquiry into the Theory and Practice of Democracy. Irving Kristol, who designed the blueprint for the conservative intellectual movement, was rewarded with $376,000 as distinguished professor at New York University's graduate school of business administration, earning a similar stipend later when he joined the American Enterprise Institute as an Olin Fellow. Over 15 years, beginning in the late 1980s, Kristol has received a total of $1.4 million in 16 Olin grants.

'Traditional Values'

The donors support a predictable set of values. Bradley explicitly states that it is 'devoted to strengthening American democratic capitalism', and seeks to help 'public policy research supporting free enterprise, traditional values and a strong national defence'. The Foundation believes in 'moving towards personal responsibility' and away from 'centralized, bureaucratic, "service-providing" institutions', which it sees as 'disenfranchising citizens' who thereby become either 'victims or clients'. It wants 'choice' for people (this emphatically does *not* mean abortion, as in 'pro-choice' legislation supported by the left).

Examples would include school vouchers so that parents can use them to educate their children in the schools of their choice, including religious ones. Parents could take the public school on offer or voluntarily supplement the vouchers to pay for better educational establishments. The Foundation also calls for social security 'reform', emphasizing private accounts. The point is to shift all public institutions towards the ethic of individual freedom of choice. Bradley also appreciates the ideological value of traditional religion, and gives dozens of grants directly to churches and to 'faith-based organizations', mostly, but not entirely local.

Bradley's strategy (which could as easily apply to any of the neocon galaxy) was summed up on the excellent Media Transparency site:

> Bradley funded the authors and writers who could set the terms for national debate on key issues of public policy, the think tanks that could develop specific programs, the activist organizations that could implement those programs, and the legal offices that could defend those programs in court, as well as carry out legal offensives against other targets.[17]

In its own words, in order to 'defend and advance freedom' (that is, support US defence and security policy, including the 'war on terrorism') Bradley gives large sums to the American Enterprise Institute in Washington, the Hoover Institution at Stanford and the School for Advanced International Studies (SAIS) at the Johns Hopkins University. The SAIS was Paul Wolfowitz's place of refuge when in exile from government and before assuming the presidency of the

World Bank. Francis Fukuyama and Zbigniew Brzezinski are both teachers at SAIS.

In a general way, the neocon right supports the rollback of progressive legislation and displays a certain genius and contrarian logic in naming its institutions, so that they sound not just innocuous, but positively progressive (perhaps a case of vice paying homage to virtue?). For example, the Independent Women's Forum is anti-choice, anti-feminist and encourages women's subservience to their husbands. The American Civil Rights Institute, which has been already mentioned, 'created to educate the public about racial and gender preferences', in fact, fights against preferences for minorities or for women. The 'Centre for Equal Opportunity' and the 'Centre for Individual Rights' are also Bradley grant recipients with similar aims and similar feel-good names. The 'Citizens for a Sound Economy' are the foot soldiers fighting for tax cuts.

Whenever neocons talk about 'reform' (of taxes, welfare, justice, social security, minority rights, or whatever) they invariably mean abolition, abrogation, dismantling or privatization. A good example is Grover Norquist, who runs an outfit called 'Americans for Tax Reform'. Norquist does not so much want 'reform' as to realize his goal, which is to 'reduce government to the size where we can drown it in the bathtub' (except, of course, for the Pentagon).

Not content to defend far rightwing policies, rightwingers want the policy field entirely to themselves. Norquist further promises to 'hunt down [progressive or liberal groups] one by one and extinguish their funding sources'. He is also a formidable organizer, famous in neocon circles for his Wednesday afternoon Washington meetings at which a hundred or more conservative groups, along with Congressional staff people and other functionaries, gather for a weekly briefing and receive their marching orders. *The Wall Street Journal* refers to Norquist as 'the V.I. Lenin of the anti-tax movement' and 'the Grand Central Station of the right because all the trains run through his office'. His donors include the usual suspects among conservative foundations, and also corporations like Microsoft or AOL–Time–Warner.

Think Tanks

Neocon foundations unsurprisingly fund neocon think tanks – the Four Sisters concentrating on what one might call the Five Brothers: the Heritage Foundation and the American Enterprise Institute, the Manhattan, Cato and Hudson Institutes. There are dozens of smaller think tanks, many of them regional, which are useful for adding 'balance' in the media across the country. The journalists who cite their people rarely mention the nature and source of their money.

We may take the example of the Heritage Foundation, founded in 1973. It is not a foundation in the sense of Bradley or Olin, but rather a recipient of their grants, although it raises funds well beyond the neocon foundations and reaches out to individual donors. As of 2004, it boasted over $150 million in assets, 205 employees, 200,000 donor members, and an annual budget of about $40 million. Heritage prepared the book of legislative proposals for Ronald

Reagan's first term, nearly all of which became law. Later, it recommended 200 people who got top jobs in the Bush administration.

Heritage stresses the 'Four Ms: Mission, Money, Management and Marketing', and judging from its results, it is particularly strong in the final category. Heritage boasts that its communications and marketing department averages '6.5 media interviews every working day'. 90 per cent of its television time is on national and international networks. Heritage runs its own talk radio network, designs educational programmes for Congressional staff members, and provides a free 'confidential, high-quality service' for job placement in 'Congressional offices, trade associations, polling groups, faith-based organizations and, more recently, colleges and universities'.

Based on its recent output, one can verify that in international affairs, Heritage is pro-Paul Wolfowitz, John Bolton and the counter-terrorism bill called the US PATRIOT Act. It is anti-United Nations generally, and anti-Kofi Annan and Security Council in particular. Domestically, it works to privatize social security, weaken Medicare and welfare, reduce taxes and cut government budgets. In 2004, six members of President Bush's Cabinet spoke at various Heritage functions, including Colin Powell, Donald Rumsfeld and John Ashcroft.

The Pen is Mightier...

Publications are another weapon for the neocons and they consistently fund everything from campus newspapers to more scholarly journals like *Commentary* or *The Public Interest*. Norman Podhoretz, editor of *Commentary*, has received 13 'research fellowships' from neocon foundations for a total of nearly $800,000. News laced with ideology is provided by the *Weekly Standard*, owned by Rupert Murdoch, where Irving Kristol's son Bill is editor, the *New Criterion* and the *American Spectator*.

Donors contribute also to specific book projects or television programmes, for example those sponsored by the Hoover Institution (a TV series on Reagan received $120,000 in 2002). Articles written by Olin grantees or other neocon-backed scholars are published in such mainstream publications as *The New York Times*, *The Washington Post* and *Time* magazine. Fox News, part of the Murdoch media empire, is a 24-hours/7-days-a-week neocon presentation of the news. It is widely rumoured that when a neocon scholar produces a book, the foundations provide the funds to buy several thousand copies, so that the books go straight on to the best-seller lists and are, thus, automatically reviewed and discussed. It sounds plausible, but one has not yet found proof.

The Legal Neoliberal Eagles

The US legal establishment and the judiciary have been particular Olin targets. An early innovator, Olin funded the new university discipline 'Law and Economics' in the 1960s, and endowed the first chair at (where else?) the University of Chicago. The idea is to teach 'free market economics' as it applies to law, emphasizing 'economic efficiency and wealth maximization as the conceptual cornerstones' for judicial opinions. Ultimately, Olin and similar institutions seek to change the US legal system in order to make corporate profits and private wealth secure and untouchable, while downgrading social justice and individual rights. This is another Four Sisters effort, receiving hundreds of thousands of dollars yearly.

Other 'Law and Economics' centres exist at Universities like Yale, Harvard, George Mason, University of Virginia, Johns Hopkins, New York University, Georgetown, Princeton, Stanford and the Massachusetts Institute of Technology. This shows the exclusive investment in the 'top of society'. Only the University of California in Los Angeles has turned down an Olin programme in Law and Economics after a year's experience, complaining that it was 'taking advantage of students' financial need to indoctrinate them with a particular ideology'.[18]

For their vision to become law, the neocons need law professors, lawyers and judges in strategic locations. The outstanding vehicle for the propagation of neoliberal doctrine in legal circles is without doubt the Federalist Society. It was established in 1982 and although its website is singularly uninformative, it does admit to having at least 35,000 members who are legal professionals, 5000 law students in 180 of the US law schools, including all the most prestigious ones, and chapters in 60 cities. It does not say how many law school faculty and deans are its members. Between 1985 and 2002, the Society received 122 grants for a total of $9 million. The Director of the Federalist Society has said that without Olin, it would never have existed.

Well-known Federalist Society members include Robert Bork (also the recipient of large grants as an Olin Fellow in the Olin-funded American Enterprise Institute); Clinton's nemesis Federal Prosecutor Kenneth Starr, and Supreme Court Justices Antonin Scalia and Clarence Thomas. Along with the American Enterprise Institute, the Society also runs a programme called 'NGO Watch' aiming to challenge 'liberal' non-governmental organizations.

The neocons understand that their final victory will not be secure until the courts have made it so. Their judicial strategy, thus, concentrates on indoctrinating and recommending judges for Federal Court openings. Although it is too early to tell, Bush's choice of the young and personable John Roberts as Chief Justice of the Supreme Court may utterly change the judicial picture in the United States. Although Roberts was less clearly piloted by the Federalist Society, there is no doubt in the case of Samuel Alito, named to the Court in February 2006, a clear Society choice. The Bush Justice Department is also riddled with Society members.

The two Bush appointees, Roberts and Alito, are more than likely to reinforce the trend towards reversing certain long-standing Supreme Court decisions. Heritage, for example, estimates that it may take another decade to fully privatize social security, and many Republicans seek the overthrow of the Roe v. Wade decision that legalized abortion in 1973. The Federalist Society naturally shares these goals and its long-term agenda is to rescind a huge body of legislation passed since the 1950s, particularly in the areas of civil and individual rights, as well as to get rid of a slew of regulatory or environmental, health and safety measures covering a variety of industries.

Other grantees of neocon foundations specializing in legal issues, include Norquist's Americans for Tax Reform, 'Union Watch', the Center for Equal Opportunity, the Center for Individual Rights, Public Interest Law and Legal Reform. A larger ancillary organization called the Institute for Justice, received 80 grants for a total of $6.65 million between 1985 and 2002. It concentrates on fighting 'the intrusive presence of government in economic and private affairs' and carries out strategic litigation against regulatory measures and the 'Welfare State'.

The Koch Foundation (based on oil) has been active in funding amicus briefs ('friends of the court', open to interested parties) to the tune of $600,000 in an attempt to rescind the Clean Air Act (an effort to which Daimler–Chrysler and General Electric also contributed). The 'Fund for Research on Economics and the Environment', another Koch project, invites judges to its ranch in Montana, where they may attend a seminar or two, but also enjoy the scenery, the cuisine and the sports activities. In 2000, six per cent of Federal judges attended one of these all-expenses-paid junkets.

This may help the Kochs as well, because their oil businesses are frequently in trouble. They have been fined many times for faulty pipelines and oil spills, and they drill on federal and tribal lands. Prior to 2000, the Clinton Justice Department had come up with 97 separate violations by Koch companies of the Clean Air and Hazardous Waste laws. The Bush administration conveniently dropped all charges and the court settled for a $20 million fine, with no jail term in lieu of the $350 million and jail terms previously called for. David Koch gave $500,000 to Republican campaigns in the 2000 elections. Since both he and his brother Charles figure on the list of the 50 Richest Americans, they can also afford to support, as they do, the Federalist Society.

In the final analysis, what do the neoliberals want? Their goal is, roughly, to undo all the progressive social or environment legislation that has been enacted since the Second World War (and sometimes before that). They are relentless, but they move slowly, readily admitting in public that 'these sorts of things take decades', as they told the progressive magazine editor Robert Kuttner who shared a panel with them (Kuttner 2002).

Kuttner, calling himself the 'token liberal', participated in an event aptly titled 'Philanthropy, Think Tanks and the Importance of Ideas', featuring the heads of Heritage and the Cato, Manhattan and American Enterprise Institutes, which together receive about $70 million a year from rightwing foundation donors. The latter agreed that over the previous 20 years – from the beginning of the 1980s – well over a billion dollars had been spent on ideological production and dissemination (they did not call it that, of course), assuring the audience that 'you get a huge leverage for your dollars'.

Conclusion from a Prodigal Daughter

The present author was born and raised in the United States, of solid American 'stock', whose ancestors arrived on the country's shores more than 350 years ago. These origins, plus an adult life spent in France and Europe, provides, perhaps, a vantage point combining proximity and distance – emotionally, intellectually, geographically – for observing changing US attitudes and politics during the latter half of the twentieth century and beyond. This essay embodies the hope that readers, and above all Americans themselves, may be helped to arrive at a deeper and more objective appreciation of what the United States stands for, what it has done, and how it is seen by the rest of the world.

The dominant self-image of Americans is a combination of the melting pot and enlightenment values, with the hardy frontier spirit thrown in for good measure. Most Americans feel as though they are God's chosen people. Patriotic displays are not seen as 'corny' or embarrassing, but as bearing witness to ideals which should be universally shared by all right-thinking Americans: 'My country, right or wrong'. The United States is perhaps the only nation in the world where a prohibition on flag-burning could be seriously proposed as a Constitutional amendment without provoking hilarity.

US perceptions – at least those instilled in this author – might be summed up as follows. The American Revolutionary War was a heroic moment, inaugurating an entirely new phase in human history, and a victory won against tremendous odds. The Constitution and the Bill of Rights are unique documents, protecting hard-won freedoms. The Civil War was a harrowing moment for the country, but in spite of everything Americans managed to abolish slavery, however great the problems of racism and poverty that may remain. The US stance in the First and Second World Wars was widely seen as exemplary.

Nor could US ideology concerning personal behaviour be improved upon. You should be strong and count on yourself; you should not blame others for your failings but work hard to correct them; just as you should work hard, period. If you did so, then you could accomplish anything. That went for women as well as for men. But along with self-reliance came a duty to others, to those who needed help and were less fortunate. Especially if you were privileged, you were expected to give back generously to the community, with gratitude for what you had received. Religion generally reinforced these secular values. In the USA of the mid-twentieth century, nearly everyone went to church, as the great majority still do.

The schools did not stress (an understatement) the history of US interventionism or the negative side of national actions, racism, maltreatment of immigrants, union-busting and the early manifestations of corporate control or capitalist greed. The Vietnam War and other events caused many Americans to stop and reflect on their country's role abroad. The 1960s and 1970s were tumultuous, witnessing face-offs between new attitudes and traditional ones, and the development of a new political consciousness in significant segments of the US population.

Today, even the world of the 1970s seems barely recognizable. The question posed now is whether a return to a more accurate, though surely less innocent, view of US culture and politics will be ever possible, or, whether the changes wrought by 50 years of manufacturing and imposing neoliberal ideology are permanent, as many fear they are. Much of the United States has become mean-spirited and fearful. The leadership has, deep down, nothing but contempt for the weak. Rather than fellow creatures to whom solidarity is owed, the poor deserve what they get – which is very little indeed. The gains of the civil rights movement are beaten back. These attitudes, as Hurricane Katrina dramatically displayed to the world, will prevail, unless and until public opinion demands change.

The media fulfil their function of what media critic Herbert Schiller (1999) calls 'Dumbing down, American style'. Most people get their news exclusively from television, where the dividing line between information and entertainment is ever more tenuous, giving rise to the hideous neologism 'infotainment'. Five or six transnational corporations hold a virtual monopoly over broadcasting, and what they do not control, the religious faction does.

'Creationism' is being taught in many states to provide 'balance' to Darwinism; although, sometimes this literal, six-days, interpretation of the Bible is tempered by the sham scientific doctrine of 'intelligent design'. Religion has now, at least as far as one can tell, precious little to do with loving one's neighbour and doing unto others as you would have others do unto you. It seems increasingly about rejoicing that your neighbour will be burnt to a crisp when Christ returns, serving the sinner right; whereas you will be saved, bodily as well as spiritually.

The books in the *Left Behind* series which describe the 'Rapture', a Second Coming with added frills and thrills, are among the largest sellers in the United States, even though you may not find them on *The New York Times* best-seller lists. The people who are 'Left Behind' are those who did not experience the Rapture, which is the instant, 'in the twinkling of an eye' (the rapture logo is an eye) when the happy few are transported directly to heaven, leaving their clothes on chairs or even airplane seats in neatly folded piles. Sinners will confront the ensuing fires and floods, plagues and wars; they will die excruciatingly nasty deaths, while the foresighted – those who were 'rapture-ready' – watch from their heavenly front-row seats.[19] This doctrine is not merely crazy; it is actively destructive. Tens of millions of believers also believe that environmental disasters are good news, since they foretell Christ's return. Do not count on their numerous Congressional representatives to pass flood control measures, forbid cutting down forests or disallow drilling for oil in Alaska.[20]

Although many classically good, kind and generous people remain in the United States, the vast majority has no idea whatsoever what their country is doing at home, much less in the world at large. They have no comprehension of its political and strategic objectives, or how these take their toll on other nations and other peoples. Americans almost never receive any cultural input that does not come from America itself – for example, foreign films represent a mere one per cent of US consumption, restricted to upper-class cognoscenti. Measures of social control are generally quite effective, such as keeping two million underclass, troublesome, mostly minority men behind bars. The schools, except in wealthy districts, are collapsing, critical thought is not taught and is increasingly unwelcome. Even academia is often infested with religious cranks and the neocon thought police who threaten professors with dismissal and condemn them to a spineless 'neutrality'. Even on public radio or television talk shows, the person supposedly representing the 'left' or 'progressive' viewpoint would in Europe be considered, at best, centre–right. Herbert Schiller quotes Larry Gelbart's 'Weapons of Mass Distraction': 'Tobacco executives are only dangerous to smokers but we all smoke the news. We all inhale television. We all subscribe to what these men are putting out. They are much more dangerous.'

The ultimate goal – or at the least, the outcome – appears to be the destruction of any possibility of social cohesion and solidarity. In the disaster of New Orleans, foreign governments were quicker to offer help than was Washington. Indeed, why bother with poor, mostly black people, who were unable to escape the city? They too got what they deserved. The ideology factory is turning out goods most people buy without even knowing it. It is contaminating the rest of the world. The price is too high and we are all paying it.

And yet, nothing lasts forever. In just the past few months, at the end of 2005 and the beginning of 2006, neoliberals in the United States have taken severe hits. A lower court in Pennsylvania has thrown out a creationist lawsuit against a school board. The lobbying scandal around Jack Abramson has caught many Republican Congressional representatives in its sticky net. The prominent neoliberal called I. Lewis 'Scooter' Libby has left the government in disgrace. Iraq is an unholy mess and Bush's popularity is plummeting. Tom DeLay is no longer Republican majority leader in the House. The voters have even chucked out the Republicans in the mid-term elections of 2006.

Now, if only we can get the progressives to learn the lessons from the right's ideological successes, and to set off resolutely on their own 'long march through the institutions', as Gramsci described the building of cultural hegemony, we might get somewhere.

Notes

1 Mandelson made this declaration at a Party seminar in June 2002, and published his contribution shortly afterwards in *The Times*, 10 June 2002.

2 The Nobel Prize in economics does not, strictly speaking, exist. Since 1969, the Royal Bank of Sweden has awarded a prize 'in memory of Alfred Nobel', which doubtless explains the large number of laureates who are neoliberal economists and econometricians. Joseph Stiglitz and Amartya Sen are exceptions.

3 See http://hayekcenter.org.

4 Particularly, for example, Article 25 of the Universal Declaration of Human Rights of 1948.

5 Thus, 'freedom of speech' does not include the right to shout 'Fire!' in a crowded theatre, as a famous US Supreme Court decision made clear.

6 Hurricane Katrina revealed the social and ecological consequences of the 'economic freedom' to increase global warming, and to leave the poor to their fate.

[7] Although the Christian right will be briefly alluded to in the conclusion, this component of the US right is too broad and complex to deal with in a cursory manner, and requires a place entirely to itself. As such, it is beyond the scope of this book. A part of this Christian movement is, for theological reasons, particularly militant on the subject of Israel's right, indeed duty, to occupy the whole of 'Judea and Samaria', that is, Palestine (and neighbouring lands).

[8] This immensely long piece (almost a book) is an excellent source for seeing the entire history of the post-war world from the neocon viewpoint.

[9] For an expansion on this theme, see George (1987 and 1999), George and Sabelli (1995), as well as chapters 1 and 3 of George (2004).

[10] I am grateful to *The Ecologist* (2005: 9) for this handy compendium of Boltonisms. More detailed information can be found in the well-researched paper by Barry (2005).

[11] Cf. David Hartridge, former Director of Services Trade Division at the WTO: 'Without the enormous pressures exerted by the American financial sector, particularly companies like American Express and Citicorp, there would have been no GATS [the General Agreement on Trade in Services] and therefore perhaps no Uruguay Round and no WTO. The US fought to get services on the agenda and they were right.' Hartridge was speaking at a symposium organized by the international law firm Clifford Chance in 1997, called 'Opening Markets for Banking Worldwide'. The proceedings are no longer on the website of the firm.

[12] Europeans behave no better in any of these areas, particularly with Peter Mandelson in the position of Trade Commissioner, but this book is concerned with US neoliberalism.

[13] See the website of People for the American Way, www.pfaw.org

[14] These remarks do not apply to the Transnational Institute's US funders, particularly the Samuel Rubin Foundation which has shown admirable constancy in its commitments. It is, however, quite small compared to the neocon giants.

[15] Joyce took early retirement from Bradley in 2002 after 15 years at the helm in order to satisfy George Bush's and Karl Rove's request that he set up a new organization called Americans for Community, Faith-Centered Enterprise.

[16] An extremely useful source on both Bradley and Olin is Miller (2003).

[17] www.mediatransparency.org

[18] I have used among other sources the site of People for the American Way (www.pfaw.org) for information about foundations. Although dated, their work remains extremely useful. Heavily footnoted, all references can be found on this site for those who want to pursue the study of US neocons, at least through the mid-1990s.

[19] If you want to know how long before you are left behind to perish, do a search for 'rapture index' on www.google.com.

[20] Although as noted earlier I had planned to include a section on American religion and ideology in this chapter, this has proven impossible without doubling the length; something neither the editor nor I are prepared to contemplate.

References

Barry, Tom (2005), 'Bolton's Baggage', Information Relations Center, www.irc-online.org, 11 March.

Ecologist, The (2005), September issue.

George, Susan (1987), *A Fate Worse than Debt* (Harmondsworth: Penguin).

——— (1997a), 'Les Transnationales au coeur des institutions européennes: Cinquième colonne à Bruxelles', *Le Monde Diplomatique*, December.

——— (1997b), 'How to Win the War of Ideas: Lessons from the Gramscian Right', *Dissent*, Summer.

——— (1999), 'Brief History of Neo-liberalism', http://www.tni.org/george.

——— (2004), *Another World is Possible if ...* (London: Verso).

George, Susan and Fabrizio Sabelli (1995), *Faith and Credit: The World Bank's Secular Empire* (Boulder: Westview Press).

Hayek, Friedrich A. von (1944), *The Road to Serfdom* (Chicago: University of Chicago Press).

——— (1978), *The Constitution of Liberty* (paperback edition; Chicago: University of Chicago Press).
Herrnstein, Richard J. and Charles Murray (1994), *Bell Curve: Intelligence and Class Structure in American Life* (New York: The Free Press).
Hersh, Seymour M. (2006), 'The Iran Plans: Would President Bush go to war to stop Tehran from getting the bomb?', *The New Yorker*, April.
Krauthammer, Charles (2001), regular column in *The Washington Post*, 8 June.
Kuttner, Robert (2002), 'Comment: Philanthropy and Movements', *The American Prospect*, Vol. 13, No. 13, 15 July.
Kwiatowski, Karen (2003), 'In Rumsfeld's Shop', *American Conservative*, 1 December.
——— (2004), 'The New Pentagon Papers', 10 March, http://www.slate.com.
Miller, John J. (2003), 'Strategic Investment in Ideas: How two Foundations Reshaped America', brochure for *The Philanthropy Roundtable*, Washington DC.
Murray, Charles (1985), *Losing Ground: American Social Policy, 1950–1980* (New York: Basic Books).
PFAW (2005), 'UN-dermined: The Right's Disdain for the UN and International Treaties', Special Report, People for the American Way Foundation, http://www.pfaw.org.
PNAC (1998), Letter to President Clinton, http://www.newamericancentury.org/iraqclintonletter.htm.
——— (2000), 'Rebuilding America's Defenses: Strategy, Forces and Resources for a New Century', A Report of the Project for the New American Century, September, http://www.newamericancentury.org/RebuildingAmericasDefenses.pdf.
Podhertz, Norman (2004), 'World War IV: How it started, what it means and why we have to win', *Commentary*, September.
Raimondo, Justin (2000), 'Norman's Narcissism: Podhoretz in Love', 16 October, http://www.antiwar.com/justin/j101600.html.
Schiller, Herbert (1999), 'US as Global Overlord: Dumbing down, American-style', *Le Monde Diplomatique*, August: 5–7.
Schlafly, Phyllis (2003), 'The Impertinence of our so-called allies', Eagle Forum, 25 June.
Smith, James Allen (1991), *The Idea Brokers* (New York: The Free Press).
Weaver, Richard M. (1948), *Ideas Have Consequences* (reprint, Chicago: University of Chicago Press).
Wiener, Jon (1990), 'Dollars for Neocon Scholars', *The Nation*, 1 January.
Wolfowitz, Paul (1992), 'Defense Planning Guidance' draft, n.s.
USAT, USA Today (2005), 'American ex-diplomats urge to block Bolton nomination to UN Post', Associated Press, 28 March.

The Iron Click

American Exceptionalism and US Empire

Mike Marqusee

I am so terrified, America
Of the iron click of your human contact.
And after this
The winding-sheet of your selfless ideal love.
Boundless love
Like a poison gas.

D.H. Lawrence, 'The Evening Land', 1923

The great struggles of the twentieth century between liberty and totalitarianism ended with a decisive victory for the forces of freedom – and a single sustainable model for national success: freedom, democracy, and free enterprise. . . . The United States welcomes our responsibility to lead in this great mission. . . . The US national security strategy will be based on a distinctly American internationalism that reflects the union of our values and our national interests.

National Security Strategy of the United States, 2002

In expounding the doctrine of 'pre-emptive war' and expanding the grounds on which the United States considers itself entitled to take military action, the National Security Strategy (NSS) of 2002 was seen as a departure from the past, and in most quarters an alarming one. However, while it certainly reflects a more aggressive posture, the NSS echoes themes, that reach back to the origins of the US republic. Its unilateralism is not a novelty, but an elaboration of long-standing claims. Its underlying assumptions – that the United States embodies the 'single sustainable model', that the United States is engaged in a global mission on behalf of universal values, and that US national interests coincide with the interests of humanity as a whole – reflect an American exceptionalism that is deeply ingrained in popular conceptions of US national identity.

American Exceptionalism: The Debate

In its narrow sense, the term 'American exceptionalism' refers to the theory that the United States is an exception to the general laws that apply to capitalist societies, notably in its lack of a mass social-democratic, socialist or labour party and the weakness of collectivist ideas and class consciousness. In its broader sense, American exceptionalism envisions the United States as unique among nations and societies; a country with a special mission and therefore enjoying special duties and prerogatives. The USA becomes not merely a nation-state among other nation-states, but an idea and an ideal.

There is a vast literature on whether and to what degree US society is actually exceptional, and whether or not this is a good thing. A number of factors have been cited in attempts to explain the United States' 'exceptional' characteristics: moving frontier, absence of feudalism, availability of land, slavery, immigration, and the multi-ethnic composition of the working class. Clearly, the United States is not a society that is devoid of class conflict or immune to crisis. It is equally clear that the various factors adduced as explanations of American exceptionalism have shaped the manner in which class conflict unfolds and crises are resolved. Like all societies, the United States too has certain distinctive features. It might be said to lie at one end of a spectrum, with the Scandinavian countries at the other. The fact that in recent decades European countries have drawn closer to the US economic and social model suggests that this model is less 'exceptional' than was previously assumed. To speak of the United States as an 'exception' implies the existence of a norm or a general law of development from which it has deviated qualitatively, and identifying a norm or law of this kind is always problematic. As a perspective on US history, American exceptionalism fetishizes differences and downgrades commonalities.

What cannot be denied, however, is the presence and power, within US society, of the tenets of American exceptionalism, at both the elite and popular levels. It is a living, protean ideology. People in many countries believe their own nation to be in some sense 'exceptional', but this belief has deeper roots and greater resonance in the United States. It has shaped class relations within the country as well as popular views of the United States' place in the world. It has played a critical role in both securing domestic support for international expansion and deflecting domestic conflict. Crucially, American exceptionalism is allied today to unprecedented military power. Unlike other countries, the United States has the capacity to make real its claims to exceptional status. For these reasons, the anti-war and anti-globalization movements need to understand how American exceptionalism functions and to devise strategies to combat it.

Strikingly, in the copious studies on American exceptionalism, scant attention has been paid to its impact on or expression in the United States' relations with the rest of the world. Seymour Martin Lipset's *American Exceptionalism* (1996), the most widely reviewed treatment of the subject in recent years, contains not a single reference to US foreign policy – the armed interventions, colonial possessions, or military spending – the latter being a category in which the United States is most definitely exceptional. This silence is itself a symptom of the patterns of thought shaped by American exceptionalism.

'Americanism' and Missionary Nationalism

US nationalism shares characteristics with and performs many of the same functions as other forms of nationalism. As elsewhere, the 'imagined community' of the nation helps to incorporate and subordinate the mass of the population into a larger entity, guided by an elite. However, because of the circumstances of its emergence, US nationalism could not wear the colours of language or ethnicity, or make the territorial claims that sustained nationalisms in other lands. Instead, it posited 'America' as an idea and elevated national identity to the status of an ideology: 'Americanism'.

Richard Hofstadter has observed: 'It has been our fate as a nation not to have ideologies but to be one' (Hofstadter 1966). To its adherents, 'Americanism' is transparent and self-justifying. It is a set of assumptions one naturally subscribes to because one is 'American'. The vagueness of the category enhances its potency. It has a greater elasticity than culturally or ethnically defined nationalisms.

In general, the tenets of 'Americanism' (or 'the American creed') are similar to those recognized elsewhere as the tenets of liberal capitalism. 'Freedom', 'opportunity', 'individualism', the 'rule of law' are all corralled into the 'American' label. What is critical here is not the shifting assortment of ideas, but their perennial branding as 'American'. 'Americanism' is adaptable and expansive, liberalism and authoritarianism, assimilation and exclusion, white supremacism and multi-culturalism cohabit within it.

The designation of those who fail to conform to mainstream US ideology as 'un-American' is revealing. Thus, by virtue of their ideas or lawful activities, US citizens have been stripped not only of their civil liberties, but also of their national identity. Dissenters in other countries are frequently labelled unpatriotic or 'anti-national', but the 'un-American' charge is distinctive. The only comparable phrase is 'anti-Soviet', where a multinational state, the USSR, identified itself (like 'America') with universal ideas and claimed to embrace and liberate diverse nations, and (like 'America'), embody human aspirations in general.

One peculiarity of 'Americanism' is that it usurps the designation of a hemisphere for a single nation-state, thus appropriating 'the new world', and reducing the status of non-US 'Americans'. For all its apparent ethnic and cultural neutrality, 'Americanism' has always been culturally and ethnically inflected. Its virtues and values have been understood as the virtues and values of white Europeans, in particular, northern Protestant Europeans.

'America', from the outset, is portrayed as a unique experiment in the annals of human history. 'The citizens of America,' George Washington (1783: 484–89) had said, 'are . . . to be considered the actors of a most conspicuous theatre, which seems to be peculiarly designed by Providence for the display of human greatness and felicity.' This notion of America as the ultimate arena of human nature still informs much US commentary on US culture, in which a variety of common human traits are designated 'typically American'. Crucially, 'America' is seen as an entity with a global purpose, a mission among the nations. 'Our nation's cause has always been larger than our nation's defense',

Bush (2002) told the cadets at West Point. He added, 'We fight, as we always fight, for a just peace – a peace that favors liberty. . . . We will extend the peace by encouraging free and open societies on every continent.' As we will see, this is a claim with a long pedigree.

Though it is by definition globally expansive, this missionary nationalism insists it is not imperial. Indeed, it is part of its nature that 'America' cannot be an empire – at least not an empire like other empires. In the crucial exercise of disguising imperial realities from the US populace, American exceptionalism plays a key role. The NSS refers to an 'American internationalism that reflects the union of our values and our national interests'. In this marriage of a nation-state-turned-super-power with a set of transcendent values, America becomes a synonym for 'freedom' (and 'freedom' becomes a synonym for 'free enterprise'). Tocqueville (1835) spoke of the United States' 'Holy cult of freedom'. 'Freedom' (rather than self-defence) has been the putative motivation of nearly every US war: the campaigns against Native Americans and Mexicans, the Civil War (the battle cry on both sides), the Spanish–American War ('freedom' for Cuba and the Spanish possessions), the First World War (to make the world safe for democracy), the Second World War, the Cold War, the Vietnam War, and now the 'war on terror'.

Bush has been careful to deny any 'clash of civilizations', to disclaim American proprietorship of democracy or capitalism. He has stressed the universal reach of 'god given freedom', and then invoked the global reach of the United States as the instrument of that freedom. Ironically, Bush appeals to an old liberal vein in US thinking about the US global mission: a belief that the United States is the vanguard of human progress, a social and economic model to be exported.

'Ours was the first of the modern ideological countries, born of a revolutionary doctrine,' Gary Wills commented in the 1970s. 'We are not merely a country. We are an -ism. And truth must spread without limit; it cannot countenance error.' Americanism is 'power purified – and the saints are free of many restrictions imposed on those without proper doctrine' (Wills 1982: 426).

Foundation Myths and American Expansionism: From the Seventeenth to the Nineteenth Century

> The story of America is the story of expanding liberty: an ever-widening circle constantly growing to reach further and include more. Our nation's founding commitment is still our deepest commitment: in our world and here at home we will extend the frontiers of freedom.
>
> George W. Bush (2004), speech to Republican National Convention

John Winthrop's oft-quoted admonition of 1630, to his fellow New England colonists, is usually cited as the *fons et origo* of American exceptionalism: 'We shall be as a city upon a hill. The eyes of all people are upon us.' For Winthrop, the colonists' toe-hold on the North American continent was a moral test, and judgement awaited them if they failed it. The propulsions of Calvinism

– the light and darkness of divine election – seemed to be enhanced by the New World setting.

There is a tendency to view American exceptionalism as a Puritan inheritance, descending in unbroken continuity from Winthrop. And it does retain a religious tinge: 'America' is a chosen nation, 'Americans' are a chosen people. However, it can be argued that American exceptionalism was more profoundly shaped by Enlightenment rationalism's secular ideas, and the mastery of nature and human labour it facilitated. The United States' exceptional historic role was first proclaimed by European progressives. In *The Rights of Man* Thomas Paine (1792) argued: 'The revolution of America presented in politics what was only theory in mechanics. So deeply rooted were all the governments of the old world, and so effectually had the tyranny and the antiquity of habit established itself over the mind that no beginning could be made in Asia, Africa or Europe. . . .' The United States was seen as providing a unique opportunity for both institutions and individuals to make a fresh start, to get 'back to nature' and first principles. In 1827, an envious Goethe wrote:

> America, you are luckier
> Than this old continent of ours
> . . . you do not suffer,
> In hours of intensity,
> From futile memories
> And pointless battles.
> (Translated by Robert Bly; Ricks and Vance 1982)

A decade later, Tocqueville (1837) declared: 'the position of the Americans is quite exceptional, and it may be believed that no democratic people will ever be placed in a similar one.'

The idea of 'America' as a great social experiment conducted on a *tabula rasa* (the American hemisphere) meant that, from the beginning, its borders were in flux; it was conceived as expansionist. In 1787, John Adams (the future second President of the republic), in his *Defence of the Constitutions of the United States* mentioned the newly-formed USA as an 'experiment . . . destined to spread over the northern part of that whole quarter of the globe'.

Adams' successor, Thomas Jefferson, was one of the first to articulate the universal claims of human rights on the political stage. In later ages and remote societies, the arguments and the prose of the US Declaration of Independence, authored by Jefferson, would be echoed by peoples seeking freedom from colonial domination. But even then, the rhetoric of human rights slides into claims for national aggrandisement. Among the charges the Declaration makes against King George III is that he has blocked 'new appropriation of lands', failed to encourage migration from Europe and sided with 'the merciless Indian savages' against the 'inhabitants of our frontiers', that is, the white settlers seeking to expand the colonial domain.

In 1786, Jefferson declared that 'our confederacy must be viewed as the nest from which all America, north and south, is to be peopled'. He wrote to Monroe: 'I have ever looked on Cuba as the most interesting addition which could be made to our system of states' (quoted in Lens 2003: 2). What was envisioned here was not the spread of sovereign governments, but their incorporation into a system predicated on white supremacy. As President, Jefferson quarantined Haiti, the hemisphere's second independent republic. Haiti was an even bolder experiment in democracy than the one made on the north, but it was an experiment conducted by black slaves and not white property owners. Following the Louisiana Purchase of 1803 – in which the United States acquired a huge land mass directly from the French Empire – Jefferson sent troops to New Orleans to ensure that the reluctant inhabitants acceded to US rule. His belief that 'America, north and south, has a set of interests distinct from those of Europe, and peculiarly her own', became the basis for the Monroe Doctrine of 1823, which declared that the United States would oppose any attempt by European powers to interfere in the hemisphere's affairs, which meant the right to interfere in these affairs belonged exclusively to the United States. This founding claim to hemispheric hegemony introduced an extra-territorial definition of national self-defence, underpinned by American exceptionalism.

Enlightenment universalism was, in the context of North America, made to serve as a settler-colonial ideology. White Anglo–Saxon supremacy was ingrained in it. Roxanne Dunbar–Ortiz (2004: 37) argues that 'the origin myth' of the United States disguises the fact that the 'American revolution' was 'a split in the British empire, not an anti-colonial liberation movement'. A settler elite, dissatisfied with distant overlordship, claimed direct rule over 'their' portion of the empire. For the plebeian settler population, however, other more democratic ambitions were involved. The outcome was a hierarchical society dressed in the uniform of democracy. The founding act of the republic was, in the official memory, an anti-colonial revolution. Over many generations, this popular understanding of the nation's origins has helped make the US public resistant to the idea that the United States should be an empire, and even more to the realization that it is an empire.

In 1845, on the eve of the war against Mexico, through which it would seize what is now the southwest United States, a US newspaper editorialized that it was the 'manifest destiny' of the nation to spread from the Atlantic to the Pacific. There is a mixture here of Calvinism (the predestination of the elect), and social experimentalism, the idea that the US model was progressive and superior, and could, therefore, disregard the claims of others. In due course, the United States completed a process of territorial expansion as rapid, brutal and permanent as anything in the annals of the human race. Opposition to this process, within US society, was confined to the margins. For the vast majority of the white population, the special claim of 'America' to America was unquestioned.

Nor was the United States' reach confined to the North American mainland. According to the State Department, the country engaged in 103 overseas military interventions between 1798 and 1895 (Zinn 1996: 290–91). To protect

US shipping, the nascent republic fought battles in the Mediterranean, the Caribbean, Sumatra, Samoa, Argentina and Peru. The principles of sovereignty and self-government were always secondary to commercial interests. By the end of the nineteenth century, the United States had established bases on dozens of islands across the Pacific, and used military force to secure a foothold in the markets of China and Japan.

An American Super-Race

Tocqueville (1835; Vol. I, Part 2) had noted that Americans lived 'in a perpetual state of self-adoration'. As a result of the success and vibrancy of their great experiment, 'they have an immensely high opinion of themselves and are not far from believing that they form a species apart form the rest of the human race'. Twenty years later, Walt Whitman published *Leaves of Grass*, an innovatory, rhapsodic poem sequence in which Americans do indeed appear as 'a species apart'.

Whitman was self-consciously and professedly an 'American bard' and remains the major poet of American national identity. His thrust was democratic, egalitarian and inclusive. He celebrated and identified himself – physically, sometimes erotically – with the life in the streets. In nobody else's verse does the word 'America' recur so frequently or carry such freight. He defined 'America' (Whitman 1982: 616), of course, not merely as a territorial or civic entity, but as 'perennial with the earth, with Freedom, Law and Love'. He seems, at times, to envision Americans as a kind of super-race.

Whitman supported the Mexican War of 1846–48. He called for US troops to be stationed in Mexico to establish a regime 'whose efficiency and permanency shall be guaranteed by the United States'. He hoped this would open an avenue 'for manufacturers and commerce, into which the immense dead capital of the country will go'.

Whitman enthusiastically embraced a missionary nationalism. 'Sole among nationalities, these States have assumed the task to put in forms of lasting power and practicality, on areas of amplitude rivalling the operations of the physical kosmos, the moral political speculations of ages, long, long defer'd, the democratic republican principle. . . .' Yet this rhapsodic exponent of American exceptionalism shivered in the face of a reality in which 'we march with unprecedented strides to empire so colossal, outvying the antique, beyond Alexander's, beyond the proudest sway of Rome. In vain have we annexed Texas, California, Alaska, and reach north for Canada and south for Cuba. It is as though we were somehow being endowed with a vast and more and more thoroughly-appointed body, and then left with little or no soul' (Whitman 1871).

In a wry key, a similar anxiety was expressed by Whitman's contemporary, Oliver Wendell Holmes, who celebrated 'the young American of the 19th century' as 'heir to all old civilizations, founder of that new one which . . . is to be the noblest, as it is the last'. But then he went on to warn: 'the chief danger is that he will think the whole planet is made for him'.

Empire and Denial – From 1898 through the Cold War

Despite incessant foreign interventions, it was only in the late 1890s that the United States began to acquire foreign territory outside the continental land mass of North America. This was one of the rare periods in which the United States has spoken openly of itself as an empire. The 1890s witnessed a major depression and extensive, often violent, conflict between labour and capital, as well as the challenge of a bi-racial, agrarian Populist movement. In the same decade, immigration from eastern and southern Europe reached mass proportions and Jim Crow laws imposed segregation and subordination on African–Americans across the south.

In this context, both government and private corporations sought to promote a new, unifying patriotism. The Pledge of Allegiance was introduced in schools. It became customary to stand for the 'Star Spangled Banner' at public events. State and local Flag Days were inaugurated. At the same time, sections of elite opinion began arguing that the United States should become an empire, and a rival to the great European powers. Overseas expansion offered a remedy to the crisis of surplus capital and industrial capacity. In this decade, the United States constructed a fleet that made it the world's second greatest naval power. It annexed Hawaii, and in a brief but heavily publicized war, prised Cuba, Puerto Rico and the Philippines from the dying Spanish empire. Propaganda for the war emphasized its economic benefits to 'our farmers and workmen'. A higher gloss was offered by Rudyard Kipling (1899), who urged the United States to shoulder 'the white man's burden', and bring civilization to the dark-skinned Filipinos.

In opposition to the new US imperialism, there emerged a substantial, avowedly 'Anti-Imperialist' movement. 'I am an anti-imperialist', said Mark Twain (1900), 'I oppose putting the eagle's talons on any other land.' For the anti-imperialists, acquiring territories overseas was contrary to the principles of the United States' own anti-colonial revolution. They warned (prophetically) that the US could not be both a republic and an empire. And they frequently argued that if the United States became an empire, it would sacrifice the very qualities that had made it exceptional. To the extent that the nation acted like a European power, its citizens would forfeit the blessings of their special historic providence.

Initially, there was extensive labour support for the anti-imperialist cause, including Samuel Gompers, leader of the American Federation of Labour (AFL) and apostle of 'pure' (that is, non-political), trades unionism. Gompers feared that US workers would be undercut by cheap labour in backward countries. However, along with the bulk of the labour movement, he soon acquiesced to overseas expansion. At this crucial juncture, which saw the emergence of independent labour parties in Britain and Australia, mainstream US unionism rejected political alliances, turned away from the unskilled and the unorganized, and sought accommodation with the employers. One of the major factors in this momentous development was the impact of the Spanish War and the consequent US overseas expansion. Years later, the Populist leader Tom Watson was to observe: 'The Spanish War finished us. The blare of the bugle drowned out the voice of the Reformer.' The brevity, success and spoils of the war fuelled the new jingoism, which had a fierce racial edge. US superiority had been confirmed; white people who ruled over black people at home could now rule over black people abroad.

According to historian Charles Bergquist:

> The imperialist thrust of 1898 coincided with . . . the beginning of the long wave of capitalist expansion that lasted until the 1920s. In the Americas, this period witnessed a great burst of US investment in Latin America, US intervention to assure the separation of Panama from Colombia, the building of the Panama canal, and the consolidation of informal US control over the whole Caribbean basin.

The canal fostered the integration of the domestic market, enabled the United States to dominate Latin America and penetrate further into East Asian markets. Growth rates after 1898 shot up to 5.2 per cent per annum. US foreign trade and foreign investment expanded exponentially. Sections of the US working class who enjoyed the fruits of empire, now provided a material base for imperial ideology and American exceptionalism (Bergquist 1996: 45–77).

Filipinos, however, took the rhetoric of 'freedom' seriously and rebelled against US rule. During more than a decade of brutal counter-insurgency, a quarter of a million Filipinos had been killed, and 4200 Americans. This was ten times the number of Americans killed in the brief Spanish–American War. Yet, US history textbooks routinely assign far more space to the latter than the former. And even the Spanish–American war – with its enormous historical consequences – is treated as a self-contained incident, a curiosity, not part of the larger narrative. Thus, the US population knows little of the United States' history as an explicitly imperial power, which makes it harder for it to grasp the imperial nature of its present activities.

Openly imperial rhetoric was soon replaced by something more compatible with American exceptionalist tradition. For the most part, the United States chose to shoulder the 'white man's burden' through indirect rule and economic coercion backed by the threat of military intervention. In 1904, Theodore Roosevelt issued his Corollary to the Monroe Doctrine, anticipating the NSS in its targeting of 'rogue states':

> Chronic wrongdoing, or an impotence which results in a general loosening of the ties of civilized society may, in America, as elsewhere, ultimately require intervention by some civilized nation, and in the western hemisphere the adherence of the United States to the Monroe Doctrine may force the United States, however reluctantly, in flagrant cases of wrongdoing or impotence, to the exercise of an international police power. (Lens 2003: 204–06)

So it was no longer a question of protecting the hemisphere from European interference, but from the unwise actions of its own residents and regimes.

The rationalization was largely accepted by a US population that had been divided by the overt imperialism of the preceding years.

It was Woodrow Wilson, traditionally viewed, like Jefferson, as an idealist, intellectual and internationalist, who applied most ruthlessly Roosevelt's Corollary. America, Wilson declared, was 'the only idealistic nation in the world'. He argued that the proposed League of Nations would be based on 'American principles' which were 'the principles of mankind and must prevail'. He proclaimed 'national self-determination' as a cornerstone of the new world order, but deployed US military forces overseas more frequently than any of his predecessors, against Mexico, Haiti, the Dominican Republic, Cuba, Panama, Nicaragua and the nascent Soviet Union. In *Lies My Teacher Told Me*, James W. Loewen (1995) surveyed the scanty consideration of Wilson's record of overseas intervention in US history textbooks. Of the twelve textbooks surveyed, not one even mentioned the anti-Soviet action, although thousands of US troops had been tied up on Soviet soil for some two years. Where they do mention foreign interventions, the textbooks present them as reluctant responses to social breakdown. One of the most widely used books, *The Triumph of the American Nation*, recounts the 1914 invasion of Mexico in these words: 'President Wilson was urged to send military forces into Mexico to protect American interests and to restore law and order' (Loewen 1995: 12–27).

The United States entered the First World War only in its final year and enjoyed the boost of quick victory and access to the victors' spoils. The war facilitated the repression of the most militant and internationalist sections of the working class, such as the Industrial Workers of the World, and the co-optation of the AFL, whose members benefited from wartime increases in production. The United States emerged from the war in a position of greatly enhanced strength when compared to its European rivals. American exceptionalism was powerfully re-enforced.

Wilson, of course, failed to sell the League of Nations to the US public. 'Isolationism' became the prevalent note through the 1920s and most of the 1930s. Calvin Coolidge offered Latin America 'dollar diplomacy', though the military stick was still employed. Isolationism was always a wariness of involvement in European conflicts; no isolationist ever suggested that the United States should withdraw from the Philippines or any of its beachheads abroad. As a current of opinion it was bolstered by nativism, but also by the particular interests and preoccupations of US capital at that time. Both the 'isolationists' and the 'internationalists' of the period drew heavily on American exceptionalism. In his famous call to make the twentieth century 'the first great American century', media mogul Henry Luce – arguing against the isolationists – offered what he called 'a vision of America as a world power, which is authentically American'. He postulated 'America as the dynamic center of ever-widening spheres of enterprise, America as the training center of the skilled servants of mankind, America as the good Samaritan . . . America as the workshop of the ideals of freedom and justice' (quoted in McCrisken 2003: 21).

The Second World War discredited isolationism, but it magnified the sway of American exceptionalism. Military production finally resolved the economic and social crisis of the 1930s; the labour unions formed through militant action were incorporated. The United States was distant from the fields of battle and shielded from the devastation. It was fighting a just and necessary cause, humanity's cause, and, at the end of the great struggle, it emerged as an economic and military 'super-power'. All of this ensured the triumph of the Luce version of America's missionary nationalism.

American exceptionalism made it easy for the United States to assume the mantle of 'leader of the free world' in the Cold War competition with the Soviet Union. In the hugely influential 1947 article in which he outlined the strategy of 'containment', George Kennan suggested that Americans should feel 'gratitude to a Providence which by providing the American people with this implacable challenge, has made their entire security as a nation dependent on their pulling together and accepting the responsibilities of moral and political leadership that history plainly intended them to bear.' Under the Truman Doctrine, the United States pledged to send money, equipment or military force to countries threatened by 'attempted subjugation by armed minorities or by outside pressures', which in the first instance meant aiding the rightwing forces in the Greek civil war. 'The free peoples of the world look to us for support in maintaining their freedoms,' Harry Truman (1947) explained. In his first inaugural address in 1953, Dwight Eisenhower reminded Americans that 'destiny has laid upon our country the responsibility of the free world's leadership' (quoted in McCrisken 2003: 22). In a global battle of-isms, 'Americanism' squared off against Communism, which was defined as its antithesis.

The military spending in the Cold War helped fuel economic growth, and confirm the US as 'the land of opportunity'. Having rid itself of the organized left at the onset of the period, US labour fully subscribed to the permanent arms economy, and the ideology that went with it, as well as using its resources in the international labour movement to sabotage working-class challenges to US dominance.

The Cold War era of the 1950s and early 1960s was the heyday of American exceptionalism. Academic studies of the subject, overwhelmingly triumphalist in tone, proliferated. Sociologist Daniel Bell proclaimed the 'end of ideology' as the American model could not be superceded.

In the competition with the Soviet bloc, it was vital that the United States distinguish itself from the old European empires (one reason it refused to back Britain and France during the Suez crisis). Here, the already established traditions of American exceptionalism made it easier for people in the United States (if not elsewhere), to persuade themselves that their role in the world was benign, and could be played by no other nation. Henry Steel Commager, a liberal, exclaimed:

> The record is perhaps unique in the history of power: the organization of the

> United Nations, the Truman Doctrine, the Marshall Plan, the Berlin airlift, the organization of NATO, the defence of Korea, the development of atomic power for peaceful purposes – these prodigious gestures are so wide and so enlightened that they point the way to a new concept of the use of power. (Quoted in Wills 1976)

In entering the Korean war in 1950, Truman had insisted that what motivated the United States was 'basic moral principle', and definitely not any wish for 'domination'. Fifteen years later, announcing the despatch of US troops to the Dominican Republic to topple an elected government, Lyndon Johnson (1965) solemnly declared: 'Over the years of our history our forces have gone forth into many lands, but always they returned when they were no longer needed. For the purpose of America is never to suppress liberty, but always to save it.' The denial of empire and the insistence on the American exception echo down the years. Richard Nixon (1994: 30) wrote in his memoirs that 'the US is the only great power without a history of imperialistic claims on neighbouring states'. Sandy Berger (1999), Bill Clinton's national security advisor, insisted: 'We are the first global power in history that is not an imperial power.' Shortly after the invasion of Iraq, Donald Rumsfeld (2003) insisted to Al Jazeera: 'We're not a colonial power. We've never been a colonial power.' Colin Powell (2003) agreed: 'We have never been imperialists. We seek a world in which liberty, prosperity and peace can become the heritage of all peoples.' Both men seemed astonished and offended that anyone could think otherwise.

Vietnam and After: Crisis and Revival of American Exceptionalism

Explaining the war in Vietnam to his fellow Americans, Johnson (1966) assured them: 'We have no territory there, nor do we seek any. . . . We want nothing for ourselves . . . we fight for values and we fight for principles.' But the platitudes of American exceptionalism were to be profoundly shaken by Vietnam. Not only did the United States lose the war to a poorer, darker people, but the populace for the first time became aware of the immorality and brutality of its government's foreign policy. In the context of widespread and unquestioned assumptions about what 'America' meant in the world, this was a profound shock. Cold War liberalism, which had given birth to the Vietnam nightmare, was stripped of its aura of idealism. Coupled with the black freedom struggle of the era, Vietnam made apparent a huge disparity between 'America' in theory and the United States in practice. In 1975, a traumatized Daniel Bell proclaimed the end of American exceptionalism: 'There is no longer a manifest destiny or mission. We have not been immune to the corruption of power. We have not been the exception . . . our mortality lies before us' (quoted in Zuckerman 1997: 14–17).

In the years to come, the Vietnam syndrome – according to which, the US population remained reluctant to expose US soldiers in large numbers to danger overseas – acted as restraint on direct foreign intervention. In one sense, it was rooted in a popular recognition of the limits of US power, and the fallibility of US leaders. But it also re-enforced the tradition of empire by indirection, and ensured that Americans remained at a safe remove from the realities and consequences of US policy. Under these conditions, American exceptionalism could revive.

Gerald Ford, Jimmy Carter, and Ronald Reagan all began their presidencies by advocating the need for the United States to return to its basic principles. All of them promised – but only Reagan seemed to deliver – a return to a pre-Vietnam America (McCrisken 2003: 40–130). In his inaugural address, Carter pledged himself to 'international policies which reflect our own precious values'. He presented 'human rights' as the new driving force in US foreign policy. He described the new posture as 'compatible with the character of the American people. Our country will be a leader in the world standing up for the same principles on which our nation was founded.' But under Carter, 'national security' usually trumped 'human rights'. His administration opposed embargoes on Uganda and South Africa, extended most favoured nation status to China, aided Zaire and Indonesia, and initiated policies that his successor later escalated: opposition to the Sandinista regime in Nicaragua and support for the Afghan mujahideen. The famous Camp David agreement did little for the Palestinians, but did bring Egypt under the US umbrella, making it a top recipient of US military aid. In his last State of the Union address, in 1980, Carter joined the list of Presidents who have modified and extended the US prerogatives embodied in the Monroe doctrine: 'Any attempt by any outside force to gain control of the Persian gulf region will be regarded as an assault on the vital interests of the United States of America,' he said, 'and such an assault will be repelled by any means necessary.'

Reagan's faith in American exceptionalism was undisguised and unqualified. He liked to talk about America as 'the city on the hill'. In his inaugural address, he promised to make America, once again, 'the exemplar of freedom and a beacon of hope'. The United States has 'a destiny and a duty, a duty to preserve and hold in sacred trust mankind's age-old aspirations'. Speaking to the United Nations, he told the world that Americans 'have never been aggressors. We have always struggled to defend freedom and democracy. We have no territorial ambitions. We occupy no countries' (quoted in McCrisken 2003: 85–91). In his 'crusade for freedom' against the Soviet nemesis, Reagan massively increased military spending; the ensuing economic recovery helped ensure his re-election in 1984 under the slogan 'America is back'. He welcomed both the Contras and the mujahideen to the White House as 'the moral equivalents of our founding fathers'.

The collapse of the Soviet Union ushered in a new wave of triumphalist American exceptionalism. The US model had outlasted all its competitors, who now sought to emulate it. Now it was the 'end of history', instead of ideology, that was declared. As US forces led the assault in the Gulf, the first President Bush (1991) told Congress: 'The hopes of humanity turn to us. We are Americans; we have a unique responsibility to do the hard work of freedom.' In the aftermath of victory over Saddam Hussein, George W. Bush declared that America possessed 'a saving grace which makes us still exemplary to other nations'. Daniel Bell recanted his 1975 recantation, affirming that American exceptionalism was alive and well, and rooted in the fact that the United States was a 'complete civil society, perhaps the only one in political history'.

After taking office in 1993, Clinton explained that 'the over-riding purpose' of his foreign policy would be 'to expand and strengthen the community of market-based economies' and 'enlarge the circle of nations that live under . . . free institutions'. Americanism was thus linked to globalization, and seen as the export of the US economic model. The key US successes of the Clinton years were the passage of North American Free Trade Agreement (NAFTA) and the Uruguay round of General Agreement on Tariffs and Trade (GATT). Along with this economic 'enlargement' went the continued exercise of military prerogatives, as and when convenient. Clinton authorized the use of force on more occasions than any of his post-Vietnam predecessors. In deference to the Vietnam syndrome, these actions relied mainly on air power rather than troops on the ground. They were also carefully smothered with the rhetoric of American exceptionalism. In his address on the Dayton Agreement, in November 1995, Clinton told US citizens:

> From our birth, America has always been more than just a place. America has embodied an idea that has become an ideal. . . . Today, because of our dedication, America's ideals – liberty, democracy, peace – are more and more the aspirations of people everywhere in the world. It is the power of our ideas – even more than our size, our wealth and our military might – that makes America a uniquely trusted nation.

In the years to come, Clinton and Madeleine Albright, his Secretary of State, would frequently describe the United States as 'the indispensable nation' (McCrisken 2003: 159–82).

None of the central neocon postulates about the United States' role in the world is novel, such as, America as an agent of global freedom, specifically of 'free enterprise', America as a modern social model which must be propagated, America as a world power that remains distinctively American. Down the generations, these notions have formed the common currency of both liberal and conservative US opinion. The universal claims, embedded in American exceptionalism, have paved the way for an empire that denies its existence. This denial is re-enforced in countless ways in everyday life. You will look in vain in the USA for the kind of visible legacies of empire – statues, street names – that litter European cities.[1]

11 September

The living influence of American exceptionalism was starkly displayed in the US response to 11 September. The year before, a poll had showed that only 4–5 per cent of US citizens considered foreign affairs as the most pressing issue facing the nation (McCrisken 2003: 180).

In the absence of a global context, and, in particular, of any understanding of the role of the United States in the Middle East and Central Asia, the 11 September attacks seemed a case of motiveless malignity. CNN showed footage of a woman running from smoke and debris, and crying, 'America doesn't do this. America doesn't kill innocent people.' She was genuinely bewildered, and her bewilderment reflected a world-view fostered by American exceptionalism.

In his address to Congress after the attacks, Bush (2001) posed the question: 'Why do they hate us?', and replied:

> They hate what we see right here in this chamber: a democratically elected Government. . . . They hate our freedoms: our freedom of religion, our freedom of speech, our freedom to vote and assemble and disagree with each other. . . . As long as the United States of America is determined and strong, this will not be an age of terror; this will be an age of liberty, here and across the world . . .. The advance of human freedom – the great achievement of our time, and the great hope of every time – now depends on us. . . .

In this construction, the atrocities of 11 September were made not merely to appear as attacks on the lives of innocents or on the US government, but on 'American values', which, as ever, were also claimed as universal (or civilizational) values. It was argued (demanded) that anyone who shared these values should automatically support the United States in its chosen response to the terrorist attack. Those who demurred were condemned as 'anti-American'. The United States was under assault because of its exceptional nature. It seemed that the same special destiny that made America admired and trusted by other nations, now made it the object of resentment, envy and hatred.

In response to 11 September, the display of national emblems became ubiquitous, and in some contexts *de rigueur*. The corporate media branded their coverage of the crisis with US flags and logos shrieking, 'America Under Attack' or 'America Strikes Back'. From baseball to pop music, there was hardly a facet of US culture that was not mobilized to support 'national unity', 'national resolve', and the distinctiveness of the 'American way of life'. Although there were certainly chauvinist and xenophobic responses to the bombings in Madrid and London, these did not provoke a similar mood in either country. (In London, there was hardly a Union Jack on display; polls showed that most Londoners believed the attack was linked to the US–UK policy in Iraq, and not to a hatred of 'British values'.)

In the wake of 11 September, and before the NSS of 2002, the United States redefined 'self-defence', and the superpower's military prerogatives. It claimed the right to attack (invade and occupy) countries alleged to harbour people involved in terrorist acts against the United States. This was a power the United States explicitly denied to others. It would not accept, for example, that India, in the wake of a terrorist attack on its soil, had the right to respond by a military strike against Pakistan. Yet this assertion of imperial right went virtually unchallenged in the United States, except by Noam Chomsky and the far left. The willingness of US intelligentsia to casually endorse a doctrine and a practice that could never be sustained as a norm of international behaviour spoke volumes about the uncritical acceptance of long-standing American exceptionalist claims, and the historical–geographical myopia they have engendered.

Bush's posture drew on widely accepted notions of American exceptionalism, and that helped him to secure (at least initially), wide domestic support for 'the war on terror'. Here, the USA appeared, once again, as an ism, as the upholder of universal values, as a special nation with distinctive and exclusive prerogatives. The official opposition's fear of challenging these notions helped render their arguments against Bush hesitant and ineffective.

On 10 April 2003, in the course of his 'mission accomplished' speech, declaring victory in Iraq, Bush told his audience: 'Other nations in history have fought in foreign lands and remained to occupy and exploit. Americans, following a battle, want nothing more than to return home.' It should not have been hard to expose this bogus claim, and the false promise that went with it – but Bush's mainstream critics, burdened with a deference to American exceptionalism, were unable to do so.

Colluding or Contesting? 'Americanism', Liberals and the Left

No other empire, in its heyday, encountered the degree of internal dissent with which the US empire has had to contend – in 1898, during Vietnam, in relation to Central America in the 1980s, and in opposition to the invasion of Iraq. The US elite has often had to work hard to secure domestic support for its international interventions. Repeatedly, American exceptionalism has come to its aid.

In the 1930s, social crisis gave rise to a contest between left and right over the ownership of 'America' and 'Americanism'. During the popular front period, the CPUSA, the dominant organization on the US left, played down its revolutionary rhetoric, and sought to establish itself as a homegrown people's movement for social justice. The official slogan of the era was 'Communism is twentieth-century Americanism'. The left claimed the Founding Fathers and Lincoln as its own. It presented itself as the vanguard, not in a global class struggle but, in the unfolding American experiment, the expanding circle of freedom that was 'America'. One of the missions of the popular front was to 'Americanize' a seemingly alien movement (Marxism, socialism). The left fretted that its ethnic roots were showing, and that these roots betrayed a heritage that was less than authentically American.

In emphasizing their national credentials, the Communists were part of a wider movement. The New Deal encouraged interest in US history and culture, and a new regionalism in the arts. It sponsored large-scale narrative paintings in public spaces and a wide array of folkloric activities. Alan Lomax, a folk music archivist and proselytizer, enjoyed both access to the Roosevelt White House, and close ties to the CPUSA. He said: 'John Henry told his captain, A man ain't nothing but a man.' Leaving aside the fact that in the late eighteenth century,

Robert Burns, a Scottish Republican, had declared 'A man's a man for a' that', what is remarkable is how easily even this progressive version of the national narrative turns expansive. Lomax (2003: 57) repeated with admiration a tall tale from the old frontier:

> 'The boundaries of the United States, sir?' replied the Kentuckian. 'Why sir, on the north we are bounded by the aurora borealis, on the east by the rising sun, on the south by the procession of the equinoxes and on the west by the day of judgement'.[2]

In adopting the rhetoric of Americanism, the left conceded dangerous ground, not so much to backward looking nativism as to the emboldened American imperialism that emerged after the Second World War. The Cold War split the liberal–left coalition of the New Deal and isolated the Marxist and radical left. The claims on Jefferson and Lincoln, the protestations of 'Americanism', wilted in the face of domestic repression. The left was demonized as alien and stripped of its American credentials, as it was ideologically outside the Cold War consensus. The USA and USSR self-consciously confronted each other as ideological (not just military or economic) rivals. The long-established universal claims of 'Americanism' were pitted against the universal claims of Soviet ideology. In these circumstances, loyalty to the USA was tied to acceptance of the latest version of missionary nationalism, whose terms both the liberals and the left had helped entrench.

In the labour movement, the Cold War purge led to mass expulsions, splits and a historic de-politicization from which US unions are still recovering. Nationalist paranoia and superpower prerogatives merged with long-term consequences for US political culture. The divergence of the US polity from its European counterparts was deepened, and the centre of gravity pushed to the right, where it has stayed. The way was paved for the routine acceptance of huge peacetime military expenditure. There was barely a whisper of domestic dissent when the United States overthrew the non-Communist, moderately nationalist regimes of Mossadegh in Iran, in 1953, and Arbenz in Guatemala, in 1954, and invaded Lebanon in 1958.

By colluding in the demonization not only of Communism and Marxism, but of anyone who opposed the Cold War, or failed to genuflect before the altar of American exceptionalism, the liberals helped create the political culture in which 'liberal', itself, eventually became a dirty word. They handed the right a devastatingly flexible ideological trump card: 'Americanism' – a means to de-legitimize radical, non-conformist and especially avowedly internationalist ideas.

While the excesses of McCarthyism were eventually curbed, its assumptions remained in place. They came under huge stress during the Vietnam War. Indeed, much of the bitterness that characterized the anti-war movement in the United States sprang from the abrupt collapse of American exceptionalist claims, for which the generation reared on Cold War liberalism was entirely unprepared.

The discovery that the US was a bloodstained empire was traumatic. But, in subsequent years, that trauma was largely reshaped in popular culture in ways that displaced it from the context of US empire. It became an 'American tragedy', marked much more by the loss of 58,000 US lives than two million Vietnamese. In the reactionary version, the war was lost at home, due to the weakness and lack of patriotism of the left. In the liberal versions (*Apocalypse, Now*; *Coming Home; Platoon*), the war is a psychodrama, an arena for an existential struggle for the American soul. The question why the United States was in South-East Asia is rarely addressed. The Vietnamese and their struggle for self-determination are invisible.

The culture of 'patriotic dissent' remains powerful in the United States, and has been strongly in evidence during the post-11 September anti-war movement. US flags are numerous and prominent in demonstrations; the focus is on US casualties. The thrust of the argument is often that the war is bad for people in the United States, and the suffering of Iraqis appears peripheral. This is more than the kind of tactical adjustment to parochial concerns that, rightly or wrongly, one sees in struggles all over the world. It reflects and re-enforces the circumscribed moral arena established by American exceptionalism. Once again, there is a competition with the right for the claim to 'Americanism'. And once again, there is a fear that opposition to the war in Iraq might be construed as lack of faith in 'American' ideals and norms.

There are, of course, other traditions of dissent in the United States, traditions that reject American exceptionalism, among them: the International Workers of the World's (IWW) opposition to the First World War, DuBois' rejection of the Cold War, and Malcolm X's explicit critique of the category of 'American' ('You're not Americans,' he told black audiences in the 1960s, 'you're the victims of America'). There has always been a black exception to the American exception. Martin Luther King often invoked the uniqueness of the American dream, and conflated it with the humanist dream. He spoke of America's 'promissory note' and how it had to be redeemed. But he was also an internationalist. His principal political model was M.K. Gandhi, and he was inspired by the anti-colonial struggles of the era. In his last years, he moved towards a more explicit internationalism and a sharper critique of American imperialism.

American 'Insularity'

No one likes us—I don't know why
We may not be perfect, but heaven knows we try
But all around, even our old friends put us down
Let's drop the big one and see what happens

We give them money but are they grateful?
No, they're spiteful and they're hateful
They don't respect us, so let's surprise them
We'll drop the big one and pulverize them

Asia's crowded and Europe's too old
Africa is far too hot
And Canada's too cold
And South America stole our name
Let's drop the big one
There'll be no one left to blame us

Randy Newman, 'Political Science', 1970

Anatole Lieven called American exceptionalism the American public's 'intense solipsism'. Here, foreign suffering is largely unreal, and global injustice often invisible. Sometimes, as in US sports, the outside world disappears altogether, or is subsumed by America itself: the climax of a baseball competition played exclusively among north American cities is dubbed 'the world series'.

A National Geographic survey (NGN 2002) in 2002, revealed a significant gap in global awareness between young Americans and young people in comparable societies. Only one in seven young Americans could find Iraq (13 per cent), Iran (13 per cent), or Israel (14 per cent), on a map of the Middle East.[3] On a map of Europe only 37 per cent could locate Britain. In addition, a majority of young Americans grossly overstated the US population. Thirty per cent put it at one to two billion. Respondents in all other countries were better able to identify the US population than were young Americans. Nonetheless, a majority of young adults in the United States (59 per cent) believe that Americans, in general, know the same amount of geography as (31 per cent), or more than (28 per cent) people in other countries. Only 11 per cent of young adults in the United States reported using the internet to keep up with world events, compared to 25 per cent in other countries.

This disparity takes on particular significance in light of the quantity and quality of foreign news coverage in the US media. According to *Newsweek*, during the 20 years prior to 11 September, newspaper editors and television executives reduced foreign coverage by 70 to 80 per cent. A Harvard University study shows that the amount of time devoted to international news on network television shrank from 45 per cent of total news coverage in the 1970s, to 13.5 per cent in 1995. While the media hyped globalization, it kept Americans increasingly in the dark about global realities. Media executives blamed the trend on popular parochialism, but when the Pew Research Center asked Americans, in 1996, about what kinds of stories they regularly followed, 15 per cent named international news, compared to 16 per cent for 'Washington politics', 14 per cent for 'consumer news', and 13 per cent for 'celebrity news' (Shaw 2003).

The veil obscuring the view of the outside world from within the United States is drawn by the media, educational institutions, and popular fictions of all sorts. It is also kept in place by the Americans' relatively low frequency of foreign travel. One reason for this is that holiday entitlement is meagre in the United States (usually two weeks compared to the European standard of five). Thus, the weakness of labour materially re-enforces American exceptionalist perceptions.

Even after the shock of 11 September and the debate that led up to the Iraq war, a substantial proportion of the US populace remains unaware of global opinion. When Americans were asked which candidate in the 2004 election they thought people around the world would prefer, only 35 per cent assumed that more would prefer Kerry, 25 per cent thought more would prefer Bush, and 39 per cent thought the views were evenly divided. In fact, Kerry was the overwhelming popular choice among all of the United States' traditional allies – with margins ranging from 10–1 (France and Norway), to 3–1 in Britain and 2–1 in Japan (PIPA 2004).

However, US attitudes towards the outside world cannot be reduced to 'insularity'. Even in the weeks after the Iraq invasion, surveys confirmed that the majority of Americans continued to prefer a multilateralist approach to world affairs. Presented with three options for the US role in the world, only 12 per cent agreed that 'as the sole remaining superpower, the US should continue to be the pre-eminent world leader in solving international problems'. On the other extreme, only 11 per cent thought that 'the US should withdraw from most efforts to solve international problems'. A decisive 76 per cent believed that 'the US should do its share in efforts to solve international problems together with other countries'. As in other polls, a majority (62 per cent) agreed with the view that 'the US plays the role of world policeman more than it should'. Presented with the argument, 'the US has the right and even the responsibility to overthrow dictatorships,' only 38 per cent agreed, while 57 per cent disagreed (PIPA 2003).

Attitudes to foreign aid illustrate some of the paradoxes of popular understanding of the US role in the world. In a PIPA poll taken in 2000, 61 per cent said foreign aid spending was 'too much', 7 per cent said it was 'too little' and 26 per cent 'about right'. But the catch here is that people in the United States believe that US foreign aid is much greater than it actually is. When asked what proportion of the federal budget goes to foreign aid, the median estimate was 20 per cent – more than 20 times the actual amount. Only 5 per cent of respondents estimated, correctly, an amount of 1 per cent or less. This extreme misperception was common to all demographic groups. Even among those with postgraduate education the median estimate was 8 per cent. When asked what percentage should be spent the great majority stated figures many times the actual amount. So, in one sense, Americans are in favour, quite overwhelmingly, of a massive increase in foreign aid, a policy never advocated by any mainstream politician, nor promoted in the media (PIPA 2001).

Another poll indicates that 70 per cent would be willing to pay an extra \$50 a year, per income tax paying household, to help meet the Millennium Development Goals on world hunger. However, a key proviso is that 'other countries were willing to give this much' as well. This reflects the continuing belief that the United States bears more than its share of the burden borne by the human race. Americans assume that as a percentage of GNP, the United States gives substantially more than other developed countries, whereas the opposite is the case (PIPA 2005). Despite these facts, and thanks not only to media silences, but also to the assumptions of American exceptionalism, the United States is seen as a patsy, a nation whose inveterate generosity is exploited by others. The entrenched disparity between national self-image and national reality disarms the US population and perverts the generous impulses it shares with others.

Similar contradictions are illustrated in US responses to the Abu Ghraib revelations of 2004, which severely tested the assumptions of American exceptionalism. In a poll in July of that year, soon after the damning photographs were published, 66 per cent said that the United States should abide by the international law that 'governments should never use physical torture', while 29 per cent found that standard 'too restrictive'. 77 per cent believed that a soldier 'ordered to take an action against a detainee that the soldier believes is in violation of international law should have the right to refuse to follow the order'. The majority rejected most forms of coercion even when a detainee might be withholding information critical to stopping a terrorist attack on the United States. 58 per cent rejected the use of threatening dogs, 75 per cent, forcing detainees to go naked – both techniques formally approved by the Secretary of Defense. However, only 35 per cent were aware that Rumsfeld had approved of making detainees go naked, 45 per cent that he had approved of using threatening dogs, and 55 per cent that he had approved of hooding and stress positions. Among those who knew that Rumsfeld had approved of these measures, 60 per cent favoured his removal. Among those who thought that he had not approved any of them, 26 per cent favored his removal (PIPA 2004b). Thus Rumsfeld survived Abu Ghraib, as did the widespread belief that torture was an aberration, an exception to America's exceptionalim.

A Distorting Mirror: US Self-Perception

Ironically, American exceptionalism obstructs perceptions of what is actually exceptional or at least distinctive in US society. It renders the country's peculiar features invisible to most Americans. Take the absence of universal health care. To most people in the United States, access to medical care is a major anxiety, even though the country has more than twice as many doctors and nurses per head than the United Kingdom and ten times as many as India. And it spends lavishly, devoting 15 per cent of GDP to health care, a higher proportion than any other country. A profligate and chaotic health care system, governed by the priorities of private profit, excludes 14 per cent of the population – the 45 million Americans without health insurance – and leaves most of the rest with only partial and often expensive coverage. The Institute of Medicine estimates that at least 18,000 Americans die prematurely each year, solely because they lack health insurance (IOM 2004).

American exceptionalism inhibits a comparative understanding of the United States. The assumption that the United States is the model democracy means that developments and improvements made elsewhere are largely unknown or regarded as irrelevant. Antiquated, undemocratic features such as the 'federal system' become totemic.

American exceptionalism obstructs knowledge and understanding of US history, and the pattern of its involvements abroad, especially any perception of the United States as acting, like any other imperial power, on the basis of self-interest. Each intervention is presented as an altruistic response to a crisis. Since, there is no American empire, no pattern, habit or system of extra-territorial domination, the motive for each intervention is assessed at face value. Given America's special status among nations, the exercise of explicitly American prerogatives (as indicated in the NSS) seems as natural to many Americans today, as did westward continental expansion to their nineteenth-century forebears. American exceptionalism makes it easier for people in the United States to believe that the United States is doing the world a favour by intervening, that it does so from benign motives, and that it has a right to seek to engineer the world in its image.

Maintaining the Informal Empire

In recent years, the fact that America is an empire has become less of a secret, even to Americans. Commentators, such as, Robert Kaplan and Niall Ferguson have urged the United States to abandon its blushes and face up to its imperial responsibilities. They argue that empires have been and can be benign, and that the United States is a liberal empire, or, in the words of Michael Ignatieff, 'an empire lite, a global hegemony whose grace notes are free markets, human rights and democracy'. The appeal of this new imperial rhetoric seems largely restricted to sections of the intelligentsia, both liberal and conservative. Bush and US spokespersons are careful to avoid or refute it, most Americans are uncomfortable or bewildered by it. For the foreseeable future, explicitly imperial rhetoric will remain difficult to reconcile with the self-image fostered by American exceptionalism – a self-image that has proved hugely valuable in disguising the realities of US foreign policies and securing domestic acquiescence to them.

It is also a severe handicap in securing support from those in Asia, Africa and Latin America where anti-colonial movements have shaped public discourse. Like other imperial powers, the United States relies not only on force, but also on the voluntary collaboration of partners and clients. Its rule requires some measure of consent from the elites of other societies, and sometimes broader support as well. Here, the mythologies of American exceptionalism prove their use in an alien setting.

From the earliest days of the United States, the ideas of democracy and 'free enterprise' were intertwined with each other and with Americanism. In the uni-polar era of neoliberal globalism, that triadic association has been recreated – with the United States now posited as the premier model and global homeland of consumerism and unregulated capitalism, as the embodiment of the prosperity and modernity to which other societies aspire. The paradox of American exceptionalism – its claims to both uniqueness and universality – makes the components of US national identity transportable and, at the same time, brand them in many minds as indelibly 'American'.

In India, for example, the ongoing neoliberal reform of the economy has been accompanied by the abandonment of non-alignment, and a more or less rapid deepening of friendship with the United States. In early 2006, during a visit to New Delhi by George W. Bush, Indian Prime Minister Manmohan Singh agreed to a deal on nuclear collaboration with the United States and followed that up by voting with the United States against Iran – a long time strategic ally – at the International Atomic Energy Agency (IAEA). Singh described the Indian policy as motivated by 'enlightened self-interest', a formulation which went with the grain of Indian elite thinking in that it justified India's deal with the United States in terms straight out of Adam Smith.

For elites in India, as elsewhere, the United States exercises attraction as both partner and model. As 'the land of opportunity' it appears to combine the virtues of formal (and stable), democracy with the unbridled acquisition of personal wealth. And as the gap between rich and poor has grown in both the United States and the developing world, the elites of the south seek to emulate the US model of the gated community, constructing protected islands of affluence amid poverty and insecurity, and, at the same time, aligning themselves with or at least acquiescing to US imperial policies. This is only possible because the American empire is an informal one, and is cloaked in the imperial denial of American exceptionalism.

What is often dubbed anti-Americanism is actually an objection to the claims of American exceptionalism, in particular, a scepticism about the disavowal of empire, and a resistance to the special powers and exemptions the US grants itself. Conversely, what might be called pro-Americanism often takes the form of the strident championing of those claims. Some polemicists depict America as the *ne plus ultra* of successful democratic modernity, and anyone who demurs is 'anti-American'. The European identification of the United States with a noble global cause and destiny can be traced back to the end of the eighteenth century. However, in those days it was invoked by the most progressive and humanistic forces in Europe, whereas today it is the property of the reactionary and callous.

Conclusion

It is important to emphasize that the zealots of American exceptionalism do not have it all their own way in the United States. There is a widespread and growing unease about unilateralism. There is a greater hunger, than in the past, for a non-mythic version of US history (witness the phenomenal sales of Howard Zinn's *People's History of the United States*), and increased referral to non-US news source (millions of hits on BBC and Guardian websites). As in other societies, and for similar reasons, there is a greater internationalist consciousness, reflected in awareness of environmental and development issues. Significantly, the huge migration from the south, in the last two decades, means that large numbers in the United States enjoy living links with non-US and non-European histories.

American exceptionalism fatally compromises the humanist universalism it claims as America's cause. Culturally and emotionally, it curtails human solidarity. More than ever, 'Americanism' is a prison that the US citizenry needs to break out of – in its own interest and in the interests of the victims of US policy. A purposeful self-redefinition of US national identity will require:

(i) A frank encounter with the facts of US history, especially the history of US intervention abroad

(ii) A recognition that the United States is an empire and that US citizens live in an imperial metropolis

(iii) A conscious renunciation of American exceptionalism.

There is an understandable temptation to adopt a softened or liberal form of American exceptionalism, but history shows that this should be resisted. What is needed is a consciously selective, critical approach to US traditions – with a willingness to admit and draw on non-US traditions. That process can be aided by an increased interchange between the United States and global lefts. In many respects, more of this is happening now than ever before.

Of course, internationalism cannot be merely rhetorical or abstract. Dissent in the United States must speak in an American idiom – but that is not the same as speaking in the idiom of Americanism.

Notes

[1] Unlike its predecessors, the United States never cultivated an imperial or colonial service. Instead, the duties of empire have fallen on the military, the corporate sector and the professional publicists: firepower, free enterprise and disinformation. This sometimes leaves the United States ill-equipped to deal with the realities of empire. The failure to make realistic plans for the aftermath of the invasion of Iraq can be ascribed, partly, to an obtuseness about the outside world and a concomitant willingness to believe one's own propaganda (including the national narrative of the United States as a non-imperial, liberating force), both fostered by the inheritance of American exceptionalism.

[2] It should be noted that Lomax left the United States in 1950, escaping the Cold War witch-hunt. He travelled and recorded folk songs in a variety of cultures, developed an internationalist theory of folk music, and became a pioneer of what would later be known (and marketed) as world music.

[3] The survey also showed that young Americans were substantially less likely to know that the Taliban and Al Qaeda movements were based in Afghanistan than their peers in Sweden, Britain, Italy, Germany or Canada. However, it is worth noting that young people in Britain and Canada performed only slightly better than their US counterparts on the test – suggesting that there is a general anglophone 'insularity' (itself enhanced by US power).

References

Adams, John (1787), 'Preface', *A Defence of the Constitutions of Government of the United States of America* (London).

Bell, Daniel (1975), 'The "Hegelian Secret": Civil Society and American Exceptionalism', in Byron E. Shafer (ed.), *Is America Different?: A New Look at American Exceptionalism* (Oxford: Clarendon Press).

Berger, Sandy (1999), 'American Power: Hegemony, Isolationism of Engagement', The Council on Foreign Relations, Office of the Press Secretary, 21 October, http://www.mtholyoke.edu/acad/intrel/bergheg.htm.

Bergquist, Charles (1996), *Labor and the Course of American Democracy: US History in Latin American Perspective* (London: Verso).

Bush, George H.W. (1991), Address Before a Joint Session of the Congress on the State of the Union, 29 January, available at John Woolley and Gerhard Peters, *The American Presidency Project* (online), University of California at Santa Barbara, http://www.presidency.ucsb.edu/ws/?pid=19253.

Bush, George W. (2001), Address to a Joint Session of Congress and the American People, Office of the Press Secretary, Washington DC, 20 September, http://www.whitehouse.gov/news/releases/2001/09/20010920-8.html.

——— (2002), 'President Bush Delivers Graduation Speech at West Point', Office of the Press Secretary, 1 June, http://www.whitehouse.gov/news/releases/2002/06/20020601-3.html.

——— (2004), 'President's Remarks at the 2004 Republican National Convention', New York, Office of the Press Secretary, 2 September, http://www.whitehouse.gov/news/releases/2004/09/20040902-2.html.

Dunbar–Ortiz, Roxanne (2004), 'The Grid of History: Cowboys and Indians', in J.B. Foster and R.W. McChesney (eds), *Pox Americana: Exposing the American Empire* (New York: Monthly Review Press).

Hofstadter, Richard (1966), *Anti-Intellectualism in American Life* (New York: Vintage).

IOM, Institute of Medicine (2004), *Insuring America's Health*, 14 January, http://www.iom.edu/?id=19175.

Johnson, Lyndon B. (1965), 'Remarks in Chicago at the Cook County Democratic Party Dinner', 3 June, available at John Woolley and Gerhard Peters, *The American Presidency Project* (online), University of California at Santa Barbara, http://www.presidency.ucsb.edu/ws/index.php?pid=27017.

——— (1966), *Public Papers of the Presidents of the United States: Lyndon B. Johnson, 1965*, Vol. I, entry 172 (Washington DC: Government Printing Office): 394–99.

Kennan, George (1947), 'The Sources of Soviet Conflict', published pseudonymously in *Foreign Affairs*.

Kipling, Rudyard (1899), 'The White Man's Burden', reprinted in *The Works of Rudyard Kipling* (Ware: Wordsworth Editions, 1994).

Lens, Sidney (2003), *The Forging of the American Empire* (reprint; London: Pluto Press).

Lipset, Seymour Martin (1996), *American Exceptionalism: A Double-Edged Sword* (New York: W.W. Norton).

Loewen, James W. (1995), *Lies My Teacher Told Me: Everything Your American History Textbook Got Wrong* (New York: The New Press).

Lomax, Alan (2003), *Selected Writings*, edited by Ronald D. Cohen (New York: Routledge).

McCrisken, Trevor B. (2003), *American Exceptionalism and the Legacy of Vietnam: US Foreign Policy Since 1974* (New York: Palgrave Macmillan).

NGN, National Geographic News (2002), 20 November, http://news.nationalgeographic.com/news/2002/11/1120_021120_GeoRoperSurvey.html.

Nixon, Richard M. (1994), *Beyond Peace* (New York: Random House).

Paine, Thomas (1792), 'Introduction', Part the Second, *Rights of Man*.

PIPA, Program on International Policy Attitudes (2001), 'Americans on Foreign Aid and World Hunger: A Study of US Public Attitudes', 2 February, http://65.109.167.118/pipa/pdf/feb01/ForeignAid_Feb01_rpt.pdf.

——— (2003), 'The PIPA/Knowledge Networks Poll: The American Public on International Issues', 29 April, http://www.pipa.org/onlineReports/AmRole_World/USRole_Apr03/USRole_Apr03.rpt.pdf.

——— (2004a), 'The PIPA/Knowledge Networks Poll: the American Public on International Issues', 21 October, http://www.pipa.org/OnlineReports/Iraq/IraqRealities_Oct05/IraqRealities%20Oct04%20rpt.pdf.

——— (2004b), 'The PIPA/Knowledge Networks Poll: The American Public on International Issues', 22 July, http://www.pipa.org/OnlineReports/Terrorism/Torture_Jul04/Torture_Jul04_pr.pdf.

——— (2005), 'The PIPA/Knowledge Networks Poll: The American Public on International Issues', 29 June, http://www.pipa.org/OnlineReports/ForeignAid/WorldPoverty_Jun05/WorldPoverty_Jun05_rpt.pdf.

Powell, Colin (2003), 'Remarks', delivered at The Elliott School of International Affairs, George Washington University, 5 September, US Department of State Press Release, http://www.state.gov/secretary/former/powell/remarks/2003/23836.htm.

Ricks, Christopher and William L. Vance (eds) (1992), *The Faber Book of America* (London: Faber and Faber).

Rumsfeld, Donald (2003), Secretary Rumsfeld Interview with Al Jazeera TV, News Transcript, US Department of Defense, 25 February, http://www.defenselink.mil/transcripts/2003/t02262003_t0225sdaljaz.html.

Shaw, David (2003), 'Foreign News Shrinks in Era of Globalization', *Los Angeles Times*, 27 September, http://www.commondreams.org/headlines01/0927-03.htm.

Tocqueville, Alexis de (1835), *Democracy in America*, Vol. I.

Truman, Harry S. (1947), 'Address before a Joint Session of Congress', 12 March, http://www.yale.edu/lawweb/avalon/trudoc.htm.

Twain, Mark (1900), 'An Anti-Imperialist', reprinted in Jim Zwick (ed.), *Mark Twain's Weapons of Satire: Anti-Imperialist Writings on the Philippine–American War* (Syracuse NY: Syracuse University Press, 1992).

Washington, George (1783), *The Writings of George Washington from the Original Manuscript Sources, 1745–1799*, edited by J.C. Fitzpatrick, Vol. 26 (Washington DC: Government Printing Office, 1931–1944).

Whitman, Walt (1871), 'Democratic Vistas', reprinted in Ricks and Vance (1992: 179–80).

——— (1982), 'Leaves of Grass' (1891–92), in *Walt Whitman: Complete Poetry and Collected Prose* (New York: The Library of America).

Wills, Gary (1976), 'Introduction to Lillian Hellman's *Scoundrel Time*', reprinted in Ricks and Vance (1992).

Zinn, Howard (1996), *A People's History of the United States*, second edition (Harlow: Longman).

Zuckerman, Michael (1997), 'The Dodo and the Phoenix', in Rick Halpern and Jonathan Morris (eds), *American Exceptionalism?: US Working-Class Formation in an International Context* (London: Macmillan).

The Ideological Banners

Political Terrorism and the US Imperial Project

Achin Vanaik

You are terrifying yourself with ghosts and apparitions, while your house is the haunt of robbers.

Edmund Burke

11 September 2001 is a distinctive event for three reasons. Outside of wartime, one cannot recall a single act responsible for so many civilian casualties.[1] Never before had any non-state actor inflicted so much damage. Not in living memory had the US homeland suffered so serious an assault of foreign origin. This international terrorist act was rightly condemned worldwide. In historical retrospect, however, its most profound political impact may well have been that it provided the US government the opportunity to unfurl fully, a banner – the 'Global War on Terrorism' (henceforth GWOT) – that it hoped would prove extremely effective in justifying future US foreign policy behaviour. A great human tragedy was being manipulated for ulterior purposes. The relationship between this banner of war on terror and the US imperial project is what we need to grasp and is what this chapter sets out to do.

The US government's immediate response (within twenty-four hours) to 11 September was not to declare it an 'international crime against humanity', whose culprits had to be captured and punished. Instead, it described the assault as a first salvo in a war against the United States, which, therefore, had to be countered by a GWOT which could last '8 to 10 years'. The words 'war' and 'global' were deliberately chosen. As long as a war is on, you are entitled to act militarily on every occasion. You do not have to be attacked again in order to retaliate. And now the battleground was to be the whole globe. Moreover, Washington declared that it would make no distinction between the actual perpetrators of terrorism and the country that may be hosting them. The moral, legal and political significance of this declaration has not yet been fully appreciated.

Morally, there are always degrees of responsibility and, therefore, different degrees of culpability assigned and different levels of punishment meted out. The welfare department of the Nazi government was not as accountable for the concentration camps as the ministry directly controlling them. The lowly orderly, ushering victims into the gas chambers, does not bear the same level of responsibility as the commandant of that concentration camp. The murderer and the accessory to the murder do not share equal responsibility. General state sponsorship must be distinguished from the more autonomous acts of the terrorist group in question. These are elementary principles of jurisprudence. Morally and legally, the United States was not entitled to overturn recognized international law and violate militarily the sovereignty of another country, like Afghanistan. But politically, the way was prepared to transform a conflict between the US state against a non-state entity, like Al Qaeda, into a war between the United States and *other states* of its choosing. The United States declared that its GWOT was a 'just war' project.[2] The war against Afghanistan, being a part of this larger project, automatically became a just war. It was left to other intellectuals, US and non-US, to do special pleading for justifying the assault on Afghanistan while the US government itself was justifying a much larger global project!

In effect, the United States gives itself a *carte blanche* to attack anyone it decides is guilty, whenever, wherever, with whatever means, and for whatever duration. Four years after invading Afghanistan, and more than two years after occupying Iraq, President George Bush (2005) turned his gaze on other 'culprits' who must now 'watch out': 'State sponsors like Syria and Iran have a long history of collaboration with terrorists, and they deserve no patience from the victims of terror. The United States makes no distinction between those who commit acts of terror and those who support and harbor them, they're equally as guilty of murder.'

11 September was not the first time the United States announced a war on terror or used this claim to justify foreign policy behaviour. When President Reagan pronounced the Soviet Union an 'evil empire', he also accused it of being the wellspring of international terrorism – as a sign of evil. But since the USSR was a world power, of equal status, with which the United States had to negotiate on several fronts, it was generally left to unofficial, civil society sources to hammer home the message about Soviet sponsored terrorism.[3] After the Cold War, and the US pre-eminence, there is no need for Washington to exercise similar moderation about the dangers of terrorism, either in its rhetoric or in the actions it proposes to deal with it.

Political terrorism is certainly a problem. But how serious or widespread is it? Who are the primary culprits? What are its principal forms? To grasp the duplicitous purposes to which the GWOT is being put, we have to understand the deceits and misrepresentations, the limitations, confusions, and absences that are part of the discourse on political terrorism, emanating even from respectable sources such as UN resolutions and reports.

What is Political Terrorism?

Political terrorism is an historical phenomenon and must be understood as such. The modern period unlike the pre-modern one, is truly the era of mass politics. Vast numbers of people, in varying ways and combinations, enter the political arena with qualitatively greater regularity and frequency, with a much more profound effect than ever. Political violence, thus, takes on newer forms (for example, the greater scale and frequency of genocide in modern times), carries newer meanings, and leads to very different results. But even modern political terrorism has its distinctive trajectory. It emerged in Europe where it originally expressed what *states* did to their peoples, for example, the 'Great Terror' during the French Revolution. In the late nineteenth and early twentieth centuries, terrorism came to be characterized as the behaviour of non-state actors carrying out selective political assassinations. In the middle third of the twentieth century, it was an instrument used by groups fighting perceived colonialists – the Bengal revolutionaries, Zionists, Kenyan Mau Mau, FLN in Algeria, EOKA in Cyprus, etc. It was only in the late 1960s that Middle-Eastern terrorism by overwhelmingly secular, non-state actors, emerged (Halliday 2004). But all through modern history, states have repeatedly carried out terrorist acts and campaigns.

Given this history of variable forms, agents, victims, purposes and effects of political terrorism, it has become impossible to find a definition which satisfies all cases or is universally acceptable.[4] Nevertheless, a 'working definition' of political terrorism, not pretending to total comprehensiveness or complete accuracy, can heuristically serve as guide to our response to it. This is perhaps the best we can aim for, as a brief survey of the definitional difficulties involved will confirm.

Terrorism is connected to the two key notions of terror/intimidation and violence. Political terrorism is carried out for political ends or purposes. Depending on how one understands these two notions of terror/intimidation and violence, conceptions can be broad or narrow. A broader notion of violence (beyond the restricted notion of physical injury or deaths to people, or the threat thereof) can justify notions about the 'violence/terrorism of poverty', or the 'violence/terrorism of social discrimination', and so on. It is also useful to distinguish between terrorist regimes and terrorist acts and campaigns (repeated acts as part of an overall tactic or strategy of combat). To talk of terrorist regimes is to talk of the institutionalization of terror/intimidation and it would pertain, therefore, to deeply undemocratic regimes.[5] But terrorist acts and campaigns are often carried out by democratic regimes, usually as part of their foreign policy behaviour. International terrorism occurs when the citizens or governments of more than one country are involved, or when existing territorial boundaries are contested. Such terrorism involves intimidation and/or violence, but violence conceived of in the restricted sense, bracketed above.

The agents of terrorist acts/campaigns can be the individual, the group or larger collectivities like state apparatuses or agencies. But the US State Department's definition of terrorism excludes the state as agent and refers to: 'Premeditated, politically motivated violence perpetrated against noncombatant targets by subnational groups or clandestine agents, usually intended to influence an audience' (*PGT* 2001: vi).

Thus the United States can excuse itself and also allies like Israel. It can justify attacking some states by claiming i) that some states *sponsor* terrorism and the United States will list them; and ii) that are no differences between agents or subnational groups carrying out terrorism and the states that sponsor or harbour them. The State Department definition uses the term 'noncombatants' instead of 'civilians', allowing it to claim that attacks on soldiers, temporarily off-duty, say in a military base, is a form of terrorism. The definition makes no reference to terrorization/intimidation, which can only affect humans so that violence against 'noncombatant targets' of any kind, such as, property, can also count as terrorism.

The United Nations' Secretary General's *High-Level Panel on Threats, Challenges and Change, Final Report* has this definition of terrorism:

> Any action, in addition to actions already specified by the existing conventions on aspects of terrorism, the Geneva Conventions and UN Security Council Resolution 1566 (2004), that is intended to cause death or serious bodily harm to civilians or non-combatants, when the purpose of such an act, by its nature or context, is to intimidate a population or to compel a government or an international organization to do or to abstain from doing any act. (UNSG 2004)

This definition does implicitly acknowledge that states can be culprits. But by insisting that *intention* is paramount, a convenient loophole is provided since states can and do claim that their intention is never to harm civilians. If this happens, it is regarded a tragic side-effect of the real purposes of the action – hence the term 'collateral damage'. However, the intention behind an attack on an airplane (or on a port facility) may be to destroy some crucial cargo (or disrupt enemy oil supplies). But, in so far as such actions involve the deaths or even the danger of death to civilians, why should they be exempted from the charge of terrorism? In Afghanistan, the United States used means they knew were going to kill large numbers of civilians, but claimed this was not terrorism since they had no intention to kill civilians – an argument that, unfortunately, found endorsement from all too many US intellectuals, including political philosophers. However, the philosophical gap between intentionally and *knowingly* killing civilians (undertaking military actions that you know are going to cause civilian casualties – 'collateral damage') is not so great as to allow such hypocrisy to get by, especially when the number of Afghan civilians killed were more than three times that killed on 11 September.

Terrorism is also about terrorization/intimidation. This automatically broadens the scope of actions that can be considered terroristic. Torture is undeniably a form of terrorism. Combatants can be subject to torture and, therefore, are not completely excluded from the range of actions considered terroristic. Nuclear weapons have rightly been called 'weapons of terror'. Their very existence constitutes a terrorist threat. This is so not only because as weapons of mass destruction they do not discriminate between civilians and combatants, but also because they are weapons of torture when configured as battlefield nuclear weapons. Their use or the threat of their use on combatants is immoral, unacceptable and terroristic. The point is that the distinction between civilians and combatants, though necessary, is not sacrosanct.

As the history of terrorism shows, political assassinations are a form of terrorism. Numerous governments as well as non-state actors have done this. The Israeli government makes a systematic use of such political assassinations against Palestinians, which the CNN and BBC call 'targeted killings', even as they describe the actions of Palestinian suicide bombers as 'murder' and 'terrorism'. In the case of assassinations, the issue of the ethics of terrorism surfaces making the seemingly natural assumption that terrorism must always be judged as immoral problematic. Why should a victimized country not see Presidents and Prime Ministers or senior government officials of another country waging an unjust war against it and its population, as legitimate targets? Why should the assassination of people guilty of great international crimes (an entirely just accusation against many a leader of democratic and authoritarian countries) by the victimized citizens be always deemed unethical, regardless of context and circumstance? The Officer's Plot against Adolf Hitler, in 1944, was correctly described as a terrorist act. But why should one disapprove of it?

So where do we stand on this issue of terrorism? We must satisfy ourselves with a reasonable working definition which encompasses all possible agents, including states and their apparatuses; which applies to the overwhelming majority of cases that we recognize as terrorist; which is objective, independent of the subjective beliefs and attitudes of the perpetrator; which uses a narrow conception of violence pertaining to the injury, death or the threat of either to human victims; and, which is pejorative and condemnatory. In short, we can simply understand political terrorism as those acts by any agency that are geared to some political purpose and are unacceptable and unjustifiable morally because they threaten or actually use violence, usually indiscriminate, against innocent unarmed civilians.[7]

Differentiating State and Non-State Terrorism: The Universality of the Phenomenon

There is state sponsored terrorism and state directed or executed terrorism. The terrorism of states is different from that of non-state individuals or combat groups. When carried out by the latter, it is essentially 'propaganda by the deed', that is, publicity is its lifeblood. They are meant to be public events and responsibility for them is usually acknowledged. These acts send messages in two directions – against the enemy and its support bases – but also to the home population to raise its morale. State executed terrorism is usually (though not always), uni-directional and aimed at sending a message of futility to the enemy in its struggle. If the first is the terrorism of the weak, the second is the terrorism of the strong. States usually do everything to avoid their terrorist acts from becoming public knowledge, since this would damage them politically, though there are occasions when states are quite happy to have such acts publicized in order to express their own determination to undertake all necessary means against the 'enemy'. Such is certainly the case with the actions of the Israeli government against Palestinians in the Occupied Territories, for example, the brutal air sorties, tank assaults on populated centres, as well as planned assassinations.

Furthermore, the scale of state terrorism is far greater than that of non-state terrorism. Although the means available to states are so much greater, the main reason that the scale of state terrorism is so great and why it is more capable of being justified or disguised as not terrorism at all is because the ends to which the terrorism of the state is harnessed are so much more grandiose, like protecting the 'national interest', 'defending the free world', 'defeating the Communist threat', 'fighting against capitalist imperialism', etc. The 11 September attacks, ironically, confirm this point since here Al Qaeda was sending a general message to the 'US Satan', rather than carrying out an act with a more specific purpose, like demanding the release of prisoners. This made it very different from other non-state terrorist attacks in the past. Nevertheless, the biggest danger that confronts us today and tomorrow is not non-state terrorism, but the scale and frequency with which states carry out terrorist acts and campaigns! Even when it comes to use or threat of the use of nuclear weapons, the biggest danger that remains is posed by nuclear weapons possessing states (although the danger of non-state actors getting their hands on such weapons is not to be dismissed altogether).

Yet, guilty states do succeed in persuading much of their populations that the real problem is the terrorism of non-state actors; and the role of the mass media, in shaping everyday public discourse, reinforces this misconception. States may, it is claimed, make 'mistakes', or occasionally be guilty of 'human rights excesses', but terrorism is not what they engage in. Such a view flows almost inevitably (barring the minority dissenting media) from the very nature of the relationship between the media, its working professionals, its owners and the government. Mainstream media is characterized by a powerful bias in favour of the 'official' nationalism of governments and it generally endorses how they interpret and analyse matters.

But there is an additional factor of some importance here. The international terrorism of states is conducted generally at a distance from the domestic population and is targeted on a specific geographical area. It lacks that sense of *randomness* in time and place that characterize non-state terrorism. Bombings in a city could affect anyone regardless of who they are or what they think. By contrast, state terrorism is seemingly directed against a distant designated enemy. The apparent randomness of non-state terrorism, its 'uncontrollable' violence, generates a greater sense of public fear. Actually, such non-state terrorism is never entirely random. After the invasion of Iraq, European bombings took place in Spain and Britain whose governments were allies of the United States, not in Sweden or in countries not part of the 'coalition of the willing'. Similarly, Muslim militants attack the Indian part of Kashmir or India itself, not Nepal or Sri Lanka.

Terrorism, then, is a universal problem demanding not a selective but a universal response – morally, emotionally and politically. Morally, there can be no double standards. One must condemn both the terrorism of Al Qaeda on 11 September, and the terrorism unleashed by the US government in Afghanistan and Iraq. One must condemn the brutalities of the Israeli government and the suicide bombings by Palestinians that kill civilians. Indeed, double standards imply that the stronger party gets away with its terrorism, while the weaker side is condemned. This is also politically disastrous because it only reinforces and widens the anger of the aggrieved side, deepening the belief that, in the absence of international and impartial mechanisms of just punishment for all agents of terrorism, the only way to punish the 'strong' is to use terrorist means. Emotionally, a universalist response to acts of terrorism by non-state (11 September attacks) or state actors (the Holocaust) is often the sentiment of 'never again'. But this can either mean 'never again to *my* people' or 'never again to *any* people' (see Mamdani 2004: 10–11). Precisely because the response of so many Americans and Israelis is the first one, their governments can carry out blatant atrocities on opponents, with considerable confidence of obtaining substantial domestic support.

The only effective way to tackle political terrorism is to tackle the political context giving rise to such actions. There can be no military or 'deterrent' solution to terrorism. Terrorism is not a pathology, although it can have a pathological dimension. Similarly, terrorism is not a specific or cultural phenomenon, but a universal and political phenomenon. The tendency today, in many circles, to see terrorism as a special characteristic of Islam or Muslims is absurd, obscene, and deeply counterproductive.

Evaluating the Terrorist Danger: Terrorism and Covering Ideologies

Not only is our greatest terrorist problem posed by states rather than non-state actors, today its most dangerous dimension is the shield that the GWOT provides for US actions. Terrorism is a means of political violence. It is not in itself an ideology. It therefore requires some kind of ideological cover to justify and sanction it. The perpetrators of terrorist acts and campaigns, whether state or non-state, use all kinds of covers – from religious belief systems to secular ideologies such as nationalism, national security, anti-communism and anti-imperialism. Even 'promoting democracy' provides a disguise. But, at least, when such ideological banners are used, terrorist behaviour can then be criticized and opposed in the name of a 'correct' interpretation of these very ideologies. But the shield provided by a GWOT *militarizes* the manner in which a 'solution' is sought, thus making the use of one kind of terrorism (a particular form of political violence) to combat another kind more likely.

Even worse, this GWOT is one of the crucial ideological banners being used by the United States to justify thinking and behaviour aimed at establishing its informal global empire. That there is an empire project is no shibboleth of the left. Many of the more prominent intellectuals of the right and the centre now openly use the term 'Empire'. The left clearly opposes the project. The right and much of the centre in the United States, Europe and Japan are supportive of it for reasons that, in more academic terms, would come under the 'hegemonic stability thesis'. Here, US dominance is presented as a necessary public and universal good, providing that necessary global order and stability without which there can be no overall progress or accumulating prosperity. Isn't the United States itself a great model of democracy and prosperity?

But sections within the rightwing and centrist groups (including the conservative Republican right in the United States) are alarmed at how the current US administration, influenced by neoconservatives, is pursuing this goal.[8] Criticism is now becoming fiercer since US forays into Afghanistan and Iraq have 'backfired'. There is now greater worldwide public hostility towards the United States than ever before. There are more tensions between the United States and its allies, actual and potential, because unilateralist inclinations clash with multilateralist desires. In the name of fighting global terrorism there has been a serious erosion of civil liberties by the United States i) externally (witness Abu Ghraib and the revelations of ill treatment of prisoners at the Guantánamo base, and even of illegal incarceration of 'suspects' in allied countries); and ii) domestically (the PATRIOT Act and recent revelations in the United States itself about illegal forms of surveillance over the domestic population), creating more internal dissent and weakening the 'model' that the country is supposed to represent internationally. The GWOT banner to cover this imperial project is thus proving to be more tattered than imagined earlier, although it remains immensely useful for that project. The dispute between neoconservatives and others on the right and at the centre is not about the illegitimacy or dishonesty of that banner, but about how judiciously it should be used to serve the needs of Empire-building.

From the end of the Cold War onwards, as pointed out in the introduction to this book, six distinct ideological banners have emerged to provide cover for US imperial behaviour – 'humanitarian intervention', 'weapons of mass destruction', 'global war on terrorism', regime change 'in the name of democracy', 'failed states' and 'war on narcotics'. The establishment of global hegemony requires not just the ability to use incontestable force, but also the ability to extract consent from those over whom hegemony is to be exercised. Hence, the importance of such larger ideological claims of doing good to the world order. The consent sought is from three 'population zones'. Firstly, there is the US population. Then, there is the population of the area that is the specific target of imperial assault. Here, the preferred banner for eighteenth-, nineteenth- and early twentieth-century colonialisms was 'tutoring the less civilized races/peoples' for the future. Finally, outside of the imperial homeland and the specific target area of imperialism, there is the broader 'international public' of countries – friendly, hostile or merely neutral.

A single rationale, no matter however overarching, will have uneven ideological efficacy in these three population zones. In contrast to all the other five ideological rationales for US Empire-building, it is the GWOT that can have the strongest domestic resonance, even as its external ideological value is by no means insignificant.

An Excellent Framing Device for the Imperial Project

The United States differs from other advanced imperial powers in two crucial respects. There is, first, an extremely deep-rooted sentiment pervading the nation and spreading across all sections of society, men and women, young and old, black and white, left and right – that is, American exceptionalism. This is the belief that the United States is the greatest and the best of all societies. Like all powerful myths, it has a measure of plausibility because there are aspects of US society that are distinctively admirable. But the belief is fundamentally mistaken and betokens a profound, if unconscious, arrogance.[9] This exceptionalism, however, is simultaneously a kind of universalism, giving a strongly messianic character to US foreign policy thinking and behaviour. In no other country in the world is the 'national interest' also seen as a cosmopolitan universal interest (Anderson 2002)! All Presidents and administrations, whether Democratic or Republican, and despite the presence of more hard-boiled 'realists' in prominent official positions, have been dominated by this belief in US exceptionalism–universalism. It remains pervasive today both among neoconservatives and their conservative and liberal opponents. This belief precludes any other conception or analysis about the nature of the US role globally and historically, and is reinforced by the victory in the 'good fight' against Communism. The United States cannot, on this account, ever be accused of being structurally imperialist. It can make mistakes and cause unfortunate suffering, but even its imperial projects and ambitions must be seen as fundamentally benign in intent and purpose.

The second difference is that despite this pervasive exceptionalism–universalism, no other advanced industrialized democracy has a general public so insular, so ignorant (thus, fearful of what it cares little to understand) and so indifferent to the rest of the world. Electoral abstention rates in the United States are among the highest, and its general political culture more 'privatized' than in other democracies. This general political passivity is a boon to elites in domestic politics, but a serious handicap for its external imperial ambitions. Here, US imperialism must harness an *aroused* nationalism, hence the immense importance of ideological banners portraying the basic justness of the imperial project. The Cold War had to be fought in the name of 'defending the Free World against the Communist threat'. The exaggeration of that threat and public fear of Communism was always more irrational and much greater in the United States than in Europe and Japan, although Communist parties and left ideologies were stronger in the political life and systems of the latter regions.

The hardware for the United States' global imperial role is its structure of military bases (over 730 in over 140 countries), the incredible level of expenditure on defence (its 2005–2006 budget will be over $500 billion), its militarization–nuclearization efforts or search for 'full-spectrum dominance' in space, and its effort to establish a global imperial army headed by Washington but involving forces from as many other countries as possible, hence the 'coalition of the willing', whose political–diplomatic value is more important than its military support. But the software for its imperial project is even more important. Of the six ideological banners cited earlier, two are much more strongly pivoted on exploiting the domestic public's sense of fearfulness – the need to prevent 'enemies' of the United States from acquiring or keeping weapons of mass destruction, and the need to wage a GWOT.

As a framing device for the pursuit of Empire, the GWOT possesses certain advantages over alternative banners, including its most serious competitor in the game of domestic mobilization – 'WMDs in enemy hands'. The two are obviously not exclusive. Indeed, the Bush administration has used both these claims, shifting from one to the other, to justify its invasion and occupation of Iraq. But the first, nevertheless, has inestimable advantages when it comes to patriotic mobilization for imperial adventures.

To advocate a GWOT is to advocate a prolonged war over the years, even decades; its very longevity is a political asset. There is no early solution, even when 'the problem' is arbitrarily and selectively identified by the United States. This makes it a fitting replacement for playing the role that the 'Communist threat' once did. Indeed, US actions – the invasion and occupation of Iraq and its support for the Israeli occupation of Palestine – are guaranteed to provoke terrorist behaviour among their non-state actor opponents, constantly providing the fuel of real-life events to legitimize an ongoing GWOT. If the 'Communist threat' potentially knew no boundaries, the same holds true for terrorism. The geography of the 'terrorist threat' is much wider than the one offered by the other legitimizing discourses of Empire; especially since the US government has made it a point to eliminate the distinction between terrorist agents themselves and the countries suspected of harbouring them. Given the decentralized character and networks of Al Qaeda and similar groups, dozens of countries may be targeted. And post-11 September, the US government, in its official document the *National Strategy for Combating Terrorism*, has drawn up just such a long target list: 'The al-Qaida network is a multinational enterprise with operation in more than 60 countries' (*NSCT* 2003: 7).[10]

The 'enemy' state need not be threatening military action or even intending such action against the United States. It is enough that it harbours actual or suspected terrorists to justify a US military assault. Thus, this GWOT carries within it the logic of 'pre-emptive' and 'preventive' military warfare. It is not at all a coincidence that once this declaration of a GWOT found widespread acceptance amongst various governments and large sections of their publics, the United States would bring out its *National Security Strategy* document barely a year after 11 September, which for the first time officially endorsed Washington's right to wage pre-emptive and preventive wars, in brazen contempt and violation of international law and the UN Charter.[11]

The GWOT, precisely because it aims to address a real internal threat (unlike the cause of exporting democracy), provides a much stronger moral (and, therefore, much more effective) domestic foundation for US foreign policy behaviour. It is much more able to create and sustain a high-minded self-righteousness on a mass scale at home. This is by no means an easy task given that the United States is an immigrant society of great ethnic mix. It is also a fast expanding population, now that the era of restricted immigration (1924–65) is long over, with all the cultural diversity and flux that this creates. It is, thus, much more strongly in need of a unifying political discourse, not aligned in its basic conceptual elements to any *particular* community sensibility. Given the United States' remarkable geographical isolation (and hence security) coupled with its exceptionalist self-image and insularity, popular mobilization for imperial purposes, that is, a nationalism in the service of expansionism, has always required a hostile external enemy (an anti-American bogey), whose threat and danger must be magnified well beyond what it actually is. There has always been an apocalyptic element, a paranoid character to US public political discourse, especially when it comes to foreign policy.

This paranoid dimension gives significant appeal to the crude 'good versus evil' formula that so many US politicians are wont to use. But embedded social characteristics are not the only reason for such post-Cold War absolutes. During the Cold War period there were structures, personnel and attitudes that strongly influenced policy-making and policy-shaping circles. All these can now be grafted on to the new enemy of 'terrorism' to give it a similar character of a 'life-and-death struggle' that the Cold War was said to represent, thus sustaining structures and vested interests that came into being in that earlier context.

The domestic advantages of this banner of fighting terrorism do not stop here. No other appeal can be as effective in justifying the erosion of democratic rights at home. In an important, if an *indirect*, manner, such internal repression is necessary for the US Empire project. The geo-economic dimension of US imperialism is the establishment and consolidation of a neoliberal world order. But economic neoliberalism has its inescapable political corollary. The shift in the relationship of forces between capital and labour in favour of the former requires not just the deregulation of capital by the state, but also the repressive regulation of labour and a greater 'policing' of the underclass and the 'losers' from this reorganization of capitalism. This requires greater legal sanction for increasing the capacities of the state to carry out such surveillance and repression when required. The GWOT helps divert popular frustrations arising from the neoliberal economic shift into channels that better suit the US state, as well as helping to promote such repressive internal legislation as the PATRIOT Act.

If, geopolitically, the United States must become the world policeman, then geo-economically it must remain the world banker, maintaining the dollar as world currency. But to successfully play these roles, the US government must maintain a strong control over its own populace. The GWOT, while it is a powerful instrument of domestic mobilization, also promotes state terrorism in the course of the fight against the 'enemy'. This state terrorism must usually be disguised or interpreted as something other than terrorism. However, there are cases, like Israel, when disguise is unnecessary because, in this case, *collective* moral insensitivity has reached extraordinary heights. Indeed, without such an established collective moral debasement it would not have been possible for the Israeli population to justify to itself the reality of an illegal and brutal occupation that is now the longest ever in modern history. For state elites, such collective moral insensitivity is the best of situations. There is then no need to hide one's actions and little fear of domestic opposition of any meaningful sort, given the state of domestic acceptance, even approval, for state terrorist acts/campaigns.

Externally, the Empire project is strongly pivoted on the United States' unique military supremacy. From the late 1990s onwards, the United States has dramatically escalated its specific nuclear preparations, upwards into space through the construction of a Ballistic Missile Defense (BMD) system, and downwards through development of battlefield, mini- and micro-nukes, as well as research into new generation weapons. The deployment and possible use of nuclear weapons is being integrated into its general planning of conventional warfare scenarios, with the United States more willing than ever to contemplate the use of nuclear weapons against non-nuclear states/targets, 'rogue' states/targets, possessing or suspected of possessing or capable of developing WMDs, whether nuclear, biological or chemical (Iran, North Korea, sub-state groups that might acquire rudimentary WMD weapons). Raising fears about 'nuclear terrorism' provides excellent cover for the United States' own deeply irresponsible nuclear behaviour, especially since such fears, though greatly exaggerated, do possess a real measure of plausibility.[12] In fact, since the US would be the most likely target of such non-state terrorism, one cannot rule out the possibility that the US government would carry out a pre-emptive nuclear attack in some third world country precisely to show its determination to use such weapons in order to forestall any such future attack.[13] To be sure, if there were to be any such an attack even by non-nuclear WMDs, the US government would almost certainly use nuclear weapons against its deemed adversary.

As part of its normalized foreign policy discourse, the current Bush administration has deliberately made misleading connections between 'outlaw/rogue states', 'terrorism' and 'weapons of mass destruction'. Such designated outlaw regimes are portrayed as extremely dangerous to the US public because they would (even if they had not done so already) develop and use weapons of mass destruction or sponsor terrorist actions against the United States. Hence, President Bush's forthright declaration: 'we are determined to deny weapons of mass destruction to outlaw regimes, and to their terrorist allies who would use them without hesitation' (Bush 2005). As for the seven most culpable state sponsors of terrorism, these are supposed to be Iran, Iraq, Syria, Libya, Cuba, North Korea, and Sudan (*NSCT* 2003: 18).

If the primary excuse for invading Iraq was the presence of WMDs, then the exposure of this lie has only led to a shift in the rhetoric of justification, wherein Iraq is presented as the seedbed of global terrorism, necessitating therefore the presence of the United States as an occupying force till 'victory over terrorism' is achieved. That prior to the invasion, there was not only no connection between the Saddam Hussein regime and Osama bin Laden, but the fact that bin Laden had repeatedly and publicly denounced the ruthless albeit secular regime of Hussein as anti-Islamic was conveniently ignored. After the occupation the very fact of armed resistance against the occupation has been presented as proof that the battle lines are now drawn between the forces of good (the United States and its Iraqi and other allies) and terrorist evil: 'The terrorists regard Iraq as the central front in their war against humanity. And we must recognize Iraq as the central front in our war on terror' (Bush 2005).

The GWOT, then, is a legitimizing discourse of immense value to the US government both domestically and externally. Empire-builders always require moral self-deception, in order to believe that imperial expansion is a public good, not merely a matter of narrow self-interest. A long-term and sustained imperial project requires an equally long-term and sustainable principle of self-deception, and here the only serious competitor to the GWOT's appeal is the 'military humanist' banner of 'exporting democracy' via 'humanitarian intervention' and 'regime change'. But humanitarian interventions and regime changes once undertaken are completed soon enough. Not so the global war on terrorism. Once again, the concluding part of the strategy document on combating terrorism spells it out: 'The campaign ahead will be long and arduous. In this different kind of war, we cannot expect an easy or definitive end to the conflict. . . . We will be resolute. Others might flag in the face of the inevitable ebb and flow of the campaign against terrorism. But the American people will not.' For, what is at stake is 'the very notion of civilized society. The war against terrorism, therefore, is not some sort of 'clash of civilizations'; instead, it is a clash between civilization and those who would destroy it' (*NSCT* 2003: 29). This, then, is the twenty-first-century version of a rather shop-worn trope – the 'civilizing mission' of colonial expansionism. But that was the 'white man's burden'. Today we have the 'American burden'.

And at the geographical heart of this imperial project lie the overwhelmingly Muslim populated regions of West Asia or the Middle East (the most important prize), and Central Asia. The temptation to demonize Islam and Muslims has, therefore, proven irresistible. Terrorism is now being ever more loudly and insistently linked to the supposed peculiarities of Islam as religion, and to the 'culture' of 'Islamic societies'.

Demonizing Islam and Muslims

Crucial to the US imperial project is the control of the geopolitical 'pivot of Eurasia' – Central and (especially) West Asia. Here, barring Israel, the countries are Muslim majority states where mass hostility to the United States is the greatest, and many of the reigning governments, while despised for their authoritarian rule, are subservient to the United States. Having successfully weakened secular oppositional currents (whether radical nationalist or leftwing) during past decades, the United States and allied governments are now opposed by a range of Islamist movements and groups. Terrorism is no monopoly of Muslim insurgent groups, which even a casual survey of Hindu and Buddhist extremism in South and South-East Asia, of Irish, Basque and Corsican extremism in Europe, and of South American insurgencies, would reveal. But for the cause of Empire these are either regions of much lesser geopolitical importance, or areas where its overall authority is much more comfortably ensconced.

Selective highlighting of 'Islamic terrorism' has become necessary to provide a justification for focusing US political–military attention on this 'hotbed' of 'global terrorism'. The term 'Islamic terrorism' is a contemptible misnomer. There is really no such thing anymore than there is 'Christianic' or 'Buddhistic' or 'Hinduistic' or 'Judaic' terrorism. Such terms falsely link a system of religious belief to terrorism when what we have are terrorists who interpret ideologies and belief systems, religious or secular to justify their actions. Thus, the accurate description is of Muslim or Hindu or Jewish or Buddhist or Sikh or Christian or 'secular' terrorists and terrorisms. Linking Islam, rather than some Muslims, to terrorism can be seen as somewhat counterproductive since it is so important for the United States to have client regimes in Central and West Asia. It hardly pays to insult the religious identities and sentiments of the populace, whether elites or masses.

Official White House discourse on the subject of Islam and terrorism is thus two-faced. There are references to Islam as a 'noble faith' and of 'Islamic radicals' distorting the religion. So the war the United States is waging against them is also for the sake of 'true Islam' and of Muslims themselves. At the same time, there is no hesitation in proclaiming Muslim terrorists as world enemy number one! 'The murderous ideology of the Islamic radicals is the great challenge of our new century' Bush (2005: 4) has proclaimed. Here a straight line is being drawn between terrorism and a radical interpretation of Islam. Apparently, we need not worry about the terrorist potential of Hindu, Sikh, Buddhist, Jewish or Christian radicals. Could it be that the injustices of US foreign policy contribute to the grievances of Muslims and turned them towards terrorism or extremism? No, radical Islam is at fault, not the US behaviour. Therefore, the United States cannot change this state of affairs since it has no errors of its own to correct. Besides, it would be fruitless in the face of such bloody-mindedness:

> Over the years these extremists have used a litany of excuses for violence – the Israeli presence on the West Bank, or the US military presence in Saudi Arabia, or the defeat of the Taliban, or the crusades of a thousand years ago. In fact, we're not facing a set of grievances that can be soothed or addressed. We're facing a radical ideology with inalterable objectives: to enslave whole nations and intimidate the world. No act of ours invited the rage of the killers – and no concession, bribe or act of appeasement would change or limit their plans for murder. (ibid.)

For Dale Eikmeyer (2005), who served on the 'Global War on Terrorism Planning Team' at the US Central Command, between January and April 2004, the civilized world is facing a 'global Islamist insurgency' whose aim is to 're-establish a pan-Islamic caliphate'. Since one cannot deal with these radicals, and since their political grievances are irrelevant, the only thing to do is to finish them off, and 'drain the swamp' whose two main feeders are the Islamist cells and the madrasas or religious schools. Thus, Eikmeyer approvingly refers to a speech by Donald Rumsfeld, US Secretary of Defense, who 'accurately identified the core question when he asked whether US forces were killing terrorists faster than Islamists could produce them' (Eikmeyer 2005: 4).[14]

Such attitudes guiding practice are guaranteed to generate more hostility against the United States in the Muslim world. Why then, in spite of this political deficiency, is the demonization of Islam, Muslims and Arabs so necessary? What the US establishment most fears is the decline of popular support and growing opposition domestically to its imperial project, more so than even rising opposition worldwide. Although external opposition cannot be dismissed, but as in the case of Vietnam, it is the strength of domestic opposition that ultimately tilts the scales. Howsoever counterproductive the demonization of Islam and Muslims in West and Central Asia is, it is invaluable for mobilizing support domestically, and in those countries of Western Europe where anti-Muslim racism is on the rise.[15] It also helps in generating support from an Indian elite increasingly influenced by rightwing Hindu communalist intolerance against Muslims and Islam, and in winning over Russian governmental support (given the Chechen issue where the Chechnyans are mostly Muslims) and Chinese governmental acquiescence (given Beijing's concern over unrest in its Muslim majority Xinjiang province). Moreover, functions can be separated. The US administration can make official declarations from time to time about its respect for Islam, while US civil society structures like the media and academia can take the lead in spreading anti-Muslim and anti-Islamic sentiments among the broader populace.[16]

There is an obvious historical reason why the tendency in the West to demonize Islam and Muslims is as strong as it is. From the eighteenth to the mid-twentieth centuries, the Muslim world provided the strongest and most successful resistance to Western colonial expansion – significantly more so than in the areas populated by the adherents of other world religions. In West Asia, the existence of the Ottoman Empire provided protection, and when it collapsed, the Turkish Republic emerged, at its core, as an independent, uncolonized, albeit weak, country. Elsewhere after the First World War, foreign (British and French) rule had to be exercised informally and indirectly through 'mandates to rule', that is, 'protectorate' status given to many of the countries emerging after the break-up of the Ottoman Empire. During the interwar period, the strongest upheavals (brutally suppressed) against colonial rule were in West Asia (Iraq in the 1920s, Palestine, 1936–39). In Central Asia, Afghanistan and the Caucasian regions were most resistant to British and Russian rule.

Muslim countries (including Indonesia) were among the first group of countries to obtain independence in the mid-twentieth century. West Asia, ever since 1945, has been the area of such great strategic importance to the United States that it has invested enormously in maintaining its overall control. Thus the United States has intervened repeatedly – from CIA collusion to overthrow Iran's elected Mossadegh regime in 1953 and the military intervention to support the Chamoun government in Lebanon in 1958 to the invasions of Iraq in 1991 and 2003. As if this was not enough, it has supported, and continues to support, some of the most authoritarian regimes in the region, such as the former Shah of Iran, the Baathist regime of Saddam Hussein himself till 1991, the Wahhabi regime of Saudi Arabia, as well as its unflinching strategic support since 1967 for maintaining Israel's regional dominance.

This consistency of US-led Western aggression in West Asia has led to a corresponding consistency of resistance and mass hostility. The *ideological* character of this resistance has been variable – the rise and decline of radical, secular nationalism, of Pan-Arabism, of socialist and Marxist inspired movements, and the current rise of Political Islam. The term 'Political Islam' is far superior to 'Islamic Fundamentalism' or 'Muslim Fundamentalism' for it is politics not religious fundamentalism that has been the driving force of resistance.

Central, also, to the current Western discourse of demonization is the notion of *jihad*. Both George Bush and Tony Blair use this otherwise unfamiliar term with growing frequency in their public pronouncements. Like most Westerners, they take it to mean the Quranic equivalent of a 'holy war' against unbelievers. In actual fact, the Quran talks of *al-jihad al akbar* (the Greater jihad) and *al-jihad al asghar* (the lesser jihad). The greater jihad means an inner struggle for self-mastery, to overcome personal/human weaknesses and achieve greater piety and virtue in an imperfect world. The lesser jihad is properly translated not as 'holy war' but as 'just war' to be fought for self-preservation. As a slogan for popular mobilization it appears at crisis points in the history of the development of Muslim societies in interaction with other (Muslim and non-Muslim) powers. Thus, its use, although aimed at unifying the Muslim *ummah* or community, has never been exclusively directed against non-Muslims, but against both Muslim and non-Muslim forces perceived to be unjust (Mamdani 2004: 50–54).[17]

The current call for jihad by Al Qaeda is as much against Saudi Arabia's and Egypt's rulers as against the governments of Israel and the United States. According to Mamdani, there have been five occasions when a mobilizing call for jihad achieved some success. The first was by Saladin in response to the First Christian Crusade of the eleventh century and was directed against the Christian 'infidels' and outsiders. The second was in the late seventeenth century in the Senegambia region of West Africa when Sufi leaders (*Marabout*) in Berber North Africa moved their forces southwards to unify the region against Muslim West African rulers, who were collaborating in the slave trade with European powers. The third jihad in the mid-eighteenth century was waged by Wahhabi Islamist rulers (the House of Saud) seeking an alliance with a rising Britain against the Sunni Muslim Ottoman rulers and against Shia heretics. The fourth jihad was declared by the al-Mahdi (Messiah) of Sudan in the late nineteenth century to promote an anti-colonial struggle against the joint Turkish–Egyptian administration that was itself being subordinated to the British. The fifth jihad (supported by the United States) was launched in Afghanistan in the 1980s by Islamist rebels and directed against Communists, Soviet and Afghan. Today, the supporters of US Empire-building in West and Central Asia falsely claim that terrorism is the practical–ideological expression of commitment to Islam's notion of jihad.

Let us put things in perspective. For all their 'shock value' and undeniable moral obscenity, 11 September, the Madrid bombings of March 2004, the London bombings of July 2005, cannot constitute a serious, let alone mortal, threat to Western societies. Forces like Al Qaeda lack the capacity to carry out actions that could result in a significant political transformation where they most want it, namely overthrowing key pro-US regimes like Saudi Arabia and Egypt that are their real *bêtes noires*. Their terrorism is political activity 'on the cheap' – an attempt to undermine public morale in the West and to cash in on the widespread public hostility to US foreign policy among Muslim masses in countries suffering under the yoke of authoritarian pro-US client regimes.

After March 2003, terrorist acts have been deliberately carried out in countries whose governments are *allies* of the United States in the invasion–occupation of Iraq, to drive a wedge between the public and their governments. 11 September was a gigantic strategic–political mistake, an enormous gift given by the minor thugs (Al Qaeda) to the most powerful dons (the US foreign policy establishment) of global rightwing reaction. The Madrid bombings did successfully affect the election results with the new Spanish government withdrawing its forces from Iraq. The London bombings do not seem to have significantly altered the pre-existing distribution of sentiment – the hostility to or support for Britain's involvement in Iraq. But, in the short term, it did enhance Prime Minister Blair's domestic popularity ratings. Given the essential impotence of this 'terrorism of the weak' vis-à-vis the basic social, economic and political structures in the West, grossly exaggerating its actual threat is all the more indefensible.

A remarkable study carried out by Robert Pape on 'suicide terrorism' shows how untenable the presumed link is between Islam/Muslims and terrorism.[18] The world leaders in suicide terrorism are the Tamil Tigers of Sri Lanka. Some 95 per cent of suicide terrorism is aimed at foreign occupiers, and is demand, not supply, driven. It is driven by the fact of occupation and its reinforcement, not by the 'Islamic supply' of religious fanatics. Of the 462 'successful' suicide attacks since 1980, most are 'first-time' volunteers, not seasoned fighters. Sustained and brutal occupation, and not the peculiarities of Islamic theology create a constant reservoir of suicide bombers. Before the occupation by the United States, Iraq had no suicide terrorist attack in its history. There were 20 such attacks in Iraq in 2003, 48 in 2004, and over 50 in the first five months of 2005. Most of the suicide terrorists are Iraqi Sunnis and Saudis.

The United States has 150,000 troops in the Saudi Arabian peninsula (including the Gulf states) and another 130,000 in Iraq, while it supports Israel's military occupation and control of Palestine. It is this US and Israeli presence that fuels suicide terrorism, not any presumed cultural–Islamic rejection of 'Western values'. Otherwise Iran with a population (70 million), three times that of Iraq, or Saudi Arabia, would be the 'hotbed' of Al Qaeda type terrorism, which it is not. Although Sudan is ruled by Political Islamists (and Osama Bin Laden lived there for three years), it does not produce Al Qaeda type terrorists. Two thirds of all suicide attacks are from countries where the United States has stationed large troop contingents. Much of the remaining one-third are in Israel–Palestine. When the occupier and the occupied are of different religions, demonization of the occupied by the occupier is likely to take place. But Pape also points out that once the occupation ends, terrorist attacks stop. In Lebanon, between 1982–86 there were 41 suicide attacks. But after the United States withdrew its troops in 1986, there were none. Similarly, once Israel withdrew from southern Lebanon, Lebanese suicide attacks stopped.

Our Tasks

Two tasks lie ahead. First, we need to expose the US manipulation of the discourse on terrorism in order to serve its own Empire-building project. Immediately after 11 September, ordinary Americans suddenly raised a very important question: why do they hate us? This 'they' might number tens of millions of 'outsiders' who might not condone what happened, but were not surprised by the attacks. The answer to that question was simple. What so many 'outsiders' hate about the United States is its government's foreign policy, that's it! But precisely to prevent such public self-questioning about foreign policy, the intellectual, political and media establishments immediately went into overdrive to provide false answers. 'They' hate us, it was declared, because they hate our way of life, envy our freedoms and prosperity. This diversion was absolutely essential for preserving the benign (popular and elite) self-perception of what motivates US behaviour abroad that so greatly buttresses its expansionism. If this self-perception is sufficiently punctured, it could lead to a massive transformation for the better, of not just US foreign policy behaviour, but also of its domestic society and polity.

The things to admire about the United States pertain primarily to the internal characteristics of US politics, culture, society and its technological and scientific capacities and practices. Successive US governments, during and after the Cold War, have inflicted immense sufferings and promoted terrible injustices worldwide, all in the name of freedom, and now, in that of the GWOT. Since all imperial projects can only sustain themselves in the long-term through popular consent, defeating the American Empire project means denying it such consent everywhere, and especially within the United States itself. The GWOT must be exposed for the fraud that it is because it aims to disguise and justify Empire-building and itself promotes and legitimizes the arrogant and terrorist behaviour of the United States (and many of its allies), which extends and deepens the hatreds that sustain the terrorism of many non-state actors.

Our second task, then, is to create the conditions whereby international terrorism will significantly diminish, even if it does not permanently fade away. Here, the biggest problem is what to do about the terrorism of states? Ignoring the terrorism of powerful states – United States, Britain, Russia, Israel, China, India, *et al.* – and focusing only on how to defeat group terrorism will not suffice. The 'problem management' approach of certain governments, while superior to the United States' 'ideologization' and 'militarization', is still inadequate to tackling group terrorism.[19] Good intelligence gathering and sharing, and clandestine secret service activities will not do. Political terrorism has to be dealt with primarily in *political* not managerial ways.

Whether one is talking of Iraq, Palestine, Kashmir, Jaffna, Chechnya, Afghanistan, the Basque region, the Balkans, or anywhere else, one has to search for a *just* solution. And what would be a just solution cannot be a function primarily of power, which is always asymmetrically distributed. It has to be a function of the moral, political and historical merits respectively of the case at hand as disputed by the main protagonists. As long as there are those who believe that power can trump justice, and impose its 'final solution', the cycle of conflicting and rival terrorisms will continue.

International terrorist acts, no matter who perpetrates them, are best seen as international crimes against humanity. It then follows that we have to put in place international laws that are comprehensive, non-partisan and fair, and establish institutions that can give effect to these laws impartially. The existing body of the United Nations Security Council Resolutions, counter-terrorism conventions and protocols, while providing a 'base' of sorts, are inadequate in several respects, most notably in their refusal to sufficiently recognize and properly deal with the central problem of state terrorism. And what about the International Criminal Court (ICC)?

Strengths and Weaknesses of the ICC

The ICC is a treaty-based organization created by the Rome Statute on 17 July, 1998 when 120 countries voted for its existence. 21 abstained, including India, and 7 voted against including the United States, China, Iraq and Israel. These 5 named countries remain outside the ICC, which came into force on 11 April 2002 when over 60 countries ratified it.[20] The ICC can carry out investigations, prosecutions and judicial sentencing against individuals (only) who are culpable of crimes like 'genocide', 'war crimes' and 'crimes against humanity' that come under its purview. While terrorism is not specifically identified, clearly much of what constitutes terrorism would qualify as crimes against humanity. Prominent state leaders, including heads of states, are not exempt from ICC purview. Nor can the accused shelter behind the excuse of following the orders of superiors, military or civilian. The ICC can issue arrest warrants to nationals of non-member states if suspected of wrongdoing against member-states. A senior US government official can be accused of an international crime even though the United States is not a member-state.

Although the United Nations helped set it up, the ICC is substantially independent of it, where power politics crucially shapes Security Council decisions. The International Court of Justice, unlike the ICC, was created to deal with disputes among nations, and not to prosecute individuals. The ICC complements national judiciaries by undertaking investigations and prosecutions for the crimes that come under ICC purview when states are unable or unwilling to do so. While the death penalty is excluded, it can give sentences of up to 30 years imprisonment to be served in national prisons of member-states.

The ICC Statute does not conflict with the provisions of the UN Charter. This is appropriate because the ICC must respect the claims of national sovereignty, but also inapt because it cannot prevent political manipulation in the United Nations. The United States, under President Clinton, initially took part in creating the ICC and signed it, hoping to subordinate it to the Security Council and the US veto. The final compromise regarding the relationship of the Security Council to the ICC was enough to make President Bush pull the United States out in his first term of office, and Washington continues to work systematically to undermine it. The Security Council can 'refer' a situation to the ICC when it suspects that one or more crimes covered by its Statute have taken place. Permanent members of the Security Council like the United States and China, though not members of the ICC, can nonetheless refer individuals from other countries (members or not) to the ICC. The Security Council also has the power to 'defer' (through a one-year renewable suspension) a case that is being tried at the investigating or prosecuting stage. The Security Council can do this to protect certain individuals from certain countries, on the condition that nine assenting votes in the Security Council are cast and no permanent member vetoes the deferment.

Theoretically, the ICC is freer from political manipulation than the Security Council or United Nations or other 'international' political or legal institutions. But it faces other limitations. Non-members of the ICC need not cooperate with it, and, without such a cooperation, the accumulation of evidence against their nationals will only be hindered. The ICC also has no machinery for implementing its decisions. It must rely on the cooperation of states to implement orders and sentences, to arrest suspects, identify and locate witnesses, give evidence, facilitate voluntary appearances, examine sites, unearth graves, conduct searches, and so on.

How many states will muster the courage to help the ICC to investigate crimes committed by powerful individuals of other powerful countries? How many will arrest and hand over visiting high officials who might have committed crimes on their territory or on that of other member states? Can one imagine a senior US official (say, Kissinger) receiving such treatment? General Pinochet, the ex-President of Chile, who masterminded the bloody coup that overthrew the democratically elected government of Salvador Allende in 1973 and established ruthless military rule, was extradited to his home country despite being arrested in Europe in accordance with progressive national laws holding him responsible for crimes against European nationals in Chile.

On 3 August 2002, the US Congress passed the American Service Members' Protection Act (APSA) stipulating that the United States can withdraw aid to countries that sign and ratify the ICC, and prohibits US citizens from cooperating with it.[21] The United States has also sought to bypass the ICC by using its political, economic, diplomatic and military clout to secure Bilateral Immunity Agreements (BIAs) with over 50 countries, whether or not they had joined the ICC. These agreements forbid these countries to surrender US nationals to the ICC, or cooperate with it where US citizens are concerned. India quietly signed a BIA with the United States on 26 December 2002 declaring that neither the United States nor India would cooperate with the ICC. No public information or media criticism accompanied the deal, nor was the issue raised in the Indian Parliament. The then US ambassador to India, Robert Blackwill, nonetheless, had the unmitigated gall to say: 'India and the US share the strongest possible commitment to bringing to justice those who commit war crimes, crimes against humanity and genocide' (see Uma 2004).[22]

How are we to evaluate the establishment of the ICC? Despite its limitations, it still represents an important effort to combat international terrorism in a lawful, universalist and impartial manner. It is superior both to international human rights commissions, whose conclusions and judgements only have the status of recommendations, and to *ad hoc* international tribunals arbitrarily set up by victorious states to prosecute selectively identified criminals, but which never examine the atrocities committed by the victors themselves. The Nuremberg and Tokyo Tribunals after the Second World War, or the more recent trials of Slobodan Milosevic and Saddam Hussein are pertinent examples.

Despite the United States and India not acceding to the treaty banning landmines, its ratification by so many other countries de-legitimized and greatly reduced the presence of such weapons. A stronger and regularly functioning ICC, more confident of its own future survival, would set up valuable and accumulating precedents. It could also consider extending its legal ambit to include the illegitimate 'aggression' of states, and 'terrorism', conceived of in a more comprehensive manner than before. It might become more willing to indict powerful individuals from powerful countries as 'suspects' to be investigated, even if the prospects of actually investigating or prosecuting them remain distant. Such highlighting of the possible culpability of the powerful, would, in itself, be of great political and symbolic value.

Ultimately, the existing relationship of forces between countries has to be altered. Thus, strengthening the ICC and genuinely advancing the struggle against international terrorism becomes integrally linked to the overarching effort to defeat the US imperial project. An internationally tamed United States, much more mindful of its limitations and regretful of its foreign policy infamies, would be good for the rest of the world, and for US society itself.

Notes

[1] Hiroshima and Nagasaki took place in a wartime situation. This in no way justifies what are, undoubtedly, the greatest single acts of violence against civilians.

[2] To this day the US government has not publicly released incontrovertible evidence that Al Qaeda was responsible for the 11 September attacks, leading some circles to wildly speculate about the identity of the 'true' culprits, some even seeing the 'hidden hand' of American official agencies. The US government almost certainly has convincing evidence of Al Qaeda culpability, but releasing this would have created a public precedent. Washington needs the political flexibility to accuse others of terrorism without having to worry about providing public proof in all cases.

[3] A key text aimed at popularizing just this message was *The Terror Network* by an American journalist, Claire Sterling (1981) who had close connections with the CIA. Her claims were publicly supported by then CIA chief, William Casey and US Secretary of State, Alexander Haig.

[4] According to Whitaker (2001), correspondent for *The Guardian* unlimited, 'A recent book discussing attempts by the UN and other international bodies to define terrorism runs to three volumes and 1,866 pages without reaching any firm conclusion.'

[5] I therefore disagree with Noam Chomsky who frequently refers to the United States as a terrorist state, indeed, as being among the worst of such terrorist states. See Chomsky (2001).

[6] On 22 August 1978, the Sandinistas took over the National Assembly in Managua, Nicaragua, holding its members ransom in return for the then dictator Anastasio Somoza broadcasting its prepared political communiqués and releasing political prisoners. Safe passage to the airport for flying out was to be given to the prisoners and the commandos, in return for the release of hostages. Not only did this take place, but a massive and spontaneous public cavalcade lined the route to the airport vociferously cheering the Sandinistas in defiance of the Somoza government. This act in which no civilian was hurt marked the turning point in the struggle to overthrow the dictatorship, arousing and expressing massive opposition to it. It was the outcome of this very act that it greatly enfeebled the dictatorship, which fell shortly afterwards in early 1979. This was clearly a terrorist act, but one whose consequences were profoundly politically beneficial. There is clearly in certain cases a complex issue of the 'ethics of terrorism' that needs to be handled in all its complexity, and not dismissed as an untenable or irrelevant issue through a denial that such acts constitute terrorism.

Any discussion of the 'ethics of terrorism' must presuppose an ethically neutral definition of terrorism. For a more systematic and detailed discussion of this thorny and complex issue, see Vanaik (2002). I also present there a more comprehensive and more precise definition, wherein what can be said to constitute the terrorist act is not simply determined by the nature of the target (innocent victims), but can also be determined by the means chosen (WMDs), the issue of disproportionate force, and the crucial element of surprise that is inherent in many terrorist acts. That definition, any more than the others, would not be expected to secure universal assent.

[7] If international terrorism means the taking of innocent civilian lives outside of one's own home country, then since the end of the Second World War, no country or set of countries (leave aside non-state actors) comes close to matching the record of the US government. The number of foreign civilians killed by US government actions runs into the millions (over 1 million killed in the Korean war, over 3 million civilians killed in Indochina), and more millions would have to be added to the count if one takes into account US support for authoritarian regimes killing their own peoples through death squads and military personnel trained by the United States. In Afghanistan, during the US-led invasion and bombings, the tally of civilian deaths is conservatively estimated at over 10,000, while President Bush has himself recently and publicly acknowledged that some 30,000 Iraqis (certainly an underestimate) have died during the invasion and military occupation. The United States also has the worst record of any country when it comes to using WMDs, not just nuclear, but chemical agents and outlawed weapons such as landmines, cluster and shrapnel bombs, 'daisy cutters' that suck out all oxygen on the area they fall on, depleted uranium shells, white phospho-

rus, etc. No American leader or senior official has ever faced punishment for any of these international crimes.

8 Conservative Republicans admire neoconservatives for their 'moral clarity' and 'commitment', but fault them for 'conceptual overreach' (too much missionary zeal in foreign policy) and 'lack of pragmatism' (too willing to use military power and too trusting in its efficacy). The more intelligent among such Conservative Republicans also reject the neoconservative approach to tackling terrorism, while never being self-reflexive enough to perceive how terrorist behaviour has always been central to US foreign policy behaviour. Neocons are pilloried for arguing that 'terrorism is terrorism', and for refusing to understand that it has 'root causes' that do need to be tackled. Such conservative voices have been disturbed by the neocon interpretation of counter-terrorism as 'war' requiring national mobilization of moral and material resources, instead of (like the British and other European governments) seeing counter-terrorism as a much more restricted field of 'problem management'. Stefan Halper and Jonathan Clarke are two such 'traditional' conservatives. See Halper and Clarke (2004: 17–22, 275–81).

9 Two ingredients of this exceptionalism are particularly important. There has to be a historical amnesia or rationalized unconcern about the United States' brutal past, from the decimation of the native populations to its numerous and ruthless depredations in the nineteenth and early twentieth centuries in Latin America and the Pacific. A specifically anti-black racism is also inescapable, since the conditions of a majority of blacks (not of all peoples of colour) is a standing refutation of any claim that the United States is the 'land of opportunity' par excellence, where individual or group failure to prosper is essentially the fault of the individual or group itself.

10 Since Al Qaeda is not the only terrorist group that the United States has outlawed and declared war upon, the list of countries that can be targeted, should the United States so desire, is even longer.

11 In February 2003, the *National Strategy for Combating Terrorism* document officially enshrined the principle of pre-emptive attacks against designated terrorists. 'The United States will constantly strive to enlist the support of the international community in this fight against a common foe. If necessary, however, we will not hesitate to act alone, to exercise our right to self-defense, including acting preemptively against terrorists to prevent them from doing harm to our people and our country.' (*NSCT* 2003: 2). Nor will the United States be bound in its behaviour by the international counter-terrorism conventions and protocols and UNSC Resolutions that it otherwise endorses. It reserves the right to carry out 'special tasks above and beyond the requirements' of such international documents (*NSCT* 2003: 19).

12 After 11 September most alarmists warning about the danger of nuclear terrorists have had combat groups and not states in mind. This exaggerated alarmism has three objective effects: (a) It helps to justify the possession of nuclear weapons by states, for example, to provide deterrence against such non-state nuclear terrorism; (b) It diverts attention away from the behaviour, attitudes and thinking of these state elites. The implicit assumption that such terrorists are frighteningly irresponsible, when compared to those who run states, is simply nonsensical and belies all historical evidence; (c) It lets the concept of nuclear deterrence as advocated, defended or practised by state elites, off the hook. Deterrence is simply a way of rationalizing the adoption of a fundamentally terrorist way of thinking about nuclear weapons and security. It was Winston Churchill who once said that after the advent of nuclear weapons, 'peace would be the sturdy child of terror'. In spite of the changed circumstances after 11 September, it is not some distinctive breed of footloose or insane nuclear terrorists that is the source of the greatest nuclear danger, but the routinized and disguised terrorism of deterrence thinking and behaviour by otherwise ordinary, sane, humane and ethical people.

But having said this, there still remains the question of how we judge the possibilities of nuclear, chemical, biological or radiological terrorist acts by non-state actors. Technically, there remain many barriers that make it extremely difficult for combat groups to handle such agents of destruction. Politically, there remain the various factors that promote self-limitation in such groups and individuals, as distinct from state actors. Nevertheless, we can no longer rule out with the same confidence or equanimity the possibility of such acts of terrorism in the future or their partial equivalents, such as the conventional bombing or destruction of a civilian nuclear energy plant.

[13] An updated Pentagon Planning document, the 'Doctrine for Joint Nuclear Operations' of March 2005 whose contents were revealed in a story carried in *The Washington Post* of 11 September 2005, confirms that such pre-emptive action has been made part of a doctrine. At the moment it has yet to obtain an official imprimatur but could well do so soon enough. It is at any rate indicative of US thinking at the highest levels.

[14] Rumsfeld's speech was reported under the heading 'Remarks at the International Institute for Strategic Studies' in *The Boston Globe*, 8 September 2004.

[15] The 2004 Presidential elections in the United States announced the rise of an overlapping bloc of rightwing Christian Evangelism and upper working class–lower middle class whites facing socio-economic decline who supported the Republicans. Christian Evangelists are committed to strong alignment with Israel and concerned about the 'cultural degeneration' of the United States. Hostility to Islam and Muslims among them is not difficult to arouse. The second part of this electoral bloc has frustrations that were easily enough displaced into similar opposition to this 'cultural degeneration'. They also have a growing fear of further decline into the real working class-underclass of US society, which is peopled by blacks and Latinos. Overt racism is no longer publicly acceptable. But a sublimation of their emotions into anti-Arab/anti-Muslim racism demonization is acceptable, indeed increasingly promoted by mainstream media and public culture in today's United States. See Lieven (2002).

By declaring an international war against terrorism, the United States can also be accused of making a grave strategic error, for it has now blurred the lines between non-state 'national terrorists' who are fighting for some national liberation cause (be it Chechnya or Kashmir), and are not targeting the United States, and those non-state terrorist groups that are targeting the United States and its citizens. By lumping them together it is pushing them to make international connections between themselves to protect against a now common opponent. The United States should, from its security point of view, be trying its best to separate and divide the two categories of 'national' and 'international' terrorists from each other. But eliding this distinction and extending the geographical list of terrorists to be attacked becomes necessary if the 'war on global terrorism' is to serve as justification for imperial–global interventions and activities.

[16] The US government (whether Democrats or Republicans) is waging a war almost entirely against Muslim terrorism. Its support for Israel's use of brutal terrorist means against Palestinians has been unflinching and continuous. Such double standards hardly go unnoticed in West Asia and elsewhere. Till recently, there were 36 organizations on the US State Department's proscribed list, of which 24 are Muslim. The rest are, apart from the Basque ETA and the Northern Irish paramilitaries, leftist groups mostly in Colombia, Peru, Nepal and India. There are no Christian, Buddhist, Hindu or Tamil (Sri Lanka) extremist groups on this list. The State Department also lists 26 countries whose nationals are said to represent an 'elevated security risk'. Except for North Korea, all the rest are Muslim countries. Although the United States does distinguish between ethnically similar South and North Koreans and between 'good' and 'bad' Cubans, no such political discrimination is applied to the citizens of the other 25 Muslim countries. In December 2002, the United States added Armenia to this list. The Armenian Ambassador to the United States immediately raised an outcry and simply pointed out by way of counter-argument that Armenia was a Christian country. Armenia was immediately removed from this list. See Chapter 6 titled 'The War Against (Muslim) Terrorism' in Mann (2003).

[17] This, and the following paragraph, have been drawn from Mamdani (2005).

[18] See the interview conducted by Scott McConnell (2005) with Associate Professor, Robert Pape of the University of Chicago, and author of *Dying to Win* (2005). Pape's conclusions are all the more discomfiting to the Empire lobby because he is certainly

no radical or anti-imperialist leftist. Pape compiled the first complete database on every suicide terrorist attack around the world from 1980 to early 2004 from various language sources – English, Arabic, Hebrew, Russian, Tamil.

[19] The view that 'terrorism is itself an ideology', and, therefore, for its upholders (the designated terrorists) an unalterable mindset, and equally the militarization of the issue, that is, that 'terrorism is terrorism', allow governments to justify their repressive and sometimes terrorist behaviour against selected opponents. These governments disregard the political context (from Chechnya to Kashmir), and their own culpabilities in making that context what it is. It is not a coincidence that a number of democracies after 11 September, such as Britain and India, followed the United States in legislating unjustified restrictions on civil liberties in the name of anti-terrorism action. States also make scapegoats of various groups to cover up their own deficiencies and their own anti-social behaviour. European governments have pushed forward a rightwing racist programme against Muslim migrants and citizens. India has targeted poor Bangladeshi migrants for brutal state treatment as potential terrorists and 'infiltrators' when their only crime is illegal entry in desperate search of a better livelihood. The US government benefits from such 'extension by example' of its perception of terrorism, since these governments are not going to challenge the illegitimacy of the notion of a US-led 'global war on terrorism'.

[20] So far, some 50 per cent of African countries, 73 per cent of countries in Europe (East and West) and in the Commonwealth of Independent States (CIS) have joined the ICC, as well as Canada and most of Latin America. Some 37 per cent of the island states in Oceania have also joined. Apart from the United States, the biggest laggards are North African, Middle Eastern and Asian countries, where China and India have set a bad example. The more countries that join the ICC, the more will be the effectivity of its work.

[21] APSA famously endorses 'any necessary action to free US soldiers' handed over to the ICC. Theoretically, this could lead to US commandos raiding Dutch prisons (the ICC's permanent seat is in the Hague) in search of US service members under ICC indictment. In Holland, APSA is dubbed 'The Hague Invasion Act'.

[22] Blackwill is also a key figure in the current Bush Administration pushing for a long-term strategic alliance between the US and India.

References

Anderson, Perry (2002), 'Internationalism: A Breviary', *New Left Review*, No. 14, March–April.

Bush, George W. (2005), 'War on Terror', speech delivered to the National Endowment on Democracy (NED), Washington DC, 6 October.

Chomsky, Noam (2001), 'New War on Terror', *The Spokesman*, No. 73: 25–46.

Eikmayer, D. (2005), 'How to Beat the Global Islamist Insurgency', *Middle East Quarterly*, Winter.

Halliday, Fred (2004), 'Terrorism in Historical Perspective', available at the *Open Democracy* website, 22 April.

Halper, Stefan and Jonathan Clarke (2004), *America Alone: The Neo-Conservatives and the Global Order* (Cambridge: Cambridge University Press).

Lieven, Anatol (2002), 'The Push for War', *London Review of Books*, Vol. 24, No. 19, 3 October.

McConnell, Scott (2005), interview with Robert Pape, *The American Conservative*, http://amconmag.com/2005_07_18/article.html.

Mamdani, Mahmood (2005), *Good Muslim, Bad Muslim* (New York: Pantheon Books).

Mann, Michael (2003), *Incoherent Empire* (London: Verso).

NSCT, National Strategy for Combating Terrorism (2003), February, available at http://www.whitehouse.gov/news/releases/2003/02/20030214-7.html.

Pape, Robert (2005), *Dying to Win: The Strategic Logic of Suicide Terrorism* (New York: Random House).

PGT, Patterns of Global Terrorism (2001), US Department of State, Washington DC.

Sterling, Claire (1981), *The Terror Network: The Secret War of International Terrorism* (New York: Holt, Rinehart, and Winston).
Uma, Saumya (2004), *International Criminal Court and India*, Women's Research and Action Group Publications, Mumbai, September.
UNSG, United Nations Secretary General (2004), *High-Level Panel on Threats, Challenges and Change, Final Report*, 1 December.
Vanaik, Achin (2002), 'The Ethics and Efficacy of Political Terrorism', in Eric Hershbery and Kevin Moore (eds), *Critical Views of September 11: Analyses from Around the World* (New York: Social Science Research Council).
Whitaker, Brian (2001), World Dispatch, 7 May, http://www.guardian.co.uk/elsewhere/journalist/story/0,7992,487098,00.html.

The Empire of Fear

Zia Mian

Whatever they fear from you, you'll be threatened with.

Seneca (4 BC–AD 65)

Introduction

In late February 2001, a year after President George W. Bush took office, his Secretary of State, Colin Powell, spoke on the subject of Iraq and its military capabilities. Ten years had passed since the Gulf War, a decade marked by international inspections aimed at finding and destroying Iraq's weapons of mass destruction and missile programmes, stringent sanctions that restricted its access to basic military equipment, as well as denying it many vital civilian goods that has caused countless deaths and enormous suffering among Iraq's people. Powell explained that the United States believed Saddam Hussein's regime 'has not developed any significant capability with respect to weapons of mass destruction', and that Iraq's leader was even 'unable to project conventional power against his neighbors' (Powell 2001).

Powell was not alone in the assessment that there was no military danger from Iraq to its neighbours, or to the United States. In late summer of that year, National Security Advisor Condoleezza Rice told *CNN* (*Late Edition with Wolf Blitzer*, 29 July 2001): 'let's remember that his [Saddam's] country is divided, in effect. He does not control the northern part of his country. We are able to keep his arms from him. His military forces have not been rebuilt.'[2] Few would have disputed this judgement, yet, over the next two years, the Bush administration was able to convince many Americans that a desperate and broken Iraq was an imminent and mortal threat that could only be confronted by war.

In this chapter, we look at how the fear of weapons of mass destruction was used by the Bush administration to organize public support for its war on Iraq in 2003. We trace the sources for this policy towards Iraq, the pressure for a more militarized US foreign policy and the role played by key figures in the Bush administration who belonged to a hard-line conservative group calling itself 'The Project for A New American Century'.

The media played a central role in the creation of public opinion in favour of a war on Iraq. We need to enquire into what public understanding and misunderstanding of basic issues connected to the war against Iraq reveal about the media, and especially, how misperceptions about the war are linked to watching television channels like Fox and CNN.

The nuclear fears that moved the Bush administration and which it used to build public support for its war, are widely shared, run deep and have a long history. We look briefly at the way these have been expressed in US culture and have mobilized an anti-nuclear movement for the six decades since the atomic bomb was first invented and used by the United States to destroy the Japanese cities of Hiroshima and Nagasaki.

Iraq was not the only instance of desperate US efforts to prevent another country from acquiring nuclear weapons. These efforts are as old as the bomb itself. We trace this history and then look at the case of Iran, the newest arena for US efforts to police the proliferation of nuclear weapons capabilities. President Bush has said that the acquisition of nuclear weapons would be 'intolerable', and many hear echoes of the rhetoric used against Iraq before the war in 2003. However, the threat of the use of nuclear weapons has become more challenging, as terrorist groups like Al Qaeda are now seen as seeking nuclear weapons.

A broader assessment of US policy on nuclear weapons makes clear that there is much more at stake than the aim simply to reduce and end the threat of nuclear weapons. The determination of the US leadership to keep and modernize US nuclear weapons, to allow chosen allies and friends to retain and develop these weapons, and to use sanctions and military force to prevent other states from even trying to acquire knowledge about these weapons, are at the heart of US policy. We look, in particular, at the way the United States has been aiding the development of nuclear capability in India and Israel.

We conclude by reflecting on the demands for the elimination of nuclear weapons and the kind of politics this might require.

How the White House set out to 'Educate the Public'

According to the US National Coordinator for Counterterrorism, Richard Clarke, at a cabinet meeting on the day after the 11 September 2001 attacks on the United States, Defense Secretary Donald Rumsfeld talked about 'getting Iraq', arguing that there were 'no decent targets for bombing in Afghanistan', and proposed 'we should consider bombing Iraq instead'. This suggestion was not rejected by President Bush, who 'noted that what we needed to do with Iraq was to change the government, not just hit it with more cruise missiles' (Clarke 2004: 30–31).

The early positions within the government were described by a senior Bush administration official in an interview:

> Before September 11th, there wasn't a consensus Administration view about Iraq. . . . There were those who preferred regime change, and they were largely residing in the Pentagon, and probably in the Vice-president's office. . . . Then, in the immediate aftermath of the eleventh, not that much changed. . . . Some

> initial attempts by [Deputy Secretary of Defense] Wolfowitz and others to draw Iraq in never went anywhere, because the link between Iraq and September 11th was, as far as we knew, nebulous at most – nonexistent, for all intents and purposes. (Lemann 2003)

President Bush's speech writers were asked at the end of 2001 to make a case for war against Iraq, to be included in the forthcoming State of the Union Address (Borger 2003). In the January 2002 speech, Bush declared that the United States confronted an 'axis of evil', naming North Korea, Iran and Iraq. North Korea and Iran received one sentence each in the speech, and the real focus was Iraq (Sanger 2002). The problem, President Bush declared, was that: 'Iraq continues to flaunt its hostility toward America and to support terror. The Iraqi regime has plotted to develop anthrax, and nerve gas, and nuclear weapons for over a decade (Bush 2002a).' He went on to say that 'by seeking weapons of mass destruction, these regimes pose a grave and growing danger. They could provide these arms to terrorists, giving them the means to match their hatred. They could attack our allies or attempt to blackmail the United States' (ibid.). These arguments were to be repeated over the next year with even greater force and detail.

Vice President Dick Cheney returned from the Middle East, and on 24 March 2002, appeared on three major Sunday public-affairs television programmes bearing similar messages on each. On CNN's *Late Edition* he offered the following comment on Saddam: 'This is a man of great evil, as the President said. And he is actively pursuing nuclear weapons at this time.' On NBC's *Meet the Press*, he said: '[T]here's good reason to believe that he continues to aggressively pursue the development of a nuclear weapon. Now will he have one in a year, five years? I can't be that precise.' And on CBS's *Face the Nation*: 'The notion of a Saddam Hussein with his great oil wealth, with his inventory that he already has of biological and chemical weapons, that he might actually acquire a nuclear weapon is, I think, a frightening proposition for anybody who thinks about it' (Lobe 2005).

A few months later, speaking at the United States Military Academy at West Point, President Bush made a more general point that revealed the real fears of the United States:

> When the spread of chemical and biological and nuclear weapons, along with ballistic missile technology – when that occurs, even weak states and small groups could attain a catastrophic power to strike great nations. Our enemies have declared this very intention, and have been caught seeking these terrible weapons. They want the capability to blackmail us, or to harm us, or to harm our friends. (Bush 2002b)

The reason why proliferation must be prevented, for President Bush and leaders before him, is that 'even weak states and small groups could attain a catastrophic power to strike great nations.' What is left unsaid here is, of course, that some 'great nations,' most notably the United States, have long had the 'catastrophic power' to destroy weak nations, and the goal is to keep things that way.

The fear that the spread of weapons of mass destruction and especially nuclear weapons might allow 'weak states' to counter the ambitions and interests of 'great nations' is almost as old as the atomic bomb. President Bush's words echo an argument advanced 50 years ago, in one of the earliest studies about how the atomic bomb might affect international relations. It was argued that atomic weapons were a grave danger to the United States, not just because 'regular rivals on the same level' might acquire these 'absolute weapons' (as the Soviet Union and Britain had already done by then), but that 'possibly some of the nations lower down in the power scale might get hold of atomic weapons and change the whole relationship of great and small states' (Dunn, Brodie, *et al.* 1956: 5). To prevent this has been an important goal of US policy, and that of the other nuclear weapons states, as each developed its own weapons.

In late July 2002, Sir Richard Dearlove, head of M.I.6, the British Secret Service, and newly returned from Washington, explained at a meeting of British Prime Minister Tony Blair and his top advisors, that the Bush administration had decided to attack Iraq, 'military action was now seen as inevitable'. In what has come to be known as the Downing Street memo, Dearlove explained that 'Bush wanted to remove Saddam through military action, justified by the conjunction of terrorism and WMD'. He continued, 'the intelligence and facts were being fixed around the policy' (Smith 2005).

This plan was to unfold over the next several months, with leaders in the United States and Britain emphasizing, what Dearlove had called, a 'conjunction of terrorism and WMD threat' from Iraq. Britain joined the United States' drive to war, despite the recognition at that meeting by the British Foreign Secretary Jack Straw that 'the case was thin. Saddam was not threatening his neighbors, and his WMD capability was less than that of Libya, North Korea or Iran.' This reflected the assessment by the British Foreign Office in early 2002 that there was no hard evidence that Iraq had stockpiles of weapons of mass destruction.

To coordinate the case for war in the United States, in August 2002, White House Chief of Staff Andrew Card set up the White House Iraq Group; the members included Karl Rove (senior political advisor to Bush), Condoleezza Rice and her deputy (now National Security Advisor) Stephen Hadley, Lewis Libby (chief of staff to Dick Cheney), and communications strategist Karen Hughes, among others. Its mission was to organize US strategy on Iraq, and according to one participant, to 'educate the public' about the danger posed by the Saddam Hussein regime (Gellman and Pincus 2003).

This group of key officials planned the speeches on Iraq by the administration, and the reports and papers laying out policy. The focus was to be the threat of weapons of mass destruction. How this came about was explained later by Deputy Secretary of Defense Paul Wolfowitz, when he revealed that 'the truth is that for reasons that have a lot to do with the US government bureaucracy we settled on the one issue that everyone could agree on which was weapons of mass destruction as the core reason' (Tannenhaus 2003).

The first major speech was on 26 August 2002, delivered by Vice President Cheney, to a conference of the US military veterans: 'there is no doubt that Saddam Hussein now has weapons of mass destruction. There is no doubt he is amassing them to use against our friends, against our allies, and against us.' It was a question of when, not if, such an attack would come, Cheney seemed to say, as he summoned up the vision of the Japanese attack on the US fleet at Pearl Harbour, claiming: 'Only then did we recognize the magnitude of the danger to our country.' Now, he argued, 'time is not on our side. Deliverable weapons of mass destruction in the hands of a terror network, or a murderous dictator, or the two working together, constitutes as grave a threat as can be imagined' (Cheney 2002).

On 8 September 2002, *The New York Times* ran a story under the headline 'US Says Hussein Intensifies Quest for A-Bomb Parts'. It reported that: 'More than a decade after Saddam Hussein agreed to give up weapons of mass destruction, Iraq has stepped up its quest for nuclear weapons and has embarked on a world wide hunt for materials to make an atomic bomb, Bush administration officials said' (Miller, *et al.* 2002). The report went on that 'hard-liners' in the administration were afraid that 'the first sign of a "smoking gun" . . . may be a mushroom cloud.'

The hardliners went on major news and current affairs television programmes that day and conjured up what is perhaps the most fearful image of our times, the mushroom cloud produced by an exploding atomic bomb. Condoleezza Rice on CNN (*Late Edition with Wolf Blitzer*, 8 September 2002) argued that 'We do know that he [Saddam Hussein] is actively pursuing a nuclear weapon . . . there will always be some uncertainty about how quickly he can acquire nuclear weapons. But we don't want the smoking gun to be a mushroom cloud.' On CBS television (*Face the Nation*, 8 September 2002), Defense Secretary Donald Rumsfeld explicitly linked Iraq, terrorism, weapons of mass destruction and 11 September, arguing that

> Iraq is a terrorist state on the terrorist list. It is a state that is developing and has developed and possessed and, in fact, used weapons of mass destruction already. . . . If you go back to September 11th, we lost 3,000 innocent men, women and children. Well, if – if you think that's a problem, imagine – imagine a September 11th with weapons of mass destruction.

In early October 2002, the same images and language were deployed by President Bush. In a nationally televised speech from Cincinnati, Ohio, President Bush claimed that 'America must not ignore the threat gathering against us . . . we cannot wait for the final proof – the smoking gun – that could come in the form of a mushroom cloud' (Bush 2002c).

This view was propounded not just in interviews and speeches on major television stations by leading figures, it also figured large in official policy documents. In September 2002, the *National Security Strategy of the United States* was released. It announced that 'We must be prepared to stop rogue states and their terrorist clients before they are able to threaten or use weapons of mass destruction against the United States and our allies and friends' (US Government 2002: 14). The message of threat and pre-emption was repeated again and again, the report claiming that 'We must deter and defend against the threat before it is unleashed' and 'We cannot let our enemies strike first.'

The US public opinion responded to this determined effort to portray an imminent nuclear threat from Iraq to the United States. A poll, in late September 2002, found that 80 per cent of Americans thought Iraq already had the capability to use weapons of mass destruction against US targets (PIPA 2002).

There was some dissent from within government, but it failed to reach the major media. An October 2002 report based on extensive interviews with officials claimed

> a growing number of military officers, intelligence professionals and diplomats . . . have deep misgivings about the administration's double-time march towards war [and] charge that administration hawks have exaggerated evidence of the threat that Iraqi leader Saddam Hussein poses – including distorting his links to the al-Qaeda terrorist network – have overstated the amount of international support for attacking Iraq and have downplayed the potential repercussions of a new war in the Middle East. (Strobel, *et al.* 2002)

These officials were categorical that 'the US government has no dramatic new knowledge about the Iraqi leader that justifies Bush's urgent call to arms'. They took issue with particular statements by President Bush, Vice President Cheney, Secretary of Defense Rumsfeld and National Security Advisor Condoleezza Rice.

This assessment was subsequently confirmed publicly by Paul Pillar, the US National Intelligence Officer for the Middle East from 2000 to 2005, the person responsible for coordinating US intelligence assessments on Iraq. In 2006, he observed that 'intelligence was misused publicly to justify decisions already made' by the Bush administration. Pillar has described the claims by senior officials and the administration as being 'at odds' with the intelligence community's judgements. He revealed, in particular, that 'the greatest discrepancy between the administration's public statements and the intelligence community's judgments concerned . . . the relationship between Saddam and al Qaeda', and was categorical that 'the intelligence community never offered analysis that supported the notion of an alliance between Saddam and al Qaeda' (Pillar 2006: 15–27). According to Pillar (ibid.: 21–22):

> Well before March 2003, intelligence analysts and their managers knew that the United States was heading for war with Iraq. It was clear that the Bush administration would frown on or ignore analysis that called into question a decision to go to war and welcome analysis that supported such a decision.

Tyler Drumhellar, a senior CIA officer, has confirmed and added to Pillar's account. He has revealed that in September 2002, the head of the CIA, George Tenet, told President Bush and Vice President Cheney that they had good reason to believe Iraq had no ongoing programme for weapons of mass destruction. The source for this information was the Foreign Minister of Iraq, a paid CIA agent. Three days later, according to Drumhellar, the White House told the CIA that 'this isn't about intel[ligence] anymore. This is about regime change' (Mazzetti 2006).

However, as Pillar makes clear, the intelligence community chose to bend with the wind (Pillar 2006: 22). It did not take a stand against the Bush administration's pressure, or ensure that Congress and the public understood what was happening. No senior intelligence official chose to follow the example, set 35 years earlier by Daniel Ellsberg, who had revealed the Pentagon Papers showing that successive US officials had been lying in public about US policy in Vietnam. This disclosure had helped end the Vietnam war. If they had similarly been made public, the intelligence assessments on Iraq could have allowed for a more informed public debate about the Bush Administration's claims about weapons of mass destruction in Iraq, and its policy of choosing war.

On 11 October, the US Congress passed a resolution which cited 'Iraq's demonstrated capability and willingness to use weapons of mass destruction, the risk that the current Iraqi regime will either employ those weapons to launch a surprise attack against the United States or its armed forces or provide them to international terrorists who would do so', and authorized President Bush to 'use the armed forces of the United States as he determines to be necessary . . . to defend the national security of the United States against the continuing threat posed by Iraq' (CJR 2002).

In his State of the Union speech in January 2003, President Bush summoned the same fears:

> Evidence from intelligence sources, secret communications, and statements by people now in custody reveal that Saddam Hussein aids and protects terrorists, including members of Al Qaeda. Secretly, and without fingerprints, he could provide one of his hidden weapons to terrorists, or help them develop their own. Before September the 11th, many in the world believed that Saddam Hussein could be contained. But chemical agents, lethal viruses and shadowy terrorist networks are not easily contained. Imagine those 19 hijackers with other weapons and other plans – this time armed by Saddam Hussein. It would take one vial, one canister, one crate slipped into this country to bring a day of horror like none we have ever known. (Bush 2003a)

Lest anyone doubt that Saddam Hussein was capable of using weapons of mass destruction, President Bush recalled that 'the dictator who is assembling the world's most dangerous weapons has already used them on whole villages – leaving thousands of his own citizens dead, blind, or disfigured' (ibid.).

Iraq's use of chemical weapons, against Iran in the Iran–Iraq war, and against Iraqi Kurds in the late 1980s, was a recurring argument used by President Bush and other policy makers in their drive to scare people into a war. They did not mention, of course, the US–Iraq relationship at the time when these weapons were actually being used. A *Washington Post* investigation revealed that during the 1980s, 'the administrations of Ronald Reagan and George H.W. Bush authorized the sale to Iraq of numerous items that had both military and civilian applications, including poisonous chemicals and deadly biological viruses, such as anthrax and bubonic plague' (Dobbs 2002).

They did not explain (nor were asked to explain) why, when Iraq had been making 'almost daily use' of chemical weapons against Iran, the United States, according to a National Security Council official, 'actively supported the Iraqi war effort', with billions of dollars and 'by providing military intelligence and advice to the Iraqis' (ibid.). As *The New York Times* reported, 'American military officers said President Reagan, Vice President George Bush and senior national security aides never withdrew their support for the highly classified program in which more than 60 officers of the Defense Intelligence Agency were secretly providing detailed information on Iranian deployments, tactical planning for battles, plans for air strikes and bomb-damage assessments for Iraq,' while, at the same time, 'the C.I.A. provided Iraq with satellite photography of the war front' (Tyler 2002). Similarly, Iraq's use of chemical weapons against the Kurds, most notoriously in 1988 against the town of Halabjah, was made possible by increased US military assistance.

On 31 January 2003, President Bush met with British Prime Minister Tony Blair and, according to an official memo of the meeting, Bush explained that 'the military campaign was now penciled in for 10 March. This was when the bombing would start' (Van Natta 2006). Bush also discussed with Blair ways of provoking a confrontation with Iraq. The memo records President Bush suggesting 'flying U2 reconnaissance aircraft with fighter cover over Iraq, painted in UN colors', and then, 'if Saddam fired on them, he would be in breach.' The memo notes that Bush also proposed bringing out a defector, who could talk about Iraq's weapons of mass destruction, and even raised the possibility of assassinating Saddam Hussein.

The decision to go to war was kept secret for over month as the United States and Britain sought, and failed to get, UN Security Council support for an attack on Iraq. The process of educating the public about the threat from weapons of mass destruction, especially nuclear weapons from Iraq, and the need to pre-empt any possible threat, continued. It culminated in the 17 March 2003 address to the nation by the President, announcing the war on Iraq. Bush (2003b) said:

> The Iraq regime continues to possess and conceal some of the most lethal weapons ever devised . . . it has aided, trained and harbored terrorists, including operatives of al-Qaeda . . . using chemical, biological or, one day, nuclear weapons, obtained with the help of Iraq, the terrorists could fulfill their stated

> ambitions and kill thousands or hundreds of thousands of innocent people in our country, or any other. . . . With these capabilities, Saddam Hussein and his terrorist allies could choose the moment of deadly conflict when they are strongest. We choose to meet that threat now, where it arises, before it can appear suddenly in our skies and cities.

In this manner, the United States brought war to Iraq. Despite the certainties displayed by President Bush, a year of direct US occupation, and the efforts of 1400 US experts from the Defense Department, the Department of Energy, national weapons laboratories and intelligence agencies turned up no weapons of mass destruction (Gellman 2004).

Subsequent investigative reporting by *The Washington Post* (Gellman and Pincus 2003) found 'a pattern in which President Bush, Vice President Cheney and their subordinates – in public and behind the scenes – made allegations depicting Iraq's nuclear weapons program as more active, more certain and more imminent in its threat than the data they had would support.' There was also the sin of omission, according to *The Washington Post*, 'on occasion administration advocates withheld evidence that did not conform to their views.'

Whose Idea Was It Anyway?

The Bush strategy on Iraq did not have its origins in 2001. It was rather based on ideas and arguments about Iraq and nuclear weapons that had been developed and promoted for several years in the late 1990s, by a group calling itself 'The Project for a New American Century' (PNAC). Founded in 1997, this network of conservative politicians, academics and policy brokers involved people who were later to become central figures in the Bush administration – Vice President Dick Cheney, Defense Secretary Donald Rumsfeld, Lewis Libby, Paul Wolfowitz (now President of the World Bank), Zalmay Khalilzad (the ambassador to Afghanistan, now appointed ambassador to Iraq), and Jeb Bush (PNAC 1997).

A major initiative of this group was to change the US policy that had been in place since the end of the first Gulf war in 1991, and had relied on sanctions and inspections to discover and destroy Iraq's weapons of mass destruction programmes. They laid out their thinking in a letter to President Clinton in January 1998 (PNAC 1998). In this letter, they argued that 'current American policy toward Iraq is not succeeding' in controlling the threat from Saddam Hussein's weapons of mass destruction. In their judgement, such failure could have disastrous consequences for the United States:

> If Saddam does acquire the capability to deliver weapons of mass destruction, as he is almost certain to do if we continue along the present course, the safety of American troops in the region, of our friends and allies like Israel and the moderate Arab states, and a significant portion of the world's supply of oil will all be put at hazard.

The Project for a New American Century proposed to the President that:

> The only acceptable strategy is one that eliminates the possibility that Iraq will be able to use or threaten to use weapons of mass destruction. In the near term, this means a willingness to undertake military action as diplomacy is clearly failing. In the long term, it means removing Saddam Hussein and his regime from power. That now needs to become the aim of American foreign policy.

As described earlier, as soon as members of PNAC, such as Rumsfeld, a signatory to the letter, came into office and found an opportunity, they sought to put this strategy into effect. The war on Iraq, and the importance given to weapons of mass destruction as the justification for that war, was a direct result of their efforts.

However, there is more to PNAC than the war on Iraq. The PNAC name and statement of principles are clearly meant to echo the ideas laid out by Henry Luce in his famous 1941 essay, 'The American Century' in *Life* magazine. In their founding statement, PNAC focused on the shared concern of its members that 'American foreign and defense policy is adrift'. Their purpose was clear, 'We aim to make the case and rally support for American global leadership' (PNAC 1997).

In particular, PNAC is worried that the United States, after the Cold War, may not have, what they describe as, the 'resolve to shape a new century favorable to American principles and interests'. They lament, in particular, the unwillingness of Americans 'to embrace the cause of American leadership'. What is needed for such leadership is 'a military that is strong and ready to meet both present and future challenges; a foreign policy that boldly and purposefully promotes American principles abroad; and national leadership that accepts the United States' global responsibilities.'

PNAC is by no means alone in this view. It just brings together some of the most prominent and influential proponents of it. There are many others who support an imperial role of the United States and are frustrated by the unwillingness of many Americans to take up their responsibility. For instance, the historian Niall Ferguson in his book *The Colossus: The Rise and Fall of the American Empire* laments the fact that 'the United States has acquired an empire, but Americans themselves lack the imperial state of mind' (Ferguson 2004: 29). There is, he says somewhat sadly, among Americans 'the absence of a will to power'.

US leaders, who seek a more willing national embrace of the imperial role, have struggled long and hard to find something to stand in for the missing 'will to power'. The problem, as Eqbal Ahmad pointed out, was that 'imperialism has not been a good word in American political culture. People do not identify with it' (Ahmad 1991: 12–13). He explained the options open to US decision-makers to create an 'imperial state of mind', noting that 'to become palatable, [empire] has to draw on citizens' anxieties and their sense of mission'. Ahmad recalls the advice Senator Arthur Vandenburg gave to President Harry S. Truman, who was trying to increase military spending and preparedness in the late 1940s as part of the policy to strengthen US power and confront the Soviet Union. Vandenberg told President Truman that to create American public support for the Cold War, 'You've got to scare the hell out of them.'

US politics through the Cold War bears witness that this advice was often followed. Crisis has followed crisis, seemingly inexorably, with the United States facing missile gaps and bomber gaps, a 'red menace', and a yellow peril', to name only a few fears. A pattern has become obvious. As Richard Barnett observed in the early 1970s, 'in mustering public support for national security policy, national security managers find it necessary alternately to frighten, flatter, excite, or calm the American people.' American national security managers, Barnett suggested, 'have developed the theater of crisis into a high art' (Barnett 1971: 267).

The World As We Know It

There is no doubt that the Bush administration was successful in mobilizing public fears over weapons of mass destruction, especially nuclear weapons, and the possibility of nuclear terrorism, in its effort to generate support for its war on Iraq. But it is important to understand the scale of this success and the role of the media in shaping the acceptance of these messages.

The Program on International Policy Attitudes (PIPA 2003) conducted public opinion polls through much of 2003 to look at public understanding of the issues associated with the build-up and start of the US war in Iraq. In January, it found that a majority of Americans (68 per cent) believed that Iraq played an important role in the 11 September attacks, and some (13 per cent) even thought there was 'conclusive evidence' of this. A subsequent study found that about 20 per cent of Americans believed Iraq to have been directly involved in the 11 September attacks, and a majority (65 per cent) thought Iraq had given some kind of support to Al Qaeda in its attack, or was somehow linked. After the war had started and the United States had occupied Iraq polling showed that about half of Americans thought the United States had actually discovered proof in Iraq that the Saddam Hussein government had been linked with Al Qaeda.

The polls also revealed that about a third of Americans believed that weapons of mass destruction had been found in Iraq (even though none had been found). About a fifth actually believed that Iraq had used weapons of mass destruction in the war. Despite the large protests around the world against the US war, and the failure of the Bush administration to win international support, almost a third of Americans believed that a majority of people in the world were in favour of the US war with Iraq.

PIPA polling showed that about 60 per cent of Americans had, at least, one of these three basic misperceptions about the Iraq war, namely, that Iraq had been linked to Al Qaeda and 11 September, that weapons of mass destruction had been found and that the world supported the US war. Only 30 per cent of Americans had none of these misperceptions.

To study the origin of these misperceptions, PIPA used polling in June,

July, and August–September 2003 to try to examine whether people's opinions on these issues were connected to their choice of media for getting news. The results are stunning. Among Fox television viewers, 80 per cent had one of these misperceptions of the Iraq war. In sharp contrast, only about 20 per cent of people who got their news from National Public Radio and PBS television had the same mistaken views. It is striking that less than half of those who got their news from television, regardless of the network, had no misperception. People who relied on print media were only somewhat better informed, 47 per cent still had one of the three basic misperceptions.

These misconceptions about what actually went on in Iraq are reflecting something more complex than just where Americans get their news. The misunderstandings about the real situation are not connected to party-political affiliation or identity. The most important correlation is whether people support the President or not. It is the single largest factor that accounts for these misconceptions – 68 per cent of people who said they supported President Bush thought the US had actually found evidence that Saddam worked with Al Qaeda, and a third of them thought the United States had found evidence of weapons of mass destruction.

The underlying phenomenon shaping public opinion seems to be the measure of trust in and support for the President. Public misperceptions about Iraq's weapons of mass destruction, its links to Al Qaeda and international opinion about the war among those who support the President increase with exposure to the news. Misperception among those who are opposed to him falls with the more news they get, regardless of its source. The media, in short, seem only to strengthen a prior willingness to trust or be sceptical about President Bush.

Polling data also reveals a profound public ignorance about nuclear weapons, despite the seemingly endless coverage given in recent years to the nuclear threat from Iraq and from possible nuclear terrorism. A 2004 PIPA poll found considerable ignorance about global nuclear geography. Large majorities of the public know Russia and China have nuclear weapons. But the list of perceived nuclear armed states then moves to North Korea (74 per cent) and Pakistan (59 per cent). More Americans mistakenly think Iran has nuclear weapons (55 per cent) than know that Britain has them (52 per cent), or are aware that India (51 per cent), Israel (48 per cent) and France (38 per cent) actually have these weapons. The polls also show that over 40 per cent of Americans believe Japan and Germany have nuclear weapons.

It also found that most Americans have little idea of the size and character of the US nuclear arsenal. When asked, 'How many nuclear weapons do you think the US has in the US, or on submarines, that are ready to be used on short notice?', more than half offered an estimate of 200 weapons or less. In fact, the United States has about 6,000 nuclear warheads, with some 2,000 on high alert. It should be noted that when asked how many nuclear weapons the United States should have, the median answer was 100, half the number of weapons that people thought the United States actually had.

This 2004 poll found that almost 60 per cent of Americans did not know that a commitment to disarmament was part of the 1970 Nuclear Non-Proliferation Treaty (PIPA 2004). However, over 80 per cent thought eliminating nuclear weapons was a good idea and almost 90 per cent said the United States should 'do more to work with the other nuclear powers toward eliminating their nuclear weapons'. A 2005 Pew Survey found that 70 per cent of the public supports signing an international treaty to reduce and eliminate all nuclear weapons, including those of the United States (RCPP 2005).

Nuclear Fears

Nuclear fears run deep in the United States. These fears are as old as the bomb itself and have been fed both by the government and the nuclear complex that has sought to garner support for a larger and more capable nuclear arsenal supposedly to defend against other nuclear states, and those who would oppose the bomb in all its aspects. This is what makes nuclear fear a powerful force, if it can be mobilized.

The American nuclear weapons programme was created during the Second World War out of the fear that Germany under the Nazis might be able to build an atomic bomb. The programme was a secret until the first bombs were used to destroy Hiroshima and Nagasaki. The support for this action was overwhelming; according to opinion polls in 1945, over 80 per cent of Americans supported the bombings (Bird and Lifschultz 1998: xxxviii).

The fearful nature of nuclear weapons, with one bomb able to destroy an entire city, was suddenly evident to all. There were many articles and essays written against the bomb by prominent public figures, political activists, scientists, writers, poets and theologians, and many letters to the editor by ordinary people (see, for instance, ibid.: 237–311). They saw the terrible logic that was being unleashed on the world. A.J. Muste (1998: 311), the great pacifist activist, wrote that the bomb had created a 'logic of atrocity', and asked:

> what can we say to any nation which may launch atomic bombs . . . against us under the conditions of frightful, unbearable tension which will presently exist in the world unless the threat of atomic war is extinguished. How can we possibly persuade anyone else or ourselves that if we have atomic bombs at all we shall not use them if we deem it expedient? There is not the slightest guarantee even that we shall not launch bombs first, take the offensive, if a sharp international crisis develops.

A year after the atomic bombing of Japan, President Truman, threatened the Soviet Union (which had been a US ally during the Second World War and did not have nuclear weapons) with nuclear attack if it did not withdraw its troops from Iran. The United States adopted and continues to maintain till today a declared policy of being prepared to use nuclear weapons first in a conflict. It has also made it repeatedly clear that it would use nuclear weapons even against countries that do not have them. Writing in 1981, Daniel Ellsberg, who worked on US nuclear war planning in the early 1960s, observed that '*every* president from Truman to Reagan, with the possible exception of Ford, has felt compelled to consider or direct serious preparations for possible imminent US initiation of tactical or strategic nuclear warfare, in the midst of an ongoing, intense non-nuclear conflict or crisis' (Ellsberg 1981: iv). US Presidents since then have been no different – President George H.W. Bush threatened Iraq with nuclear weapons in the first Gulf War, President Clinton threatened North Korea, and President George Bush threatened Iraq and, recently, Iran.

There were other powerful early responses to the use of the atomic bomb. Most notably, *The New Yorker* in August 1946 gave over its entire issue to John Hersey's essay 'Hiroshima', the story of half a dozen survivors of the atomic bombing of the Japanese city. It was read out over the radio in four installments, and published as a book that became a best-seller and was re-printed over and over again. But, as the historian of the anti-nuclear movement Lawrence Wittner (1993: 58) notes, 'it did not change the minds of most Americans about the bombing. Instead, it reinforced the predominant emotions about nuclear weapons that had already become widespread among Americans: awe and, especially, fear'.

These efforts to alert people to the terrible consequences of the coming of the atomic bomb galvanized an enduring anti-nuclear movement (Wittner 1993, 1997, 2003). In the aftermath of Hiroshima, the anti-nuclear movement focused on the threat and consequences of nuclear war. Scientists and physicians played a prominent role in explaining the terrible effects of a nuclear explosion – the blast, heat, radiation and the nuclear fallout. They brought the death and destruction home by mapping Hiroshima on to each city and explaining that there was no defence. The anti-nuclear movement created for the public the image of 'the world as Hiroshima' (Weart 1988: 242). The purpose seems to have been, in physicist Eugene Rabinowitch's phrase, 'scaring men into rationality' (Wittner 1993: 59).

Journalism, literature, cinema and television all found abundant material in the powerful images and ideas associated with nuclear weapons (Lifton and Mitchell 1995). But the most powerful medium was the visual. The mushroom cloud became an iconic symbol of the nuclear age. *Hiroshima/Nagasaki, August 1945*, the 1970 documentary that was the first film to use footage actually taken by Japanese cameramen at the time of the bombing, was shown on the twenty-fifth anniversary of the bombing. It attracted one of the largest audiences ever for US public television and had a real impact on people's thinking (ibid.). But the film that may have shaped how most Americans imagine the effect of nuclear weapons was *The Day After*. Broadcast on Sunday, 20 November 1983, it showed the effects of a nuclear attack on the city of Lawrence, Kansas. The film ends with a stark reminder to viewers that 'The catastrophic events you have witnessed are, in all likelihood, less severe than the destruction that would actually occur in the event of a full nuclear strike against the United States' (Emmanuel n.s.). The film was apparently watched by half the adult population of the United States.

Many other films about a possible nuclear attack followed. After the end of the Cold War, the focus shifted from a nuclear war between the United States and Soviet Union to the threat of nuclear terrorism, in Hollywood films such as *Broken Arrow* (1996), *The Peacemaker* (1997) and *The Sum of all Fears* (2002). It has become a common theme on popular television shows, most notably the Fox channel's action series, *24*. The 2002 series centred on a plot by a terrorist group to set off a nuclear weapon in Los Angeles, subsequent seasons have dealt with terrorists seeking to use chemical, biological and nuclear weapons. *The New York Times* called it 'one of the best series on television' (Stanley 2003). In 2005, the show had an average viewing audience of 12.1 million, with peak audiences of over 15 million, and DVD sales of earlier series have apparently been in the millions (Amdur 2006).

Like so much of the discussion and writing, *The Day After* and other movies before and since have focused on the threat and the effects of a nuclear attack on the United States. Inevitably, they require the viewers to identify with those in the film as possible victims of a nuclear attack who must seek to survive. It is a perspective that politicians can use to call for public support of all possible means to defend the United States from nuclear threat.

Controlling the Bomb

The bomb is not just about fear. It is also about the power to create fear. In the six decades it has been a nuclear weapons state, the United States has created a vast, diverse and massively destructive nuclear arsenal and made detailed plans to use these weapons, while also seeking to restrict the spread of nuclear weapons to other states.

Once the bomb had been built and used to destroy the Japanese cities of Hiroshima and Nagasaki, it came to be seen by US leaders as a profound new instrument of national power. On being told of the destruction of Hiroshima by the atom bomb, President Harry Truman called it 'the greatest thing in history' Sherwin 1987: 221). After the war, it was seen as the 'winning weapon' by the United States, and soon afterwards, by some other states (Herken 1982). Nuclear weapons have, since then, come to define for most people the subsequent phase of world history and be seen as the iconic 'weapon of mass destruction'.

Recognizing the power of the bomb, the United States sought from early on to restrict other states from gaining access to it. Even before the bomb was produced, General Leslie Groves, who was in charge of the Manhattan Project, proposed that the United States should try to acquire total control of all the known uranium supplies in the world, and thus, stop any other state from accessing the raw material from which nuclear weapons can be produced (Rhodes 1986). But it was clear even then that uranium reserves were far too common around the world for the United States to be able to control all of them.

Recognizing that its monopoly would not last, the United States turned to the newly created United Nations in order to exercise international control over the spread of atomic weapons. On 24 January 1946, in the first General

Assembly resolution, the United Nations called for the elimination of nuclear weapons and of all other weapons of mass destruction. The United States soon proposed a plan for disarmament. It called for all other states to commit never to make nuclear weapons and to open all their nuclear facilities to inspections, and, once this system was established, it agreed to give up its own weapons. This poorly cloaked effort to preserve US monopoly for as long as possible, while trying to ensure no other state would or could build them, came to naught.

The US fear of other states gaining nuclear weapons was great and there were calls for unprecedented measures, including pre-emptive war. A 1946 report for the US Joint Chiefs of Staff (JCS 1947) argued that:

> Traditionally, the policy of the United States is one of non-aggression and, as a result, in the past we have awaited attack before employing military force. Because such forbearance in the future will court catastrophe, if not national annihilation, it is necessary that, while adhering in the future to our historic policy of non-aggression, we revise past definitions of what constitutes aggression calling for military action.

The report went on to suggest that future war planning should be based on the recognition that 'the processing and stockpiling of fissionable material in a certain quantity by a certain nation at a certain time may not constitute an aggressive act (incipient attack) while the same acts by another nation at another time may, upon their discovery, call for swift action in the national defense' (ibid.). In short, the development of nuclear capabilities in another country under some circumstances could be sufficient grounds for pre-emptive attack by the United States. To this end, the United States needed 'first, protection against surprise and, second, the ability to attack with overwhelming force before an enemy can strike a significant blow.'

The report was explicit about what was required. It called for legislation from the US Congress that would 'make it the duty of the President of the United States, as Commander in Chief of its Armed Forces after consultation with the Cabinet, to order atomic bomb retaliation when such retaliation is necessary to prevent or frustrate an atomic weapon attack upon us.' In other words, the United States should be required by law to launch a nuclear attack as part of a preventive war strategy.

The obvious concern was the Soviet Union. There was a debate in the United States in 1947 about whether to attack the Soviet Union with nuclear weapons, in order to both check its rise and to prevent it from acquiring its own nuclear arsenal. Threats were made but never carried out, and then, in 1949, the Soviet Union tested its own nuclear bomb. The age of mutually assured destruction was born.

By the early 1960s, the USA and the Soviet Union had been joined as nuclear armed states by Britain and France, but both were allies and elicited no concern from the United States. In fact they received some US support. Things changed when it seemed that China might soon be ready to test nuclear weapons.

Once again, thoughts turned to war as an option to prevent a state from acquiring nuclear weapons. In April 1963, the US Joint Chiefs of Staff developed plans for conventional air attacks and a tactical nuclear attack on Chinese nuclear weapons facilities, and there was a similar report from the State Department in 1964 (Le May 1963; Rathjens 1964). Other options proposed were sanctions, infiltration, subversion, sabotage, and invasion. None of these plans were put into effect, and in 1964, China tested nuclear weapons for the first time.

In 1968, the US and the Soviet Union agreed on a Nuclear Non-Proliferation Treaty. Peter Clausen (1993: 93–94), a historian of the NPT, has noted that for the United States the timing of this initiative was linked to its pursuit of its interventionist policies and global interests: 'it was no accident that the period of the treaty negotiations corresponded to the high water mark of America's postwar global activism . . . the spread of nuclear weapons in a region of vital interest to the United States could increase the risks of containment and threaten American access to the region.'[65] This is not to say that the use of force was to be abandoned. In 1970, the year the NPT entered into force, Harold Agnew, Director of the Los Alamos National Laboratory, suggested that 'if people would prepare the right spectrum of tactical weapons, we might be able to knock off this sort of foolishness we now have in Vietnam and the Middle East or anyplace else' (cited in Metzger 1972: 54).[1]

A decade after the end of the Cold War, US nuclear weapons designers and military planners began pushing for new designs, using arguments couched in similar strategic terms. Paul Robinson (2001), the Director of the Sandia National Laboratory and Chairman of the Policy Subcommittee of the Strategic Advisory Group for the Commanders-in-Chief of the US Strategic Command proposed developing a special low-yield 'To Whom It May Concern' nuclear arsenal, directed at Third World countries. Stephen Younger (2000), Director of the Defense Threat Reduction Agency and former Associate Laboratory Director for Nuclear Weapons at the Los Alamos National Laboratory, has argued that in the post-Cold War world, the United States needs new kinds of low-yield nuclear weapons because it faces 'new threats', and the continued US 'reliance on high-yield strategic [nuclear] weapons could lead to self-deterrence, a limitation of strategic options.'

The US 'Nuclear Posture Review 2002' recommended continued reliance on nuclear weapons for the indefinite future 'to achieve strategic and political objectives', and mandated new facilities for the manufacture of nuclear bombs, research into new kinds of nuclear weapons, new delivery systems, and much more (NPR 2002). It laid out a new strategy, in which nuclear weapons were to be used to 'dissuade adversaries from undertaking military programs or operations that could threaten US interests or those of allies'. It named as possible targets, Russia, China, North Korea, Iraq, Iran, Syria and Libya, and opened the door to the use of nuclear weapons in response to 'sudden and unpredicted security challenges'.

The Report explains that 'the proliferation of NBC [nuclear, biological, chemical] weapons and the means of delivering them poses a significant challenge to the ability of the United States to achieve these goals' (ibid.). However, even this does not make clear how nuclear weapons, in the hands of states in these regions, could be a threat to the United States. Michael May, the Director Emeritus of the Lawrence Livermore National Laboratory (the second major US nuclear weapons laboratory) and Michael Nacht, former Assistant Director of the US Arms Control and Disarmament Agency in the Clinton administration, have done so, explaining that:

> Since the cold war, the top US military priority, as stated in congressional testimonies, has been to deploy the world's most effective power projection forces. These forces have been used in the Balkans, the Persian Gulf and central Asia. A power projection force operates in or near hostile territory. . . . Any power projection force needs air bases and ports of debarkation and logistics centers for sustained operations. These facilities must be rented or conquered. Their number is limited – a handful in Iraq, and not many more in east Asia, seven or so in Japan, some bases in South Korea, and a few others. These facilities are highly vulnerable even to inaccurate nuclear missile attacks. (May and Nacht 2005)

In short, nuclear weapons in the hands of states opposed to US policy are a constraint on US capability to project military power in their region. As a Bush administration official put it more directly: 'It is a real equalizer if you're a pissant little country with no hope of matching the US militarily' (Keller 2003).

Iran is the current arena of conflict for US policy in order to restrict the spread of nuclear capabilities to states that it sees as a potential threat. It is one of the 'axis of evil' states identified by President Bush in his 2002 speech. He described it as a state that 'aggressively pursues' weapons of mass destruction and 'exports terror' (Bush 2002a). President Bush has declared that the 'stated goal' of US policy is that 'we do not want the Iranians to have a nuclear weapon, the capacity to make a nuclear weapon, or the knowledge as to how to make a nuclear weapon' (Fathi, Sanger and Broad 2006). Secretary of State Condoleezza Rice (2006) has clarified US concerns, arguing that 'the Iranian regime must not acquire nuclear weapons. The vital interests of the United States, of our friends and allies in the region, and of the entire international community are at risk, and the United States will act accordingly to protect those common interests.' It is not hard to imagine which 'vital interests' of the United States, and of its 'friends and allies in the region' are 'at risk.' It is clearly important to current conceptions of US interests and those of its clients in the Middle East (for example, Saudi Arabia, Kuwait, United Arab Emirates) that Iran is a major producer of oil and gas (it has almost 10 per cent of global oil reserves), is a part of the Middle East, borders on the Caspian Sea, and is a key oil and gas producing region of the world in its own right (Klare 2001). With a nuclear arsenal, Iran would change the power politics of both regions.

But there is more at stake than a potential loss of US control over significant global sources of oil and gas. Henry Kissinger (2006) worries that if Iran were to acquire nuclear weapons, it 'would be able to use nuclear arsenals to protect [its] revolutionary activities around the world', and in time, 'all significant industrial countries would consider nuclear weapons', and 'have the ability and incentives to declare themselves as interested parties in general confrontations'. In short, Kissinger fears that with nuclear weapons other countries would be able to do what presently only the United States and handful of other nuclear armed states feel able to do, and this would, he argues, 'make the management of a nuclear-armed world . . . infinitely more complex.'

To forestall Iran's nuclear programme, the United States has chosen to try to prevent the current Iranian regime from having full control over the nuclear fuel-cycle, even for civilian purposes, claiming (rightly) that there is an intrinsic dual-use character of key nuclear technologies, especially uranium enrichment, which allow them to be used for either civilian (nuclear energy generation) or military (nuclear weapons) purposes. But, while the United States has sought to restrict enrichment technology (including the technology for separating plutonium, the other material that can be used for making nuclear weapons, from spent nuclear fuel) in its drive against Iran, no such efforts have been directed at other non-nuclear states that have developed uranium enrichment or plutonium separation technologies (for example, Germany, Japan, Holland, and recently Brazil). Should their governments choose, these states could make a nuclear weapon sooner than Iran. The US Director of National Intelligence, John Negroponte, noted in early June 2006 that 'the estimate we have made is some time between the beginning of the next decade and the middle of the next decade they might be in a position to have a nuclear weapon', that is, Iran is still five to ten years away from being able to make a nuclear weapon, should it choose to do so (BBC 2006).

This US concern is a far cry from US policy towards Iran's nuclear ambitions in the late 1970s, when the country was ruled by Reza Pahlavi (the Shah of Iran), a close ally of the United States. Some of the officials in the Bush administration now, most notably Vice President Cheney and Defense Secretary Donald Rumsfeld, were in President Ford's administration and supported a multi-billion dollar deal to help Iran build a large nuclear energy industry that would have given it access to material and technology needed for making nuclear weapons (Linzer 2005). This deal was cancelled when the Shah was overthrown in the 1979 revolution.

The cause for concern is the revelation that for almost two decades Iran has had a secret programme to enrich uranium; enriched uranium can be used to make nuclear fuel for civil nuclear reactors or, at higher levels of enrichment, as fuel for nuclear weapons. Iran's actions are at odds with the commitments it made when it signed the Nuclear Non-Proliferation Treaty. The International Atomic Energy Agency and the United Nations Security Council have called on Iran to suspend all its uranium enrichment activities and resolve outstanding questions about the history and purpose of its nuclear programme (UNSC 2006). The United States is pushing for the UN Security Council to impose sanctions and keeps open the option of using force to compel Iran to comply (Baker 2006). It has been frustrated by opposition from Russia and China to the use of major sanctions or force.

Having failed in its initial efforts to muster Security Council support to confront Iran, the United States offered to join Britain, France and Germany in talks with Iran on its nuclear programme, if Iran suspended its uranium enrichment programme. But this was driven less by recognition of the need to resolve the crisis diplomatically, than by the compulsion to build international support for a more coercive approach. *The New York Times* (Sanger 2006a) reported that:

> During the past month, according to European officials and some current and former members of the Bush administration, it became obvious to Mr. Bush that he could not hope to hold together a fractious coalition of nations to enforce sanctions – or consider military strikes on Iranian nuclear sites – unless he first showed a willingness to engage Iran's leadership directly over its nuclear program and exhaust every nonmilitary option.

Given the recourse to war in Iraq, it is perhaps no surprise that, as one former US official told *The New York Times*, 'it came down to convincing Cheney and others that if we are going to confront Iran, we first have to check off the box [of talks]' (ibid.).

There are indications that the United States has begun preparing for the use of force against Iran. *The Washington Post* reported (Baker, Linzer and Ricks 2006) that the Bush administration was 'studying options for military strikes against Iran'. It claimed that

> two main options are under consideration, according to one person with contacts among Air Force planners. The first would be a quick and limited strike against nuclear-related facilities accompanied by a threat to resume bombing if Iran responds with terrorist attacks in Iraq or elsewhere. The second calls for a more ambitious campaign of bombing and cruise missiles leveling targets well beyond nuclear facilities, such as Iranian intelligence headquarters, the Revolutionary Guard and some in the government.

The *Washington Post* report claimed that 'Pentagon planners are . . . contemplating tactical nuclear devices.'

The veteran reporter Seymour Hersh (2006) claims in the *The New Yorker* magazine that 'intensified planning for a possible major air attack' has begun, and that 'Air Force planning groups are drawing up lists of targets, and teams of American combat troops have been ordered into Iran, under cover, to collect targeting data'. Hersh revealed that 'one of the military's initial option plans, as presented to the White House by the Pentagon this winter, calls for the use of a bunker-buster tactical nuclear weapon, such as the B61–11, against underground nuclear sites.' A Pentagon advisor told Hersh of a 'resurgence of interest in tactical nuclear weapons among Pentagon civilians and in policy circles.'

These reports have been confirmed on 18 April 2006. At a White House Press conference, President George Bush was asked 'when you talk about Iran, and you talk about how you have diplomatic efforts, you also say all options are on the table. Does that include the possibility of a nuclear strike? Is that something that your administration will plan for?' President Bush replied: 'All options are on the table' (Bush 2006).

These reports have rightly stirred many fears. Many believe the Bush administration is trying to repeat the strategy used for mobilizing public support for the war on Iraq. Zbigniew Brzezinski (2006), the hard-line former National Security Advisor, has warned: 'If there is another terrorist attack in the United States, you can bet your bottom dollar that there also will be immediate charges that Iran was responsible in order to generate public hysteria in favor of military action.'

Brzezinski also points out that a US attack on Iran 'in the absence of an imminent threat . . . would be a unilateral act of war.' He argues:

> If undertaken without a formal congressional declaration of war, an attack would be unconstitutional and merit the impeachment of the president. Similarly, if undertaken without the sanction of the United Nations Security Council, either alone by the United States or in complicity with Israel, it would stamp the perpetrator(s) as an international outlaw(s). (ibid.)

Towards the end of 2006, the US succeeded in getting Russia and China to go along with a Security Council Resolution threatening a limited and mild set of sanctions if Iran did not stop its enrichment programme. But this in no way hampers the US from pursuing its war plans, indeed it can be seen as the diplomatic complement of its wider political-military strategy.

A similar logic has played itself out in the case of North Korea, the third state (along with Iraq and Iran) in President Bush's January 2002 'axis of evil'. North Korea is, Bush declared, 'a regime arming with missiles and weapons of mass destruction, while starving its citizens'. What he did not explain was that North Korea was arming partly as a response to US threats, including the use of nuclear weapons. The first nuclear threats were made in the Korean War, barely five years after the bombing of Hiroshima and Nagasaki; in 1950, President Truman said the United States would use 'every weapon we have' against North Korea, if things went badly, and towards the end of the war, in 1953, President Eisenhower declared that the United States would 'remove all restraints in our use of weapons' if North Korea did not come around (Pincus 2006).

The Korean War ended in a stalemate, and has still not formally ended. Korea was divided, with the United States occupying the southern part of the country. Starting in 1957, the United States armed its forces in South Korea with nuclear weapons. By the early 1990s, it became clear that North Korea was building a nuclear weapons capability and, in March 1993, North Korea announced its intention to withdraw from the NPT. The United States began to consider military action to end the programme, including a possible attack on North Korea's nuclear facilities. In early 1994, US Defense Secretary William

Perry announced that he had ordered military preparations and warned that the US was looking at 'grim alternatives' (Smith 1994). President Clinton later explained, 'We actually drew up plans to attack North Korea and to destroy their reactors and we told them we would attack unless they ended their nuclear programmes' (Monaghan 2002).

A 1994 agreement to freeze and dismantle the North Korean nuclear weapons programme and prospects for improved US–North Korean relations soon suffered a setback with the victory of the Republicans in the US Congressional elections in 1994. The Republicans rejected the deal negotiated by the Clinton administration and sought to end funding for it (Greenhouse 1994). The Bush administration took an even harder line with North Korea after coming to power in 2001, including trying to discourage South Korea from improving its relations with the North (French 2001). In the wake of the 'axis of evil' speech, the United States repeatedly claimed it sought a diplomatic settlement and would not invade North Korea, but did not explicitly rule out attacks on North Korean nuclear facilities (Dinmore and Ward 2003).

With China, Russia, Japan and even South Korea refusing to accept the US use of force against North Korea, a diplomatic process finally yielded an agreement. In September 2005, North Korea agreed to 'abandon all nuclear weapons and existing nuclear programs', and the United States and North Korea committed to 'respect each other's sovereignty' and 'to normalize their relations'. However, veteran Korea watcher Selig Harrison (2006) reported, 'It was no secret to journalists covering the September 2005 negotiations, or to the North Koreans, that the agreement was bitterly controversial within the [US] administration and represented a victory for State Department advocates of a conciliatory approach to North Korea over proponents of "regime change" in Pyongyang.'

It came as no surprise, then, that the conciliatory posture was short lived. A few days after the agreement was reached, the US Treasury Department imposed severe financial sanctions against North Korea in an effort to isolate the country from the international financial system and squeeze its leadership and economy. The North Korean response was defiance – they prepared a long range missile test.

This, in turn, prompted former Secretary of Defense William Perry and former Assistant Secretary of Defense Ashton Carter (both of whom served in the Clinton administration) to ask: 'Should the United States allow a country openly hostile to it and armed with nuclear weapons to perfect an intercontinental ballistic missile capable of delivering nuclear weapons to US soil?' They argued, 'We believe not . . . . the United States should immediately make clear its intention to strike and destroy the North Korean Taepodong missile before it can be launched. . . . It undoubtedly carries risk. But the risk of continuing inaction in the face of North Korea's race to threaten this country would be greater' (Carter and Perry 2006). Others argued that instead of attacking the missile, as it was readied for testing, the United States should focus on more important targets, like North Korea's nuclear reactors: 'Those reactors could produce enough plutonium for several dozen nuclear warheads a year. They must not be allowed to operate. Preemption would make good sense against them' (O'Hanlon and Mochizuki 2006).

On 9 October 2006, North Korea carried out its first nuclear weapons test (Sanger 2006b). The failure of US policy could hardly have been more complete.

While Iran and North Korea currently occupy international attention, there are other sources of nuclear fear. It is no longer just the states that want the capability to match the United States. Other political actors have Hiroshima on their minds. There are claims that there is an intercepted message, in which Osama Bin Laden talks of planning a 'Hiroshima' against America (Rosen and Engelberg 2001). It was discovered after the US invasion of Afghanistan in 2001 that three scientists from Pakistan's nuclear weapons programme had been there to meet Taliban and Al Qaeda leaders (Burns 2001). There was a possibility that several others may have had similar ties with Al Qaeda (Frantz, Risen and Sanger 2001). There are also fears about the security of Pakistan's nuclear facilities, its nuclear weapons, and the fissile material used to make them (Frantz 2001). It has been suggested that should the present Musharraf regime fall and radical Islamic groups look ready to seize power, United States may try to intervene and capture Pakistan's nuclear weapons (Hersh 2001). The prospect of nuclear terrorism will not disappear, even after the problem over Iran's nuclear ambitions is resolved.

With a Little Help from My Friends

There are some countries that have nuclear weapons but elicit no US fears. Britain and France are obvious examples who were already US military allies before they acquired the weapons, and at a time when nuclear proliferation was not a serious concern. Much can be learned by looking at the more recent cases of the United States accepting and even fostering the nuclear ambitions of some chosen states. US policy towards the nuclear weapons programmes of India, Pakistan and Israel offers a simple way to see the anomaly that is the attack on Iraq and the threats against Iran.

India began laying the base for its nuclear energy and nuclear weapons programme soon after its independence in 1947. Its early progress was facilitated by the US Atoms for Peace Program, which trained nuclear scientists and engineers and provided a research reactor. In the early 1960s, amid US concerns about China's first nuclear weapons test, the US Atomic Energy Commission considered helping India with 'peaceful nuclear explosions', involving the use of US nuclear devices under US control (Perkovich 1999: 52–53). For their part, senior officials in the State Department and the Pentagon went so far as to consider 'the possibilities of providing nuclear weapons under US custody' to India (ibid.: 92). The plan envisaged to help India modify aircrafts to drop nuclear weapons, train its crews, and provide dummy weapons for practice runs, and information on the effects of nuclear weapons for use in deciding targets. These ideas were eventually not taken up.

India went ahead with its own nuclear weapons programme and, in 1974, carried out its first nuclear weapons test. In May 1998, India conducted another five nuclear tests and announced it was now a nuclear armed state. US law required sanctions to be imposed on any state that tested nuclear weapons. But they were at best nominal in the case of India.

In the spring of 2000, President Clinton made what was the first visit to South Asia by a US President since 1978, and differences on nuclear weapons were set aside. The United States made it clear that it was willing to pursue a new relationship with nuclear India. A joint statement in 2000 declared: 'India and the United States will be partners in peace, with a common interest in and complementary responsibility for ensuring regional and international security' (*UIR* 2000). In 2001 there was an agreement to permit greater joint military planning, joint military operations, and the supply of US weapons and military technology to India (Sipress 2001).

The development of a security alliance between the United States and India took another step forward with the January 2004 'Next Steps in Strategic Partnership' agreement. This committed the United States and India to 'expand cooperation' in civilian nuclear activities, civilian space programmes, and high-technology trade, as well as on missile defense. US officials have made clear the purpose of this agreement, as a senior official has put it: 'Its goal is to help India become a major world power in the 21st century. . . . We understand fully the implications, including military implications, of that statement' (Reuters 2005).

Former senior US officials have pointed out the inference that can be drawn from this new US effort to 'help India'. Robert Blackwill (2005), who served in the Bush administration as US ambassador to India and then as Deputy National Security Advisor for strategic planning, wondered, for instance, 'Why should the US want to check India's missile capability in ways that could lead to China's permanent nuclear dominance over democratic India?' His advisor drew a direct analogy to the critical role of US support for the nuclear programmes of Britain and France during the Cold War, and argued:

> If the United States is serious about advancing its geopolitical objectives in Asia, it would almost by definition help New Delhi develop strategic capabilities such that India's nuclear weaponry and associated delivery systems could deter against the growing and utterly more capable nuclear forces Beijing is likely to possess by 2025. (Tellis 2005: 35)

This plan took another step forward with the 18 July 2005 joint statement by President Bush and Prime Minister Manmohan Singh of India. The two leaders announced a deal in which the United States would change its own laws and try to amend international controls that have for 30 years restricted nuclear trade with India. This deal, if approved by the US Congress and the Nuclear Suppliers Group of countries, will enable India to strengthen both its civil and military nuclear capabilities.

The history of Pakistan's nuclear weapons programme tells a similar story about how far the United States is willing to go in turning a blind eye to proliferation, when a state seeking nuclear weapons is willing to support what the United States sees as its key interests. Pakistan set out to make nuclear weapons in the early 1970s, in part, driven by fears about India's nuclear ambitions. The United States tried to stop Pakistan from acquiring the basic technology to make highly enriched uranium and to separate plutonium (Spector 1984: 70–110). But the 1979 Soviet invasion of Afghanistan and Pakistan's willingness to support the United States in its proxy war against the Soviet Union changed all that. The United States lifted its non-proliferation sanctions on Pakistan, poured billions of dollars of economic and military aid into the country, and supported the military dictatorship of General Zia ul Haq. The nuclear weapons programme was no longer an issue, as Leonard Weiss (2006), the former Staff Director of the US Senate's Governmental Affairs Committee said, in testimony to the Congress:

> the lifting of sanctions against the Pakistanis coupled with a $3.2 billion aid package sent them the message that they could continue with their nuclear weapons acquisition activities with the US government doing little to stand in their way as long as they continued funneling assistance to the mujahideen and did not embarrass us by setting off a nuclear explosion.

It took the end of the Afghan war and the collapse of the Soviet Union for sanctions to be restored on Pakistan (Kux 1998). By then, Pakistan had acquired nuclear weapons and radical Islam had taken root.

Through the 1990s, Pakistan faced growing economic and political crises, a spiralling debt burden, a growing balance of payments problem, and the rise of militant Islamist groups. Pakistan was described as on its way to becoming a 'failed state'; General Anthony C. Zinni, Commander-in-Chief of US Central Command (which encompasses Pakistan) worried in 2000: 'If Pakistan fails we have major problems . . . hardliners could take over, or fundamentalists or chaos' (Priest 2000). One fear was that victory for radical Islam or chaos in Pakistan could mean that its nuclear weapons could fall into the hands of groups hostile to US interests in the Middle East, and globally. But no action was taken.

After the 11 September attacks, the United States needed Pakistan's support to wage war against the Taliban and Al Qaeda in Afghanistan. The United States rescheduled hundreds of millions of dollars of Pakistan's debt, approved a $300 million credit line for private investors, over $100 million to help patrol borders and fight drug trafficking, and $600 million in foreign aid (Wines 2001). In June 2003, coinciding with an official visit by President Pervez Musharraf, the United States rewarded Pakistan's support in the 'war against terrorism' with a further $3 billion aid package, of which half was military in nature (Sanger 2003).

Washington has been willing to overlook Pakistan's continued development of nuclear weapons and testing of ballistic missiles. It has also been muted in its response to the sale of Pakistan's uranium enrichment technology to Iran, North Korea, and Libya (and perhaps other states), and, in some of these cases, even a nuclear weapons design, by A.Q. Khan, a key figure in Pakistan's nuclear weapons programme (Broad, Sanger and Bonner 2004). After A.Q. Khan confessed, General Musharraf placed him under house arrest while pardoning him at the same time.

There is an even more telling example of US support for a state that has acquired nuclear weapons in the face of international opposition. It is the one country in the Middle East that has nuclear weapons and elicits no US fears. Israel now has the largest nuclear arsenal outside of the five major nuclear weapons states. It is believed to have up to two hundred nuclear weapons, long-range ballistic missiles, as well as aircrafts capable of delivering nuclear weapons, and submarines that can launch nuclear cruise missiles (*BAS* 2002).

There have been repeated demands from the international community that Israel give up its nuclear weapons and sign the Nuclear Non-Proliferation Treaty. It is the only state in the Middle East that is not a signatory to the Treaty. There are also long-standing demands for the Middle East region to become a nuclear weapons-free zone. A 1998 UN General Assembly Resolution on the Middle East called on 'the only state in the region that is not a party to the NPT to accede without further delay and not to develop, produce, test or otherwise acquire nuclear weapons' (UNGAR 1998). 158 states supported the call. Only 2 states were opposed to it: Israel and the United States.

The United States supports Israel, despite Israel pursuing policies and actions that it normally condemns and seeks to reverse. Israel has still not ended its occupation of the Palestinian territories, captured in 1967. It was ready to use nuclear weapons in its 1973 war (Hersh 1991). In 1982, Israel's invasion of Lebanon led to the deaths of about 20,000 people (Ross 1982). Israel has had a policy of assassinations and bombings directed against Palestinian leaders in third countries. In October 1985 it conducted an attack on the headquarters of the Palestinian Liberation Organization in Tunis, with US-supplied jets, in which over 70 people were killed (Prial 1985). In mid-2006, Israel again invaded Lebanon causing deaths and injuries of civilians on a mass scale.

The United States has also extended Israel economic and military support. It has given some 70–80 billion dollars of military and economic aid to Israel over the past two decades, and is currently granting Israel well in excess of 3 billion dollars a year. Israel has access to information on US military technologies (Green 1988). It may even have had access to US and French nuclear weapons design and test expertise (Arnett 1996: 15). The US–Israel cooperation has become closer with time. In 1998, the United States signed a Memorandum of Agreement with Israel, committing itself to 'enhancing Israel's defense and deterrent capabilities', and 'upgrading the framework of the US-Israel strategic and military relationship, as well as the technological cooperation between them' (USIMOA 1998). This included a US understanding to provide 'ways and means of assuring and increasing Israel's deterrent power by supplies of modern technology and weapons systems' (Diamond 1999). It is hard to read this as anything but active US support for Israel's nuclear weapons capabilities.

Towards Freedom from Nuclear Fear

American novelist and critic, E.L. Doctorow (1986: 327–32), has suggested that in the decades since the atomic bomb was first built and used, nuclear weapons have become a central part of the politics, economy and culture of the United States: 'We have had the bomb on our minds since 1945. It was first our weaponry and then our diplomacy, and now it's our economy. How can we suppose that something so monstrously powerful would not, after years, compose our identity?' The fear of this 'monstrously powerful' technology, captured vividly in the image of the mushroom cloud, makes it amenable to manipulation by political leaders to mobilize public support.

But the bomb, as weapon, diplomacy, economy and identity, has not gone unchallenged in all this time. Many seek to free themselves from nuclear fears. The anti-nuclear and peace movements have been a powerful force in US politics. In particular, it has been a fundamental obstacle confronting US leaders whenever they have considered using nuclear weapons. A testament to their power is evident in the judgement by McGeorge Bundy, President Kennedy's National Security Advisor, that 'no president could hope for understanding and support from his own countrymen if he used the bomb' (Wittner 2004; also 1993, 1997 and 2003).

The proof of its success is evident in the change in public perceptions about nuclear weapons over the past 60 years. There is now widespread support for the elimination of all nuclear weapons and a rejection of their use. A 2005 poll found that two-thirds (66 per cent) of Americans believe no nation should have nuclear weapons, and 60 per cent of younger people, those aged between 18 and 29 years, now disapprove of the bombing of Hiroshima (Lester 2005).

At the same time, key officials who have been responsible for preparing the United States to wage nuclear war have become public critics of nuclear weapons. Robert McNamara served as US Defense Secretary, and, as a nuclear cold warrior, had been responsible for a large build-up of the nuclear arsenal in the 1960s. He was a key player in the Cuban Missile Crisis, where the United States threatened to launch nuclear war against the Soviet Union. Given the catastrophic character of such a war, many believe it was perhaps the most dangerous moment in the history of humanity. McNamara (2005), now, says, 'I would characterize current US nuclear weapons policy as immoral, illegal, militarily unnecessary, and dreadfully dangerous.'

No opponent of US nuclear weapons policy is, perhaps, more striking than General Lee Butler (1999), who had the responsibility of all US Air Force and Navy nuclear weapons as Commander-in-Chief of the US Strategic Air Command (1991–1992) and then of the US Strategic Command (1992–1994). Butler now believes that 'nuclear war [has] no politically, militarily or morally acceptable justification.'

In the face of public demand for the elimination of nuclear weapons, and support for this goal from prominent former officials, why does the United States keep nuclear weapons and insist on its right to use them? General Butler has offered an explanation. It is a rare first-hand account of the darkness at the heart of the nuclear weapons complex. He writes:

> I have no other way of understanding the willingness to condone nuclear weapons except to believe that they are the natural accomplices of visceral enmity. They thrive in the emotional climate born of utter alienation and isolation. The unbounded wantonness of their effects is a perfect companion to the urge to destroy completely. They play on our deepest fears and pander to our darkest instincts.

For Butler, the continued reliance on nuclear weapons by the United States is due to the presence of a nuclear complex. The institutions that make and plan to use nuclear weapons are, he says, 'mammoth bureaucracies with gargantuan appetites and global agendas . . . beset with tidal forces, towering egos, maddening contradictions, alien constructs and insane risks.'

Today, the United States both clings to its nuclear weapons and rightly lives in fear of the bomb it first brought into the world and tried to use, in order to establish its dominance. The elimination of nuclear weapons cannot succeed as long as the United States insists on retaining and improving its nuclear arsenal, supports the nuclear ambitions of its friends and allies, and tries to deny these weapons to those it sees as enemies. In a world in which the United States insists that nuclear weapons are fundamental to its power and security, and that of its friends and allies, there is no argument that will reliably persuade others to give up these weapons, or to not acquire them in the first place.

To add to the danger from states that seek to emulate the United States and the other nuclear weapon states, by developing the capacity to wage nuclear war, and so gain national power and prestige, there is now the threat of nuclear armed Islamist political groups and movements. For these religious zealots, nuclear weapons may represent the ultimate tool with which to confront the United States and force a change in its policies.

To end the nuclear danger in all its forms will require people everywhere to put down the banners of nation and faith, and embrace a greater shared identity. This was recognized 50 years ago, in the words of the manifesto by Bertrand Russell and Albert Einstein (Russell and Einstein 1955), where they wrote:

> We have to learn to think in a new way. We have to learn to ask ourselves, not what steps can be taken to give military victory to whatever group we prefer, for there no longer are such steps; the question we have to ask ourselves is: what steps can be taken to prevent a military contest of which the issue must be disastrous to all parties?. . . . We appeal as human beings to human beings: Remember your humanity, and forget the rest.

Note

[1] Cited in Metzger (1972: 54). For US planning for use of nuclear weapons against Vietnam, see Hayes and Tannenwald (2003: 52–59) and for the declassified docu-

ments on US military planning for use of nuclear weapons, see the website of Public Education Center: http://www.publicedcenter.org/stories/vietnam-nukes/.

References

Ahmad, Eqbal (1991), 'Introduction', in Phyllis Bennis and Michel Moushabek (eds), *Beyond the Storm* (New York: Olive Branch Press).

Amdur, Neil (2006), 'The Twist for "24" may be in its Ratings', *The New York Times*, 14 January.

Arnett, Eric (1996), 'Implications of the Comprehensive Test Ban for Nuclear Weapons Programmes and Decision Making', in Eric Arnett (ed.), *Nuclear Weapons After the Comprehensive Test Ban: Implications for Modernization and Proliferation* (Oxford: Oxford University Press).

Baker, Peter (2006), 'Iran's Defiance Narrows US Options for Response', *The Washington Post*, 13 April.

Baker, Peter, Dafna Linzer and Thomas E. Ricks (2006), 'US Is Studying Military Strike Options on Iran', *The Washington Post*, 9 April.

Barnett, Richard (1971), *Roots of War: The Men and Institutions Behind US Foreign Policy* (New York: Penguin).

BAS, The Bulletin of Atomic Scientists (2002), 'Israeli Nuclear Forces, 2002', September–October.

BBC (2006), 'Iran bomb "within next 10 years"', 2 June, http://news.bbc.co.uk/go/pr/fr/-/2/hi/middle_east/5039956.stm.

Bird, Kai and Lawrence Lifschultz (eds) (1998), *Hiroshima's Shadow* (Stony Creek, CN: The Pamphleteers Press).

Blackwill, Robert D. (2005), 'A New Deal for New Delhi', *The Wall Street Journal,* 21 March.

Borger, Julian (2003), 'How I Created the Axis of Evil', *The Guardian,* 28 January.

Broad, William J., David E. Sanger and Raymond Bonner (2004), 'A Tale of Nuclear Proliferation: How Pakistani Built his Network,' *The New York Times*, 12 February.

Brzezinski, Zbigniew (2006), 'Been There, Done That', *The Los Angeles Times*, 23 April.

Burns, John F. (2001), 'Pakistan Atom Experts Held Amid Fear of Leaked Secrets', *The New York Times*, November 1.

Bush, George W. (2002a), 'The President's State of the Union Address', 29 January, http://www.whitehouse.gov/news/releases/2002/01/20020129-11.html.

——— (2002b), 'President Bush Delivers Graduation Speech at West Point', New York, June 1, http://www.whitehouse.gov/news/releases/2002/06/20020601-3.html.

——— (2002c), Remarks by the President on Iraq, Cincinnati Museum Center, Cincinnati Union Terminal, Cincinnati, Ohio, 7 October, http://www.whitehouse.gov/news/releases/2002/10/20021007-8.html.

——— (2003a), 'The President's State of the Union Address', 28 January, http://www.whitehouse.gov/news/releases/2003/01/20030128-19.html.

——— (2003b), Remarks by the President in Address to the Nation, 'President Says Saddam Hussein Must Leave Iraq Within 48 Hours', http://www.whitehouse.gov/news/releases/2003/03/20030317-7.html.

——— (2006), 'President Bush Nominates Rob Portman as OMB Director and Susan Schwab for USTR', White House, 18 April, http://www.whitehouse.gov/news/releases/2006/04/20060418-1.html.

Butler, Lee (1999), 'The False God of Nuclear Deterrence', *Global Dialogue*, Vol. 1, No. 2, Autumn.

Carter, Ashton B. and William J. Perry (2006), 'If Necessary, Strike and Destroy: North Korea Cannot Be Allowed to Test This Missile', *The Washington Post*, 22 June.

Cheney, Dick (2002), Remarks by the Vice President to the Veterans of Foreign Wars, 103rd National Convention, 26 August, http://www.whitehouse.gov/news/releases/2002/08/20020826.html

CJR, US Congress Joint Resolution (2002), H.J.RES 114, 11 October, http://usgovinfo.about.com/library/weekly/bliraqreshouse.htm

Clarke, Richard (2004), *Against All Enemies: Inside America's War on Terror* (New York: The Free Press).

Clausen, Peter A. (1993), *Nonproliferation and the National Interest: America's Response to the Spread of Nuclear Weapons* (New York: Harper Collins).

Diamond, Howard (1999), 'New US–Israeli Strategic Dialogue Announced; Israel Acquires New Submarine', *Arms Control Today*, July–August.

Dinmore, Guy and Andrew Ward (2003), 'Pyongyang Warns of "Total War" if US Attacks Nuclear Facilities: US "Retains Options"', *The Financial Times*, 7 February.

Dobbs, Michael (2002), 'US had Key Role in Iraq Build-up', *The Washington Post*, 30 December.

Doctorow, E.L. (1986), 'The State of Mind of the Union', *The Nation*, 22 March.

Dunn, Frederick S., Bernard Brodie, Arnold Wolfers, Percy E. Corbett and William T.R. Fox (1956), *The Absolute Weapon: Atomic Power and World Order* (New York: Harcourt, Brace and Company).

Ellsberg, Daniel (1981), 'Call to Mutiny', in E.P. Thompson and Dan Smith (eds), *Protest and Survive* (New York: Monthly Review Press).

Emmanuel, Susan (n.s.), '*The Day After*', The Museum of Broadcast Communications, http://www.museum.tv/archives/etv/D/htmlD/dayafterth/dayafter.htm.

Fathi, Nazila, David E. Sanger and William J. Broad (2006), 'Iran Reports Big Advance in Enrichment of Uranium', *The New York Times*, 12 April.

Ferguson, Niall (2004), *The Colossus: The Rise and Fall of the American Empire* (New York: Penguin).

Frantz, Douglas (2001), 'US and Pakistan Discuss Nuclear Security', *The New York Times*, 1 October.

Frantz, Douglas, James Risen and David E. Sanger (2001), 'Nuclear Experts in Pakistan May Have Links to Al Qaeda', *The New York Times*, 9 December.

French, Howard (2001), 'Seoul Fears US Is Chilly About Detente with North', *The New York Times*, 25 March.

Gellman, Barton (2004), 'Iraq's Arsenal Was Only on Paper', *The Washington Post*, 7 January.

Gellman, Barton and Walter Pincus (2003), 'Depiction of Threat Outgrew Supporting Evidence', *The Washington Post*, 10 August.

Green, Stephen (1988), *Living By the Sword: America and Israel in the Middle East 1968-1987* (London: Faber and Faber).

Greenhouse, Steven (1994), 'Republicans Oppose Deal with Koreans', *The New York Times*, 27 November.

Harrison, Selig S. (2006), 'North Korea: A Nuclear Threat – Is Kim Jong Il ready to provoke a regional crisis? An exclusive account of what Pyongyang really wants', *Newsweek International*, 16 October.

Hayes, Peter and Nina Tannenwald (2003), 'Nixing Nukes in Vietnam', *Bulletin of Atomic Scientists*, May–June.

Herken, Gregg (1982), *The Winning Weapon: The Atomic Bomb in The Cold War 1945-1950* (Princeton: Princeton University Press).

Hersh, Seymour M. (1991), *The Samson Option: Israel's Nuclear Arsenal and American Foreign Policy* (New York: Random House).

——— (2001), 'Watching the Warheads', *The New Yorker*, 5 November.

——— (2006), 'The Iran Plans', *The New Yorker*, 17 April.

JCS, Joint Chiefs of Staff Evaluation Board (1947), 'The Evaluation of the Atomic Bomb as a Military Weapon', The Final Report of the Joint Chiefs of Staff Evaluation Board for Operation Crossroads, 30 June, http://www.trumanlibrary.org/whistlestop/study_collections/bomb/large/documents/fulltext.php?fulltextid=27.

Keller, Bill (2003), 'The Thinkable', *The New York Times*, 4 May.

Kissinger, Henry (2006), 'A Nuclear Test for Diplomacy', *The Washington Post*, 16 May.

Klare, Michael (2001), *Resource Wars: The New Landscape of Global Conflict* (New York: Metropolitan Books).

Kux, Dennis (1998), 'Pakistan', in Richard Haass (ed.), *Economic Sanctions and American Diplomacy* (New York: Council on Foreign Relations, 1998): 157–76.

Le May, General Curtis (1963), Joint Chiefs of Staff, 'Study of Chinese Communist Vulnerability', April 1963, http://www.gwu.edu/~nsarchiv/NSAEBB/NSAEBB38/document6.pdf.

Lemann, Nicholas (2003), 'How it Came to War', *The New Yorker*, 31 March.

Lester, Will (2005), 'Poll: Most in US Oppose Nuclear Weapons', Associated Press, 31 March.

Lifton, Robert Jay and Greg Mitchell (1995), *Hiroshima in America: A Half Century of Denial* (New York: Avon Books).

Linzer, Dafna (2005), 'Past Arguments Don't Square With Current Iran Policy', *The Washington Post*, 27 March.

Lobe, Jim (2005), 'Dating Cheney's Nuclear Drumbeat', http://www.tomdispatch.com/index.mhtml?pid=9301.

McNamara, Robert S. (2005), 'Apocalypse Soon', *Foreign Policy*, May–June: 29–35.

May, Michael and Michael Nacht (2005), 'The Real Nuclear Threat Is To America's Bases', *Financial Times*, 22 September.

Mazzetti, Mark (2006), 'Prewar Intelligence Ignored, Former CIA Official Says', *The New York Times*, 22 April.

Metzger, Peter (1972), *The Atomic Establishment* (New York: Simon and Schuster).

Miller, Judith, *et al.* (2002), 'US Says Hussein Intensifies Quest for A-Bomb Parts', *The New York Times*, 8 September.

Monaghan, Elaine (2002), 'Clinton Planned Attack on Korean Nuclear Reactors', *The Times* (London), 16 December.

Muste, A.J. (1998), 'Has it Come to This?', in Bird and Lifschultz (1998).

NPR, Nuclear Posture Review (2002), excerpts on www.globalsecurity.org/wmd/library/policy/dod/npr.htm.

O'Hanlon, Michael E. and Mike Mochizuki (2006), 'Preemption and North Korea', *The Washington Times*, 28 June.

Perkovich, George (1999), *India's Nuclear Bomb* (Berkeley and Los Angeles: University of California Press).

Pillar, Paul (2006), 'Intelligence, Policy, and the War in Iraq', *Foreign Affairs*, March–April.

Pincus, Walter (2006), 'N. Korean Nuclear Conflict Has Deep Roots: 50 Years of Threats and Broken Pacts Culminate in Apparent Atomic Test', *The Washington Post*, 15 October.

PIPA, Program on International Policy Attitudes (2002), 'Americans On The Conflict With Iraq', 2 October, http://www.pipa.org/OnlineReports/Iraq/IraqConflict_Oct02/IraqConflict%20Oct02%20rpt.pdf.

——— (2003), 'Misperceptions, the Media and the Iraq War', 2 October, http://65.109.167.118/pipa/pdf/oct03/IraqMedia_Oct03_rpt.pdf.

——— (2004), 'Americans on WMD Proliferation', 15 April, http://www.pipa.org/OnlineReports/WMDProliferation/WMD_Prolif_Apr04/WMDProlif_Apr04_rpt.pdf.

PNAC, Project for a New American Century (1997), 'Statement of Principles', 3 June, http://www.newamericancentury.org/statementofprinciples.htm.

——— (1998), Letter to President Clinton, http://www.newamericancentury.org/iraqclintonletter.htm.

Powell, Colin (2001), 'Press Remarks with Foreign Minister of Egypt Amre Moussa', Cairo, Egypt, 24 February 24, http://www.state.gov/secretary/former/powell/remarks/2001/933.htm.

Prial, Frank J. (1985), 'Israeli Planes Attack P.L.O. in Tunis', *The New York Times*, 2 October.

Priest, Dana (2000), 'An Engagement in 10 Time Zones', *The Washington Post*, 29 September.

Rathjens, G.W. (1964), 'Destruction of Chinese Nuclear Weapons Capabilities', US Arms Control and Disarmament Agency, 14 December, http://www.gwu.edu/~nsarchiv/NSAEBB/NSAEBB1/nhch6_1.htm.

RCPP, Research Center for the People and the Press (2005), 'America's Place in the World 2005', November, http://people-press.org/reports/display.php3?PageID=1016.

Reuters (2005), 'US unveils plans to make India "major world power"', 26 March.

Rhodes, Richard (1986), *The Making of the Atomic Bomb* (New York: Simon and Schuster).

Rice, Condoleezza (2006), Statement by Secretary of State Condoleezza Rice, 31 May, http://www.state.gov/secretary/rm/2006/67088.htm.

Robinson, C. Paul (2001), *A White Paper: Pursuing A Nuclear Weapons Policy for the 21st Century*, Sandia National Laboratory, 22 March, http://www.sandia.gov/media/whitepaper/2001-04-Robinson.htm.

Rosen, James and Stephen Engelberg (2001), 'Signs of Change in Terror Goals went Unheeded', *The New York Times*, 14 October.

Ross, Jay (1982), 'War Casualties Put at 48,000 in Lebanon', *The Washington Post*, 3 September.
Russell, Bertrand and Albert Einstein (1955), *The Russell–Einstein Manifesto*, 9 July, http://www.pugwash.org/about/manifesto.htm.
Sanger, David E. (2002), 'The State Of The Union: The Overview; Bush, Focusing On Terrorism, Says Secure US Is Top Priority', *The New York Times*, 30 January.
——— (2003), 'Bush Offers Pakistan Aid, But No F-16's', *The New York Times*, 25 June 25.
——— (2006a), 'For Bush, Talks with Iran were a Last Resort', *The New York Times*, 1 June.
——— (2006b), 'North Korea Says It Tested a Nuclear Device Underground', *The New York Times*, 9 October.
Sherwin, Martin (1987), *A World Destroyed: Hiroshima and the Origins of the Arms Race* (New York: Vintage Books).
Sipress, Alan (2001), 'US Seeks to Lift Sanctions on India: Aim is to Bolster Military Relations', *The Washington Post*, 12 August.
Smith, Michael (2005), 'Blair planned Iraq war from start', *The Sunday Times,* 1 May.
Smith, R. Jeffrey (1994), 'Perry Sharply Warns North Korea', *The Washington Post*, 31 March.
Spector, Leonard S. (1984), *Nuclear Proliferation Today* (New York: Vintage Books).
Stanley, Alessandra (2003), 'Television Review: Countering Terrorists and a Dense Daughter', 28 October.
Strobel, Warren P., Jonathan S. Landay and John Walcott (2002), 'Some In Government Doubt Iraq Evidence: Say Administration Hawks Have Exaggerated The Threat', *Pittsburgh Post-Gazette*, 9 October.
Tannenhaus, Sam (2005), Deputy Secretary Wolfowitz Interview with Sam Tannenhaus, *Vanity Fair*, 9 May.
Tellis, Ashley (2005), *India as a New Global Power: An Action Agenda for the United States* (Washington DC: Carnegie Endowment for International Peace).
Tyler, Patrick E. (2002), 'Officer Say US Aided Iraq in War Despite Use of Gas', *The New York Times*, 18 August.
UIR (2000), *US–India Relations: A Vision for the 21st Century*, White House website, http://www.pub.whitehouse.gov/uri-res/I2R?urn:pdi://oma.eop.gov.us/2000/3/21/25.text.1.
UNGAR, United Nations General Assembly Resolution (1998), A/RES/53/80, Risk of Nuclear Proliferation in the Middle East, 4 December.
UNSC (2006), UN Security Council Presidential Statement, 29 March, UNSC, S/PRST/2006/15, http://www.un.org/News/Press/docs/2006/sc8679.doc.htm.
US Government (2002), *The National Security Strategy of the United States of America*, http://www.whitehouse.gov/nsc/nss.html.
USIMOA (1998), US–Israel Memorandum of Agreement, 31 October, Center for Nonproliferation Studies, Monterey, http://cns.miis.edu/research/wmdme/isrl_moa.htm.
Van Natta, Don (2006), 'Bush was set on a path to war, memo by British adviser says', *The New York Times*, 27 March.
Weart, Spencer R. (1988), *Nuclear Fear: A History of Images* (Cambridge, MA: Harvard University Press).
Weiss, Leonard (2006), 'Testimony on the A.Q. Khan Network', House Committee on International Relations, Subcommittee on International Terrorism and Nonproliferation, 25 May.
Wines, Michael (2001), 'Leasing, if not Building, an Anti-Taliban Coalition', *The New York Times*, 18 November.
Wittner, Lawrence (1993, 1997, 2003), *The Struggle Against the Bomb: A History of the World Nuclear Disarmament Movement*, 3 volumes (Stanford, CA: Stanford University Press).
——— (2004), 'The Power of Protest', *Bulletin of Atomic Scientists*, July–August.
Younger, Stephen M. (2000), *Nuclear Weapons in the Twenty-First Century*, LAUR-00-2850, Los Alamos National Laboratory, 27 June.

Humanitarian Intervention and US Hegemony

A Reconceptualization

Mariano Aguirre

> The strongest is never strong enough to be master all the time, unless he transforms force into right and obedience into duty.
>
> Jean-Jacques Rousseau, *The Social Contract*

Over the last decade and a half, international debate on the protection or abandonment of victims of mass human rights violations has become more intense. The serious situations in Somalia, Rwanda, the Balkans, Haiti and sub-Saharan Africa have forced the different actors in the international community to take sides politically and legally on this issue. This is not a simple issue as it affects national sovereignty directly (whether the international community has the right or not to intervene in a state), and also because humanitarian issues have been used on numerous occasions as an excuse for defending private economic or geopolitical interests. To this complexity should be added the way the United States, and its main partner, the British government, have manipulated the concept of humanitarian interventionism.

By deliberately confusing interventionism with humanitarian action, and by combining it with war operations, not to mention regime changes and supposed compliance with UN resolutions, the US and UK have in fact degraded the trend that has developed in the last fifteen years towards the international community assuming greater responsibility to protect victims. At the same time, Washington has tried to include 'humanitarian intervention' as another concept in its menu for taking action on the international scene – on some occasions to intervene and on others to avoid its multilateral responsibilities.

A criticism frequently heard is that humanitarianism is essentially an excuse for powers like the United States to justify their interventions. The issue however, is more complex. On the one hand, from the time of George Bush Senior's Presidency up till now, and including Bill Clinton's reign, Washington has responded warily to international pressure demanding protection for populations in danger of genocide, and other crimes against humanity. On the other hand, these three Presidents have used humanitarian crises to legitimize the claim that the United States is the core country without which little or nothing can be done within the international system.

To this must be added the fact that Bush Junior's government, with the collaboration of some intellectuals and journalists, has manipulated the concept of humanitarianism to equate it with and to bring it closer to the notion of interventionism, implying war operations and possible regime changes. This manipulation has been instrumental in projecting the United States as the leader of the international system and as the supreme judge in the interpretation of international law.

The concepts and policies that have been explicitly and implicitly manipulated are those of 'humanitarian intervention' and 'peacekeeping', as they have also been arbitrarily linked to 'regime change' and 'democracy'. This confusion distorts public debate on all these questions. Furthermore, this confusion is fomented by some governments, as well as by certain intellectual and journalistic circles. The outcome is, on the one hand, a discretionary use of these concepts in order to cover up policies and, on the other, a widespread, often wholesale, rejection of humanitarian intervention in leftwing and 'alternative' circles.

This process of reconceptualization has been developed in conjunction with other processes, namely:

1. *Delegitimation of the United Nations* as the main instrument for implementing international law and also as the forum where the decision whether to use force or not in defence of genocide victims, by applying Chapter VII of the UN Charter, should be taken.
2. *Legitimation of NATO* as an extension of US power to replace the United Nations in decision-making processes and to set up a firewall against any attempt to establish an international force under UN mandate.[1]
3. *Promotion of the idea that the only State in the world system that can assume leadership in the face of its problems is the United States.* Thanks to the mainstream media, some think tanks and government officials, there is a consensus in the United States, which extends to much of the rest of the world, that the actor that has the last word in world affairs is the United States. It can encourage negotiations (for example, in the Palestinian–Israeli conflict), promote humanitarian intervention, or block it. It is presumed to be best equipped to confront international terrorism.

It is precisely through these three assumptions that the ideological banner of 'humanitarian intervention' has been woven and then used to justify and promote the United States' imperial role.

Manipulating Concepts

Was the United States' military intervention in Iraq a punishment – because Saddam Hussein's government did not comply with UN resolutions, because it had nuclear weapons, or because it was a dictatorship that oppressed its people? Or, was it a punitive war provoked by the 11 September attacks in 2001, a preventive action against a 'terrorist' state with weapons of mass destruction? Or, yet again, a coercive form of promotion of democracy in the Arab world? Or, perhaps, a war for geopolitical interests which served as a focal point for a coalition of diverse groups in Washington? Last but not least, was it also a 'humanitarian war'? For any citizen who has followed the debate since 2002, any of these options could be seen as either true or false.

These questions entail as great a variety of answers as there are interests. Analysts critical of the war and those who supported it could answer at least two of these hypotheses affirmatively. More specifically, we can ask: was the purpose of the diplomatic process previous to the war (2002–2003) the destabilization of the United Nations system, thereby weakening the role of the Security Council in particular? Was the Iraq war used to deliberately divide Europe and, consequently, to promote the idea that the United States should lead a fragmented European continent?

While it is not this essay's intention to analyse the Iraq war and its context, these two questions need to be addressed. During the last fifteen years, serious confusion has arisen regarding political practices that had thus far a specific definition and clear, legal and theoretical boundaries such as, war between states or within them, humanitarian interventionism, peacekeeping operations, democracy promotion, war against terrorism and the like. These different worlds in the political constellation have now been conceptually reconfigured and have become interconnected in the single discourse justifying the attack on Iraq.

Thus, the Iraq war was initially justified as a preventive measure to eliminate weapons of mass destruction, and when these did not surface, it became a mission to establish democracy in the Middle East, as well as stop the spread of terrorism. This became almost a self-fulfilling prophecy as several armed groups began to attack the occupation forces of the United States and other countries, and President George W. Bush contended that the streets of Fallujah and Baghdad were the front line of the war against terrorism. That line has become, in 2006, the proposed bulwark of the 'long war' against terrorism.

On the other hand, before and after the war began, the US Government and some others (Italy, Spain, among others) indicated that an additional aspect of the operation was the provision of humanitarian aid. NGOs or non-governmental organizations in the United States and Europe were either helpful and willing to collect funds for work in the field, or critical of this perspective. The concept of 'humanitarianism' was used as part of the propaganda of the spin doctors to gain legitimation. As Brauman and Salignon (2004: 257) state, the concept was finally emptied of its meaning. And after analysing the US and British military actions in Iraq the President of Doctors Without Borders writes: 'The abusive use of the humanitarian aid can offer the double advantage of justifying the war and making one forget its crimes' (Bradol 2004: 29). The Iraq war, therefore, serves as the entry point for a debate on interventionism.

Interventions and War

A war is a military and political action between two or more actors, normally states, or between one state and one or more non-military actors. Morgenthau (1993: 229) wrote that '(W)ar is considered to be a contest between the armed forces of the belligerent states' and the *Encyclopaedia Britannica* (Vol. 29: 628) defines it as 'a conflict among political groups involving hostilities of considerable duration and magnitude'. A formal declaration of war is currently an old fashioned practice and most new wars are undeclared.

'Interventionism' has been defined in several ways. Schraeder (1989: 2) says that it is the 'purposeful and calculated use of political, economic, and military instruments by one country to influence the domestic politics or the foreign policy of another country'. Other definitions put more stress on the use of force: 'the use of military force by one country to interfere in the internal affairs of another country, although it connotes more generally the element of coercion or imposition in relations among states and may include political interference, economic sanctions, covert operations, and even cultural operations' (Robinson 2001: 429). Any modern definition of interventionism is related to the concepts of 'sovereignty' and 'non-interference' in the internal affairs of other states. These two concepts, strongly associated with the state, are at the base of the construction of the multilateral states system.

However, the growing interconnection and globalization of politics, economics and values have generated a discussion on the limits of sovereignty. David Held (2004: 132), a leading academic advocate of cosmopolitan democracy, considers that 'the resort to force in this sovereignty model is an option of last resort to be activated only in the context of a severe threat to human rights and obligations by tyrannical regimes, or by circumstances which spiral beyond the control of particular people and agents, such as disintegration of a state'.

Humanitarian interventionism is a controversial concept because some authors and NGOs consider the two activities as antithetical: humanitarianism means neutrality and pacifism; whereas intervention involves coercion and taking sides. Furthermore, there is the question of whether international humanitarian law can be legitimately defended by force? In general, it is assumed that humanitarian interventions are aimed at victims who need the international community to provide protection during genocide or massive human rights violations. Where would be the limits for the use of force in the name of protection?[2]

Humanitarian interventions were requested by politicians, UN Secretary-Generals and NGOs, in particular, from the 1990s onwards for situations such as Liberia (1990–1997), Northern Iraq (1991–2003), Somalia (1992–1993), the Balkans or Rwanda and the Democratic Republic of Congo (1994–1996), Haiti (1999–1997 and 2004–present), Sierra Leone (1997–present) and East Timor (1999–present).

Since the early 1990s, humanitarian intervention has become an instrument used partially and discretionally instead of universally acceptable criteria of what is 'legitimate'. Discretionality was extended to peacekeeping operations in such a way that it was not easy for non-specialists to see why, in some cases, it was essential to intervene (Kosovo), and why in others it took so long that it failed to stop genocide (Rwanda), and why, in still other cases, it is obvious that no one wants to intervene (like in Chechnya).

Neither is it easy to see, on the face of it, the difference between military missions authorized by the UN Security Council, and those carried out by NATO, or those organized by regional security organizations (like the African Union), or those that are under European Union command or those which are coalitions of armed forces from different countries without a UN mandate. After the Dayton Agreement (1995), controlled and enforced by NATO instead of the United Nations, and the Kosovo war (1999), in which UN functions were handed over to NATO, the Atlantic Alliance, for example, came to define itself as a 'humanitarian' agency.

The intervention in Kosovo was the turning point as it was used by the United States and the United Kingdom to legitimize military actions without a Security Council mandate. As a report of the Interaction Council (2002: 3) stated:

> The collective enforcement mechanisms of the UN Charter were designed to protect against the dangers of unbridled resort to military. The most serious ramification arising from NATO's resort to force in Kosovo without Security Council authorization is the possibility that other groups of States may also decide that they too have the right to use military force on humanitarian grounds and to determine for themselves the circumstance in which resort to such force is justified.

Kosovo was also a turning point for the NGOs. There had been violations of human rights but not at any stage a humanitarian crisis. David Rieff (2004: 270) writes, that though the Serbian government exercised repression against the Albanian population in the autonomous province, this did not mean that there was a humanitarian crisis. But the US and the British governments, as well as NATO, used the concept of a humanitarian war to legitimize the military operation and to set Kosovo up as an international protectorate governed by the UN Interim Administration Mission in Kosovo (UNMIK). This author considers that in Kosovo the 'humanitarian independent ideal' was transformed into a 'State oriented humanitarianism: a US style humanitarianism in which the NGOs are considered or increasingly consider themselves as servile subcontractors or collaborators of the governments'.

Another concept that has been used as a principle of justification is democracy promotion. This is a policy of legal assistance, advice and other measures that the European Union, the United States and regional organizations have adopted and practise in different ways. This concept has been ambiguously transformed by Washington into the theoretical strategic goal of its global war against terrorism. As a logical corollary, if there are dictatorships that practise violations of human rights, develop nuclear weapons and, furthermore, have terrorist tendencies or relations with potential terrorist groups, then war becomes an imperious need.

War, in these cases, could be waged to prevent the development of nuclear capacity, to punish some dictators for their repressive policies, and to sustain regional allies, as the so-called US neoconservatives imagined the future of the

Middle East after the Iraq war. The confusion, therefore, between war, humanitarian intervention, peacekeeping operations, democracy promotion and war against terrorism, is very great indeed, and for several reasons a serious one.

Firstly, because it makes it easier for powerful states, like the United States and United Kingdom, to *adapt the definition to the mission*, and not the opposite, according to the policy they want to follow. This also means using legal instruments of international law and multilateral system mechanisms as if they were items on a menu à la carte.

Secondly, because the invasion of non-legal concepts creates a serious delegitimation of international law and of legitimate multilateral mechanisms for defending populations in danger.

Thirdly, because it aligns the use of force with the fight against terrorism and democracy promotion. Terrorism is carried out by many different organizations; it is complex, international, decentralized and has diverse origins. The legal, political and cultural measures to confront it are darkened by military action, which is much more spectacular, but not necessarily more effective.

Fourthly, because the use of force conceals peaceful and cooperative formulas that could be put into practice to promote democracy. Democracy promotion, particularly by the United States, has been a counterproductive policy in the Middle East and in some other regions. The 'close association of democracy promotion with US military intervention' has created a 'backlash against policies in favour of democracy' (Carothers 2006: 67).

Saving Lives or Making War?

When the Cold War ended, a series of conflicts produced humanitarian crises in peripheral areas of the world system (that is to say, areas less developed industrially, in some cases postcolonial countries and in others ex-Communist states). From the Balkans to sub-Saharan Africa, individual and group survival of tens of thousands of people was threatened. Organized attempts to eliminate communities placed the genocide issue on the international agenda for public debate.

Since the 1980s, the issue of the State's responsibility to protect its own population had been gaining ground. Dictatorships in Southern countries, mass or selective direct killings, and the use of techniques such as making opponents disappear and killing or kidnapping their relatives proved that the State was not always a trustworthy actor in protecting its citizens.

The debate about whether the international community should substitute for the State and circumstantially violate the principle of sovereignty, in order to carry out that protection when the State does not do so, has distant origins, and it referred, in particular, to the need to intervene to save co-nationals who were in danger (see Malanczuk 1993). However, it was after the Second World War and the founding of the United Nations that the issue of the protection of people who had to flee (as refugees) from their country of origin led to the debate on what is currently called 'the responsibility to protect'.

The UN High-Level Panel on Threats, Challenges and Change indicated in 2004: 'In signing the Charter of the United Nations, States not only benefit from the privileges of sovereignty but also accept its responsibilities'. But if the State is unable or unwilling to meet its responsibilities to protect its own people, then 'the principle of collective security means that some portion of those responsibilities should be taken up by the international community' (*More Secure World* 2004: 17).

One of the most frequently confusing issues, which is too often deliberately so, is to identify humanitarian action undertaken by non-State actors with humanitarian intervention carried out by states.

Humanitarian action is the combined action of protection and assistance, in favour of victims both of disasters that have natural or technological causes as well as of armed conflicts and their direct consequences. These activities are aimed at preventing and mitigating suffering, guaranteeing subsistence and protecting victims' dignity and rights.

Humanitarian action is governed by the principles of 'humanity' (the right of all people to receive aid), 'impartiality' (impartiality in the face of political and economic pressure), 'universality' (assistance is given to people from all countries), and 'neutrality' between the parts involved. It is very important, as the lawyer Bouchet–Saulnier (2001:381) has argued, to differentiate between 'humanitarian interventions' carried out by individual states, by a coalition of states or the community of states and a UN mandate 'from relief assistance undertaken by impartial humanitarian organizations in periods of conflict'.

In the 1990s there was an intense and productive debate on humanitarian action between NGOs, the International Red Cross Committee (IRCC) and governments. The experience of the Rwanda slaughter (1993–1994) provoked serious reflection about the inefficiency and, on occasions, counterproductive work of humanitarian actors. On the other hand, the Balkans war, events in Western Africa, Afghanistan and Iraq revealed the limits of some NGOs, which agreed to work under the governments who were leading the military operations. This provoked a critical reaction, for example, from the IRCC. In 2000, Jacques Forster, IRCC vice-president said: 'Humanitarian action is designed to protect human dignity and to save lives, not to resolve conflicts, and should be clearly separated from political and military measures' (quoted in Marcos and Aristegui 2005: 19).

After the end of the Second World War, humanitarian aid was considered to be an activity that the international community exercised towards states in emergency situations. Emergency aid was seen as one aspect of official development assistance. The idea was to consolidate states as a means of promoting peace and security. But from the 1980s onwards, the State, especially in countries in the South, lost its capacities owing to internationalization of the economy and structural adjustment programmes.

Crises in some states, their incapacity to control their territory and the rise of armed groups meant that the relationship between sovereignty and international aid broke down. The international community then began to give aid without necessarily counting on the State. Development aid had been an issue that required to be coordinated with states; relief assistance, in cases of humanitarian crises and mass human rights violations had to be channelled towards non-State actors (Macrae 2001: 7–23). This process gave rise to the idea of humanitarian interference not consented to by the state where the crisis was occurring.

Humanitarian intervention or interference is a vague concept. In the 1980s the concept of the 'right or duty to interfere' was coined in order to legitimize coercive humanitarian intervention in cases of mass human rights violations. This 'right to interfere' is a legally ambiguous concept with moral overtones. The United Nations Charter, in reality, does not explicitly contemplate humanitarian intervention as 'there is no conventional norm authorizing it', but neither is there 'a common international law on humanitarian intervention accepted by the majority of States' (Oraá 1995: 108–09).

On the contrary, the Charter indicates that the three basic principles of International Law are: State sovereignty (article 2.1), non-intervention in other states' internal affairs (article 2.7), and the ban on using armed force. State sovereignty is basic for the functioning of the international system, and the principle of non-interference is enshrined in Article 2.7 of the UN Charter. After the Second World War and the process of decolonization, the issue of sovereignty became even more important.

The Chapter VII of the Charter envisages that if a state threatens peace, breaches it or commits an act of aggression, then this Chapter could be used to authorize the implementation of diplomatic and economic sanctions and, eventually, the use of armed force. The United Nations has used Chapter VI (which foresees interventions with the consent of the affected state) on occasions and Chapter VII, by categorizing humanitarian crises on the same level as threats to international peace. There is also an agreement among the states that have signed the Convention on the Prevention and Punishment of the Crime of Genocide (the so-called Genocide Convention) that this crime 'could be considered a threat to international security and as such provoke action by the Security Council' (*More Secure World* 2004: 65).

This process can lead to peacekeeping or peace enforcement operations. In the last few years, regional organizations, such as the African Union, are also gaining political ground by exercising similar powers. A peacekeeping force could be set up to guarantee the implementation of a peace agreement, or to guarantee a humanitarian corridor or to secure a border among two or more actors in conflict. Peacekeeping operations need the actors' consent and could have the authorization of the Security Council to use force. Currently 90,000 military personnel and civilians are deployed across the world in some or the other peace operation in 19 UN missions and 22 non-UN missions led by regional or security organs (CIC 2006: xiii–xiv).

A peace enforcement operation could also be decided by the UN Security Council and does not need the consent of the actors in conflict. Therefore, these operations are an imposition and, in all probability, the forces involved would need to use some degree of violence. Lt. General Roméo Dallaire (2003: 71), who commanded the UN contingent that could not stop the genocide in Rwanda in 1994, due to the lack of resources and political and economic support from the members of the UN Security Council, explains: 'No nation would be prepared to contribute to a Chapter-seven mission to a country where there were not strategic national or international interests and no major threat to international peace and security'. The lack of a clear distinction between peacekeeping and peace enforcement among the UN, governments and military officials is still generating deep problems for the missions, and it is not likely that the problem will be solved in the near future.

But as Bruce D. Jones (2006: ix), from the Center on International Cooperation writes:

> [p]eace operations are evolving into a practical international policy tool for ending war. When it works, peacekeeping saves lives and creates stability and the possibility of economic recovery. It can generate, or at least facilitate, democratic transformation. In 2005, missions of the UN Department of Peacekeeping Operations oversaw or assisted in referendums and elections in countries with populations totaling over 100 million people. . . . In short, peacekeeping matters. But this is frequently obscured by partial failures, inefficiencies, and scandals.

Humanitarian Intervention

The evolution of international treaties on human rights since 1945 and the concern of governments and civil society about mass human rights violations and humanitarian crises have led to a broad interpretation of 'acts of aggression' or 'breach of peace'. From another direction, the weakening of the State as the protector of rights, either because it attacks its own citizens or because it does not have the capacity to maintain a legitimate monopoly on the use of force, territorial control and legal order, has fostered the tendency to identify a 'threat to peace' or an 'act of aggression' with mass human rights violations in the so-called 'failed states'. This is the interpretation the Security Council gave to Somalia in 1991, in the former Yugoslavia in 1992 and in Rwanda in 1994. The US government during the Haiti crisis in 1994 justified its intervention on the basis of the claim that there had been human rights violations, as did NATO members in 1999 when they decided to intervene in Kosovo. The Security Council approved a mission to Haiti in 2004 with a 'half' peacekeeping and 'half' peace enforcement mandate.

The international action in Kosovo and the substitution of NATO was considered illegal by many lawyers from the point of view of international law.[3] The NATO intervention has also come under fire for causing more harm than good, and for exaggerating the figures about Serbian violations of human rights in order to justify the intervention (see Chomsky 2001). On the other hand, some analysts consider that though an imperfect operation, it fitted the preconditions for a lawful humanitarian mission.[4]

Humanitarian interventions not authorized by the Security Council are illegal from the point of view of international law. Moreover, human rights violations, no matter how unjust it may seem, are not explicitly mentioned in the UN Charter as a factor that disturbs peace and security. Some lawyers consider that if the Security Council does not succeed in responding to massive human rights violations, it is legitimate for members of the international community to take measures.

This broad interpretation, which is beyond the scope of the Security Council, has opened the door both to the United Nations being left to one side and to other organizations taking over its competences. As for NATO, in its strategic doctrine of 1999, it adopted the mission of defending security and democratic values outside its borders, and it included within its functions, fighting against genocide, without needing to obtain the UN Security Council's authorization. But this broad interpretation of peace and security is legally questionable. The UN Sub-Commission on Human Rights, in its 1999–92 resolution, pointed out that the right or duty to undertake humanitarian interference, especially when threats or armed force are used, lacks a legal basis.[5]

The concept of humanitarian intervention has been widely debated since the end of the Cold War. It covers three situations in contemporary discourse:

(i) Provision of assistance without the consent of the country concerned in order to alleviate acute emergencies that constitute a threat to the lives of large numbers of people.

(ii) Authorization by the Security Council for the use of force on the basis of Chapter VII of the UN Charter, in response to situations involving large-scale human rights violations in a given country.

(iii) Intervention by a state or group of states involving the use or threat of use of force on the territory of another country in response to grave, large-scale violations of human rights that are taking place there, without the prior authorization of the Security Council (*Humanitarian Intervention* 2000: 6).

It is the definition of humanitarian intervention as applied to the third situation that is the most controversial because the action may be taken without authorization. A redefinition of 'humanitarian intervention' that allows for such cases becomes:

> The threat or use of force by one or more states, whether or not in the context of an international organization, on the territory of another state:
>
> a) in order to end existing or prevent imminent grave, large-scale violations of fundamental human rights, particularly individuals' right to life, irrespective of their nationality;
>
> b) without the prior authorization of the Security Council and without the consent of the legitimate government of the state on whose territory the interventions takes place. (Ibid.)

A more advanced interpretation of humanitarian intervention would be the one provided by the Secretary-General's High-Level Panel. It states that 'there is a growing recognition that the issue is not the "right to intervene" of any State, but the "responsibility to protect" (ICISS 2001) of every State when it comes to people suffering from avoidable catastrophe'. In consequence, the Panel endorses

> the emerging norm that there is a collective international responsibility to protect, exercisable by the Security Council authorizing military intervention as a last resort, in the event of genocide and other large-scale killing, ethnic cleansing or serious violations of international humanitarian law which sovereign governments have proved powerless or unwilling to prevent. (*More Secure World* 2004: 66)

The Panel also endorsed the idea that 'deploying peace enforcement and peacekeeping forces may be essential in terminating conflicts'. Furthermore, the legitimate use of force could be required in processes of peace-building and implementation of peace agreements, and in the case of the protection of civilians when 'particularly egregious violations, such as occur when armed groups militarize refugee camps' (ibid.: 70–73).

Based on this background document, Secretary-General Kofi Annan (2005) proposed in the report *On Larger Freedom*, 'the establishment of an interlocking system of peacekeeping capacities that will enable the United Nations to work with relevant regional organizations in predictable and reliable partnership'.

The idea of 'cosmopolitan' guidelines for carrying out humanitarian intervention has been also developed. In this case, the role of a reinforced United Nations is seen as complementary to international institutions like the International Criminal Court and would involve the creation of mixed civilian and military forces (Archibuggi 2002). A coalition of experts and NGOs also are in favour of the creation of a United Nations Peace Emergency Service or stand-by force that could intervene in some cases to prevent genocide (Johansen 2005).

The United States and Interventionism

What has the United States done since the end of the Cold War in the name of humanitarian intervention? George Bush Senior decided in 1992 to intervene in Somalia, apparently having been convinced by Secretary- General Boutros Ghali (1999: 58). In the wake of a war between several internal factions, the so-called warlords, and after a famine crisis, the US marines were deployed under CNN cameras. The UN Security Council approved the mission and other countries contributed with troops.

After the end of the Cold War, the US foreign policy establishment felt the influence of the debate in the United States and Europe about a redefinition of security and the potential incorporation of other situations (for example, humanitarian crisis) and values (like, defense of human rights). The Bush Senior administration did not have any strategic purpose behind its intervention in Somalia.

Somalia was a crucial experience, as it influenced what was going to happen over the next thirteen years. The mandate was vague and the United States arrived when the famine crisis was over. US troops fought a war instead of keeping peace or even enforcing peace because their goal was ambiguous: Was it State building? Or protection of the victims? Or militia disarmament? In the end, the US army fought against the warlords, side by side with the Italian army that had more experience and were less willing to be trapped in a war situation. After a group of marines were killed, President Clinton, who had inherited the operation, decided to pull out the troops.

The Clinton administration started its mandate with a discourse in favour of strengthening the United Nations and an assertive multilateralism. Under the influence of the changes in the analysis of the world after 1989, the US establishment was caught between the values of the Wilsonian internationalist tradition, and the conventional national security responses. Clinton represented a mix of the two trends, with a stronger orientation towards realism.

After 18 US Rangers were killed in Mogadishu, Clinton prepared the Presidential Decision Directive 25 (PDD 25) rejecting those commitments with the international system, and returning to a realpolitik approach; the US would intervene only in situations that would be to its benefit, and with a clear exit strategy.

From Somalia onwards, Washington maintained a very cautious position in the face of UN and European demands to send troops to the Balkans, and particularly to defend Bosnia–Herzegovina. Karin von Hippel (2000: 23), former Political Affairs Officer to the Representative of the UN Secretary-General for Somalia indicated:

> Particularly since the deaths of eighteen US Army Rangers in Somalia in 1993 the US government has attempted to reduce its financial, military, and political commitments abroad when there is no obvious strategic interest. And in the post-Cold War world, there has been little agreement as to what exactly constitutes an obvious strategic interest.

The next stop was Haiti. After doing nothing except blocking any initiative in the Security Council that could mean sending troops to Rwanda in 1993, and practically nothing in the Balkans, Clinton reacted to demands from Boutros Ghali, the Black Caucus in the US Congress, the media, and human rights organizations and decided, in 1994, to send troops to Haiti, where President-elect Aristide had been ousted from power. Haiti was a problem for Clinton because of the flow of boat people to Florida, the angry reaction from the Cuban Americans who criticized the White House for allowing *other* immigrants into 'their' terrain, and because of the pressure from the Black Caucus who claimed that the President was not paying enough attention to Haiti because the victims were black.

Clinton looked for international consensus from France, Canada and the Organization of American States, proposing the idea that the United States should be the leader of multilateral action, and not the only actor or policeman. The US troops that went to Haiti, imposed some level of internal order, re-instated Aristide with a World Bank plan under his arm, and left the country thereafter. When Haiti was again in crisis in 2004 – and this time the aim was to expel Aristide from the country – the United States promoted, with the help of the UN Secretary-General, an international military and police force under the leadership of Brazil and Canada. This included Latin American forces, troops from Spain, Morocco, France and a small contingent from the United States. Haiti is an example of the kind of regional interventions carried out by regional powers. For Washington it is important to have a politically stable Caribbean Basin, but it does not have any interest in committing troops in countries where the general scene is as chaotic and unstructured as it is in Haiti.

The next two interventions were in Bosnia–Herzegovina, where the United States had been reluctant for years to intervene (Owen 1996). Disagreements among the allies blocked the United Nation's capacity to intervene and thus, while the UN Security Council adopted resolutions to protect genocide victims, the mandates the troops received were very limited. The outcome was the *safe haven* killings of Srebrenica in 1995. The course of the war was defined when the United States supported Croatia in its offensive against Serbia, while Europe and Washington gave Bosnia–Herzegovina the option to be the weaker state or else disappear. The Dayton Agreement (1995) was negotiated by the United States, and NATO forces guaranteed it (Holbrooke 1998). In 1999, Clinton and Blair led the NATO war against Serbia to protect the Albanian Kosovars in Kosovo. The war ended with the United Nations suborned, and with an agreement that gave military control to NATO, and not to a multilateral UN force.

The reasons for the US intervention in Bosnia–Herzegovina were the same as those that had guided the war against Serbia for Kosovo in 1999. On the one hand, to prevent chaos and violence in Bosnia because, as the Canadian professor Charles-Philippe David (2000: 10) explains, that would mean 'a threat to European stability' with flows of refugees, aggressive nationalism and risks for the future expansion of NATO. David quotes the then Deputy Secretary of State Strobe Talbott indicating that peace in Bosnia, and the US and other countries' military presence are coherent with a vision that rests on liberal values: 'A Europe unified by a shared commitment to democracy, civil society, and the free market' (quoted in ibid.).

On the other hand, Clinton and his team wanted to preserve and encourage the position of NATO as that was important for the protection of these liberal values under the leadership of Washington, and as it was important to have an organization with legitimation and power at the beginning of the process of enlargement involving Eastern Europe.

In Kosovo, the way the negotiations were conducted by the Clinton administration before the war, was denounced as expressing a clear unwillingness to find a peaceful resolution. The requirement that the US Government demanded of the Serbians at the negotiations in Rambouillet, namely that NATO troops could enter the territories of Serbia, Montenegro and Kosovo at any time, was clearly to ensure that President Milosevic would not negotiate. The US–UK–NATO coalition supported the Kosovo Liberation Army (KLA) that had a criminal profile and almost no legitimacy. At the same time, the way that military means and air warfare were conducted on behalf of humanitarian aims was dubious. NATO started an air campaign on 24 March 1999, without any authorization of the UN Security Council, and before giving enough time to a civil mission of the Organization for Security and Cooperation in Europe (OSCE). But the crucial point in Kosovo was that force was used without the authorization of the United Nations and that NATO, and not a UN force, implemented that force.

Michael Byers (2006: 42–43), professor at the British Columbia University states:

> Very little was advanced in the way of legal justifications for the air strikes, though most of the countries involved considered it relevant that the Security Council had identified the situation in Kosovo as a threat to peace and security in both Resolutions 1199 and 1203. To the degree most of the intervening powers provided a justification at all, they argued that, once the Security Council has identified a threat and demanded action from a 'problem' state, the members of the United Nations are implicitly entitled to ensure that the Council's will is carried out. The Kosovo War was condemned as illegal by Russia, China and a large number of developing countries. And so, while an implied authorization argument was floated during the Kosovo war, very few people – even those who advanced the argument – took it all that seriously.

Prime Minister Tony Blair (1999) stated at the time of the Kosovo war: 'This is a just war, based not on any territorial ambitions but on values. We cannot let the evil of ethnic cleansing stand.' Blair indicated that economic and political globalization was the framework for the beginning of 'a new doctrine of international community'. He challenged the principle of non-interference in cases of genocide, and explained what the five principles to intervene would be in the future: (a) to be sure of the case; (b) that diplomatic options have been exhausted; (c) that the military operations will be prudently undertaken; (d) that the interventionist states will be committed to a long-term operation; and (e) that there will be some national interest involved.

By issuing this list of reasons, Blair effectively put aside the principles behind a just war that have been discussed for centuries since St Augustine and St Thomas Aquinas, to the more recent writings of the philosopher Michael Walzer. Blair also mixed up operating principles (long-term involvement) with humanitarian law (matters of prudence), with political activities (exhaustion of diplomatic options), with values (prevention of genocide) and with realism (national interest). In a few months, his checklist was being tested in Chechnya.

In 1999, the Russian troops entered this autonomous Republic using brutality and extensively violating human rights. But neither the British Government nor the US Government did anything, alleging that Russia was facing 'a terrorist insurrection'.[6] Later on, Blair helped the United States in the war against Iraq without being sure about the facts regarding weapons of mass destruction, without having exhausted the diplomatic options, without any sense of prudence and with no notion of the national interest beyond reaffirming that London must be the best ally of the United States.

Ten years after the end of the war in Bosnia and seven years after Kosovo, the situation there is still highly unstable. Bosnia is weak and dependent on international aid. Kosovo is, as a matter of fact, an international protectorate of the United Nations. Violence, riots and clashes between the Albanians and Serbs and attacks against the international personnel in March 2004 indicate the fragility of the NATO force in Kosovo (KFOR) and the UN Interim Administration Mission in Kosovo (UNMIK). As is indicated in a research study (Gowan 2006), one of the problems in Kosovo is the growing divergence between the mandates for KFOR and UNMIK, and the overall decline in their resources.

The two initiatives that Washington has led in the region are still going nowhere. The Balkans have not featured in the post-11 September agenda of Bush and the neocons. To some extent, the lack of long-term projects for the Balkans reveals the same lack of long-term vision – as against the short-term objectives of promoting NATO against the United Nations, taking the lead over Europe, and showing strength to Russia – so dramatically obvious in Iraq.

Double Standards

After 11 September 2001, Washington launched wars in Afghanistan and Iraq. In both cases, the main legitimizing principle was the 'war against terrorism', but the excuses of defence of human rights and promotion of democracy were used as well.

There are several points that should be highlighted regarding these developments:

(i) Most of the resolutions and actions that were implemented in the 1990s were limited, and there was a shortfall between the mandate and the economic, political and military resources. The general feeling was one of frustration, either because of lack of willingness to protect the victims or owing to lack of alternatives.

(ii) In all cases the UN Security Council practised double standards, by approving normative resolutions, while in fact acting in a very restricted way.[7]

(iii) The role of the United States in all cases, from Somalia to Darfur in 2004, was very specific, and often subject to double standards in an attempt to: (a) involve the least number of troops (Rwanda); (b) obstruct any UN resolution that could create a precedent for future consolidation of the UN multilateral system and enable the United Nations to have more power than itself (Rwanda, Bosnia and most of the other cases); (c) sideline the Security Council (as in Kosovo) when other members of this body were not following its policies (Russia and China were against the attacks on Serbia). To bypass the Security Council, the United States used the argument that a vague Security Council resolution was enough to create 'a coalition of the willing' to intervene. (d) Promoting fast 'exit strategies', driving some missions to leave the field before the aims had been achieved, as happened in May 2005, when the United States put pressure for withdrawal of the UN troops from East Timor, with tragic results a year later (Bolopion 2006).

(iv) Bush Senior, and then Clinton, used these and other means too (such as imposing a no-fly zone over Iraqi Kurdistan without a UN mandate in the 1990s) to erode and delegitimize the United Nations. This was part of the US effort to be the only hegemonic power in a multilateral system.

Nancy Soderberg, former US official at the State Department in the Clinton administration and former Interim Ambassador to the United Nations, revealed as much in her book on the United States as a limited superpower. In every crisis that she describes, from Somalia to the Balkans and also the Israeli–Palestinian conflict, she has revealed that Clinton was cautious, reluctant to intervene or to support resolutions that could provide more resources, as in Rwanda, in order *to prevent* genocide.[8] At the same time, the Clinton administration tried to maintain the leadership of the United States while seeking allies to share its missions. Explaining the role of the United States in the 1994 crisis in Haiti, Soderberg (2005: 50) writes: 'While the world looked to the lone superpower to tackle every crisis, the United States has to set the course of the international community but then share the burdens of keeping the peace.'

Soderberg very clearly explains the hegemonic ambitions of the Democratic Presidency of Clinton. She breaks them down as follows:

(i) The United States cannot be a unilateral imperial power because of the complexity of the world order and the rise of other relevant actors such as the European Union, China and Russia.

(ii) But the United States should be the hegemonic power in this multilateral world because the European Union is weak and divided; China and Russia do not have democratic legitimation; the United Nations has real structural problems (too many voices and too much bureaucracy); and the UN peacekeepers 'cannot fight a war, nor can they enforce a peace' (ibid.: 86).

(iii) Under the 'new division of labor' of the Clinton Administration – 'The UN would be left to political negotiations where there is a peace to make and to peacekeeping when there is a peace to keep. The UN and regional organizations other than NATO would focus on institution and capacity building, and NATO and coalitions of capable forces, led by the United States, would take on the wars or so-called enforcement operations' (ibid.: 94).

(iv) Echoing Blair on values, she indicates that 'Clinton developed a new use of force to back up a new American diplomacy in areas previously considered beyond America's strategic interest'. For example, the war in the Balkans 'threatened America's core interest in stability in Europe, the credibility of American commitments, and even NATO's survival' (ibid.: 95).

Imperial Humanitarianism

The ideology of imperial humanitarianism is constructed, in short, by taking up the morally loaded issues of protecting the victims of mass human rights violations, of the need for establishing democratic regimes, of preventing the acquisitions of nuclear weapons by certain anti-Western states or groups. These concerns are then dovetailed with the apparently unquestioned truth that the United States is the only country that can and should take the lead in resolving these important problems. Justifications for this approach are then churned out from numerous sources.

Michael Ignatieff, a recently elected Canadian MP and a former Director of the Carr Center for Human Rights at Harvard University, has been writing over the last few years about the United States' historical role in promoting Democracy, even when it is accomplished by force. He explains this by referring to US exceptionalism, its historical mandate from the Founding Fathers and American idealism. For Ignatieff the United States must assume the imperial 'burden' of leading the war against terrorism, promoting democracy and preventing dictators from gaining access to the technology for developing weapons of mass destruction. Also, the United States has to shoulder this imperial burden because Europeans and Canadians are selfish freewheelers who are happily enjoying their democratic and wealthy lives, while the United States is leading the war against terrorism by fighting on the streets of Fallujah.

According to Ignatieff, the United States is the only country that understands the new kind of challenge posed by Islamic fundamentalism which is nihilist, non-State based, and breaks with the conventional idea of war, which was the conquest of the State (Ignatieff 2003, 2005; Aguirre 2005). Neoconservative ideologue Robert Kagan and academic Francis Fukuyama (before he became critical of the neoconservatives in 2005) also promoted the same ideas regarding the weakness of Europeans and the need to return to a realist world under the leadership of one power (Kagan 2003; Fukuyama 2002).[9] A decade ago, David Rieff (2005), an expert on humanitarian issues, also supported the idea that the United States should be a liberal interventionist actor to protect human rights. He followed the path of Samantha Power (2002) who, in her celebrated book *A Problem From Hell*, had presented a strong critique of the US policies of non-intervention in cases of genocide and of those who advocated such a policy.

The defining characteristics of the enemy (radical, nihilist, and fundamentalist) are also stressed by liberal philosopher Paul Berman (2004), who considers that we are at a historical point in continuing the war against totalitarianism, whose new face is radical Islam. The United States is leading the war between Freedom and Tyranny and Berman also considers that the war in Iraq was humanitarian as far as its aim was to fight Saddam Hussein's dictatorship. A supporter of the war in Iraq, Berman also thinks that Bush should use the 'humanitarian case' in a more consistent way.[10]

At the end of the day, fighting dictators, preventing the development of WMDs, effecting regime change, democracy promotion, selective humanitarian interventions and the killing of potential terrorists are intertwined political activities that configure a repressive model of internal and external non-democratic exercise of power by the United States.

This mythology of 'moral concern' helps to hide the responsibility that external actors such as the international financial institutions, corporations and some governments have in creating the conditions that drive some states to fail. The institutional crisis of some states has many of its roots in their integration into a hierarchical and exploitative international economic system. Countries like Sierra Leone, Liberia, Haiti have been suffering because of the implementation of structural adjustment policies as part of the dynamic of their inclusion in the so-called globalization process. John Tirman (2003) writes about this process:

> Globalization can undermine the ability of states to respond to crisis while creating conditions conducive to war economies. In this account, humanitarianism itself is seen then as the superficial if pervasive policing (that is, intervention) of the complex and often deteriorating situations that liberal economic and political governance (that is, globalization) has been so intimately involved in creating. Processes of globalization and processes of intervention are thus intertwined.

Conclusions

The United States has distorted an important debate on the responsibility to protect the victims of massive human rights violations and of the role of postcolonial states. It has manipulated this debate in its favour with the help of friends, such as the British Prime Minister.

Their ultimate goals have been, in the first place, to avoid universal and even private responsibilities; secondly, to erode the multilateral system; and thirdly, to use humanitarian crises to impose a broader game plan in which the mixing of concepts (such as regime change, prevention of terrorism and promotion of democracy) could be instrumental in the expansion and legitimization of US hegemony.

The moral need to respond to threats to human groups and to violations of human rights should not obscure the roots of the problems and the structural factors, both internal and external, that have created institutional crises in some states. 'Humanitarianism' should not become an ideology for justifying military interventions or a cover for the lack of interest of the international community in a country's deeper problems that require non-military solutions. As Tirman (2003) says:

> The identification of 'humanitarian intervention' with military action is, paradoxically, a tacit claim of powerlessness to do anything short of war to prevent

the streams of refugees, the genocides, the famines. It is as if to say, we will tolerate brutal regimes and human deprivation unless and until conditions are so severe that only the military can rescue the victims. This is another form of avoiding responsibility and shifting blame.

Finally, the left, as well as liberal and progressive circles, should not abandon the moral imperative to protect victims, nor the principles of democracy and international law. Manipulation of these concepts should not lead them to be dismissed altogether. We need to recognize that there *are* massive violations of human rights, that there *are* dysfunctional states that do not protect their people either due to lack of will or incapacity. Also, that the UN system lacks the administrative capacity and flexibility to respond and that power politics limit its capacities, and that, therefore, the international community has a role to play, a role that is always difficult and complex.

We need to initiate a debate between Northern and Southern actors concerning humanitarian crises, on the protection of victims based on the responsibility to prevent pogroms, massacres, genocides, and other forms of gross human rights violations, as well as on the possibilities and conditions for establishing conflict prevention policies and impartial and equitable forms of last resort interventions.[11] If we want to elaborate a political critique of the way the United States and its allies have cynically manipulated these concepts, we need to have concrete alternatives and not look the other way.

[All translations for this essay are by the author himself.]

Notes

1 This is also a complex process because previous US Governments, particularly Bush Senior's and Clinton's, pushed forward NATO, but set limits on the European allies so that they would not have access to leadership within the Organization.

2 On this controversial issue see Palwankar (2004) and Adam, *et al.* (2002).

3 Detailed information about the debate and views on Kosovo is available in 'Humanitarian Intervention', by Chris Walker, in the excellent Crimes of War Project at www: http://www.crimesofwar.org/archive/archive-humaninter.html.

4 A consistent analysis of the Kosovo crisis and the responses from UN and NATO is available in Robertson (1999: 401–24). An interesting analysis also appears in Brown (2001: 283–88).

5 An interesting history of UN peacekeeping operations can be found in Kennedy (2006: 77–112).

6 'The international community has chosen mainly to ignore Chechnya – with the notable exception of a few human rights groups', says the journalist Anna Politkovskaya (2001: xxxi).

7 One of the best juridical and political accounts of this double policy is by Higgins (1993).

8 On the role of the United States, the UN and other States see Dallaire (2003). Lt. General Dallaire pointed at Washington in the list of those responsible for the deaths in Rwanda and writes: 'the US government, which actively worked against an effective UNAMIR (UN Mission for Rwanda) and only got involved to aid the same Hutu refugee population and the génocidaires, leaving the genocide survivors to flounder and suffer'.

[9] A critique of Kagan and Fukuyama appears in 'Is Europe Betraying the United States?', TNI website, http://www.tni.org/archives/aguirre/betraying.htm.
[10] A critique of Berman and Rieff's books can be found in Holmes (2005).
[11] The priority for the ICISS (2001), in *The Responsibility to Protect* Report, is prevention.

References

Adam, Bernard, *et al.* (2002), *Militaires Humanitaires: A Chacun son Role*, GRIP (Brussels: Editions Complexe).
Aguirre, Mariano (2005), 'Exporting Democracy, Revising Torture: The Complex Missions of Michael Ignatieff', London, http://www.opendemocracy.net/conflict-americanpower/jefferson_2679.jsp.
Annan, Kofi A. (2005), *In Larger Freedom: Towards Development, Security and Human Rights for All* (New York: United Nations).
Archibuggi, Daniel (2002), 'Cosmopolitan Guidelines for Humanitarian Intervention', paper presented at the Cosmopolitan Militaries Workshop, Balliol College, Oxford, 10 July.
Berman, Paul (2004), 'Silence and Cruelty: Five Lessons From a Bad Year', *The New Republic*, http://www.tnr.com/doc.mhtml?pt=FFbfqVgaVE96UDrHCJXR%2B2%3D%3D.
Blair, Tony (1999), 'The Blair Doctrine', Public Broadcasting Service, 22 April.
Bolopion, Philippe (2006), 'Les missions de paix de l'ONU: Une efficacité qui fait débat', *Le monde*, 1 July.
Bouchet-Saulnier, Françoise (2001), *Diccionario Práctico de Derecho Humanitaria* (Barcelona: Península).
Boutros-Ghali, Boutros (1999), *Unvanquished: A US–UN Saga* (London: I.B. Tauris).
Bradol, Jean-Hervé (2004), 'Un Orden Mundial Sanguinario y la Accion Humanitaria', in Fabrice Weissman (ed.), *A la Sombra de las Guerras Justas* (Barcelona: Icaria).
Brauman, Rony and Pierre Salignon (2004), 'Iraq: en Busca de una Crisis Humanitaria', in Fabrice Weissman (ed.), *A la Sombra de las Guerras Justas* (Barecelona: Icaria).
Brown, Chris (2001), 'A Qualified Defense of the Use of Force for "Humanitarian" Reasons', in Ken Booth (ed.), *The Kosovo Tragedy* (London: Frank Cass): 283–88.
Byers, Michael (2006), *War Law* (New York: Grove Press).
Carothers, Thomas (2006), 'The Backlash Against Democracy Promotion', *Foreign Affairs*, March–April.
Chomsky, Noam (2001), 'A Review of NATO's War Over Kosovo', *Z Magazine*, April–May.
CIC, Center on International Cooperation (2006), *Annual Review of Global Peace Operations 2005* (Boulder: Lynne Rienner Publishers).
Dallaire, Lt. General Roméo (2003), *Shake Hands With the Devil* (Toronto: Random House).
David, Charles-Philippe (2000), 'At least 2001: US Security Policy and Exit Strategy in Bosnia', *European Security*, Vol. 9, No. 1, Spring.
Fukuyama, Francis (2002), 'Occidente Puede Resquebrajarse', *El Pais*, Madrid, 17 August.
Gowan, Richard (2006), 'Kosovo: In Search of a Public Order Strategy', *Annual Review of Global Peace Operations* (Boulder: Lynne Rienner Publishers).
Held, David (2004), *Global Covenant* (Cambridge: Polity Press).
Higgins, Rosalyn (1993), 'The New United Nations and Former Yugoslavia', *International Affairs*, No. 69, London: 465–83.
Holbrooke, Richard (1998), *To End a War* (New York: Random House).
Holmes, Stephen (2005), 'The War of the Liberals', *The Nation*, 14 November, http://www.thenation.com/docprint.mhtml?i=20051114&s=holmes.
Humanitarian Intervention (2000), report by the Advisory Council on International Affairs, The Hague, April.
ICISS, International Commission on Intervention and State Sovereignty (2001), *The Responsibility to Protect*, International Development Research Center, Ottawa.
Ignatieff, Michael (2003), 'The Burden', *New York Times Magazine*, 1 January.
——— (2005), 'Who are Americans to Think that Freedom is Theirs to Spread', *New York Times Magazine*, 26 June.
Interaction Council (2002), Chairman's Report on the High-Level Expert Group Meeting,

'International Humanitarian Law, Humanitarian Crises and Military Intervention', The John F. Kennedy School of Government, Harvard University, 22–23 April.

Johansen, Robert C. (2005), 'Report on the Discussion of a United Nations Emergency Peace Service' (unpublished), 5–6 February, Global Action to Prevent War, Cuenca, Spain.

Jones, Bruce D. (2006), Center on International Cooperation, *Annual Review of Global Peace Operations 2006* (Boulder: Lynne Rienner Publishers).

Kagan, Robert (2003), *Of Paradise and Power: America and Europe in the New World Order* (New York: Alfred Knopf).

Kennedy, Paul (2006), *The Parliament of Man: The Past, Present, and Future of the United Nations* (Toronto: HarperCollins Publishers).

Macrae, Joanna (2001), *Aiding Recovery?* (London: Zed Books).

Malanczuk, Peter (1993, *Humanitarian Intervention and the Legitimacy of the Use of Force* (Amsterdam: Het Spinhuis Publishers).

Marcos, Francisco Rey and Ana Urgoiti Aristegui (2005), *Manual de Gestión del Ciclo del Proyecto en la Acción Humanitaria*, Vol. 1 (Barcelona: Obra Social Fundación La Caixa).

More Secure World (2004), *A More Secure World: Our Shared Responsibility*, Secretary-General's High-Level Panel on Threats, Challenges and Change, United Nations, New York.

Morgenthau, Hans J. (1993), *Politics Among Nations* (New York: McGraw-Hill).

Oraá, Jaime (1996), 'Derecho Internacional y Posibilidades de Intervención en Situaciones de Emergencia', in Centro Pignatelli (ed.), *Convulsión y Violencia en el Mundo*, Gobierno de Aragón, Zaragoza.

Owen, David (1996), *Balkan Odyssey* (London: Indigo).

Palwankar, Umesh (ed.) (1994), *Symposium on Humanitarian Action and Peace-Keeping Operations*, International Committee of the Red Cross, Geneva.

Politkovskaya, Anna (2001), *A Dirty War* (London: The Harvill Press).

Power, Samantha (2002), *A Problem From Hell* (New York: New Republic Books).

Rieff, David (2004), 'Kosovo: el Final de una Epoca', in Fabrice Weissman (ed.), *A la Sombra de las Guerras Justas* (Barcelona: Icaria).

——— (2005), *At the Point of a Gun* (New York: Simon and Schuster).

Robertson, Geoffrey, QC (1999), *Crimes Against Humanity: The Struggle for Global Justice* (London: Penguin Books).

Robinson, William (2001), 'Intervention', in Joel Krieger (ed.), *The Oxford Companion to Politics of the World* (New York: Oxford University Press).

Schraeder, Peter J. (1989), *Intervention in the 1980s: US Foreign Policy in the Third World* (Boulder: Lynne Rienner Publishers).

Soderberg, Nancy (2005), *The Superpower Myth* (New Jersey: John Wiley and Sons).

Tirman, John (2003), 'The New Humanitarianism', *Boston Review*, December.

von Hippel, Karin (2000), *Democracy by Force: US Military Intervention in the Post-Cold War* (Cambridge: Cambridge University Press).

'And the Name for Our Profits is Democracy . . .'

Phyllis Bennis

> We own half the world, 'oh say, can you see,'
> And the name for our profits is Democracy
> So like it or not you will have to be free,
> 'Cause we're the cops of the world, boys, we're the cops of the world.
>
> Phil Ochs, 'Cops of the World', 1965

Within hours after the 11 September attacks in New York and Washington, the news was already grim. Reports flooded in from George Bush's White House, cascaded from Tony Blair's 10 Downing Street, poured out of the Pentagon, leaked copiously from the CIA. The reports were very scary. And they all came back to Iraq. Iraq was an imminent threat to the United States and to every American family. Indeed, Iraq threatened the peace and security of the Middle East region, of US allies and, in fact, of the entire world.

Baghdad possessed a complete arsenal of weapons of mass destruction (WMDs), we were told. Some of the weapons could be launch-ready in 45 minutes. Israel and, perhaps, even the United States itself were already in Iraq's crosshairs. Baghdad was purchasing uranium yellowcake and specialized aluminium tubes from Niger, proving it had restarted its nuclear weapons programme and was about to turn little nukes over to backpack-toting terrorists. Saddam Hussein had deployed mobile bio-weapons laboratories throughout his vast country, readying horrific anthrax and other germ warfare attacks. Iraq's government was a longtime large-scale exporter of international terrorism. Baghdad was in league with Al Qaeda, and Saddam Hussein was a close friend of Osama bin Laden – indeed, Iraq was pretty much responsible for the 11 September attacks. Piggybacking onto the near paralysis of fear that had already gripped the American people after the 2001 terrorist attacks, the reports added up to a terrifying picture.

Not surprisingly, given that they were either unequivocally asserted or repeatedly insinuated by the White House, the State Department, Pentagon and other top government officials, these claims were accepted by wide swathes of the American people. At various points, before and even after the US invasion, significant numbers of Americans believed that Iraq was responsible for the attacks. Large numbers even assumed that some or most of the 19 hijackers (from Saudi Arabia, Egypt and the United Arab Emirates) were actually Iraqis. Huge percentages of Americans were certain that Iraq had viable and operational – and dangerous WMDs.

That should not have surprised anyone. More than two months into the invasion, although the Pentagon's high-profile WMD-search teams had still turned up no weapons, President Bush (2003) publicly exulted that 'We found the weapons of mass destruction. We found biological laboratories. . . . We found 'em!' The triumphant claim quickly took over headlines across the country and around the world, and many Americans, at least, saw the announcement as bolstering their existing conviction that the United States had been right about the elusive weapons.

Only gradually, as the lies about nuclear weapons, yellowcake uranium, aluminum tubes, links with Al Qaeda, and all the rest, were grudgingly exposed in the mainstream press, did a new pretext emerge. It quickly became the most popular and proved to be the one with most staying power: we are invading Iraq to bring the light of US-style democracy to the benighted Middle East. What a relief!

Of course, significant sectors of US opinion, led by a quickly-emerging broad anti-war movement, never bought the claims about Iraq's alleged WMDs and link with the 11 September attacks, and stated from the very beginning that those allegations were false. But the dominant view, in both public and powerful elite circles, accepted largely without question that Iraq was somehow a threat to the United States. For many, that segued inexorably into the next step, accepting the fear-induced claim that invasion and overthrow of the government in Iraq were necessary to prevent another 11 September-style terrorist attack in the United States.

Thus, at first, among the swirling assortment of over-heated claims of WMDs, nuclear weapons, and terrorist links, the alleged US commitment to bringing democracy to Iraq was largely relegated to the sidelines. That pretext for invasion emerged only on the periphery of the broader campaign to justify the war. The problem did not lie in convincing Americans that Iraq's government was undemocratic. Saddam Hussein's history of violating Iraqis' civil and political rights was an easy sell in the United States, having already played a key role in the demonization of Iraq orchestrated to ensure public acquiescence to the 1991 war, and the ensuing years of Washington's UN-credentialed and ultimately genocidal economic sanctions. But Bush and his powerful political operatives seemed to recognize that expressing concern about Baghdad's repression and calling for democracy would not be sufficient to convince the Congress – let alone the American people – to embrace the invasion of Iraq.

So the initial justification, both before the war and even as US troops and warplanes attacked Iraq, was rooted in fear – the same fear factor that had proved so malleable and useful to the Bush administration since 11 September. The spin doctors broadcasted warnings of weapons of mass destruction aimed at the United States; publicized alarming reports of nuclear weapons about to be deployed in terrorists' backpacks, and sowed scary links between Iraq, Al Qaeda and Osama bin Laden that meant another 11 September was virtually inescapable.

The spin, while false, was for a while largely successful. US policymakers and the American people believed far more claims of an 'Iraqi threat' than the evidence ever supported. Eventually, as time passed after the initial invasion of Iraq, the lack of evidence and the growing public awareness of deliberate lies by the administration and campaigns of distortion began to make the arguments for war more difficult. Lots of people continued to believe the original claims. But eventually, as the US arms inspectors who had replaced their UN counterparts publicly failed to find evidence of WMDs, and as more information confirmed that Iraq had no links to Al Qaeda and even less to 11 September, those early 'security' justifications began to collapse.

Thus, the claim of democracy, originally the outsider in the pantheon of pretexts, moved closer to centre stage. As it shifted to a position of greater priority, democratization was itself broadened and redefined. Now we were not hearing only about 'bringing democracy to Iraq', but about the process of democratization spreading across the Arab world. Finally and inevitably we were told that imposing democracy 'over there' would safeguard our own democracy at home here – an unassailable rallying cry for a still frightened nation.

The Endless War: Eroding Democracy in the Name of Democracy

Hours after the 11 September attacks on the World Trade Center and the Pentagon, even before Washington's war of vengeance and resource control against Afghanistan was launched, the Bush team made its intention clear. In a cabinet meeting less than six hours after the first plane hit the World Trade Center, Secretary of Defense Donald Rumsfeld and other top administration officials pointed to Iraq as the top target for retaliation.

According to an aide's handwritten notes from the meeting, Rumsfeld ordered his military commanders to 'judge whether good enough hit S.H. [Saddam Hussein] @ same time – not only UBL [Usama bin Laden]. . . . Sweep it all up. Things related and not.'[1] The real target of Bush's 'war against terror', then, would be, what was primly referred to as, 'regime change' in Iraq, whether connected to the terrorist attacks or not.

War in Afghanistan would come first. Revenge aside, seizing control of Afghanistan was regarded a huge boon in consolidating US control of Central Asia's regional oil and natural gas supplies. But, in broader strategic terms, even as the post-11 September political goals of the Bush administration were totted up, Afghanistan remained largely a sideshow. The war against Afghanistan would be justified as self-defence, despite the fact that the UN Charter's definition of self-defence was far too narrowly drawn to encompass a retaliatory US war against an impoverished country. The legal definition, in Article 51, states unequivocally that a nation's 'inherent right of self-defense' is limited by two crucial qualifications. First, the right exists only '*if* an armed attack occurs', and then, only '*until* the Security Council has taken measures necessary to maintain international peace and security.' In the case of Afghanistan, while an armed attack had undoubtedly occurred, more relevant was the 'until' language of the Charter. In the UN meeting, immediately following the 11 September attacks, but weeks before the United States invaded Afghanistan, the Security Council had thus already taken those measures it deemed 'necessary to maintain international peace and security'.

And those measures did not include a call for war. When the United States called the UN Security Council into special session on the morning of 12 September, just over 24 hours had elapsed since the planes had hit the World Trade Center, a few miles south of the UN headquarters. Smoke still rose from the WTC site, casualty figures were unknown and wildly exaggerated rumours of tens of thousands of deaths were circulating. Some thought, and many hoped, that convening the Council meeting foretold a US decision to work collaboratively with the rest of the world, a decision to abjure the earlier tendencies towards unilateralism and overly eager military responses of the Bush administration. Many thought it could be the initiation of a new Bush approach to global democracy.

After all, Article 51 of the UN Charter seemed precisely drafted to deal with just such a scenario. Convening the Council so quickly after the attacks seemed to portend a US plan to engage the United Nations, and the international community as a whole to respond to this massive crime against humanity. There was no fear that anything the United States proposed to the Council might be rejected. A US request for creation of a new special global anti-terrorism tribunal, backed by a new international police enforcement unit, whose first mandate would be the identification and capture of the perpetrators of the attacks, all would have been welcomed with enthusiasm. Given the immediate collapse of all nascent international opposition to Washington's rising hegemonic power in the wake of the 11 September attacks, anything, including a US request for UN authorization for a coalition-based or even a unilateral military strike, would have been accepted by stunned and frightened diplomats and governments.

But the US-drafted resolution debated that morning did none of these things. Resolution 1368 mentioned the right of self-defence in an introductory clause, but authorized no use of force, whether by UN Blue Helmets or by anyone else. Crucially, it was not passed under the auspices of Chapter VII of the UN Charter, a prerequisite for any approval of military force. Instead, the resolution called on all states 'to work together urgently to bring to justice the perpetrators, organizers and sponsors of these terrorist attacks and stresses that those responsible for aiding, supporting or harboring the perpetrators, organizers and sponsors of these acts will be held accountable.' It went on to call on 'the international community to redouble their efforts to prevent and suppress terrorist acts including by increased cooperation'.

The Council discussion, leading up to the passage of 1368, was characterized by a unanimous condemnation of the attacks, and unanimity of support for creating the kind of cooperation needed, for what the French ambassador called, a 'global strategy' to deal with terrorism. Jamaica's ambassador Patricia Durrant, in words similar to other Council ambassadors', called on the Council to insure that 'the masterminds, and those in collusion with them, must be brought to justice, and the global community must demonstrate a solid front to defeat terrorism' (UNDPI 2001). Bringing perpetrators to justice, and using global co-operation to do so, were the consistent themes of the discussion; launching a war on Afghanistan, half a world away from the still-flaming ruins of the World Trade Center, was not on the United Nations' agenda.

But the Council was not prepared to claim the central role the Charter assigns to the United Nations to respond to real threats to international peace and security. The Security Council and General Assembly votes of passionate but undefined solidarity with Americans were followed by two weeks of uneasy silence towards the clear unilateral approach of the US government. Then, in a major speech to the Assembly on 24 September, Secretary-General Kofi Annan sounded a cautionary note. He identified the 11 September attacks as having 'struck at all our efforts to create a true international society', and called for the world, through the United Nations, to 'respond to it in a way that strengthens international peace and security – by cementing the ties among nations, and not subjecting them to new strains.' Focusing on the need to make the United Nations the central player in a global response, he went on to note that 'this Organization is the natural forum in which to build such a universal coalition. It alone can give global legitimacy to the long-term struggle against terrorism.' It was an urgent call for global democracy to rise in response to the terrorist attacks.

But the Bush administration's own version of how to respond to the attacks did not involve global collaboration or new democratic alliances based on equality and mutual respect for national sovereignty. Instead, in the short run-up to its 7 October invasion of Afghanistan, Washington would set the terms for how the United States would coerce and ensnare allies – reluctant and otherwise – to join its crusade.

In fact there was a rush to join the US 'coalition of the willing' – even before it was clear as to what it was that other nations were joining. 76 governments granted landing rights in their countries for US military operations. 23 governments offered bases for US forces involved in offensive operations. In virtually every country, whose government backed the US invasion, democracy suffered. As former Clinton administration official James Steinberg described it, the leaders 'who supported the president, particularly on Iraq, in almost every case were doing so against their domestic public opinion and they paid a price' (Baker 2006b).

Few of those governments signed up simply because they were 'willing' to help the United States go to war; almost all of them asked for and got something real and tangible in return for joining the US anti-terrorism campaign. Those who got the most tended to be those whose own commitment to democracy was the shakiest. For Washington's new 'best friends', trading base rights or landing rights to the Pentagon in exchange for a let-up in US criticism (however mild) of their own anti-democratic actions was an easy call, and quickly became the centrepiece of a new Great Game. China was quickly granted a free hand in its restive Muslim border regions. And in Chechnya, where the United States and Europe had been harshly critical of Moscow's crackdown on human rights, Russia's endorsement of Washington's 'war on terrorism' led to a rapid reversal. In the US lexicon, Chechens were now transformed from sympathetic victims of Russian repression to a collection of terrorists against whom Russia, as a US ally was standing firm. Both Pakistan and India, in and around Kashmir (at least until their regional conflict threatened to spill out of control), were suddenly immune from US criticism. Turkey gained even greater immunity for repression in its Kurdish southeast, and Uzbekistan's brutal regime won a human rights pass throughout its territory. Perhaps, most overtly (though not in the first days of the crisis), Israel's General Ariel Sharon was given a public green light by the Bush administration to steal more land, expand settlements and further brutalize the population of the occupied Palestinian territories. Around the world, newly emboldened national spin doctors justified their governments' lack of democracy and human rights violations by a kind of reverse finger-pointing – after all, don't we have the same right of self-defence that the US is making use of in Afghanistan?

And all of those brutalities paled besides the human toll that the war itself would soon entail. Less than a week after the 11 September attacks, it was already clear that the United States intended massive retaliation against the entire country of Afghanistan for the actions of Egyptian and Saudi terrorists who had lived in Hamburg, trained in Florida, and gone to flight school in the US Midwest. The US war against Afghanistan was way too late to qualify as self-defence – this was about revenge. And it was already clear who would pay the price: less than a week after 11 September, a *Los Angeles Times* headline warned 'Afghans Teeter on Edge; Aid workers fear a major US offensive could trigger mass starvation in a land where millions are already suffering'. The *Times* cautioned:

> With hundreds of thousands of Afghan refugees already on the move, food supplies in their nation running out and winter just weeks away, US military action against Afghanistan could lead to mass starvation, aid agencies warned Sunday. The UN refugee agency estimated that by Saturday as many as 300,000 Afghans had fled the southeastern city of Kandahar, the ruling Taliban movement's spiritual capital and a presumed target of any airstrikes in retaliation for last week's terrorist attacks in the United States. 'That means up to half the city's population has already left, more are following, and the mass exodus is spreading across the country as refugees head toward Iran and Pakistan,' said Yousaf Hassan, a senior official in Islamabad, the Pakistani capital, with the Office of the UN High Commissioner for Refugees. . . . 'We're talking about a huge catastrophe in the making,' said Andrew Wilder, field office director of

> the nonprofit agency Save the Children's $6-million aid program for Afghans. (Marshall and Watson 2001)

The war in Afghanistan was indeed a 'huge catastrophe' for the Afghan people. But it also had global consequences throughout and beyond Central Asia. Governments across the region, long reviled for dramatic human rights violations, such as the military dictatorship in Pakistan and the brutal junta in power in Uzbekistan, were quickly granted political endorsement from Washington officials, eager to enlist their help in the 'global war on terror'. The nuclear-armed Pakistani generals were suddenly given access to US 'security' aid as well as Apache helicopter gunships, and US concerns about the military coup that had brought General Pervez Musharraf to power were silenced (Ciarrocca 2002).

The Uzbek government of President Islam Karimov was already on the State Department's 2001 list as:

> an authoritarian state with limited civil rights. . . . The Government's human rights record remained very poor, and it continued to commit numerous serious abuses. Citizens cannot exercise the right to change their government peacefully; the Government does not permit the existence of opposition parties. Security force mistreatment resulted in the deaths of several citizens in custody. Police and NSS forces tortured, beat, and harassed persons. (USDS 2002)

Karimov used the opportunity of the anti-terrorism crusade to expand his own power and shred even further his people's already limited democratic rights. Speaking of 'the ugly face of the terrorist threat,' he said, 'handing out leaflets . . . should be recognized as being supportive of these evil-doers' (interview cited in Amnesty International 2001). Later in the war, President Bush would single out Pakistan and Uzbekistan for special praise as 'friends' of the US in the battle against terrorism (Bush 2002). Concern for democracy did not rise to the top of his agenda.

It was not only repressive military governments, but noted democracies too that benefited from the moment. Germany took advantage of Washington's post-11 September tendency to sideline previously noted human rights issues, as Berlin removed its long-standing constitutional protection against prosecution for hate speech and other crimes by avowed faith-based organizations. When a Turkish Islamist organization was the first to be banned under the new law, the excuse offered by Interior Minister Otto Schily was that it 'stirs up its members against democracy, against those of other beliefs and against the Republic of Turkey. . . . [It] endangers domestic security as well as the important interests of Germany, in particular foreign policy.' When Germany had taken similar legal actions against Scientologists, the United States, however disingenuously, had expressed grave concern. But when 'anti-terrorism' was now used to justify stripping the same protection from Germany's Constitution, and Islamists were its first victims, the United States remained consciously silent (Erlanger 2001).

Democracy, Afghan Style

When the United States first attacked Afghanistan less than a month after the 11 September attacks, democracy was not particularly high on the agenda. Revenge was a much clearer motivation. In fact, at first, the attack on Afghanistan was less about punishing Afghanistan as a nation than it was about showing the world that the United States was entering a new phase of history: that not only the bilateral reality of the Cold War, but the unilateral-but-have-to-go-through-the-motions-of-multilateralism stage of the post-Cold War era were over. On 12 September, the Bush administration announced the next phase of history – that of unchallenged unilateral militarism. It would be what the influential editor of *Newsweek International*, Fareed Zakaria, called 'a new era of American hegemony' (*Lehrer News Hour*, 11 March 2002).

The Bush administration was determined that it alone would set the terms of its war of vengeance. But its credibility depended on the claim that the 11 September attacks were somehow an attack on 'the whole world', and that, therefore, the aggressive US response was being waged on behalf of the whole world. So, while the military assault on Afghanistan remained a US operation (backed by a few hastily collected, token contingents from allied governments) the task of occupying the long-ravaged country was soon shared with NATO and the all-too-compliant United Nations. At that point, the democracy argument surfaced again. The Bush administration's minions and apologists fanned out, thundering their new-found concern about the repressive cruelty, especially against women, and the lack of democracy of the Taliban government's hard-line Islamist rule. The claims were largely true. But the hypocrisy of a government that had long supported the Taliban and other Islamist militias against the Soviet Union, and whose latest envoy to occupied Afghanistan, Zalmay Khalilzad, had himself only recently dined with Taliban delegations in Texas to negotiate multi-billion dollar pipeline deals with UNOCAL (Stephens and Ottaway 2001), was blatant.

The US claims that under normal circumstances, its invasion of Afghanistan, which was bringing an even greater humanitarian catastrophe to the already suffering Afghan people, but was aimed, in truth, to 'liberate Afghan women' and democratize the country, would have been greeted with derision. After all, just as the Taliban was sweeping to victory in Afghanistan's civil war and five years to the day his boss launched a massive war against Taliban-ruled Afghanistan, Khalilzad had been recommending rewarding the Islamist rulers because the 'Taliban does not practice the anti-US style of fundamentalism practiced by Iran. We should . . . be willing to offer recognition and humanitarian assistance and to promote international economic reconstruction. . . . It is time for the United States to reengage [the Taliban]' (Khalilzad 1996).

But the post-11 September period was not normal. The fear factor had already settled in like a thick cloud over US political life, snuffing out any hint of critical thinking. The claim that the United States was bringing 'democracy' to Afghanistan somehow seemed to stick. There were graphics to make the point.

Every Western wire service, it seemed, was inundated with photographs of exuberant Afghan women across Kabul throwing off their hated burqas. The excitement of these women was no doubt genuine. But little attention was paid to the fact that the vast majority of Afghan women, living in endemic poverty outside of the capital, had gained little or no freedom from the invasion and occupation. Wearing burqas was hardly the main issue for the desperately impoverished, overwhelmingly illiterate and entirely disenfranchised peasant women (and men) of the Afghan countryside.

New evidence piled up regarding bomb raids that hit civilians in cities and towns across Afghanistan. On 23 October 2001, Pentagon spokeswoman Victoria Clarke admitted that Navy fighter jets had 'accidentally' dropped a 1,000-pound bomb near a senior citizens centre in Herat, in northern Afghanistan. She acknowledged that the residence might in fact be the building that Pentagon officials originally described as a 'military hospital'. Clarke's disclosure came only a day after her boss, Secretary of Defense Rumsfeld, categorically denied Taliban claims that a hospital was hit in Herat. 'We have seen repeatedly things that are not true put out by the Taliban', he said. 'We have absolutely no evidence at all that would suggest that [the reported hospital bombing] is correct. I'm sure it's not' (Loeb and Graham 2001).

The violence against Afghans continued, with the US-backed Northern Alliance warlords regaining control of much of the country. The Taliban, driven from power in Kabul, resurfaced as guerrilla fighters in much of the rest of the country. But the US 'democratization' process continued, with a UN-backed election trajectory that began with the US choice of Hamid Karzai, a former consultant for UNOCAL, as chairman of the 'Transitional Administration', less than two months after its invasion of Afghanistan. In June 2002, the 'Loya Jirga' or grand council meeting was held in Bonn under UN auspices, but with a heavy US hand, resulting this time in a vote for the same US favoured Karzai as interim President of the new Afghanistan Transitional Administration. And then, in October 2004, with the fanfare almost drowned amidst the greater attention paid to the similar 'election' process in Iraq, Karzai was voted in once more as President of Afghanistan.

The United States continued its claims that its orchestrated elections, featuring ink-stained fingers held up for the world's press, amounted to democracy in Afghanistan. Karzai had little national support, little mention of opposition candidates appeared in the government-controlled media, and there was widespread evidence of election fraud. But the United Nations, under heavy US pressure, certified the election and declared Karzai the victor without a run-off. President Karzai rapidly was re-anointed 'Mayor of Kabul' as his influence remained solely in the capital and his weak government proved unable to bring even a hint of stability to Afghanistan's vast hinterlands. NATO troops moved in to back up the thousands of US occupation soldiers, and the violence continued, though it would soon be sidelined by the much larger war in Iraq. 'Democracy', for Afghans, remained a cruel joke.

Iraq Moves to the Fore: The Axis of Evil

It had been clear for some time that Afghanistan was in many ways a sideshow to the Bush administration's real goal – 'regime change' in Iraq. But before that crusade would begin, an even broader set of US global intentions emerged. On 29 January 2002, George W. Bush went before a joint session of the US Senate and the House of Representatives, for his annual State of the Union address – the first following the terror attacks of 11 September 2001.

Bush's strategic target was clear: 'regimes that sponsor terror' had to be kept from 'threatening America or our friends and allies with weapons of mass destruction'. And just which regimes he had in mind was clear too, although he acknowledged that 'some of these regimes have been pretty quiet since the 11 September. But we know their true nature.' Then he named them, identifying his official 'axis of evil' – North Korea, Iran and Iraq.

As had become the post-11 September norm, the address was all about fear. The descriptions varied, but each included a scary report of what weapons the evil governments had or sought. In two of the three cases, Bush added a horrified account of what the rulers were doing to their own people. Pyongyang was a 'regime arming with missiles and weapons of mass destruction, while starving its citizens'. Tehran 'aggressively pursues these weapons and exports terror, while an unelected few repress the Iranian people's hope for freedom'. The democracy argument hovered as part of the background.

When it came to Iraq, however, at first, democracy was not the issue. The fear-inducing warning focused solely on the military danger – not to Iraqis, or even to regional neighbours, but danger to the whole world, including to the United States itself. Baghdad, the President warned, 'continues to flaunt its hostility toward America and to support terror. . . . This is a regime that agreed to international inspections – then kicked out the inspectors. This is a regime that has something to hide from the civilized world.' And again those false claims went largely unchallenged in the mainstream press. Few reporters added caveats to their State of the Union coverage pointing out that the State Department's own 'Patterns of Global Terrorism' reports had not accused Iraq of involvement in international terrorism, that the UN arms inspectors were not kicked out by Iraq, but were warned to leave by the United States itself on the eve of President Clinton's 1998 'Desert Fox' bombing raids, and that just possibly what the regime in Baghdad was hiding was precisely that it had no viable WMDs or nuclear weapons programmes.

Bush's three top targets were very different countries, posing very different challenges. And the US response was very different to each. Of the three countries, only isolated and impoverished North Korea might have had a viable, if primitive, nuclear weapons programme in early 2002 – if not actual weapons yet, at least the likely capacity to produce them soon. Iran, while economically and militarily powerful in the region, was and remains years away from nuclear weapons capacity. More significantly, despite the later escalation of US pressure focused on Iran's nuclear power programme, Tehran was then, as a signatory to the Non-Proliferation Treaty (unlike North Korea), under intense and intrusive UN monitoring by the International Atomic Energy Agency. By 2002, Iraq had been qualitatively disarmed during seven years of find-and-destroy missions by UN arms inspectors, and had been decimated by the crippling sanctions that had left its economy in free-fall and its social fabric in shreds.

What the three countries had in common was that none of them represented a threat to the United States. But where they differed, despite being grouped in Bush's 'axis of evil', was in how they were actually viewed in the United States. Iran appeared to Americans as the glowering face of Ayatollah Khomeini, with fading images of blindfolded hostages – a long-standing enemy. North Korea was seen as just strange, a racism-tinged caricature of a country. Neither was widely viewed as a serious danger. But Iraq represented the continuing core enemy, Saddam Hussein the personification of evil who had been demonized ever since the 1990–91 Gulf crisis and the war had reversed the longstanding US support for Baghdad.

In his speech linking Iran and Iraq, long and bitter enemies, and, inexplicably, North Korea, Bush crafted an artificial 'axis' whose targeting would publicly reframe the nature and the parameters of his crusade, far beyond the war of vengeance, then already in process against the Taliban and Al Qaeda. The speech would reshape the trajectory of Washington's war from bounty-hunting in Afghanistan, to threatening invasions, overthrowing of governments, and military attacks in countries across the globe.

At first, the crusade was shaped by claims of military–terrorist threats – WMDs, links with Al Qaeda, the dread of another terrorist attack. In a speech at the Virginia Military Institute, Bush told cadets:

> a small number of outlaw regimes today possess and are developing chemical and biological and nuclear weapons. In their threat to peace, in their mad ambitions, in their destructive potential and in the repression of their own people, these regimes constitute an axis of evil and the world must confront them. (Allen 2002)

For many months, these claims were widely accepted by the Washington elite in both political parties, most mainstream media outlets, and by a majority of the American people. The assertions largely went unchallenged, at least in public, by most other governments, and they formed the basis of Bush's and Secretary of State Colin Powell's presentations at the United Nations. Even the leaders of the global governmental opposition, France, Germany and to a lesser degree Russia, did not directly challenge Bush's disingenuous allegations, relying instead on the less confrontational call for allowing UN inspectors to complete their work. Only the increasingly powerful anti-war movement, in the United States and around the globe, consistently and explicitly rejected the false claims.

But, even as the Iraq-as-military threat continued to shape the Bush administration's drive towards war, secondary and even tertiary justifications emerged, based on issues of democracy and human rights. Among their proponents were some of the small cadre of Iraqi exiles who had supported the invasion and their backers in the Pentagon and the White House. They included, of course those few, but inordinately powerful US officials who maintained colonial-style visions of remaking the Middle East in the image of Western 'market democracies'. From the beginning, these redraw-the-maps enthusiasts, led by Deputy Defense Secretary Paul Wolfowitz (now President of the World Bank) had called on the Bush administration to openly assert 'democratization' and 'ending Saddam Hussein's human rights violations' as key legitimating motives for war.

These were the same ideologically driven policymakers, who seemed truly to believe, against all evidence, that invading US troops would be welcomed in the Iraqi streets with sweets and flowers. But their claimed focus on human rights and democracy were not popular early on. Other powerful Washington political operatives understood that the American people were unlikely to embrace a large-scale and indefinite deployment of US troops to defend abstractions of democracy or human rights. So, for most top Bush officials, those high-minded goals took the pride of place only later on, when all their original rationales were beginning to crumble, exposed as lie after lie.

'So Like It or Not, You Will Have to be Free. . .'

The first explicit claims of democracy, being the primary rationale for the war in Iraq, appeared in a speech made by George Bush on 6 November 2003, when public awareness of the lies regarding weapons of mass destruction was on the rise. The speech called for a 'forward strategy of freedom,' linking his claimed commitment to democratization in the Middle East to Ronald Reagan's Cold War call for democratization in Eastern Europe. He acknowledged that earlier US policies of accommodating repressive regimes in the region 'did nothing to make us safe', but offered no indication of an actual new approach. He praised the King of Morocco and the Emirs of the smaller Gulf petro-states for their largely cosmetic steps towards narrow versions of democracy. He lauded US allies, Egypt and Saudi Arabia, for initial democratic openings, but assured them that 'working democracies always need time to develop', thus alleviating any fear of serious pressure on Riyadh or Cairo.

The speech, and the announcement of a new 'forward strategy for freedom' was designed to give a popular cover to what had already emerged as a permanent war – framing Bush's preventive 'war on terrorism', especially in Iraq, as a 'war for liberty'. It aimed to distract the American people from the sham reasons actually given for the war – the missing WMDs, the non-existent 'imminent danger', and the false claims of Iraq's links with Al Qaeda.

Much of the 'democracy' framework that Bush tried to assert about Iraq had to do with the electoral process imposed by the US occupation forces. Certainly elections are often important indices and instruments of democracy, but elections held under conditions of military occupation can never be fully legitimate. President Bush had one thing right when he said, 'All [foreign] military forces and intelligence personnel must withdraw before the . . . elections for those elections to be free and fair' (Reuters, 8 March 2005). He was talking, however, about Syrian troops in Lebanon and made no mention of a parallel need for foreign forces to withdraw from Iraq to make *those* elections free and fair. The initial plan for elections in Iraq was designed to provide a veneer of credibility and legitimacy to the continuation of US control of the country. The strategy was to elect a US-friendly government that would accept permanent US military bases in Iraq, maintain the US privatization and corporate-friendly economic regulations, and draft a US-oriented Constitution.

Implementation of the 'democratization' strategy involved, from the beginning, powerful US political operations in Iraq, designed to influence the outcome of the series of elections. Despite official US denials, it was quite clear that US financial and political influence-buying was extensive. Both the National Democratic Institute (NDI) and the International Republican Institute (IRI) launched major campaigns to help 'train' and provide 'capacity building' to various Iraqi political parties. Ostensibly those services were available to all parties, but they certainly favoured those deemed open to maintaining close ties to the US occupation authorities and those viewed as likely to move Iraq's economy towards privatization and globalization. The US Agency for International Development provided about $80 million to NDI, IRI and other similar organizations, many of them working under the auspices of the Cold War-era National Endowment for Democracy in order to 'assist' Iraqi parties in the run-up to the elections.

The election processes caused serious escalation of the sectarian divides within Iraq. In a country whose social fabric was brutally shredded by a dozen years of crippling economic sanctions, continued bombings, invasion and military occupation, the tendency to retreat from Iraq's traditional secular national identity and enter into smaller associations of religion, ethnicity, tribe, clan and family increased. The emergence of a new set of political parties, based largely on ethnic and/or religious identity, continued the fragmentation of Iraqi national identity. Washington's early embrace of Kurdish and Shi'a parties (not coincidentally based in Iraq's oil-rich zones) combined with its efforts to win the appearance of legitimacy and to undercut resistance by convincing Sunni politicians to join the electoral process, continued this process of devolution of Iraqi national identity thus national power to smaller religious and ethnic sub-groups. As sectarian violence rose in early 2006, and especially as White House threats to expand the war to Iran increased, Washington shifted some of its political support, particularly distancing itself from some of the key pro-Iranian parties. More than six months after the January 2006 election of a 'permanent' Iraqi government, fractious parliamentarians remained unable to choose a cabinet. From the beginning of the occupation, US 'democracy' efforts had the effect of dividing Iraq and Iraqis by ethnic and religious affiliations designed to undercut the once primary Iraqi national identity.

Faced with a global outcry against the 'election' process being orchestrated by the occupation forces in Iraq, the United Nations asserted that there was, in fact, a precedent for 'legitimate' elections held under military occupation. Their model of choice was the 1999 UN-run election in East Timor. But there were significant differences. UN resolutions had, since 1976, officially deemed the 1975 Indonesian occupation illegal and called on Jakarta to withdraw. The 1999 vote in East Timor was not to select a puppet 'government' to administer East Timor under continuing Indonesian occupation, but a direct referendum on whether or not to end the occupation – a choice never given to Iraqis. Additionally, the Indonesian military was under sufficient pressure so that there was little military violence during the referendum itself. (The Indonesian military's razing of much of Dili came after the election.) And the balloting was run directly by the United Nations, with the aid of thousands of UN election workers and a wide array of international monitors.

The Iraqi elections were also qualitatively different from the Palestinian election of January 2006, which brought a Hamas-led government to power. That election, held under conditions of occupation with restrictions over which Palestinians could participate, certainly faced severe challenges of legitimacy, yet conditions were vastly different. The election was run completely by the Palestinians themselves, and international observers designated it as largely free and fair. However flawed the limited institutions of Palestinian democracy that have emerged in the Occupied Territories over the last decade, there was a functioning civil society, a parliamentary structure, and a national process not directly controlled by the occupying forces. The level of occupation violence in Palestine might be very high; it is, nevertheless, generally much lower than the full-scale warfare characterizing much of Iraq.

The outcome of the election, of course, demonstrated the fraudulent character of Washington's claim about its commitment to democratization. The election was primarily a vote against the ruling Fatah party's corrupt ways and its failure to end the occupation, much more than it was a statement of commitment to the new Islamist leadership in Hamas. But, despite the internationally-acknowledged fairness of the process, Washington moved quickly to join Israel in penalizing the Palestinians for their vote. The collective punishment of cutting off international economic aid, denying Palestinians access to their own tax revenues collected by Israel and closing the border crossings, led to a serious escalation of extreme poverty, hunger and malnutrition. So much for 'democracy' as the basis for US policy.

Spreading Democracy. . .

Three years into the Iraq war, 'democratization' in Iraq and the Middle East has remained the only surviving excuse for Bush's invasion, occupation and war. Certainly part of the reason it has survived is that it was very difficult to unequivocally disprove the poetic, but vague, claim that invading and occupying Iraq was somehow a step towards 'democratization' of the entire Middle East, a region filled with authoritarian regimes and absolute monarchies. It was far easier to physically authenticate Iraq's demonstrably absent WMDs and nuclear weapon facilities, than to 'prove' that real democracy was not part of Washington's real agenda in the region.

But that was not the only reason. It would be difficult to overestimate the power of 'democracy' – always spoken of with reverence as an unassailable good – as a compelling vision for the US public at large. The war in Iraq would have global implications, global consequences, global costs. But the invasion and the war remained at its centre a US-driven crusade – and 'democracy' has a long history in American national identity, and certainly a pride of place in the list of justifications for US wars. Phil Ochs' masterpiece 'Cops of the World' was written in 1965, when the US invasion of Santo Domingo ('take the Dominican Republic, which we did. . .' was part of his in-concert intro) was immediate history, and the huge US troop build-up in South Vietnam was just underway. But it goes back further than that. Since the United States was created, the myth of the United States as a font of democracy, both globally and within its borders, has shaped Americans' self-image.

The Atlantic-to-Pacific western expansion of the United States in the seventeenth, eighteenth and nineteenth centuries, deemed the 'manifest destiny' of the white European settlers, was enabled by the genocidal slaughter of Native peoples in a transcontinental settler–colonial land grab. It was rationalized in the churches and the newspapers of the time, with the twin claims of the religious and secular righteousness of the 'civilizing mission' that would bring God to the heathen and spread democracy in the New World. It was only incidental, of course, that those same righteous white pioneers, in the name of those twin gods of Christianity and democracy, would seize the Native peoples' land to enrich and empower a new nation, now spread across a huge and fertile continent. Hundreds of years later, US global power and wealth was still rooted in the genocide and accompanying land grab against Indian nations, along with the profits accrued from centuries of a lucrative system of slavery.

American exceptionalism, in fact, is grounded in a national self-image that equates America *with* democracy. That is, a tautological belief that anything the United States does is *ipso facto* democratic precisely because the United States, the biggest/strongest/bravest/best of all the world's democracies, is doing it. While Alexis de Tocqueville may have had other, perhaps more objectively measurable, criteria in mind for defining American exceptionalism, US national identity, as understood and appropriated by US citizens themselves, has always been rooted in the mythology of democracy.

One consequence of this is that the long and ugly history of US military intervention, conquest, subjugation and occupation of other peoples' lands has never been understood by US citizens as colonialism. The forging of the United States as an independent nation in the context of its own victorious anti-colonial struggle shaped a founding mythology of democracy. As a result, every westward-thrusting and overseas foray, from the Lakota and Cherokee lands to the Philippines and Puerto Rico, was legitimated through the discourse of 'spreading democracy', whether 'from sea to shining sea' in North America, or in military invasions around the world.

Certainly there were important distinctions between the settler colonialism of what would become continental United States, and the military seizures of islands and nations across the globe. But in both cases, even when the expansion of US military power in the south Pacific, in the Caribbean, in north Asia, and eventually in Southeast Asia took on the permanence and depth of occupation, the dread word 'colonialism' was rarely heard. When the United States won control of the Philippines from Spain, and then fought long years of a brutal war to suppress nationalist resistance in the islands, its century of domination was somehow not understood (among US citizens, that is), as colonialism. When the United States seized and held Puerto Rico and Cuba, when US troops transformed the Hawaiian kingdom into an off-shore plantation for 'democracy', Dole and United Fruit, the identification of the United States as a colonial power was still not made.

The key architects of the Iraq war have continued this tradition a century later. Shortly after the US invasion and occupation of Iraq, Secretary of Defense Donald Rumsfeld famously told the Arabic satellite television Al Jazeera: 'we don't do empire'. Vice President Dick Cheney struck a similar 'we are not an empire' note at the World Economic Forum in Davos, Switzerland, telling the gathered glitterati: 'if we were a true empire, we would currently preside over a much greater piece of the earth's surface than we do. That's not the way we operate' (Getz 2005).

Interestingly, even British historian Niall Ferguson, darling of the new cadre of analysts who assert the legitimacy of a post-11 September US empire, believes that Washington's denial of its essential nature makes the country more menacing. 'The United States is the empire that dare not speak its name', he said. 'It is an empire in denial, and US denial of this poses a real danger to the world. An empire that doesn't recognize its own power is a dangerous one' (Gibbons 2003).

Ferguson has staked out the claim that empire, at least its British version, is not such a bad idea. But he also noted that while Washington claims to be in a 'unique situation' in Iraq, occupying the country and yet not overseeing an imperial project, the British had said, in fact, the same thing when they occupied Baghdad in 1917. The language of that year, he said, was 'our armies do not come into your lands and your cities as conquerors, but as liberators.'

Looking at the repeated claims, particularly from top Bush administration officials Cheney and Rumsfeld that invading US troops would be greeted in Iraq with flowers and sweets, their optimism was all too familiar. Ultimately, Ferguson said, the notion of 'conquest as a form of liberation, of building an empire of democracy, is not new. Britain did it too in its liberal heyday. What we are looking at is a second Anglophonic empire similar in many ways to the first, and that has to be recognized' (ibid.).

Democratization, it appears, could be a potent explanation for a variety of sins of the empire. As we have demonstrated elsewhere in this volume, Washington has relied, with different successes and failures at different times, on a set of excuses and justifications for its drive towards empire: terrorism, nuclear weapons, drugs, failed states and humanitarian crises – all have had their day. But democracy is different. Unlike the goal of stopping or preventing the evils of terrorism, nuclear weapons, etc., democratization is a positive goal upheld by both supporters and opponents of empire, albeit with different definitions of what democracy and democratization really mean. It is perhaps for this reason that democracy survives in the public mind to legitimize illegal wars even when other pretexts have collapsed. Certainly it is also true that it is much easier to demonstrate the concrete absence of nuclear weapons or terrorist links, than to prove unequivocally that something as amorphous as 'democratization' is a myth. But the power of persuasion inherent in the claim of 'democracy' is potent, and thus challenging that specific myth remains much more difficult.

However, there are additional bases for challenging those who would use democratization as an excuse for US war. Beyond the hypocrisy of empire denial, it is necessary to examine the inadequacies and shortcomings of US claims regarding the strength, resilience and power of its own democracy.

The claim that the United States is attacking Afghanistan or invading Iraq in order to 'spread democracy' across Central Asia and the Middle East is predicated on the assumption that US democracy is the model of what those backward regions could, should, would be like, if only they were 'democratic like us'. If 'we' were not democratic, presumably, 'we' would have no right to claim any legitimacy to spread democracy somewhere else. So the legitimacy survives largely in the minds of those who accept the view that the United States itself is the strongest, the most representative and the fairest democracy of all.

In fact, in the wake of the escalation of civil liberties violations post-11 September in the form of secret surveillance, unregulated even by secret courts, arrest without trial and indefinite detention, legalized torture, collapse of constitutional protections – any claim regarding the 'model US democracy' collapses into an oxymoron. But while the 'war against terrorism' has brought new and dangerous assaults on democratic rights once taken for granted by many in the United States, the reality is that internal democracy within the United States has always had its limitations. Recent developments have not created whole cloth, but rather enormously magnified those longstanding limitations.

Democracy has many definitions. Perhaps the most useful is the notion of a participatory government chosen by, and accountable to the interests of, the majority population, with guarantees of full protection for the rights of the most vulnerable, minority, and poorest communities. In many countries, certainly including the United States, that would mean a participatory government defending the combined interests of the poor, the working class, and most of the middle class. In a republican government, based on representative rather than participatory institutions, real democracy is always limited; in a huge population numbering in the hundreds of millions, those limitations are even pronounced. The United States has never practised participatory, popular democracy on a national scale. Such democracy exists only in isolated small towns and in a few held-over examples (such as the early presidential primary in the lightly populated state of New Hampshire), widely viewed as anachronistic. The exercise of popular power has always been indirect, and with the advent of powerful lobbies, corporate control of most media, and private campaign financing, ensuring the almost exclusive empowerment of the wealthiest, the concept of 'real democracy', for most people, becomes a bad joke.

That is not to say that the United States is 'not a democracy'. There is a proud legacy of powerful democratic struggles in the United States. Popular movements demanding and defending democratic rights, especially for marginalized sectors including African-Americans and other people of colour, immigrants, women, workers, gays and lesbians – are all key components of US history. Those movements, fighting to abolish slavery, to end wars, for the right to speak, assemble, vote, unionize and more, have won important protections, often in bloody battles with great human costs that belie the ostensibly broad existing 'democracy' of the country. Taken together, they have broadened and strengthened US democracy over three centuries or more. But all of those hard-fought battles, despite their importance, have yet to create the real, inclusive, non-discriminatory law-based democracy that so many Americans imagine their country to be.

In fact, some of the most important democratic victories are now threatened by new attacks, facing the threat of being dismantled. What is new and especially dangerous about the domestic consequences of the so-called 'war against terrorism' is that these repressive moves not only hold back the broader democratization of US society, but even threaten existing rights, stripping the US Constitution and especially the Bill of Rights of their essential guarantees. The minimum US standard for democratic rights – parallel to the basic UN covenants guaranteeing global human rights, civil, political, economic, social and cultural rights – is now at risk. The hard fought and unfinished battle for economic rights, for economic democracy in the United States, has been largely redefined, not as popular empowerment, but as the triumph of 'free markets'.

Phil Ochs' 'Cops of the World' lyrics declare that 'the name for our profits is Democracy'. The operative US version of democracy, when used to legitimize the invasion and/or occupation of variously disobedient countries, is usually asserted as 'market democracy', with an equal emphasis on multi-party elections (regardless of actual popular involvement or free choice) and 'free' trade (regardless of consequences for workers and small producers).

Democratizing the Middle East

So, how successful has been the US-orchestrated 'democratization' of post-Taliban Afghanistan? What does 'democracy' look like in Iraq, more than three years after the US invasion overthrew the existing government and set up its own version of a 'sovereign' Iraqi state? And across the Middle East, how successful has been the Bush administration's campaign to 'spread democracy' in Arab monarchies and semi-dictatorships, long armed and succoured by Washington?

In a single day in early 2006, *The Washington Post* provided partial answers to all those questions. The newspaper describes 'democracy' in Afghanistan as 'a weak government, well-armed private militias and deep ethnic and ideological divisions'. The justice system is so 'undeveloped, corrupt, highly politicized and poorly equipped' that the international human rights and accountability-focused Afghanistan Justice Project announced that the first war crimes trial 'is so fundamentally flawed in so many ways we're recommending it not to continue' (Witte 2006).

Five years after the US invasion of Afghanistan, the fiction, that conditions in that country bore any relationship to democratization, had long since been exposed. Despite the UN-backed election and the continuing occupation by US and NATO troops ostensibly there to protect Afghanistan's fledging democracy, the country has remained in a state of violence-driven fear and repression. Especially in southern Afghanistan, the resurgent Taliban was again (or is still?) a dominant force in people's lives. The US-backed government and the US occupation forces themselves had been increasingly cooperating with – and dependent on – the brutal Northern Alliance warlords in much of the country where the Taliban itself had not yet re-emerged. Opium production reached 52 per cent of the official GDP of Afghanistan in 2005 (UNODC 2005). The NATO-led International Security Force for Afghanistan (ISAF) could provide little protection and the reach of elected President Hamid Karzai did not extend much beyond the edge of the capital city. US troops, focused on their perpetually failed search for Osama bin Laden in southern Afghanistan, had long since abandoned any pretence that their mandate was primarily one of protecting Afghan civilians. By the middle of 2006, the frequency and escalating severity of US attacks on Afghan civilians was creating a rising tide of public opposition to the United States and the Kabul government it had installed.

As writer Laila Lalami (2006) describes Afghanistan in *The Nation*,

> Little seems to have changed in the past century, for now we have George W. Bush, leader of the free world, telling us, before invading Afghanistan in 2001, that he was doing it as much to free the country's women as to hunt down Osama bin Laden and Mullah Omar. Five years later, the Taliban is making a serious comeback, and the country's new Constitution prohibits any laws that are contrary to an austere interpretation of Sharia.

In Iraq, the failure of the Bush policy includes the failure to bring real democracy to that country, something that remains impossible under conditions of military occupation, while Iraq's sovereignty remains out of reach. In another article, the same day, *The Washington Post* (Fletcher and White 2006) went on to quote George Bush's claim that the sectarian and anti-occupation violence that spiked across Iraq after the bombing of the Shi'a Golden Dome shrine in Samarra was actually the fault of 'insurgents intent on disrupting Iraq's democratic process'. Despite the negative realities, the Bush administration continued to claim that their invasion and occupation of Iraq was bringing democracy to the beleaguered country. In fact, the series of elections in Iraq, for interim and then transitional governments, for a constitution, and for a 'permanent' parliament, all failed to provide credibility and legitimacy to the continued US control of Iraq.

Elsewhere in the region, that same day's *Washington Post* recognized that Bush's 'Push for Democracy Loses Some Energy'. During Secretary of State Condoleezza Rice's high-profile Middle East trip to Egypt, Saudi Arabia, Lebanon and the United Arab Emirates, the *Post* reported:

> [Rice's] call for greater democracy appeared more muted, as some of the aftershocks of the democracy push have given autocratic governments more leverage in their dealings with the United States. . . . Other foreign policy goals on Rice's agenda this week – such as seeking agreement to confront Iran over its nuclear program and enlisting Arab support for the new Iraqi government as bloody sectarian violence erupted – also appeared to overshadow the administration's democracy campaign. (Kessler 2006)

It was clear that Rice's trip contained more than a hint of desperation; it followed the overwhelming election of a Hamas majority to the Palestinian Legislative Council, and Rice largely failed to convince influential Arab governments to follow the US lead in rejecting the democratically elected Islamist-led Palestinian government. She outraged democracy campaigners throughout the region when she provided fulsome praise to Egypt's Hosni Mubarak, despite his cancelling of elections and other authoritarian moves, and to Saudi King Abdullah, despite his refusal to allow any serious reforms. *The Washington Post* noted:

> In the Arab world the impression left by Rice's trip . . . was that she was on a mission to round up support to punish a series of US enemies such as Hamas, Iran and Syria. The campaign against Hamas . . . drew particular scorn because it was seen as hypocritical to want to punish a group that had achieved power through democratic elections. . . . The skepticism in the region was reflected in the blunt questions posted to Rice by Arab journalists. In Saudi Arabia, a female journalist, dressed head to toe in a black *abaya*, demanded: 'How is it possible to harmonize the US position as a nation supporting freedom of expression and the right of people to practice democracy with your effort to curb the will of Hamas?' Egyptian Television's Mervat Mohsen also rattled off a series of tough questions. 'American calls for democracy have unwittingly brought unprecedented support for the Muslim Brotherhood, but you're not happy with the Muslim Brotherhood in power,' he said. 'Is this some kind of designer's democracy then, Dr Rice? (Kessler 2006)

And that was just one day's newspaper. So much for spreading democracy.

The failure of democratization remained the hallmark of Bush's regional strategy. By spring 2006, when Cairo was in the midst of a brutal crackdown on protesters supporting judges' demands for independence, Egyptian President Hosni Mubarak's son and putative heir apparent, Gamal Mubarak, visited Washington. Ostensibly arriving on a 'private visit', he secretly met with top Bush administration officials including Vice President Cheney, National Security Advisor Stephen J. Hadley, Secretary of State Condoleezza Rice, and President Bush himself. *The Washington Post* reported:

> The meetings came a day after stick-wielding riot police officers disrupted a demonstration in Cairo, chasing protesters, beating them and removing them. . . . Activists saw the incident as part of a broader crackdown on dissent, despite what they dismiss as cosmetic moves towards democracy intended to placate the Bush administration. . . . [Egyptian Ambassador Nabil] Fahmy called the clash an unfortunate upshot of a more democratic Egypt. (Baker 2006a)

The real problem for US officials, of course, remained not only how to pull off something that would look like multi-party elections, but how to impose 'democratic elections' that did not end up electing the wrong people. To quote Phil Ochs again, the answer is to send the 'cops of the world', who will 'find you a leader that you can elect'. That has long been the hallmark of US interventions – finding the right leader to impose, through staged or forced elections, on a recalcitrant population, a leader who would bring the people to heel and embrace Washington's agenda. The problem emerges when the people voting in those US-backed, internationally hyped elections somehow get the crazy idea that elections are supposed to be about choice, about getting to decide who you really want to have power in your country. And these days, strangely enough, this often leads to electoral victories, not for the US-anointed, English-speaking, Western-style secular 'democrats,' but rather for Islamist clerics, socially conservative, yet popular, respected for being incorruptible, and staunchly opposed to US policies in their country and the surrounding region.

The Jordanian columnist Rami Khouri (2006), writing in Beirut's *Daily Star* in February 2006, totted up the score of Washington's electoral efforts in the Middle East, in the title of his article, 'Bearded Arabs 1, American ladies 0':

> Nothing better captures the broad lines of the great contestation that now defines the Middle East than the four very telegenic characters who have criss-crossed the region during the past week: US Secretary of State Condoleezza Rice, her colleague in charge of US public policy, Karen Hughes, Hamas official Khaled Meshaal and the young Iraqi cleric Moqtada al-Sadr. . . .
>
> Two of these four Middle Eastern itinerant ideologues are slick, appointed American political figures who spend many of their waking hours preaching the benefits of democratic elections in the Arab world. Two others are bearded Arab Islamists who have come to power through the American-supported vehicle of democratic elections in the Arab world. It would seem to be a match made in heaven: bearded Arab politicos who wish to expand their own efficient constituencies and militias into governing systems that enhance the wellbeing of

> their fellow citizens; and the American ladies who combine the bouncy enthusiasm of young high school cheerleaders with the more daring inclination to engage in political genetic engineering in order to enhance the wellbeing of Arab citizens and the security of Americans, in one fell swoop.
>
> . . . .The likelihood is that this past week will go down in the record books as one in which the American ladies significantly lost ground to the bearded Arabs.
>
> . . . [T]hese Islamist leaders have more legitimacy in the Middle East than all of Rice's and Hughes' copious democratic rhetoric, and all the Marines in Mesopotamia put together.

Failure – in Palestine, Iraq, Egypt, and Saudi Arabia – continues to be the main accomplishment of the Bush administration's 'we're spreading democracy across the Arab world' claim.

And this failure does not stop the Bush administration from asserting their, now hoary, claim of 'spreading democracy' to their newest target, with blustering calls for regime change and even threats to use nuclear weapons against Iran. The combination of escalating rhetoric from Washington, spiralling deterioration of security conditions in Iraq, Bush's political problems, and an ideologically-driven pursuit of power made the possibility of a US military attack on Iran – however reckless and however dangerous its consequences – a frighteningly real possibility. And from the White House, reliance on the 'Iran might get nukes! They might give them to terrorists!' rhetoric, was backed with the familiar claim that US intervention would also bring about democratization to Iran. The 2005 Iran Liberation Act offered an initial $5 million in US assistance to organizations in Iran ostensibly committed to democracy – conveniently defined as opposing the government and welcoming the United States.

Global suspicions continue to run high regarding US claims about Iran because of Washington's lies leading to the invasion of Iraq. The Europeans do not accept Washington's spurious democratization claims, or its rhetoric applauding 'regime change'. This has led to a significant divide between the European Union negotiators and Washington on how to deal with Iran, and whether UN Security Council threats of sanctions or military strikes, or arms inspection agency cooperation, should be the basis of any agreement. But European governments and some others concerned about non-proliferation are still sold to the imaginary notion that Iran should be viewed as a nuclear threat even while agreeing that Tehran is years – perhaps a decade or more – away from an actual nuclear weapons capacity. The result was a much weakened global opposition to US war threats, even as the Non-Proliferation Treaty and international law in general fell victim to Bush's unilateralism.

Democracy and Anti-Communism

The reliance on democracy to justify war is not, of course, a new phenomenon. Throughout the years of the Cold War, the assertion of democracy was central to Washington's anti-Communist crusade. The fundamental clash of civilizations of that era was not described as an apples-to-apples battle between Communism and capitalism as competing economic systems, but rather the ideologically shaped apples-to-oranges language of a struggle between 'Communism' (read: inherently cruel, dictatorial and evil) and 'democracy' (read: motherhood, patriotism, and quasi-religious righteousness).

Democracy, in one guise or another, has been a central player throughout the overarching history of US empire. It has provided justifications for campaigns during the First and Second World Wars, through the Korean War, Vietnam, the Cold War's 'proxy wars' in places like Nicaragua and Angola, and the first US war against Iraq. It has justified several of the post-Cold War interventions ostensibly launched to protect human rights and humanitarianism, in Somalia, Haiti, and the former Yugoslavia. So what was actually new and different in the post-11 September drive towards empire was not that the Bush administration relied on 'democracy' for legitimation, but rather that it was their last choice of pretext, rather than their first option. It was asserted only after the earlier claims of WMD, nuclear weapons, links to terrorism, etc., were all proved false.

Democracy was also central in legitimating the Cold War itself. The United States was not only going to defeat the Soviet Union and the countries of the Warsaw Pact, it was going to democratize them right out from under the control of the 'Evil Empire'. The struggle against Communism provided the overarching framework, but democratization was seized upon as the weapon of choice – in all its variant forms, but especially focusing on providing support for anti-Communist regimes and pro-Western dissidents. The support was not conditioned on the recipients actually supporting democracy, but only so far they were against Communism. Thus, long-standing US backing of brutal dictators in Haiti, Nicaragua or Zaire; support for savage militias such as the Nicaraguan contras or the murderous Renamo in Mozambique; or lionizing czarist-style monarchists such as Aleksandr Solzhenitsyn – were all congruent with US 'democratization'. After all, if the epoch good-and-evil battle was between Communism and democracy, anyone who fought against Communism must be a supporter of democracy, right? It was, ultimately, a case of adopting the enemies of one's enemies, not only as friends, but as proxies. So, democracy morphed into a new, nebulous category – defined as that which stood against Communism.

After the collapse of the Soviet Union and the end of the Cold War, the framework equivalent to the battle against Communism was no longer viable, and democracy as a concept had little resonance as a strategic weapon. The world remained confused – bi-polarity no longer held sway, and genuine multi-polarity was thwarted by the seemingly unchallengeable expansion of US power. So, during most of Washington's post-Cold War military interventions, in Somalia, Haiti, the former Yugoslavia and elsewhere, the most common justification was some version of 'humanitarianism' – human rights violations were on the rise, and the US Marines were rushing to the rescue. Even in sanctions-riven Iraq, the constant bombing raids throughout the 1990s were justified in terms of global democracy. According to President Bill Clinton, the United States was 'enforcing

UN resolutions', despite the inconvenient (and rarely mentioned) fact that no UN resolution had ever created or allowed military attacks on the US- and British-imposed 'no-fly zones' in northern and southern Iraq.

What the attacks of 11 September provided, then, was a potential new framework for the latest versions of Washington's long-standing drive towards empire-seeking invasions and interventions: the 'Global War On Terror'. Most specifically, in the post-11 September world, 'Islamic terrorism' would take the place of Communism as the global bogeyman, the all-around bad guy and overall face of evil in the world. Unfortunately, for Washington's spin masters, however, even in fear stricken US minds, the Islamist terror rationale was never quite sufficient.[2] But it did, and still does, provide a basis for ratcheting up fear. Among the American people, it is a fear that is based, as is so often the case in the United States, on racism. By itself, the terrorism framework remains incomplete. So the endgame was spun as the need to 'spread democracy' in the 'terrorist sanctuaries' – primarily in the still largely repressive, and sometimes occupied, nations of the Arab and Muslim worlds of the Middle East and South Asia.

In the United States it is assumed, of course, that democracy in 'those' regions does not just grow on its own. 'We', who live in the world's best democracy, the world's democratic superpower, the good guys – have an obligation to bring democracy to those terror-lands. And how do we do it? We send the Marines. Phil Ochs was right:

> The name for our profits is Democracy,
> So like it or not you will have to be free.
> 'Cause we're the cops of the world, boys,
> We're the cops of the world.

Even after 11 September, however, Americans were still reluctant to back a deadly invasion and occupation solely to bring democracy to some 'other' people on the other side of the world, however oppressed and eager for invasion those 'others' might appear in popular discourse. Americans might not support sending US troops to die for someone else's democracy. Yet Bush found it a relatively easy bet, at least for a while, to win support for invading other countries, killing tens of thousands of civilians and risking the lives of thousands of US troops, because it would bring safety, security and protection to Americans themselves – by spreading democracy. Other countries, other peoples, all those 'others' not only live without freedom and democracy, Bush told the American people, but they represent a constant threat to 'us', to 'our' freedom and 'our' democracy.

The argument was based, however simplistically, on the notion of a 'democratic peace' – the claim that democracies do not go to war against each other. If we can just democratize all of 'them', the argument goes, we would not have to worry about 'them' attacking 'us'. It would all be so simple.

Except for Chile, where the United States backed a military coup against the oldest and most stable democracy in Latin America because it had the auda-city to elect a socialist. As Henry Kissinger infamously said, regarding Chile, 'I don't see why we have to let a country go Marxist just because its people are irresponsible.'

And except for Mossadegh's Iran in 1953, and Panama several times over, and the Dominican Republic in 1964 and so many other countries where elected governments ('democracies' according to the narrow 'democracy means elections' definition so popular in Washington) have been undermined, sanctioned, demonized and ultimately militarily overthrown by the United States.

And except for Venezuela. Recently by US officials threatening President Hugo Chávez, who was elected to office with far higher numbers and far higher voter participation levels than President Bush, do not seem terribly concerned about Venezuela's democratic government.

But the 'democratic peace' theory fails for other reasons as well. The most important fallacy in the theory lies in its failure to address the consistent willingness of 'democracies' – especially the wealthiest and most powerful – to go to war against almost anyone else, most easily against those countries they dismiss as *not really* 'democratic'. So George Bush (2004) can blithely assert:

> the reason why I'm so strong on democracy is democracies don't go to war with each other. And the reason why is the people of most societies don't like war, and they understand what war means. . . . I've got great faith in democracies to promote peace. And that's why I'm such a strong believer that the way forward in the Middle East, the broader Middle East, is to promote democracy.

But the stark reality is that impoverished countries like Iraq and Afghanistan, however undemocratic, struggling to survive years of crippling sanctions and/or decades of destructive wars, simply do not become 'democratic' under US bombs or the jackboot of US occupation. Nor do they represent even a modicum of military threat to the United States. That the war is waged against them in the name of expanding the 'democratic peace' does not make the war any more survivable for the Afghans and Iraqis who face the onslaught of 'democratic' missiles and 'democratic' tanks.

Ultimately, when all others have failed, democratization becomes the justification of last resort.

Notes

1 Notes released under Freedom of Information Act request, cited in Krugman (2006).

2 See Vanaik, 'Political Terrorism and the US Imperial Project', in this volume.

References

Allen, Mike (2002), 'Bush Resumes Case Against Iraq', *The Washington Post*, 18 April.

Amnesty International (2001), 'Central Asia: No Excuse for Escalating Human Rights Violations', October.

Baker, Peter (2006a), 'Mubarak's Son Met With Cheney, Others', *The Washington Post*, 16 May.

——— (2006b), 'Bush Reinforces Friendship with Australia', *The Washington Post*, 17 May.

Bush, George W. (2002), speech delivered on 12 March.

——— (2003), Interview of the President by TVP, Poland, White House Press Release, 29 May, available at http://www.whitehouse.gov/g8/interview5.html.

——— (2004), 'President and Prime Minister Blair Discussed Iraq, Middle East', White House Press Release, 12 November.

Ciarrocca, Michelle (2002), 'American Arms: Into Whose Hands?', February 2002, http://www.motherjones.com/commentary/columns/2002/02/arms_saks.html

Erlanger, Steven (2001), 'Germany, Under New Antiterrorist Law, Bans a Radical Muslim Group', *The New York Times*, 13 December.

Fletcher, Michael A. and Josh White (2006), 'Bush Says Iraqis Face Moment of "Choosing"', *The Washington Post*, 25 February.

Getz, Arlene (2005), '"We Must Work Together": Dick Cheney tried to strike a conciliatory note in Davos', *Newsweek* online, 26 January.

Gibbons, Fiachra (2003), 'US "is an empire in denial": Historian accuses Washington of failing to face the facts', *The Guardian*, 2 June.

Kessler, Glen (2006), 'Push for Democracy Loses Some Energy', *The Washington Post*, 25 February.

Khalilzad, Zalmay (1996), 'Afghanistan: Time to Reengage', *The Washington Post*, 7 October.

Khouri, Rami G. (2006), 'Bearded Arabs 1, American ladies 0', *Daily Star*, Beirut, 25 February.

Krugman, Paul (2006), 'Osama, Saddam and The Ports', *The New York Times*, 24 February.

Lalami, Laila (2006), 'The Missionary Position', *The Nation*, 19 June.

Loeb, Vernon and Bradley Graham (2001), 'Errant Bombs May Have Hit Afghan Civilians, US Says', *The Washington Post*, 24 October.

Marshall, Tyler and Paul Watson (2001), 'Afghans Teeter on Edge', *Los Angeles Times*, 17 September.

Stephens, Joe and David B. Ottaway (2001), 'Afghan Roots Keep Adviser Firmly in the Inner Circle: Consultant's Policy Influence Goes Back to the Reagan Era', *The Washington Post,* 23 November.

UNDPI (2001), 'Security Council Condemns, "In Strongest Terms", Terrorist Attacks on United States; Unanimously Adopting Resolution 1368 (2001), Council Calls on All States to Bring Perpetrators to Justice', United Nations Department of Public Information Release, Security Council SC/7143, 4370th Meeting, 12 September.

UNODC, UN Office of Drug Control (2005), Afghanistan Opium Survey 2005, November.

USSD, US Department of State (2002), *Uzbekistan: Country Reports on Human Rights Practices – 2001*, released by the Bureau of Democracy, Human Rights, and Labor, 4 March.

Witte, Griff (2006), 'A First Look Back at the Horror', *The Washington Post*, 25 February.

Something Out There

State Weakness as an Imperial Pretext

David Sogge

> Every ten years or so, the United States needs to pick up some small crappy little country and throw it against the wall, just to show the world we mean business.
>
> Michael A. Ledeen (in Goldberg 2002)

Out there, in the backlands of its empire, another spectre has begun to haunt America: the failing state. In its *National Security Strategy* of 2002, the White House held that 'America is now threatened less by conquering states than we are by failing ones'. The US National Intelligence Council, reflecting the consensus of top spy mandarins, saw an approaching 'perfect storm' of conflict in certain regions made possible by 'the continued prevalence of troubled and institutionally weak states' that yield 'expanses of territory and populations devoid of effective governmental control. Such territories can become sanctuaries for transnational terrorists (such as Al Qaida in Afghanistan) or for criminals and drug cartels (such as in Colombia).' In conclusion, the American spymasters predicted a world in 2020 beset by a 'pervasive sense of insecurity' (USNIC 2004: 14).

Across the Atlantic, policy elites seemed similarly spooked. The European Union's official *Security Strategy*, issued in 2003, put state failure among Europe's five 'key threats'. France's Economic Council for Defence echoed these fears, stating: 'there are no more threats to our borders' but now 'no borders to our threats' (CED 2004).[1]

Filling a gap left by the Soviet Union there is a new menace. It is another kind of barbarism. Lurking in the backstreets of Mogadishu or tribal areas of Pakistan, the barbarians may be far away, but thanks to low-cost telecommunication and porous national borders, they are, for all intents and purposes, at the gates.

Under a variety of terms – weak states, fragile states, crisis states, Countries at Risk of Instability, Low-Income Countries Under Stress – the idea of state failure has gained wide acceptability among different interest groups. From the West's idea factories – the foreign aid system, philanthropic foundations, academic research units and military and security think tanks – have come rising streams of research and proposals for action.

With an intellectual food chain to sustain it, the idea of state failure has been swimming vigorously in the mainstream, making policy waves in some important places including the Pentagon, NATO and the United Nations Secretariat. Yet, the idea has had little uptake in the non-Western places to which it refers. That is by itself significant. After all, citizens of these places have for decades, and with no help from Western powers, protested against and struggled to end the bad governance and public disorder affecting their countries.

Audible in much of today's talk about failing states are the telltale undertones of Western supremacy and condescension. Imperial intervention has returned as a fashionable idea, though usually predicated by adjectives like 'lite' or 'benign', and countenanced only if Western powers do the intervening. Some observers openly advocate the revival of colonial rule. Much of this talk is patently reactionary, but it is drawing attention to real and fundamental problems in non-Western places – polarized and feeble economies, precarious lives, social injustice, democratic deficits, crippled public services, corrupt justice systems, criminal violence and war.

Why do such conditions emerge? Why are they continually reproduced? Do states fall or are they pushed? Exploring such questions may suggest ways to shift the terms of the debate in emancipatory directions. As an idea with serious consequences, such as broader, more intrusive mandates for military interventions, it merits attention and interpretation.[2]

Some ideas can be dangerous, and need to be disposed of urgently. In nineteenth-century Europe, cholera killed hundreds of thousands of poor people because political elites clung to a theory that miasma (bad air), and not polluted water, caused the disease. The solution – effective water and sanitation systems – required heavy public investments, and thus higher taxes. Elites were, therefore, easily persuaded by miasma theory, as it implied no redistributive claims on their wealth (Evans 1987). Notions of failing states are like the miasma theory of disease, and thus candidates for the septic tank of discredited ideas.

What is at Stake?

At the heart of this talk about state failure is the definition of what the states should all be about, in whose interest should they function, and thus *for whom* they might fail or succeed. Should states exist chiefly to promote globalization's winners and to police its losers? Or, should ensuring better life chances for all citizens irrespective of the states be their chief task? The first version appears to have the upper hand. For the Western geo-strategists, non-Western states have the role and duty, before all else, to protect the West and its interests and only when such tasks are fulfilled may these states look homeward.

Further at stake are powers to enforce rules of membership in the world order, and to determine the fate of those who neglect or defy the rules. Such rules assign ranks and privileges, set agendas, define the problems and furnish the solutions. Working at deep levels, they are rarely queried, their work being equivalent to 'common sense'. Once rules form part of an everyday idiom, they give their backers enormous ideological suasion, being consistent with the observation that '*[T]he definition of the alternatives is the supreme instrument of power*' (Schattschneider 1960: 68).

Among Washington's ideological powers are those it has arrogated to itself for selecting some states and excluding others from acceptable world society. An example of such imperial judgement appeared in a 1998 *Foreign Affairs* article signed by Secretary of State Madeleine Albright. For her government, the world's nations could be assigned to one of the four categories: 'Full members of the international system; those in transition, seeking to participate more fully; those too weak, poor, or mired in conflict to participate in a meaningful way; and those that reject the very rules and precepts upon which the system is based' (cited in Guyatt 2000: 122).

The last category refers to 'rogue' or 'outlaw' states like North Korea, Syria, Iraq under Saddam Hussein and Iran under the Mullahs. Since then, however, US leaders have simplified matters even further, insisting that the political world consists of only two kinds of countries: those that cooperate with the United States and those that do not – in short, friend and foe. For today's ideologists of empire, the notion of an enemy is essential.[3]

At stake further is the rolling back of advances made in international politics: respect for self-determination, sovereign autonomy and collective self-esteem. Today's talk about failing states puts those achievements in question, it likens foreign lands to frontier territories, inviting entrance and supremacy. A failed state can evoke among some Americans a restless, 'can-do' spirit of activism abroad, reminiscent of the mythologized conquest of America's western frontier lands. That activism can range from the acquisition of client regimes to 'humanitarian intervention', guided 'nation-building', and small wars. None of these are great respecters of self-determination.[4] For the British political scientist Mark Duffield (2006), the designation 'failed state' implies eligibility for re-colonization under international supervision.

Also at stake are claims to profits and strategic advantages gained in controlling hydrocarbons, rare minerals and other natural resources, things that awaken the animal spirits of powerful outsiders. Depending on the stakes, application of the labels 'weak' and 'failing' can be selective. World petroleum politics illustrates this, for, in oil-exporting countries along the Gulf of Guinea and in West and Central Asia, disorder, injustice, criminalization and other signs of weakened public authority are notorious. Yet such places seldom figure prominently in official discussion of the problem.

Finally at stake are claims to supremacy among competing bureaucratic blocs. If talk about disorder in non-Western places is put primarily in terms of crushing security threats to Western interests, military and security establishments will emerge as Top Guns. Whereas if the talk is chiefly about boosting economic growth and investment opportunities, a bloc of state-backed mercantile agents may gain an upper hand. Institutional primacy, reflected in budgets, contracts, prestige and careers, are at stake.

'The Problem'

What drives the idea of state failure and how did it first gain purchase? Since at least the 1950s, Western scholars and policy mandarins have studied non-Western states for evidence of this ineffectiveness and instability, but rarely regarded it as a big threat. Cold War thinkers did not worry about 'chaotic' and 'unhealthy' nations, but rather about 'strong, internally stable governments', that is, states tending to be led by 'one-party Communist totalitarian governments' (Kahn and Wiener 1967: 311). Nightmare scenarios for Western policy elites have been chiefly about well-ordered, self-reliant and autonomous states, not weak and troubled ones.

But, in the early 1990s, during a crescendo of media attention for upheavals in Haiti, Nagorno Karabakh, Somalia and above all, Yugoslavia, the idea of failing states began to take off and gain altitude. Capturing attention were a handful of shrewd and well-placed public intellectuals on the right, exemplified by the travel journalist and pundit Robert Kaplan. His lurid observations about aboriginal hatreds in the Balkans and 're-primitivized man' in Africa drew huge US audiences, including people in high places. Every US embassy in Africa got copies of his 1994 article, 'The Coming Anarchy', depicting a planetary future of criminality and mayhem. President Clinton is said to have found that article 'stunning', adding that 'it makes you really imagine a future that's like one of those Mel Gibson "Road Warrior" movies'. Kaplan's writings reportedly moved Vice President Al Gore to ask the CIA to set up a major research effort, the State Failure Task Force.[5]

Still more brutality in Africa – killings in South Africa's Kwa-Zulu Bantustan, resurgence of war in Angola, and the terrible bloodletting of Rwanda in 1994 – led editorialists to stereotype distant Others along lines of Kipling's 'sullen peoples, half devil and half child'. Metaphors like 'contagion' (UK Prime Ministers Strategy Unit 2005b) or 'the swamp in which fundamentalist or messianic terrorism has been able to breed' (*Economist* 2002: 18) took the place of solid explanation.

Yet, toward the end of the 1990s, the idea seemed to lose momentum. Official concern about disorder in non-Western lands was waning and aid for them shrinking. The Clinton administration, convinced of their neoliberal efficacy, let the International Monetary Fund and World Bank steer policy on low-income countries. As Presidential candidate in 2000, George Bush said, 'I don't think nation-building missions are worthwhile'. Poor, troubled places were just not worth bothering about very much.

Then, abruptly in September 2001, the United States' leaders found they had been blindsided. Officials and pundits who had smugly regarded themselves as hard-nosed realists, knowing exactly what was going on in the world, had been caught in a deeply humiliating posture. Those narratives of societies driven by their primitive compulsions and inexplicably dysfunctional states had clearly been of no help whatsoever.

What Indicates State Failure?

Studies of state failure generate lots of distinctions and typologies. Researchers have shown a zest for taxonomy like that of Victorian butterfly collectors (Duffield 2001).[6] Most purport to identify types, rank them and suggest explanations. A sampling of mainstream writings yields a fairly consistent number of attributes of state fragility and failure.

In standard perspectives, a state fails where and when it loses its monopoly over the means of coercion. In mid-2005, a Washington DC think tank, the Fund for Peace, offered the following definition:

> A state is failing when its government is losing physical control of its territory or lacks a monopoly on the legitimate use of force. Other symptoms include the erosion of authority to make collective decisions, an inability to provide reasonable public services, and the loss of the capacity to interact in formal relations with other states as a full member of the international community. (Fund for Peace 2005)

The main upshot of all this: the state and reigning political class lose legitimacy and authority.

State fragility and failure are usually matters of degree. Fragility can change over time and across a political geography. For example, the year 2002 saw major shifts in two African countries – in the Côte d'Ivoire, the state's reach shrank to about half the national territory, as ethnic/regionalist rebel groups assumed control of the rest; in Angola, state authority expanded across almost the whole of the country, reappearing in zones from which it had been excluded by more than 20 years of anti-Communist 'rollback' war and its sequel. In Latin America, a number of states have lost full authority over certain sub-territories; parts of cities like Sao Paulo and backlands of Colombia have, for example, become no-go zones for public authorities, being fiefdoms of men with guns (see Koonings and Kruijt 2004).

Documents like the US *National Security Strategy* concentrate not so much on indicators of failing states as on the bad things that flow from them: 'poverty, weak institutions, and corruption can make weak states vulnerable to terrorist networks and drug cartels within their borders'. State failure in Africa is threatening because local civil wars may spread regionally, and badly policed borders may permit terror groups to operate freely.[7]

Other non-official analyses offer a little more detail, but operate within the same dangerous-classes-threatening-our-security paradigm. For example, in 2004, a commission of mainstream, US academics, policy specialists, bankers, lawyers and former aid agency officials published, under the auspices of a Washington think tank, a report with the portentous title *On The Brink*. It focused on three functions of government: ensuring security, meeting the basic needs of citizens, and maintaining legitimacy. If these are not performed well, threats arise to 'the welfare of citizens, the security of neighbours, and the stability of the international system'. The heart of the matter, however, is the threat to US security and economic interests (Commission on Weak States 2004).

What and Who Brings about State Failure?

In conventional narratives, state breakdown is a result of the wickedness of national politicians. They are corrupt and greedy, and have 'consciously sucked state competencies dry'. The US academic Robert Rotberg is typical in concluding: 'State failure is man-made, not merely accidental nor – fundamentally – caused geographically, environmentally or externally. Leadership decisions and leadership failures have destroyed states and continue to weaken the fragile polities that operate on the cusp of failure' (Rotberg 2002: 93).[8] In 1999, the World Bank mounted a major two-year research project on the Economics of Civil Wars, Crime and Violence. In widely cited findings, it concluded that social injustice ('grievance') explains few, if any, civil wars, rather, the main culprits are bad people and their criminal behaviour ('greed').[9]

Mainstream analyses of political disorder rely on number crunching to establish statistical correlations among variables drawn from data sets of stylized facts like 'party fractionalization' or 'discrimination', built on expert opinion. The results are hardly unambiguous.

Take the findings of the State Failure Task Force, a consortium of US academics commissioned in 1994 by the CIA. Using many data sets from the period 1958–1998, it reached hardly earth-shaking conclusions, for example, that risks of state failure are higher where living standards are low and where there is violent conflict next door. The Task Force found that 'partial democracies' were more prone to state failure than full democracies or outright autocracies. They elaborated on this failure:

> The characteristic of partial democracies that correlates most strongly with a high risk of state failure, our analysis shows, is the combination of a powerful chief executive with a relatively fractious or ineffective legislature. . . . Fitting this pattern in the 1990s were many of the recent transitional polities in Sub-Saharan Africa and the former Communist bloc, including Mozambique, Armenia, and Georgia. (SFTF 2000: vi, 14, 80)[10]

The results of these studies are taken with great seriousness. Never mind that Mozambique, Armenia and Georgia, despite acute problems, have in fact *not* drifted toward collapse – such studies frame official thinking. The *Fragile State Strategy* of USAID, for example, identifies as key sources of fragility, 'governing arrangements that lack effectiveness and legitimacy' (USAID 2005: 5).

Other search-for-correlations exercises reach rather different conclusions, simply by using other variables. A study by the Washington DC-based Fund for Peace emphasizes indicators of social injustice and abuse of human rights. Using data gathered in late 2004, the study (Fund for Peace 2005) concluded:

> Among the 12 indicators we use, two consistently rank near the top. Uneven development is high in almost all the states in the index, suggesting that inequality within states – and not merely poverty – increases instability. Criminalization or delegitimation of the state, which occurs when state institutions are regarded as corrupt, illegal, or ineffective, also figured prominently.[11]

Common Denominators

In the 1990s, faced with rising political and economic disorder in sub-Saharan Africa, ex-Yugoslavia and other troubled places, US and European policy-makers, and their media and academic associates, needed common denominators to describe these crises. Notions of state fragility and collapse answered these needs. After the attacks of 11 September 2001, and the sudden celebrity of hitherto neglected backwaters like Afghanistan, state failure notions underwent rapid revival among policy elites. Indeed they became a regular part of the Western policy idiom.

Conventional accounts pin the blame on the usual suspects – despotic and greedy leaders. Yet, a few mainstream studies have suggested that perhaps some of the malfeasance, incapacity and disorder in these troubled non-Western lands stem from factors beyond their immediate control. But, in official versions, failing states have brought misfortune on themselves. Though not as robust as notions of 'rogue' states, this talk of failing states persists because a host of powerful and well-funded Western interests – geo-strategists, military establishments, development agencies and humanitarian NGOs – rally behind its banners.

Problems with 'The Problem'

For intended audiences – foreign policy directors, military chieftains and pundits who shape policy perspectives – accounts of the problem, in the ways just sketched, evidently make sense. These mainstream analyses are routinely supplied, though demand for them may rise or fall depending on the crisis at hand. Are mainstream versions of the problem adequate? From a perspective of emancipatory global politics, there are some reasons to think they are not.

A Model Preferred by Outsiders

Mainstream talk avoids essential matters of state purposes and politics. It takes for granted an ideal type preferred by Western powers. The US political scientist Susan Woodward finds that 'the entire literature on fragile or failed states assumes a particular normative model of the state' that meets requirements of market systems and norms of 'responsibility', as determined by dominant powers. These requirements can be quite specific. States in targeted countries must enact laws favouring foreign interests, including the selling-off of public utilities to private bidders. In other words, powerful outsiders are determining rules and standards of state performance. This sets the bar high – higher by far than what Western states faced at similar periods in their evolution.

As Woodward (2005b: 5) further points out, the 'consensus model' of the state is usually posed in the technically sanitized terms of development and security policy, and not in terms of clashing interests and the need to negotiate among them. Suspended above the messy matter of politics, the model is largely irrelevant to understanding the main issues, that is, what makes states weak, and what would really be required for them to grow stronger.

Prejudicial Explanations

A look into the rogue's gallery of leading personages, in severely troubled countries, makes the greedy-and-corrupt-leaders, explanation seem plausible, even persuasive. Yet, if this voluntarist, 'big man' account of history were the only version to go by, one would have never learnt why such leaderships emerged or have remained in power and by whose help. It would be hard, for example, to explain the remark of a former US President about a Latin American *caudillo*, 'He may be a son-of-a-bitch, but he's *our* son-of-a-bitch.'

Narratives of primordial savagery and irrationality, and thus of the need of the civilized power to liberate non-Western peoples from erroneous beliefs, tribal feuding and despotic rulers, go back to the conquistadors of Latin America in the sixteenth century and to Europe's imperial scramble for Africa and Afghanistan in the nineteenth century. In paying generous attention to observers like Kaplan, media gatekeepers have drawn on such historical prejudices.

Yet, rarely did these media expose the sociology of Kaplan and his kind as sophomoric, if not simply crackpot.[12] They overlooked, for example, massive evidence that 'ethnic' violence stemmed, not from 'age-old fury' of the Kaplan school, but from calculated political stratagems. Many conflicts in Africa are illustrative: in Sudan, the United States and Israel began backing rebel armies in the 1960s; in Mozambique and Angola, the United States encouraged insurgencies backed by apartheid South Africa; in South Africa itself, a variety of Western interests promoted Chief Buthelezi and his violent Inkatha movement against Nelson Mandela's African National Congress; in Rwanda, a small political cabal enjoying ties with French elites incited the 1994 pogroms. Yet the 'anarchy' and 're-primitivized man' school ignored these histories of outside intervention.

In most mainstream versions, a grasp of history tends to be shallow. Accounts of state failure are peppered with words like 'corrupt' and 'rent-seeking', but rarely dwell on who paid the biggest bribes and whose rents were sought. A little probing into the history of a 'tribe' commonly reveals the decisive role of colonizers in creating tribalism in the first place (Vail 1989). Neglect of such matters cannot be due to ignorance or naivety. For there is no lack of published material, from political biographies to ethnographic history and judicial testimony, about colonial and post-colonial orders.

How Robust were States in the First Place?

In Africa, the colonial state emerged only after an 'unnatural birth' at a rapid tempo, usually at the point of a gun. Colonialism dispensed with pre-colonial states almost everywhere and set about organizing cheap and expedient apparatuses of domination. There was no time for organic growth of formal state institutions (Moore 2001). Bureaucratic power did not extend much beyond administrative outposts. Supervising the extraction of raw materials, taxes and labour, on behalf of foreign elites, was the state's core business.

Lacking effectiveness and legitimacy, the colonial state could hardly qualify as robust according to today's criteria. Legitimacy was merely assumed, never built or tested through public politics. Colonial rulers paid local potentates and groomed their so-called 'traditional' authority. Resistance to the colonial state – mainly in passive forms such as tax avoidance, flight, smuggling, sabotage and irreverent songs and jokes in local languages – developed from an early hour, becoming honourable traditions in many places.

Beyond Africa, states in other peripheral settings were hardly much stronger. Varieties of military, monarchical, commercial and land-owning elites have lorded it over the Balkans, most of Latin America and the southern flanks of Russia, as junior partners in imperial overrule and predation. Institutions of governance, law and public services were ramshackle and corrupt, conditions that local and foreign elites found useful. In polarized and crumbling Nepal, a country 'administered as if it were a large family business, whose only purpose was further to enrich the ruling elite' (Gregson 2002), US and British policy was basically that of arming and otherwise backing that elite, with the chief aim of keeping out rival powers.[13]

In the last decades of colonial rule in Africa, political activism did gain momentum as political parties emerged. But colonial powers forcefully curtailed most public politics. In the post-colony, traditions of anti-politics persisted. Left-leaning and secular parties (such as in Iran and Sudan in the 1950s) were rapidly decimated and repressed by juntas and monarchs acceptable to, if not actively supported by, Western interests. In the Cold War, the risks of leftwing nationalism were judged to be too high to allow space for public, competitive politics. Hence, those civil spaces were closed down, making politics a dead letter.

In the post-colonial or neo-colonial era, ingrained patterns of stunted politics, shallow bureaucracy, ineffective services and passive resistance did not go away. Systems grew along lines set by economies oriented outward, serving foreign interests and their local junior partners – the 'growth without development' path. In their broad outlines, these dysfunctional systems, and the political dead ends to which they were leading, were already clear for observers of countries like Liberia and Côte d'Ivoire in the 1960s (Dumont 1962; Clower 1966).

States as Targets for Demolition

Around 1980, after 50 years in the making, the neoliberal counter-revolution against Keynesian economic policy conquered the commanding heights in Washington and London. The United States began to vilify *most* governments, not just the state–socialist ones. Public management was no longer the solution, but seen as the problem itself. States were held to have no capacity, nor legitimacy, for steering economies. Such tasks were best left to outsiders and their local private associates. A coalition of interests, including neoliberal think tanks, easily enlisted the World Bank and the International Monetary Fund, hitherto ardent backers of state-led (but Western-supervised) growth, as leading agents of market-led dogmas.

Downsizing the State and re-engineering governance became key Western aims. For public services in low-income countries this meant – elimination or reduction of State subsidies for food, medicines and social protection, privatization of State assets, cutbacks in State payrolls, mainly of the education and health staff. Outside the State, some branches of civil society were assigned tasks to curtail State power and provide social services at no cost to the public treasury. Many Western NGOs, buoyed up by a wave of adulation for the non-profit sector, showed little regret at the neglect of public services. Meanwhile, other civil society branches, particularly trade unions, were firmly discouraged, if not eliminated.

European donors went along with this Anglo-Saxon ideological campaign, notwithstanding their nominally greater leverage in the former colonies and in the international financial institutions, where their combined votes exceeded those of the United States.

Economic collapse, disorder and State breakdown have also been planned and executed in cold blood. Western powers pursued their Cold War aims through regime change: the grooming (or assassination) of political leaders, full-scale rollback wars in Southern Africa and Central America, intimidation and removal of political actors from Khartoum to Jakarta. In disintegrating Afghanistan, US policy, for more than a decade, was essentially that of arming and otherwise backing Islamic militants against a Soviet-supported regime. The aim throughout was to weaken and eventually overturn governments prejudicial to US interests. Programmes of economic reform also proved to be massively destructive weapons. Jeffrey Sachs, the US mastermind of economic 'shock therapy' toward Eastern Europe, and the former Soviet Union, has admitted that the chief purposes of Washington's economic remedies were not 'economic' but 'strategic', that is, a geopolitical pursuit of war by other means.[14]

In terms of lost and crippled lives, economic damage and predatory governance, the devastation of the Cold War cannot be calculated with precision, but that it was catastrophic, is beyond doubt (Westad 2006).

How Enabling or Disabling is the Global Setting?

Most conventional accounts of failing states neglect their political economy in a global setting. A view of states as self-contained political islands, from which outside forces are largely excluded, does not match reality. For, in much of Africa and parts of Latin America and Asia, key instruments of sovereign authority have been dissolved or effectively transferred abroad. The control over fiscal and monetary policy has been rendered immune to local influence through legislation and binding international agreements. Governments may ratify their budgets only after approval in Washington DC. Today's typical African polity is, according to some scholars, 'neither African nor state' (Bayart 1999; Englebert 1997).

For governing elites, opportunities for self-enrichment and acquisition of means of repression have never been greater, and the risks lower, than those offered by today's global setting of largely invisible flows. This environment includes the following trends:

(i) Wide access to under-regulated, private and secret banking services that facilitate looting of public assets, tax avoidance and general capital flight;

(ii) Global demand for illicit and 'obnoxious' exports, from hard drugs to body parts, and for services, including the smuggling of people seeking jobs and better prospects;

(iii) Demand for State services enabling businesses and individuals to escape fiscal, banking, labour, environmental and other regulations. This entails commodification of sovereignty (tax paradises, export-processing zones, cut-rate licensing of ships, dumping of dangerous waste, re-casting of government bodies to assure freedom of capital flows and so forth) actively encouraged by Western governments and international financial institutions;

(iv) Feeble international control over booming markets for arms and military services, worsened by State industrial subsidies and by State breakdowns (especially in former Eastern bloc lands);

(v) Competition for oil, heightened by demand from China;

(vi) Corporate resistance to public and obligatory regulation of revenues derived from petroleum, diamonds, tropical hardwoods and other resources;

(vii) Pressures within the foreign aid system to 'move the money'.

These trends have developed on a scale and with a freedom scarcely imaginable before the advent of neoliberalism. Indeed they are the offspring of that idea, emerging in the climate of loosened and realigned public regulation. An illustration of this can be found in the bombing of US Embassies in East Africa in 1998. These could not have been financed and managed so easily without the existence of the unregulated Gulf entrepôt Dubai. The bombers could easily finance their action thanks to Dubai's trade in the East African gemstone tanzanite. A necklace of tanzanite adorning the neck of a Hollywood starlet sent Americans scurrying to jewellery shops. Fashion-driven consumers may not be directly complicit in mass murder, but their wildly glamourized free markets carry enormous risks (ASC 2003).

What are the outcomes? One is the emergence of 'rentier' regimes whose elites are focused on short-term gain and survival (see Moore 2001).[15] National authorities face few incentives to engage with citizens as sources of revenue and of legitimation. The cost – benefit calculus tilts away from domestic realms. The rewards and risks there hardly weigh up against the irresistible financial, military and political opportunities flowing from arrangements with foreign banks, suppliers, buyers, governments and international agencies.

Yet this calculus leads to weaker polities. Where externally derived 'unearned' income trumps internally 'earned' income, the reciprocity between states and citizens tends to collapse. Nigeria, Angola, Azerbaijan and other oil-exporting autocracies are cases in point. Yet even aid monies can resemble oil monies. Aid-dependent autocracies in Malawi and Uganda show many of the same symptoms. Comparative research indicates that states that 'earn' their income in taxes and fees from citizens, are, regardless of the overall level of national income, better providers of public goods than are states dependent on 'unearned' income (Moore, *et al.* 1999).

Into the Abyss

A number of case studies have indicated patterns of socio-economic shifts and shocks that can push countries toward violent conflict. The Cambridge economist Valpy FitzGerald (1999: 59) notes three key factors:

> First, the sudden widening of disparities in income or wealth within a society, which can arise both from the impoverishment of some groups or the enrichment of others. . . .
>
> Second, an increase in uncertainty as to the economic prospects of dominant or subordinate groups or both in terms of real incomes and asset ownership including access to common resources, which generates collective insecurity. . . .
>
> Third, the weakening of the economic capacity of the state to provide public goods, which undermines the legitimacy of the existing administrative system. Lack of financial resources can mean that the government no longer provides all social and territorial groups with an acceptable access to social services and economic infrastructure, nor mediates between 'winners' and 'losers' in the economic development process . . . nor even maintains law and order. In consequence, the 'social contract' no longer receives wide support, and allegiance is transferred to those actors (ranging from security companies to warlords) who can apparently fulfil more limited 'group contracts'.

All three of these factors were clearly at work in ex-Yugoslavia, Sierra Leone, Rwanda and Haiti. In places lacking a 'political contract' of citizen–state reciprocity, rulers can usually buy off discontent, or repress it. In such settings, social and economic disorder itself can become an instrument of politics (see Chabal and Daloz 1999). Interests converge around non-transparent systems of patronage that make disordered, weakened states useful instruments for domestic and foreign elites.

Yet, there are other varieties of disorder, not all of them signifying permanent breakdown and elite aggrandizement. In 2004–2005, for example, upheavals in impoverished Bolivia and the Kyrgyz Republic did not herald state collapse, but rather led to political change driven by public dissatisfaction with the old order. In a world-historical perspective, such episodes are perfectly normal. Attempts to forestall them or to shore up a status quo may, therefore, be doomed, or even perverse.

Distorted Governance

Greedy despots, ethnic feuding and non-delivery of public services certainly exist. But in themselves they do not explain why states weaken and break down. Arguing that states are fragile because they lack effectiveness and legitimacy is circular. Many non-Western states are artefacts of penetration and domination by Western powers for over hundreds of years. The neglect of these histories as well as of the rise of global circuits of trade and finance, labour markets and communication in the mainstream versions leads to obfuscation of the origins and the drivers of disorder and malgovernance.

As it settles and establishes connections everywhere, making the world one place, Western capitalism concentrates on income, wealth and status. Countries become polarized places of 'insiders' and 'outsiders'. Managing the resulting stress and upheaval in peripheral zones falls to nominally sovereign governments there. Yet, to fulfil Western imperatives, these states have seen their sovereign powers and effectiveness cut back, if not dissolved altogether. Real lines of authority and systems of incentives are oriented outward and upward, toward powerful core states. If colonial and Cold war legacies of distorted governance are factored into these cumulative processes, conventional accounts of State failure would look not only unconvincing, but also deliberately misleading.

Solutions

Failed or not, all types of states are vital for today's kind of hegemonic empire. Security strategists like the US conservative Philip Bobbitt (2002) may envision market-led utopias without sovereign states, but most Western geo-strategists would shudder at the thought. States with full juridical sovereignty under international law, as British historian of global politics Peter Gowan points out, have been key to legitimizing the US hegemonic project. As systems of formal rules, states continue serving as 'organizing centres of national capitalism' (Gowan 2004: 97).

States not only facilitate Western economic strategies, but also police and curtail things Western interests do not like: flows of people seen as threatening to Western security, or labour markets or flows of goods deemed undesirable. States in non-Western parts of the world are expected to cooperate as enforcers of these rules. Those unwilling to do so may find themselves redefined as weak or failing and thus, as part of the problem. They then face consequences.

Empire's Industrial Strength

In cases they define as refractory (a 'rogue' state), neoconservatives tend to favour armed intervention, not only to change a specific regime, but also *pour encourager les autres*. Harvard Professor of National Security and Military Affairs Stephen Rosen (2002) puts it as follows: 'The maximum amount of force can and should be used as quickly as possible for psychological impact – to demonstrate that the empire cannot be challenged with impunity... [W]e are in the business of bringing down hostile governments and creating governments favourable to us.'

A relevant question is *how* the United States intends to bring down governments it does not like. Today, the risks of *overt* intervention seem obvious. Whence covert intervention and low-intensity war may be poised for a comeback, after a spell on the benches following its triumphs in savage rollback wars of the 1980s in Southern Africa, Central America and Afghanistan. Countries like Somalia and Sudan, with politicized Islam a ready vehicle for mobilization, seem likely candidates for covert operations. Security doctrines, in any event, are shifting, inspired in part by the discourse of failing states. In 2006, US military strategists began talking in chorus about 'the long war', thus re-branding the 'war on terror' to suit new military mandates and budgetary ambitions. For the NATO powers, according to a Canadian military strategist, future military operations will require the following:

> [A] blend of the political, economic, social, military and technological skills used in unconventional operations to establish whatever the conditions for success might be. As an aside, who is to say that the whole paradigm of conventional versus unconventional warfare will not reverse itself, where the majority of Western military forces of the future will be equipped, organized and trained to fight a terrorist or insurgent foe as matter of routine?. . . The conventional threat might be the terrorists and insurgents, and the unconventional the massed military formations of anybody silly enough to present such a target-rich environment to the devastating abilities of modern military forces. (Leslie 2005: 9)

US military strategists have struggled to devise a coherent doctrine of 'small wars' or 'low-intensity conflict', since at least the 1930s. Yet, as the German political scientist Jochen Hippler (2006) observes, those shifting doctrines fail to resolve fundamental imperial dilemmas: How can US-friendly 'stability' be promoted through destabilization? How can viable, popularly legitimate states be built through US domination over those states?

Faced with these puzzles, some strategists and pundits advocate solutions of an old-fashioned kind. After 11 September 2001, several of them called for a revival of colonial rule (Wolf 2001; Cooper 2002; Mallaby 2002; Fukuyama 2004). As ideologues such as Paul Wolfowitz, a mastermind of the US occupation of Iraq, now command institutions tasked with 'development', the odds of such ambitions getting serious consideration seem to be getting lesser.

Nevertheless, calls to take up the rich man's burden have had, as yet, little effect in high places. As the colonial powers surmised, in the last decades of their rule in Africa, when faced with rising pressure to deliver on their promises of broad improvement for their colonial subjects, today's project of *direct* imperial rule is unaffordable.

Empire Lite

The geo-strategic mainstream's preferences converge around solutions that are less risky and expensive than direct rule for the rich and secure countries anyway. Although obscured by talks of heavy burdens nobly assumed by reluctant but beneficent interveners (see Ignatieff 2003), most risks and expenses are to be borne over a long term, by the targeted states themselves.

Official approaches show a range of options, ranging from institution-building to State-building to nation-building. As in the Cold War, most are premised on containment and not on resolution of problems. Today's proposals are a blend of beefed up justice systems and policing, political re-engineering and 'capacity building'. For the European Union, the preference is for multilateralism and rules enjoying international legitimacy – that is, avoidance of Anglo-Saxon posses and their unilateralist gunslingers. British official discourse emphasizes prevention, stabilization and collaborative action among the G8 countries, European Union, United Nations, NATO, IMF/World Bank and regional groupings such as the African Union (UK Prime Minister's Strategy Unit 2005a).

Official US strategy statements emphasize the long term and call for stronger institutions for security, law and order. Also considered priorities are the setting up of better systems of gaining and analysing information. But in contrast to European approaches, US guidelines tend to read like management checklists. They say almost nothing about preventing crises, and in contrast to some European statements, nothing whatsoever about 'external drivers', such as global financial circuits (USAID 2005; OCRS 2005).

The Humanitarian Impulse

In 1927, the German political thinker and Nazi sympathizer Carl Schmitt (1976: 53) argued: 'The concept of humanity is an especially useful ideological instrument of imperial expansion, and in its ethical-humanitarian form it is a specific vehicle of economic imperialism.' Such acute, if cynical, reasoning has been applied many times over in the twentieth century, with particular frequency in recent decades. US-led sanctions and war against Iraq may have cost hundreds of thousands of lives, which were claimed as necessary for humanitarian purposes.

Yet, imperial drives are not always those of cold calculation. Other impulses can surge up. Images of people suffering in faraway places, if widely broadcast to Western audiences, can leave decision makers with no choice but to act, even if there is no geo-strategic advantage to be gained. An example was the pell-mell American invasion of troubled Somalia in late 1992, following intense media attention to hunger and mayhem there. Launched with the heart-warming motto 'Restore Hope', and lots of military bravado about 'kicking ass', it ended with humiliation, and no hope restored. The humanitarian impulse can sometimes drive realpolitik to such lengths. Not all 'solutions' proffered for State failure can be dismissed as imperial pretexts. Yet, because Western responses to State failure are commonly packaged in the language of humanitarianism, and humanitarian agencies recruited into what are patently military–political adventures, the two impulses are hard to distinguish.[16]

Nation-building tasks normally fall to the aid-and-development industry. Police and military forces sometimes play supporting roles. But talk of failing states has transformed the issue of development into a matter of security. Strategies to tackle pre- and post-conflict situations have brought forth other new missions, agencies and task forces. In mid-2005, the Bush administration created the Office of the Coordinator for Reconstruction and Stabilization in the Department of State as a 'force multiplier' for the government's civilian response to pre- and post-conflict situations. Its job is to make post-conflict states 'democratic and market-oriented', with ambitions no less than to change 'the very social fabric of a nation' (OCRS Director Carlos Pascual quoted in Klein 2005).

As development actors become agents of security, so too are security services becoming development agents. The US military used to be mandated for just one task – combat. But, in November 2005, with little fanfare, the Pentagon announced that 'stability operations are a core US Military mission' that will, henceforth, enjoy 'priority comparable to combat operations'. This recasting of US military doctrine was required to stop terrorist groups from 'setting up shop in so-called ungoverned areas, or failing states, around the world' (Deputy Assistant Secretary of Defense for Stability Operations Jeffrey Nadaner, quoted in Scarborough 2005). 'Winning the peace' may now be part of the military's core business, but winning on socio-political fronts is hardly a sure thing. As Loren Thompson, a US defence expert at the Lexington Institute in Arlington, put it, 'people who are good killers tend not to be good mediators' (quoted in *CSM* 2005).

Problems with the 'Solutions'

Where an ideology of empire has defined the course, it follows that there will be horses selected and bred to run them. In the case of political instability and governance deficits, generations of 'solutions' and 'problems' have followed each other in close, incestuous succession. When combined, these solutions form knots of crippling, even fatal, tensions. Susan Woodward (2005a: 7) assigns the chief causes of State fragility and failure to:

> the domestic consequences of two global trends: one, systematic efforts over the past 25 years to reduce the capacity of states for the purpose of economic liberalization and the other, increased international demands on governments, including a growing reliance on states to manage threats to international security.

Since the late 1970s, market fundamentalist measures to scale back and privatize governance have been promoted as non-negotiable imperatives. Outcomes of market fundamentalism for low-income countries have been, contrary to what was advertised, seriously harmful – slowed, and sometimes negative growth of output,[17] rising joblessness, worsening inequality in income and assets,[18] capital flight, and exposure to economic shocks. These factors reinforce one another, with cumulative effects, including effects on the public sector and governance.

A ground level view comes from the Kyrgyz Republic, where market fundamentalist 'reform' has been exceptionally intense since the early 1990s. A group of villagers told World Bank researchers:

> Well-being is what we had in the past; we had enough money then, prices were low, health care was free, and doctors were very polite. Education for children was free too. People respected each other. There were a lot of children and youths. Everybody had a job, wages were paid on time, nobody's rights were abused and nobody wanted to leave town. . . . Poverty results in suicide, hunger, death, lack of money, lack of hope. Things are getting worse everyday. People are afraid of starvation, lack of heating, ethnic unrest. People bite one another like dogs. (Rysakova, *et al.* 2002: 285)

Outcomes for State capacities and political legitimacy in low-income countries have likewise been, on balance, negative. At the behest of Western donors, public institutions have been squeezed by austerity budgets, segmented incoherently into hundreds of projects, by-passed by special management units, NGOs and consulting firms, and robbed of their best managers and technicians by foreign firms and agencies.

Bleeding States Dry

The Western insistence that the states part with their money has further weakened state capacities. With exceptions such as occupied Iraq and Afghanistan, low-income countries are expected to regard the repayment of their foreign debt as their highest priority. This drain on public revenues can be crippling. It discourages private investment and vital investment in public infrastructure that investors require. Inevitably, debt affects domestic politics. A recent update of the 'debt boomerang' draws two conclusions: 'Heavy debts make it difficult for governments to prevent and recover from conflict [and] . . . pressure governments to impose austerity policies that have resulted in riots and violent police crackdowns' (Anderson, *et al.* 2005: 22–23).

Western imperatives divest poor states of their money in other ways. Such states typically depend on trade taxes for a quarter to a third of their revenue. Yet international financial institutions have compelled them to shift tax burdens from external trade to internal consumption, such as through the Value Added Tax. Such measures were supposed to leave governments fiscally no worse off, but they have proven to be pure swindles. Reviewing data since 1975, two IMF economists concluded in 2005 that 'low income countries . . . very largely failed to recover from domestic sources such revenue as they have lost from trade reform' (Baumsgaard and Keen 2005: 18). The poorer the country, the less revenue its government recovered.

Legacies of Bad Ideas

With self-reliance disallowed, governments in low-income countries have to rely even more on donors for loans, grants and policy formulas. And as the World Bank's own research has shown, many of its standard ideas are unfit for human consumption. In 2005, after decades of actively and coercively imposing strategies to promote agrarian exports, a major World Bank publication concluded that a 'development strategy based on agricultural commodity exports is likely to be impoverishing in the current agricultural policy environment' (Aksoy and Beghin 2005: 3). Detailed studies confirm the kinds of catastrophes that can occur where donors rule. A 1998 internal evaluation of World Bank efforts in Malawi, for example, concluded that 'the Bank's approach to Malawi . . . impoverished the smallholder sector' (WBOED 1998: 2). In other words, the World Bank made millions of poor people even poorer.

Behind these imposed formulas is an arrogance of power, a belief that 'the ten best World Bank economists can't be wrong', and donor officials' complete exemption from punishment if policies fail or do outright harm. Being driven by ideology, attitudes of intellectual invincibility and juridical impunity, it is, therefore, unsurprising that Western officials have imposed policies without any serious consideration of, let alone respect for, actual problems.

Governance without Politics

Weak states and politics have frequently been made weaker through calculated efforts directed from Washington. Meeting resistance to their structural adjustment programmes, the citadels of the foreign aid system set about, in the 1980s, to empower central banks and finance ministries and insulate those economic control rooms from domestic politics. This meant sidelining legislatures. Deprived of any real powers over budgets and economic policy, parliaments were allowed to determine such things as public holidays and the choice of national anthems. Development choices are, in any case, effectively removed from public debate.

One factor strongly predictive of State failure, according to the US State Failure Task Force, may have gained destructive power, thanks to this re-engineering of governance. Late in the 1990s, the World Bank and others tempered their enthusiasm for rolling back the public sector, and for neutralizing legislatures. But, by then, much of the damage had already been done.

While political accountability has been oriented upward and outward, to foreign economic actors and aid systems, downward accountability has been limited largely to hollow, manipulated elections. This has weakened government legitimacy and authority, already dented by poor performance in the delivery of healthcare, education and other public goods. Citizens are also broadly aware of elite self-enrichment through self-dealing in the privatization of public assets. The decline of State services and legitimacy is further undercut by reduced tax effort. When combined with rising insecurity, as freelance militias and criminal gangs fill the vacuum left by poorly supported, corrupt and abusive police or soldiers, the political class is almost guaranteed the loss of public confidence.

Such trends hardly favour the emergence of open politics, let alone a sense of a 'political community'. Where all political parties offer the same economic formulas, and thus, differ only by ethnic affiliation or by the personalities of the 'big men' leading them, competitive politics can be unattractive and even dangerous. Organizations of 'civil society' (selectively supported from abroad) may pre-empt space for indigenous local politics. Hence the observation that in a fragile political setting there may be 'too much civil society, too little politics' (Langohr 2004).

Frequently missing in mainstream solutions are means to stop or reverse the cumulative, self-reinforcing damage done to states and societies by powerful outsiders' intrusive and coercive practices.[19] Economic insecurity can not only damage social trust and solidarity ('People bite one another like dogs'), but also tease out fears and resentments ripe for political mobilization – against State authorities and especially against people of other ethnicities and/or religious persuasions. It is no accident that most of the countries high on the lists of fragile and failing states, such as that of the Fund for Peace/Foreign Policy (2005), have been prime targets of orthodox economic programmes.

The Garbage Can

These programmes' catastrophic outcomes are now better documented and even acknowledged at the commanding heights of the foreign aid system that had imposed them. Hence the advent of new, 'failsafe' versions, with a poverty focus, local 'ownership' enhanced by consultation with 'civil society' and so forth. To end the pretence that the poorest countries will someday repay their official debts, Western powers have responded with modest efforts at debt relief incommensurate with the problems at hand.[20] Such shifts of accent may sometimes offer openings at the margins, but essentials of the market fundamentalist solution – economies and polities subordinated to foreign actors – are retained (see, for example, Gottschalk 2005).

In this, the careers of many mainstream formulas fit the 'garbage can model' of public policy-making. This is a chaotic and wasteful pattern seen among poorly regulated organizations. First, problems to be tackled are identified in unclear or conflicting ways, commonly because they are defined only in terms of the solutions on offer. Second, concrete ways and means to produce desired policy outcomes are poorly understood. Third, those responsible for policy come and go continually, arriving cohorts routinely disparage the formulas and 'solutions' of the outgoing cohorts. No promoter of a solution can be held to account if the solution fails or backfires; indeed most policy mandarins are rewarded. Cleaning up the mess is somebody else's problem.

There is little to suggest that things might go differently for fragile states. A 2005 internal assessment of World Bank effectiveness in 'Low Income Countries Under Stress' concluded that Bank programme designs and supervision were not up to the job. In essence, the Bank showed little respect for the depth and complexity of problems it claimed to address (WBOED 2005: 15). The record of the IMF is even worse. Yet, despite such criticism, and claims that the aid system has abandoned the coercive 'Washington Consensus', there are no signs of major departures from neoliberal formulas. For the time being, decent jobs and public services will remain aspirations, not programmes for the here-and-now.

In prospect then is a continual stream of experimental 'solutions' that generate new problems, reinforce old ones, and deflect attention from the chronic, powerful drivers of State fragility at global levels. It is to those upper levels, where no one can be effectively held to account, that much power and authority have been relocated.

Militarized Protectorates

From Southeast Asia to Central America to Africa, imperial adventures in the twentieth century spawned insurgencies and counter-insurgencies. These included botched decolonization, local sub-imperial grabs of territories, and autocratic regimes (Noriega, Milosevic, the Taliban) that later seemed no longer so useful for the Western powers that had supported them in the first place. The pretexts for installing protectorates have been many, and highly disputed. But there is no doubt that managing protectorates is today a major given in world politics.

Armed takeovers to shore up weak states has only seldom been the geostrategists' method of choice. Yet today, military–civilian trusteeship under multilateral auspices has many precedents, ranging from deployment of short-term task forces (for example, UN in Cambodia in 1991–1993, a series of UN missions in Haiti from 1993 onward) to direct rule (for example, Kosovo since 2000, and the UN forces in East Timor in 1999–2002).

For the United States, an important advantage of multilateral intervention and protectorate governance is to bring other Western powers and, in some cases, the United Nations, into its strategies. Indirect rule through such configurations helps lower risks and costs in US lives and money. And they can help reproduce and re-legitimize US hegemony, not only over non-Western, but also over other Western nations.[21]

Multilateral takeovers have eased transitions to political independence in a few cases such as Namibia and East Timor.[22] Yet there emerge recurring patterns of failure which include:

(i) military collaboration blind to its violence-inducing effects, for example, as inequalities, collective humiliation and counter-violence grow worse;[23]

(ii) post-conflict demobilization efforts guided by norms of cheapness and expediency, not through decent employment or other means of social inclusion;

(iii) underestimation and relative neglect of formal and informal capacities for continued violence, and of needs for fundamental transformation of state–citizen relations;[24]

(iv) the destabilizing and corrupting force of 'disaster capitalism' seen in many post-conflict settings – an updated version of market fundamentalist 'shock therapy'.

The case of Bosnia–Herzegovina illustrates how protectorates can be driven into dead ends. Run under a consortium of Western foreign ministries since 1995, Bosnia has become an aid-driven colony suffering 'disaster capitalism' with attendant corruption and poverty. In the ten years since the war, employment has stagnated at about 60 per cent of pre-war levels. For poor people the main options have been precarious informal livelihoods or emigration. Although its policies have been dominant, the World Bank blames the mess on 'powerful interest groups' including criminal gangs and trade unions. The UNDP, by contrast, identifies the main source of Bosnia's economic malaise in an imposed ideology, particularly a macro-economic orthodoxy based on 'doctrinaire' criteria, 'part of a haphazard and inconsistent "shock therapy" programme'. The UNDP sees viable alternatives, involving domestic markets and demand-led development, but concludes that 'Bosnia–Herzegovina has been prevented from doing so by the policy of the "internal" international community' (UNDP 2003: 94).

Nevertheless, proposals for a bigger, bolder trusteeship are receiving wider attention.[25] These are commonly coupled with telling criticisms of expediency-driven, short-term solutions that have proven to be no solutions at all. Two Stanford University academics advocate well-financed, long-term neo-trusteeship for failed states, not under impartial UN auspices, but under that of a 'lead state' or regional organization (Fearon and Laitin 2004). Another US political scientist (Paris 2004) starts from a critique of capitalism and the incompatibility of market forces and stability, but arrives at a similarly authoritarian brand of trusteeship.

Conclusion

This chapter has sketched the rise of an idea that, while driven by dubious intentions, refers to real things. Geo-strategists' talk about failing states may be likened, using a poetic paraphrase, to ideological gardens with real frogs in them. For the wretchedness visited upon millions, whose states and public orders have decayed or imploded, has been real. That such unnecessary human suffering can trigger genuine altruism and expressions of solidarity is not in doubt. Yet the mainstream paradigm of state failure relegates citizens to the sidelines; indeed they and their leaders get most of the blame for their misfortunes. Among Western geo-strategists, State failure ignores global history in the service of an idealized global future favouring Western interests. Thus the idea often does provide pretexts for powerful outsiders to impose 'solutions' that lead to the very things that weaken states and public order – inequality, exclusion, an impoverished public sector and illegitimate governance.

Will the idea of failing states be around by the year 2010? This will depend not on its power to explain crises and generate effective responses. This chapter has argued that the idea is seriously flawed in both these respects. Rather, its longevity will depend on its power to keep animating coalitions across powerful diplomatic, military, financial, NGO and media blocs. Yet, as it continues to license these blocs' global reach, and to mask their own roles in disorder and maladministration, the idea is unlikely to gain endorsement in the subaltern lands it purports to describe.

Notes

1 Thanks to Susan George for this reference.

2 Together with other contributions to a book like this, about rationales for empire, this chapter starts from a premise that ideas matter. Ideas can constitute interests. If interests underlying them attract a sufficient coalition, then ideas can become real, gaining hands and feet. A prominent theorist of international politics, Alexander Wendt, argues that we should 'begin our theorizing about international politics with the distribution of ideas, and especially culture, in the system, and then bring in material forces, rather than the other way around. The importance of this ultimately lies in perceived possibilities for social change' (Wendt 1999: 371).

3 In this a prevailing ideology in Washington resembles that of the German political philosopher Carl Schmitt (1888–1985). This authoritarian thinker, once regarded as the 'crown jurist' for the Nazi movement, emphasized the unity of political leaders and *volk*, the pointlessness of parliamentary democracy, and the importance of identifying and opposing enemies, mainly the foreign 'other'.

4 Drives to intervene are not, of course, confined only to big powers. Sub-regional powers have also intervened in neighbouring countries to 'restore order', such as in 1997, when Angola deployed troops in Congo–Brazzaville, and in 1998, when South Africa invaded Lesotho.

5 Besteman (2005: 239), footnotes 2 and 3 cite several other writers.

6 One such taxonomy (Gros 1996) included: 'Anarchic state' (Somalia); 'Anaemic state' (energy sapped by counterinsurgency groups – Haiti); 'Phantom or Mirage state' (semblance of authority – Congo Zaire); 'Captured State' (which only represents part of the polity, like Rwanda and Burundi), and 'Aborted state' (failed even before consolidated – Bosnia and Angola).

7 The Security Strategy pays more attention to 'rogue' states, since these promote global terrorism. Rogue states are recognizable in that they 'brutalize their own people and squander their national resources for the personal gain of the rulers; display no regard for international law, threaten their neighbours, and callously violate international treaties to which they are party; are determined to acquire weapons of mass destruction, along with other advanced military technology, to be used as threats or offensively to achieve the aggressive designs of these regimes; sponsor terrorism around the globe; and reject basic human values and hate the United States and everything for which it stands.' (US Government, 2002: 14).

8 Official views in Europe often echo this perspective. A semi-official Dutch policy body, the Advisory Council on International Affairs concludes: 'State failure is chiefly the work of people. . . . Power holders in the country choose to misuse their position in the state in favour of themselves and their group. They thereby undermine the state structure until it disintegrates.' (AIV–CAVV 2004: 92).

9 See: http://www.worldbank.org/research/conflict/papers/civilconflict.htm

10 This groups has since been re-baptized as the Task Force on Political Instability.

11 This study draws on a variety of academic research projects including the *World Conflict and Human Rights Map* produced by a study centre at Leiden University in the Netherlands.

12 See Bringa (2005) and Besteman (2005) for telling critiques of Kaplan's writings.

13 Thanks to Praful Bidwai for calling attention to the example of Nepal.

14 About collapse in the Soviet Union and eastern Europe, a probing television interviewer drew from Sachs the statement that Washington's chief purpose, pursued

through the IMF and USAID, was not to revive those countries' economies, but to 'finish off' the Cold War agenda. BBC *Hardtalk*, 22 January 2003.

[15] Unsurprisingly, business elites in *peripheral countries* with weak states usually shun the long, risky path of local investment/accumulation. In this they follow today's economic elites in *core countries*, where the attractions of the casino economy of stock-market capitalism generates 'a central contradiction of "actually existing neoliberalism": its inability to promote strong accumulation.' (Duménil and Lévy 2004: 264).

[16] In the 1990s, a debate erupted about the harnessing of humanitarianism in the service of geopolitics. The issue is hardly new. In 1918, the US Government secretly began planning 'regime change' against the Bolsheviks in Russia. The plan involved both military action and medical and food aid. President Woodrow Wilson received the following cynical counsel from his Secretary of State: 'Armed intervention to protect the humanitarian work . . . would be much preferable to armed intervention before this work had begun.' Cited in Williams (1973: 94).

[17] More than four out of every ten low-income countries showed negative per capita growth rates in the period 1980–2002 (Milanovic 2005), in contrast to their much stronger performances in prior decades. Catastrophic economic performances in the former Soviet republics and southeast Europe also illustrate these effects. Economists affiliated with the World Bank (Milanovic 2005 and Easterly 2005) conclude that IFI programmes have had *no positive effects* on recorded growth.

[18] A main theme of Chua (2004).

[19] An exception was the response of the Royal African Society, London, to the crescendo of plans and promises to spend more for Africa; in 2005, it issued 'A Message to World Leaders: What about the Damage We Do to Africa?' The message: 'It's not just about thinking up good things we should do to Africa – its about the bad things we should stop doing.' See http://www.royalafricansociety.org.

[20] See, for example, a major study of debt relief efforts (1990–1999) carried out by the Dutch Foreign Ministry's Policy and Operations Evaluation Department (Netherlands Ministry of Foreign Affairs 2003).

[21] Thanks to Achin Vanaik for drawing attention to these aspects of multilateral rule.

[22] Frequently mentioned as a triumph of peacemaking, Mozambique's 'civil war' was largely a calculated rollback war. This was demonstrated in October 1992, when fighting came to a prompt end, as Pretoria, not the insurgent forces, decided that enough was enough.

[23] Detailed in the case of Rwanda by Uvin (1998); see also Schnabel and Ehrhart (2006).

[24] In today's Afghanistan, for example, 'the focus of the international community has been misplaced. In particular, the pressure of donors on the Ministry of the Interior has been nowhere near as strong as that exerted over the Ministry of Finance' (Giustozzi 2004).

[25] See, for example, Nossel (2003), advocating UN Trusteeship Council control over Liberia, a country that, as of 2006, showed signs of political revival without Bosnia-like trusteeship.

References

AIV–CAVV (2004), *Falende Staten: Een Wereldwijd Verantwoordelijkheid*, report no. 35, May (The Hague: Advisory Council on International Affairs–Advisory Committee on Issues of Public International Law).

ASC, African Studies Centre, Leiden (2003), *Failed and Collapsed States in the International System*, December, Center of Social Studies (Coimbra University), CIP–FUHEM (Madrid) and Transnational Institute (Amsterdam), http://www.tni.org/reports/failedstates.pdf.

Aksoy, M. Ataman and John C. Beghin (eds) (2005), *Global Agricultural Trade and Developing Countries* (Washington DC: The World Bank).

Anderson, Sarah, *et al.* (2005), *Debt Boomerang 2005: How Americans Would Benefit from*

Cancellation of Impoverished Country Debts, Washington DC, Institute for Policy Studies (Discussion Draft, 27 October).

Baumsgaard, T. and M. Keen (2005), 'Tax revenue and (or?) trade liberalization', *IMF Working Paper* 05/112.

Bayart, Jean-Francois (1999), 'Africa in the world: A history of extraversion', *African Affairs*, Vol. 99, No. 395.

Besteman, Catherine (2005), 'Why I Disagree with Robert Kaplan', in C. Besteman and H. Gusterson (eds) *Why America's Top Pundits Are Wrong: Anthropologists Talk Back* (Berkeley: University of California Press): 83–101.

Bobbitt, Philip (2002), *The Shield of Achilles: War, Peace and the Course of History* (London: Allen Lane).

Bringa, Tone (2005), 'Haunted by the Imaginations of the Past', in C. Besteman and H. Gusterson (eds), *Why America's Top Pundits Are Wrong: Anthropologists Talk Back* (Berkeley: University of California Press): 60–82.

CED, Le Conseil Economique de la Défense (2004), *Présentation et programme de travail 2004–2005*, http://www.defense.gouv.fr/sites/ced/

Chabal, Patrick and J.P. Daloz (1999), *Africa Works: Disorder as Political Instrument* (Oxford: James Currey).

Chua, Amy (2004), *World on Fire: How Exporting Free Market Democracy Breeds Ethnic Hatred and Global Instability* (New York: Anchor).

Clower, Robert (1966), *Growth Without Development: An Economic Survey of Liberia* (Evanston: Northwestern University Press).

Commission on Weak States and US National Security (2004), *On the Brink: Weak States and US National Security* (Washington DC: Center for Global Development).

Cooper, Robert (2002), 'Why we still need empires', *The Observer*, 7 April.

CSM, *Christian Science Monitor* (2005), 'New military goals: "win the peace"', 16 December.

Duffield, Mark (2001), *Global Governance and the New Wars: The Merging of Development and Security* (London: Zed Books).

——— (2006), Remarks at seminar on 'Peacebuilding Processes and State Failure Strategies', Centro de Estudos Sociais, University of Coimbra, Portugal, 31 March.

Duménil, Gérard and Dominique Lévy (2004), 'The Nature and Contradictions of Neoliberalism', in Leo Panitch, *et al.* (eds), *The Globalization Decade* (London: Merlin Press).

Dumont, René (1962), *L'Afrique noire est mal partie* (Paris: Éd. Du Seuil).

Easterly, William (2005), 'What Did Structural Adjustment Adjust?: The Association of Policies and Growth With Repeated IMF and World Bank Adjustment Loans', *Journal of Development Economics,* Vol. 76, No. 1, February: 1–263.

Economist, The (2002), 'A Survey of America's World Role', 29 June.

Englebert, Pierre (1997), 'The Contemporary African State: Neither African nor State', *Third World Quarterly*, Vol. 18, No. 4: 767–75.

European Union (2003), *A Secure Europe in a Better World: European Security Strategy*, December, EU, Brussels, http://ue.eu.int/uedocs/cmsUpload/78367.pdf.

Evans, Richard (1987), *Death in Hamburg: Society and Politics in the Cholera Years, 1830–1910* (Oxford: Clarendon Press).

Fearon, James and David Laitin (2004), 'Neotrusteeship and the Problem of Weak States', *International Security*, Vol. 28, No. 4: 5–43.

Ferguson, James (1990), *The Anti-Politics Machine: 'Development' Depoliticization, and Bureaucratic Power in Lesotho* (Cambridge: Cambridge University Press).

FitzGerald, Valpy (1999), 'Global Linkages, Vulnerable Economies and the Outbreak of Conflict', *Development*, Vol. 42, No. 3: 65–70.

Fukuyama, Francis (2004), *State Building: Governance and Order in the Twenty-First Century* (New York: Profile Books).

Fund for Peace/Foreign Policy (2005), 'The Failed States Index', July–August, http://www.foreignpolicy.com/

Giustozzi, A. (2004), '"Good" State vs. "Bad" Warlords? A Critique of State-Building Strategies in Afghanistan' (London: Crisis States Programme, LSE), http://www.crisisstates.com/Publications/wp/wp51.htm.

Goldberg, Jonah (2002), 'Baghdad Delenda Est, Part Two: Get On With It', *National Review* online, 23 April.

Gottschalk, Ricardo (2005), 'The Macro Content of PRSPs: Assessing the Need For a More Flexible Macroeconomic Policy Framework', *Development Policy Review*, Vol. 23, No. 4: 419–42.

Gowan, Peter (2004), 'The American Campaign for Global Sovereignty', in Leo Panitch, *et al.* (eds), *The Globalization Decade: A Critical Reader* (London: Merlin Press): 295–321.

Gregson, Jonathan (2002), *Blood Against the Snows: The Tragic Story of Nepal's Royal Dynasty* (London: Fourth Estate).

Gros, J.-G. (1996), 'Towards a Taxonomy of Failed States in the New World Order: Decaying Somalia, Liberia, Rwanda and Haiti', *Third World Quarterly*, Vol. 17, No. 3.

Guyatt, Nicholas (2000), *Another American Century?* (London: Zed Books).

Hippler, Jochen (2006), *Counterinsurgency and Political Control: US Military Strategies Regarding Regional Conflict*, INEF Report, 81/2006 (Duisburg: Institute for Development and Peace, University Duisburg–Essen).

Ignatieff, Michael (2003), 'The American Empire (Get Used to It)', *The New York Times Magazine*, 5 January (cover story).

Jackson, Robert H. (1990), *Quasi-States: Sovereignty, International Relations and the Third World,* Cambridge Studies in International Relations (Cambridge: Cambridge University Press).

Kahn, Herman and A. Wiener (1967), *The Year 2000: A Framework for Speculation on the Next Thirty-Three Years* (New York: Macmillan).

Klein, Naomi (2005), 'The Rise of Disaster Capitalism', *The Nation*, 2 May.

Koonings, Kees and Dirk Kruijt (eds) (2004), *Armed Actors: Organized Violence and State Failure in Latin America* (London: Zed Books).

Langohr, Vickie (2004), 'Too Much Civil Society, Too Little Politics', *Comparative Politics*, Vol. 36, No. 2, January: 181–204.

Leslie, Andrew (2005), *Thoughts on the Future of the Canadian Forces* (Montreal: Institute for Research on Public Policy), http://www.irpp.org/events/archive/jun05NGO/leslie.pdf.

Mallaby, Sebastian (2002), 'The Reluctant Imperialist', *Foreign Affairs,* March–April.

Milanovic, Branko (2005), *Why Did the Poorest Countries Fail to Catch Up?* (New York: Carnegie Endowment For International Peace), http://www.carnegieendowment.org/pubs.

Moore, Mick (2001), *Political Underdevelopment: What Causes 'Bad Governance'*, March (Brighton: The Institute of Development Studies).

Moore, Mick, *et al.* (1999), *Polity Qualities: How Governance Affects Poverty* (Brighton: The Institute of Development Studies).

Netherlands Ministry of Foreign Affairs (2003), *Results of International Debt Relief 1990–1999*, Policy and Operations Evaluation Department, IOB Evaluation No. 292 (The Hague: Netherlands Ministry of Foreign Affairs).

Nossel, Suzanne (2003), 'A Trustee For Crippled States', *The Washington Post*, 25 August.

OCRS, Office of the Coordinator for Reconstruction and Stabilization (2005), *Post-Conflict Reconstruction Essential Tasks*, April (Washington DC: US Department of State).

Paris, Roland (2004), *At War's End: Building Peace after Civil Conflict* (Cambridge: Cambridge University Press).

Rosen, Stephen (2002), 'The Future of War and American Military', *Harvard Magazine*, May–June, Vol. 104, No. 5.

Rotberg, Robert (2002), 'The New Nature of Nation-State Failure', *The Washington Quarterly*, Summer.

Rysakova, J., *et al.* (2002), 'Kyrgyz Republic: Crumbling Support, Deepening Poverty', in D. Narayan and P. Petesch (eds), *Voices of the Poor: From Many Lands* (Washington DC: The World Bank and Oxford University Press).

Scarborough, Rowan (2005), 'Nation-building elevated', *The Washington Times*, 14 December.

Schattschneider, E.E. (1960), *The Semi-Sovereign People: A Realist's View of Democracy in America* (New York: Holt, Rinehart and Winston).

Schmitt, Carl, (1976), *The Concept of the Political* (translation) (New Brunswick: Rutgers University Press).

Schnabel, Albrecht and Hans-Georg Ehrhart (eds) (2006), *Security Sector Reform and Post-Conflict Peacebuilding* (Tokyo: United Nations University Press).
SFTF, State Failure Task Force (2000), *State Failure Task Force Report: Phase III Findings*, College Park, Maryland.
Torres, Magüi Moreno and Michael Anderson (2004), *Fragile States: Defining Difficult Environments for Poverty Reduction*, PRDE Working Paper 1, Poverty Reduction in Difficult Environments Team, Policy Division, UK Department for International Development.
UK Prime Minister's Strategy Unit (2005a), *Investing in Prevention: An International Strategy to Manage Risks of Instability and Improve Crisis Response*, February (London: Cabinet Office).
——— (2005b), *CRI Decision Support and Risk Assessment,* Countries at Risk of Instability Programme (London: Cabinet Office).
UN Department of Economic and Social Affairs (2005), *Development Challenges in Sub-Saharan Africa and Post-Conflict Countries*, Report of the Committee for Development Policy on the seventh session, 14–18 March.
UNDP, United Nations Development Programme (2003), *Bosnia and Herzegovina Human Development Report* (New York: UNDP).
USAID, US Agency for International Development (2005), *Fragile States Strategy* (Washington DC: USAID), http://www.usaid.gov.
US Department of Defense (2005), *Directive Number 3000.05 on Military Support for Stability, Security, Transition and Reconstruction Operations*, http://www.nps.edu/CSRS/PDF/DoDD300005.pdf.
US Government (2002), *The National Security Strategy of the United States of America*, http://www.whitehouse.gov/nsc/nss.html.
USNIC, US National Intelligence Council (2004), *Mapping the Global Future, Report of the National Intelligence Council's 2020 Project*, Washington DC, www.cia.gov/nic.
Uvin, Peter (1998), *Aiding Violence: The Development Enterprise in Rwanda* (West Hartford: Kumarian Press).
Vail, Leroy (ed.) (1989), *The Creation of Tribalism in Southern Africa* (London: James Currey).
Wendt, Alexander (1999), *Social Theory of International Politics* (Cambridge: Cambridge University Press).
Westad, Odd Arne (2006), *The Global Cold War: Third World Interventions and the Making of Our Times* (Cambridge: Cambridge University Press).
Wiedenhoff, Andreas and Javier Nino–Perez (2005), *State Failure: A Variety of Opportunities to Act*, EU internal document for a meeting of EU Political Directors in Luxembourg, January.
Williams, William Appleman (1973), 'American Intervention in Russia 1917–1920', in *History as a Way of Learning* (New York: New Viewpoints).
Wolf, Martin (2001), 'The need for a new imperialism', *Financial Times*, 9 October.
Woodward, Susan L. (2005a), 'Introduction to the Workshop', *Workshop on State Failure: Reframing the International Economic and Political Agenda*, Program on States and Security, Ralph Bunche Institute, Graduate Center, City University of New York, 9–10 May, http://web.gc.cuny.edu/ralphbuncheinstitute/pss/papers/Woodward_memo.pdf.
——— (2005b), *Fragile States: Exploring the Concept*, paper for international seminar, 'Failing States or Failed States? The Role of Development Models', FRIDE, Madrid, 12 December, http://www.fride.org/eng.
WBOED, World Bank Operations Evaluation Department (1998), *Malawi: The World Bank and the Agricultural Sector, Impact Evaluation Report*, No. 17898 (Washington DC: The World Bank).
——— (2005), *Improving the World Bank's Development Effectiveness: What Does Evaluation Show?* (Washington DC: The World Bank).

The Internationalization of the War on Drugs

Illicit Drugs as a Moral Evil and a Useful Enemy

David Bewley–Taylor and Martin Jelsma

To the amazement of the older nations of the earth, we have . . . enacted new legal prohibitions against the oldest vices of man. We have achieved a body of statutory law which testifies unreservedly to our aspiration for an absolutely blameless . . . life on earth.

Walter Lippmann, 'The Underworld as Servant', in *Forum*, 1931

Success in this mission area will not only stem the flow of illegal narcotics on US streets, but also deny a source of funding that terrorist groups may use to finance their operations.

General Bantz J. Craddock, US Army Commander, SouthCom, 2005

These operations met none of the goals or objectives outlined in the policies that called for these military endeavors. Interdiction operations aimed at the illegal drug supply achieve nothing of consequence. . . . Further militarization of the drug war is not the answer. . . . It's time to take the responsibility for America's drug war from the hands of the military generals and give it to the Surgeon General.

Lt. Col. Stephen P. Howard, US Air Force, 2001

Introduction

For nearly 20 years now much attention has been devoted to understanding the multiple realignments produced by the end of the Cold War. Since 2000, focus has naturally shifted towards the 'diplomacy' of George W. Bush. Influenced greatly by neoconservative thinking, the Bush administration's general disregard for the widely accepted role of the United Nations in post-Cold War transnational affairs has been emblematic of the unilateralist impulse underpinning US foreign policy during his Presidency, especially his first term. Indeed, even before the 'allied liberation' of Iraq fractured the international community, Washington's selective approach towards international law, notably its withdrawal from the Kyoto treaty, its repudiation of the 1972 ABM treaty, and the unprecedented 'unsigning' of the convention establishing an International Criminal Court, had put great stress on US relations with its traditional allies, as well as on the functioning of the multilateral system itself.

The aim of this chapter is to explore a facet of US foreign policy that has had a profound, and often damaging, impact on relations with many countries around the world, yet within the current international context has remained paradoxically reliant upon the United Nations for both legitimacy and global reach – the long running war on drugs. It explores not only the rationale and negative implications of the very visible militarized US fight against drug production in Afghanistan and Colombia, but also the more low key 'below the radar' policy debates between the United States and other nations within the UN drug control framework. As will be discussed, a growing reluctance by many European states recently, to continue to buy into US style zero-tolerance policies on drug use has resulted in the emergence of transatlantic tensions within the international organization.

The chapter begins by deconstructing the evolution of what has been called the global drug prohibition regime: a US influenced international treaty system based on the 1961, 1971 and 1988 UN drug control conventions. Today the vast majority of world states count themselves as members of this regime (Nadelmann 1990: 503). Yet, by locating contemporary trends within a broad historical context it becomes clear that many European states have been actually reluctant to wholeheartedly embrace the moralist-driven prohibitive philosophy that for nearly a century, the United States has worked so hard to internationalize. Indeed, in the early phases of the development of the current drug control system, inertia from European states did much to thwart US efforts to export its domestic policies to the rest of the world. Even after 1945, when US hegemony ensured considerable success in determining the form of the contemporary system, many European states agreed to adhere to its prohibitive principles and norms, only because drug control was not high enough on the policy agenda to warrant confrontation with Washington.

A similar dynamic has characterized relations between drug producing nations and the United States. While it was President Nixon who first declared the war on drugs, its militarization only began halfway through the 1980s, when the US military were brought in to train personnel for counternarcotics operations in the Andes. From that point until 11 September 2001 the war on drugs proved especially useful in the years between the Cold War and the War on Terror. It bridged an ideological gap in terms of justifying US military operations, bases and interventions abroad.

While this was the case, the end of the Cold War also coincided with, and in some respects produced in many states around the world, a redefinition of national priorities. The spread of HIV/AIDS amongst injecting drug users (IDUs), resentment, especially in South America, towards US conditionality and sovereign states' commitment to the war on drugs, and a growing awareness of the ineffectiveness of repressive anti-drug efforts to reduce the illicit market, have all contributed to an erosion in global support for the US-style zero-tolerance anti-drug ideology. The emergence of more pragmatic and less punitive approaches to the drugs issue, under the banners of 'harm reduction', 'decriminalization' and 'alternative development', have led not only to increased tensions with the United States, but also a weakening of, and the beginnings of possible change in, the current global drug control regime, a process for which 'Europe' may become the epicentre. Yet, in spite of this growing isolation, the regime still retains Washington's full and energetic backing. This is even more so now that neoconservatism influences policy formulation and the Bush administration moves to merge the anti-drugs and anti-terror agendas. Indeed, as we shall see, the two pillars of the war on drugs for the United States still stand tall – its moralist roots and its usefulness to legitimize its military presence and interventions in certain regions.

The Moralistic Impulse

Since the beginning of the twentieth century, influential anti-narcotics groups and individuals within the United States have successfully worked to locate the source of their national drug problems beyond the boundaries of 'American Society'. The intention has been to deflect blame for domestic drug problems and ultimately eliminate behaviour deemed morally unacceptable by the dominant Protestant culture. As the historian David Musto (1999: 248) notes, 'Projection of blame on foreign nations for domestic evils harmonized with the ascription of drug use to ethnic minorities. Both the external cause and the internal locus could be dismissed as un-American.' Indeed, a powerful moralistic impulse certainly underpins the US crusade to export the prohibitive paradigm.

Although US interest in the development and maintenance of an international system for drug control can be explained in part by the desire to limit the flow of illegal drugs into the United States itself, proselytization and the desire for the transnational replication of US style prohibition has remained a constant feature. Contemporary international legislation, embedded in the UN drug control treaties, has gone a considerable way towards realizing this goal. Yet, while UN policies are constructed on the foundations of a long line of US influenced international agreements, it was only the possession of hegemonic superiority that created the political atmosphere necessary for the globalization of US anti-drug ideals.

Acquisition of the Philippines, after the Spanish–American war of 1898, prompted the internationalization of the evolving US doctrine of drug prohibition. With a transnational outlook focused through the lens of exceptionalism, it seemed clear that now the United States as a major global power had a moral duty to rectify what it perceived as the immoral use of narcotics in one of its protectorates. This increased interest overseas actually forced the United States to accelerate the implementation of domestic policies. After all, how could Washington export prohibitive ideals and become an example to the world when its own house wasn't in order? Early recognition of the truly international nature of the drug issue compounded the ever-present evangelical zeal to ensure that the United States embarked upon what was effectively a crusade to attain wide ranging transnational commitments. These, it was hoped, would include not only rules regulating the production, manufacture and trafficking of psychoactive substances deemed to be incompatible with American moral values, but also the prohibition of their use for anything other than medical and scientific purposes. Consequently, for over a century, an eclectic mix of individuals, government agencies and interest groups have sought to influence the legal approach to drug use adopted within the boundaries of sovereign states.

The *League of Nations* Era

Prior to 1945 progress to this end was mixed. Efforts to establish widely accepted transnational legislation and norms concerning the control of certain drugs met with only limited success. Nonetheless, the three decades between the United States' first moves to convene an international meeting on drugs at Shanghai in 1909 and the outbreak of the Second World War in Europe were significant. The often strained work with the League of Nations and its associated drug control apparatus went a long way to determine the paradigmatic guidelines inherited by the post-war UN drug control system.

Indeed, the League's philosophy and accompanying legislation reflected the US preference for supply-side approaches to drug control. Ideologically, this externalization of blame suited the morally inspired United States more than other, particularly European, countries. The League's supply-side bias was in no small measure due to US endeavour. But pragmatic European governments who agreed in principle to the need for some form of regulation of the international drug trade pursued the strategy predominantly because it placed the onus of responsibility on the drug producing states, and thus minimized interference into domestic affairs.

Accordingly, US efforts to outlaw the production and non-medical use of drugs met with a lukewarm response from traditional colonial powers, particularly France, Great Britain, Portugal and the Netherlands, all of which operated lucrative drug monopolies in overseas possessions. Reflecting dissatisfaction with the attitude of the Europeans the Americans referred to them as 'the old opium bloc' and pejoratively called meetings of the League's Opium Advisory Committee the 'smugglers' reunion. According to one historian, the British approach to the opium question reflected 'a mixture of pragmatism, expediency and cultural disdain' (Walker III 1994: 10–11). Prefiguring the wider contemporary debate, as late as 1929, the Dutch saw the US belief that drug smuggling could be completely eliminated in Indonesia as unenforceable.[1]

Differences in attitudes could also be seen within the domestic sphere. In the United States, the influential 1914 Harrison Narcotic Act set the tone for future drug policies. The Act, very much a product of the Progressive era and now widely regarded as the starting point for US drug prohibition, was seen to be a 'routine slap at a moral evil' (Musto 1999: 65). Although debate still surrounds the framer's intent, it was clearly more than the tax and licensing statute introduced by Francis B. Harrison. Furthermore, while the Harrison Act itself left the status of the drug addict unchanged it was not long before energetic lobbying by various anti-narcotics organizations as well as the Treasury

Department forced a series of crucial Supreme Court decisions (Bertram, *et al.* 1996: 69). These saw the Act's original taxation powers enforced in such a way as to limit doctors' use of drugs for the 'maintenance of mere addiction' (Musto 1999: 65, 68).[2] Prohibitionist groups within the United States, thus, successfully transformed what was largely a 'medical model for controlling drug use into a punitive law enforcement paradigm for outlawing drug use through coercion and force' (Bertram, *et al.* 1996: 68).

Meanwhile some European nations explored domestic approaches not based solely on law enforcement and prohibition, casting aside the 'sin and evil' appellations often applied by US counterparts at the time. A 'British System' consisting of a combination of punitive and treatment measures was neatly described as 'policing and prescribing' (Whynes 1991: 2). Other European states also followed their own paths. In Italy, for example, the 1923 Drug Act contained no criminal sentences for the possession or use of drugs and while the 1930 Penal Code stiffened trafficking sanctions, drug use still went largely unpenalized (MacCoun and Reuter 2001: 231).[10] The US moral authoritarianism might have been received more appreciatively in another European era, but in the first decades of the twentieth century most of Europe was culturally on another wavelength. As Walter Lippmann (1967) noted in 1931: 'To the amazement of the older nations of the earth, we have . . . enacted new legal prohibitions against the oldest vices of man. We have achieved a body of statutory law which testifies unreservedly to our aspiration for an absolutely blameless . . . life on earth.' The same author pointed at the criminogenic effects of US Puritanism at the time, attributing the 'high levels of lawlessness' to 'the fact that Americans desire to do so many things which they also desire to prohibit'.

The stories about gangs and mafia expanding control over entire cities in the United States obviously were no inspirational picture for European policy makers:

> The unenforceable laws that attempted to prohibit alcohol, gambling, drugs and commercialized sex also made risks small for the host of politicians, police officers, and gangsters profiting from the newly created illegal markets. America had clearly become a land of criminal opportunity by the 1920s. . . . The repeal of alcohol prohibition was a notable but rare admission in America that moral ideals are no match for human ingenuity and human nature. (Woodiwiss and Bewley–Taylor 2005: 6–7)

Alcohol prohibition in the United States lasted from 1919 to 1933,[3] much of the same period that the United States was busy trying to replicate internationally the same model for drugs through the League of Nations. Understandably, it met with considerable reservations. Thus, despite concerted efforts the lofty expectations concerning the exportation of US style policy were to remain largely unfulfilled. Ironically, this was the case even though many domestic drug control laws within European states were passed to fulfil obligations made at international meetings instigated by various US delegations.[4]

Limited US success can be attributed to a number of other interrelated factors as well. First, for most of the League's lifetime the United States simply lacked sufficient international muscle to dictate its drug control policies and thereby export the concept of prohibition. Secondly, although delimiting international rules regulating the production, manufacture, distribution and use of licit drugs[5] and making efforts to eliminate the trafficking of illicit drugs,[6] the League 'had no real, lasting power to discipline unreasonable nations' (Block 1989: 331). This was a product of the third factor to be considered: a general absence of faith in a collective system. The dominant European nations were unwilling to surrender national sovereignty over domestic drug control or, as noted, even relinquish profitable opium monopolies in their colonies. The combination of all three factors was to result in international legislation that did not impinge upon the principles of national sovereign rights in any significant way.

The League's drug control system, like the United Nation's today, relied upon voluntary adherence. However, in the absence of a widely accepted international norm concerning drug use and crucially the non-existence of a hegemonic actor interested in and capable of encouraging adherence to policies to control it, national drug legislation remained largely the province of individual governments.

While the conditions necessary to facilitate the creation and maintenance of a global prohibitionist norm were missing within the international environment before 1945, the outbreak of war in Europe, and the resulting temporary transfer of the League drug control bodies to Washington were portents of a realignment in the dynamics of the international control movement. It was only after the global balance of power in the post-war world was restructured in favour of the United States that the nation was transformed, from being simply one important player in the League's system, into the driving force behind transnational drug control. Symbolic of this shift was US success in finally persuading Allied nations to terminate opium monopolies, and the imposition of US style drug control polices in the territories of conquered Axis powers, including a Japanese version of the Harrison Act after VJ Day.

US Hegemony and UN Drug Control

By 1945, the United States occupied a newly found position of prominence within the international community as a whole. Its economic, military and political strength ensured the nation played a crucial role in the functioning of the post-war world. The issue of drug control, although apparently not high on the post-war agenda for reconstruction, was consequently an area that was to be greatly affected by the shift in the balance of power away from the established European foci to the United States.

The central role that the United States played in the creation of the United Nations Organization ensured that the wider transition in the global power balance was mirrored in the sphere of international drug control. Although other states were important in the foundation of the United Nations, the Charter was very much the handiwork of the United States (see Bennis 2000: 1–21). Indeed, the Charter 'was perceived as a reasonably accurate reflection of US interests and values and the UN was widely viewed within the US as an important tool for the exercise of the leadership that was expected of the world's pre-eminent power' (Gregg 1999: 5). In viewing the United Nations in this way, the United States set about developing the international system in line with US views on drug control, gaining success unachievable before the acquisition of superpower influence. US prominence in the Organization ensured that US delegations to its policy making body, nowadays called the Commission on Narcotic Drugs (CND), had a considerable impact upon the creation and implementation of the UN system and sought to develop a global regime that reflected its own morally inspired and law enforcement led approach.

This process to internationalize the doctrine of prohibition was an important, but largely ignored, facet of the US quest to determine the contours of new post-war global order and impose self-determined rules upon the international system and sovereign nations within it. It is widely acknowledged that the close of the Second World War saw the United States exploit 'hegemonial stability' to create and sustain multilateral regimes in the fields of trade and money. Both the Bretton Woods monetary system and the open world trade regime, centred on the General Agreement on Tariffs and Trade (GATT), amply demonstrate this fact. While these and other similar regimes enjoy significant attention, the global drug prohibition regime, a product of the same international political environment, remains largely ignored.

The rules and norms of the UN treaty system owe much to the efforts of the United States after the Second World War. US activity between 1945 and the early 1960s certainly moved a considerable way towards the creation of an international control framework anchored to the doctrine of prohibition (see Bewley–Taylor 2001; McAllister 2000, Bruun, *et al.* 1975: 132–48). The US crusade blended well at the time with the Islamic approach to alcohol and drugs dominant in a number of countries in the Middle East, and with anti-colonial sentiments in Asia, in which domestic opium use was in part perceived to be a colonial heritage due to the enforced opening of the opium markets at the time of the highly profitable colonial opium regimes. The period, while marked by both vicious infighting within the United Nations' drug control bureaucracy (McAllister 2000: 156–211) and the chilly dynamics of the Cold War (ibid.: 183; Bewley–Taylor 1999: 147–71), was a crucial stage in the development of a global prohibitionist norm, and the construction of the bedrock of the current regime – the 1961 Single Convention on Narcotic Drugs.

The UN Conventions

The 1961 Single Convention on Narcotic Drugs replaced previous international agreements that had been developing piecemeal since the early years of the twentieth century, but also included new provisions not contained in earlier treaties, creating a stricter zero-tolerance and more prohibitively oriented system for control (McAllister 2000: 204–18; Bewley–Taylor 2001: 136–64). It also extended the existing control systems to include the cultivation of plants that were grown as the raw material of narcotic drugs, thereby placing a special burden on the traditional producing countries. The cultivation and extensive traditional use of opium poppy, coca and cannabis at that time was largely concentrated in Asia, Latin America and Africa. The Single Convention aimed to phase out non-medical use of these plants from the planet in a period of 15 years for opium, to 25 years for coca and cannabis. Traditional use, which included widespread traditional medicinal purposes of all three plants, was defined as 'quasi-medical' practice which had to be terminated.

The Convention was bolstered by an amending Protocol in 1972, and today the regime consists of these instruments plus the 1971 Convention on Psychotropic Substances and the 1988 Convention against Illicit Traffic in Narcotic Drugs and Psychotropic Substances, both of which are based upon the 1961 legislation. The 1971 Psychotropic Convention was conceived in response to the diversification of drugs, and introduces controls over more than a hundred largely synthetic drugs – many of them produced by the pharmaceutical industry – like amphetamine-type stimulants and Ecstasy, barbiturates, hallucinogens, tranquilizers like diazepam, etc. In sharp contrast to the 1961 Convention, the Conference negotiating the 1971 treaty decided to completely leave out control measures for the cultivation or production of psychotropic substances. If the underlying logic of the 1971 Convention would have prevailed at the time of the 1961 Convention, coca would never have become a controlled substance, and many social conflicts in the Andean region since that time would have been prevented. The 1988 Trafficking Convention tightened the control regime significantly by introducing the obligation to criminalize all facets of trade prohibited under the 1961 and 1971 treaties, including them as criminal offences in national legislation punishable with criminal sanctions. It also contains provisions against money-laundering and the diversion of precursor chemicals, and agreements on mutual legal assistance.

Ambiguity within the Conventions as well as different interpretive perspectives on many clauses provides some flexibility, at least on the consumption side of the drug chain, for signatory nations (Krajewski 1999; Dorn and Jamieson 2000; De Ruyver, *et al.* 2002). Yet while there is clearly national variation in policy, the existence of the global drug prohibition regime does a great deal to restrict freedom of action at the national level. A useful way to understand the impact of the regime is to compare it with the domestic situation in the United States between 1919 and 1933. It has been argued that the Single Convention stands in much the same relationship to worldwide drug prohibition that the Eighteenth Amendment and the Volstead Act stood in relation to alcohol prohibition. Just as the Eighteenth Amendment restricted the way US states created alcohol policy, so UN legislation limits the way sovereign states approach drug laws (Levine 2002).

Washington's influence in the formulation and perpetuation of the current regime cannot be underestimated. It is true that other nations also favour the prohibitive zero-tolerance approach to drug policy. These states have formed a curious alliance including, Japan, Sweden, many ex-Soviet states, most Arab and African nations and quite a few Asian countries. It is difficult, however, to imagine any of these countries playing such an influential role within the regime. Yet, as noted earlier, it is also important to recall that the treaty regime does enjoy an impressive level of adherence among all UN member states. This raises an obvious question. Why, while still reluctant to embrace US-style prohibitive approach to the use of certain drugs, have so many nations become Parties to the Conventions? Part of the explanation can be found in the fact that the UN system does much to regulate the licit trade in pharmaceutical drugs. Non-signatory states thus would have significant problems to obtain access to essential medicines such as morphine. Furthermore, 'Governments of all types, all over the world, have also found drug prohibition useful for their own purposes' (Levine 2003: 147–48). The concept provides a rationale for the expansion of police and government powers. The process of demonizing illicit drugs allows state managers to construct a simplistic, and hence politically safe, focus for policies targeting a wide range of complex and ongoing social problems like poverty and crime. Drugs, to quote the title of a book by the Scandinavian authors Nils Christie and Kettil Bruun, can therefore be regarded as 'The Useful Enemy'.[7]

Global Enforcement

These factors, however, do not entirely explain the apparent universal acceptance of a prohibitive norm. The political costs of non-adherence to a UN norm, added with coercive measures applied by the United States, have played an important role.

The image of the United Nations as a benevolent organization has been crucial to the functioning of the global drug prohibition regime. As Inis L. Claude, Jr. (1994: 196) observed, 'While the voice of the United Nations may not be the authentic voice of mankind, it is clearly the best available facsimile thereof, and statesmen have by general consent treated the United Nations as the most impressive and authoritative instrument for the global version of the general will.' By employing rhetoric stating that those drugs defined as illicit are a 'danger to mankind' (*UN Conference* 1964: 300) and that the United Nations' ideals consequently 'transcend the traditional concerns of the international community' (International Conference on Drug Abuse 1988: iii, 1) the supporters of the regime can exert considerable pressure on nations to conform to the established norms of behaviour regarding control policies. States that flout the principles of the regime and refuse or fail to abide by its norms and rules can be labelled as deviants. They thus risk condemnation by those members of the international community who adhere to the recognized standard of behaviour. The 'reputational effects' of non-compliance are important because by reneging on their commitments, under a regime or even deviating from the spirit of the regime, nations are likely to weaken their stature and forfeit potential future gains from cooperation (Keohane

1984: 94). The practice of linking or 'nesting' drug control with other issue areas makes cost and cooperation important concerns. Violating a particular agreement or norm of the regime can have consequences beyond the drug issue and may affect a state's ability to achieve goals elsewhere. States are willing to accept regime rules when they perceive the cost of compliance to be cheaper than non-compliance (see Bewley–Taylor 2001: 171–74).

This issue of cost is heightened when a hegemon is included in the equation. Washington's energetic support for the drug control regime ensures that states are often keen to seek compliance. Today the United States arguably often acts as a global enforcer for the International Narcotics Control Board (INCB). Established by the 1961 Single Convention, one of the Board's key roles is to monitor national compliance with the drug control treaties. It regularly attempts to counter its lack of formal powers by effectively shaming governments into fulfilling what it interprets to be their treaty obligations. Thus, the United States' ongoing interest in the issue effectively gives the United Nations' drug control framework the teeth that international endeavour prior to 1945 had lacked. Deviation can prove costly when US co-operation in other international issue areas is at stake: 'Open defection from the drug prohibition regime would . . . have severe consequences: it would place the defecting country in the category of a pariah "narcostate", generate material repercussions in the form of economic sanctions and aid cut offs, and damage the country's moral standing in the international community' (Andreas 1999: 127–28).

In order to help ensure compliance in its war on drugs the US administration maintains the disciplinary mechanism of drug certification. According to the process, enacted by the US Congress in 1986, countries failing to fully cooperate with US anti-narcotics efforts or not taking sufficient steps on their own to meet the terms of the UN conventions, face mandatory sanctions. These include not only the withdrawal of most US foreign assistance, but also US opposition to loans those countries seek from multilateral development banks. The administration can waive sanctions against a country, if it determines that it is in the 'vital national interests' of the United States (Spencer 1998). Countries that have appeared on the list of de-certified nations include Burma, Afghanistan, Colombia, Nigeria, Guatemala, Mexico, and most recently, Venezuela. The selection procedure for inclusion in one of the categories of the certification system is highly politicized, and mainly works as a threat to coerce countries to comply with specific US demands. For example, each year Peru is forced to eradicate a specified number of hectares of drug crops. Also, when cannabis decriminalization appeared on the political agenda in Jamaica, that country was required to abstain from adopting any such legislation. Extradition of national citizens to the United States from countries like Peru and Jamaica to face drug charges is also required. Even the Netherlands once appeared on the certification list in the category of 'emerging threats' together with North Korea and Cuba, when the United States apparently needed an additional tool to influence Dutch decisions about the US Forward Operation Location (FOL) on Curaçao and Aruba (see below), and the extradition of Dutch citizens accused in the United States of selling Ecstasy.

The certification mechanism is widely resented, especially in Latin America and it has become a constant nuisance on the agenda of American Summits and in the Organization of American States. The CICAD, the drug control body of the OAS has, for that reason, developed its own multilateral evaluation mechanism (MEM), in which US performance is measured against the same criteria as other nations. It seems likely that it will become more difficult for the United States to maintain this unilateral instrument, and this is perhaps why its coercive function is being increasingly transplanted to bilateral trade agreements between the United States and Latin American countries. These now almost per definition include drug control conditionality clauses.

Conditionality has of course long played a crucial role in the internationalization of the war on drugs. To be sure, the persistence of the global drug prohibition regime has relied upon the readiness of nations to rate the drug issue as less important than US cooperation in other fields – often trade but also military. Much of the United States' success at globalizing its drug prohibition policy is attributable to a lack of widespread and forcible opposition. This is, however, not to say that cooperation is indicative of complete agreement. Rule following differs significantly from an exercise of empathy. The ideas of Kettil Bruun, Lynn Pan and Ingemar Rexed are worth recalling here. In their seminal 1975 book *The Gentlemen's Club: International Control of Drugs and Alcohol,* they observed: when a 'superpower' exhibits a high degree of involvement 'there is unlikely to be much resistance or unresponsiveness on the part of countries appealed to for support, unless such support is contrary to national interests. Generally speaking, co-operation with the US in drug control matters does not conflict in any significant way with the interests of other Western countries and is therefore readily provided' (Bruun, *et al.* 1975: 142).

European Compliance

It can be argued that many European nations became parties to the UN Conventions, particularly the 1961 and 1971 Conventions, because at the time of signing such action was not contrary to their national interests. It seems likely that many signatory nations considered the stringency of some parts of the Single Convention acceptable, in as much as it did not dramatically affect domestic approaches to drug use at that time. Its main impact was to be felt in Southern traditional opium and coca producing countries, not in Europe. It should be remembered that the document had been developing for over a decade and came into force just as changing cultural and socio-economic conditions in many European nations began to impact patterns of illicit drug use.

Additionally, lobbying by the principal European pharmaceutical manufacturers ensured that their interests regarding the production and distribution of licit manufactured drugs were protected during the drafting stages. On this aspect of international control the concerns of Britain, Switzerland, West Germany, the Netherlands and Italy neatly coincided with those of the hegemonic United States (McAllister 2000: 209). European nations were also willing to put their name to the 1971 Treaty because, while the Single Convention imposed strict controls on nations producing organic drugs, the 1971 legislation only imposed loose controls on psychotropics and minimized the impact on domestic laws:

> The most important manufacturing and exporting countries tried everything to restrict the scope of control to the minimum and weaken the control measures in such a way that they should not hinder the free international trade . . . the 1971 Convention consists of two treaties: one for "street drug" hallucinogens in Schedule I and one for pharmaceuticals in Schedule II, III and IV. There are extremely strict control measures for Schedule I substances and very weak ones for Schedule II and III substances and nothing for Schedule IV substances. The provisions of the 1971 Convention do not allow the monitoring of the movements of international shipments which are necessary for the prevention of their diversion. (Bayer 1989: 21, 24)

It could even be argued that the scientifically questionable distinction between so-called 'narcotics' controlled by the 1961 Convention and 'psychotropics' under the 1971 Convention, was largely invented because the pharmaceutical industry resisted the idea that their products might be subject to the stringent controls of the Single Convention and, therefore, lobbied effectively for a separate legal instrument. Concerted efforts to weaken the 1971 treaty provisions by the United States, Britain, Canada, West Germany, Switzerland, the Netherlands, Belgium, Austria and Denmark ensured that pharmaceutical interests remained relatively unharmed (Sinha 2001: 25; McAllister 2000: 226–34).

Much the same can be said for European nations becoming parties to the 1988 Convention against Illicit Traffic. The increase in drug trafficking during the 1970s and 1980s meant that most states agreed upon the need for some form of international agreement to address the problem. Active US involvement in the negotiations helped ensure that the intent of the Convention was to harmonize national drug laws and enforcement actions around the world in an attempt to decrease illicit drug trafficking through the use of criminalization and punishment (Sinha 2001: 33). Thus, despite being regarded by some as part of the 'Americanization' of national criminal justice systems, the interests of European states generally coincided with that of Washington (Stewart 1990: 338; Woodiwiss 2003: 19; Nadelmann 1993: 469–70).[10]

Militarization of Drug Control

While such a coincidence of interest may have existed with regard to international protocols during the 1980s, the United States remained largely isolated in its preference for energetically recruiting the military into overseas anti-drug efforts. President Nixon first declared a 'war on drugs' in 1968, basically in response to the 'flower power' anti-war movement and a domestic heroin epidemic brought home from the war the United States was conducting in Southeast

Asia against its then-number-one national security threat – Communism. The nature of this war on drugs changed soon:

> Three years after declaring war, Nixon took what has proven to be the pivotal step in setting the nation on its inexorable march toward militarization; he proclaimed drug trafficking to be a 'national security' threat. . . . The linking of drugs to national security provided the rationale that future presidents would use to justify expanding the role of US armed forces; and protecting national security remains the rallying cry of those who want to provide more money and more firepower to those waging the war on drugs. (Zirnite 1997)[40]

Actual deployment of US military abroad started only in 1983 when Special Forces were first sent to the Andes for counternarcotics training. At that time a first version of the 'narcoguerrilla' theory was already being developed to assure a blending of the anti-drug mission with counterinsurgency objectives in the Andean region. President Reagan subsequently issued a National Security Decision Directive (NSDD-221) in April 1986 that declared drug trafficking a 'lethal' threat to the United States. The Directive set into motion Operation Blast Furnace in July–November 1986, which was to become the 'first publicized employment of US Army combat forces on the sovereign soil of another country to conduct joint anti-drug efforts' (Abbott 1988: 103). Six helicopters and 150 troops were sent to Bolivia for what was ultimately a failed attempt to destroy some cocaine labs.

The Pentagon was fully thrust to the front lines of the drug war with the National Defense Authorization Act (NDAA) for FY1989 by President George Bush, Senior. This made the Department of Defense (DOD), the single lead agency responsibility for monitoring, detecting and intercepting illicit drugs transports. This decision led to a dramatic increase in the number of military assets and personnel dedicated to the counter-drug effort: the start of a real 'war' on drugs. According to the General Accounting Office (GAO 1993a), 'Funding for DOD's surveillance mission and its associated flying hours and steaming days has increased from about $212 million in fiscal year 1989 to an estimated $844 million in fiscal year 1993 – nearly a 300 per cent increase.'

The period can be seen as the 'honeymoon' period of the DOD and the counter-drug mission. In its heyday, about half of all AWACS flying hours were dedicated to drug interdiction missions. 'The timing for large-scale military involvement was excellent: the Cold War was drawing to a close, freeing up large amounts of assets, but the dramatic drawdown had not yet begun' (Corcoran 1997).[11] The anti-Communist rationale for high military budgets and operations abroad was in trouble after the fall of the Wall, the same year that the Pentagon was given a significant anti-drugs role. In December 1989, the United States invaded Panama to topple the government of General Manuel Noriega. One of the main reasons given for the invasion was Noriega's involvement in drug trafficking.

The honeymoon was short. In the course of 1993, the GAO undertook a thorough review which led to devastating conclusions: 'Measured against interdiction success rates and supply reduction goals, the investment in the flying hours and steaming days that support DOD's mission is out of proportion to the benefits it provides.' According to the report, interdiction success at deterring the cocaine flow has been more symbolic than real: 'The hope that military surveillance would make a difference has proven to be overly optimistic.' The GAO has made an explicit recommendation to Congress that 'in light of the negligible contribution that military surveillance has made to the drug war', DOD's involvement in interdiction 'should be significantly reduced' (GAO 1993a).

The Clinton administration took office in 1993, and 'determined that a controlled shift in emphasis was required – a shift away from past efforts that focused primarily on interdiction in the transit zones to new efforts that focus on interdiction in and around source countries' (White House 1995), a conclusion was formalised in Presidential Directive 14 later that year (White House 1993). Subsequent years saw a decline in counter-drug funding for DOD of some 24 per cent between 1993 and 1999. DOD flight hours allocated to tracking illegal drug shipments in transit areas declined from about 46,000 in 1992 to some 15,000 in 1999, a 68 per cent drop (GAO 1999).

The conclusion reached by the GAO in 1993 still seems valid: 'military surveillance has not demonstrated that it can make a contribution – to either drug interdiction or to the national goal of reduced drug supplies – that is commensurate with its cost . . . [A]dding military surveillance to the nation's interdiction efforts has not made a difference in our ability to reduce the flow of cocaine to American streets' (GAO 1993b).

After dedicating 15 years of his military career to counternarcotics efforts, US Air Force Major Daniel L. Whitten (1999) has not become convinced of its usefulness:

> During the past two decades the administrations in power have continued to escalate the military's involvement in this fight. . . . Interdiction has been the primary military application for more than 15 years. And after all this time we have not had a serious impact on the drug market if price and availability are an indicator. That stability in price is a profound indicator of our ineffectiveness in drying up drug supplies. . . . In my opinion the military interdiction effort is an extremely expensive and ineffective mission for our forces to perform.

A military colleague of Major Whitten at the Air University arrived at the same conclusion: 'These operations met none of the goals or objectives outlined in the policies that called for these military endeavors. Interdiction operations aimed at the illegal drug supply achieve nothing of consequence.' The author, an Air Force officer who took time off to study the effects of interdiction, started from a fully supportive position, but, after six months, concluded: 'Further militarization of the drug war is not the answer. . . . It's time to take the responsibility for America's drug war from the hands of the military generals and give it to the Surgeon General' (Howard 2001).

US Military Infrastructure

US drug policy, unfortunately, was not handed over to the health authorities. The National Drug Control Strategy for 1998–2007 still delegates to the DOD, particularly the US Southern Command (SouthCom), operations related to the interruption of illicit drugs production and transport. This is not because other officials had been able to argue successfully that those operations in fact were effective in reducing the availability of illegal drugs, but rather because they served other useful purposes in Latin America for which another post-Cold War justification was difficult to find – the maintenance of an infrastructure of military bases, in the form of Forward Operating Locations (FOLs), military training and exercises, and military intelligence collaboration.

In June 1999, the Colombian newspaper *El Espectador* quoted a US State Department source as saying, 'The new counterdrug bases located in Ecuador, Aruba and Curaçao will be strategic points for closely monitoring the guerrillas' steps and their constant incursions into Venezuela, Panama, Brazil, Peru and Ecuador.' One State Department document to which *El Espectador* had access revealed: 'So as not to divert the missions, which will initially focus on counterdrug efforts, and in order to avoid polemics in the international arena and Congress, military intelligence work against the FARC and the ELN will mainly be framed in relation to their status as "narcoguerrillas"' (*Espectador* 1999).

In February 1998, before FOL negotiations began, an Air Force official made a series of recommendations that now appear to have been prescient. Referring to the increasing importance of South American petroleum, he said that if 'military attention follows this shift in vital interest . . . forward basing will be found woefully lacking.' Regional commands 'must be proactive immediately in the establishment of new bases'. The 'selection and development of four or five central bases with at least minimal infrastructure is the first step to ensuring forward access.' The same official emphasized that it is better to negotiate contracts with host nations before a crisis strikes, 'anticipating the need for access and beginning dialogue without time constraints. Laying the political groundwork and obtaining initial approval is the first half of the process.' In times of crisis, he added, 'the Armed Forces can further improve possibilities for access by helping to 'sell' the idea of a threat in the host nation' with the goal of gaining approval for expanded use of the site (Goffus 1998).

Mixing Drugs with Terror

Plan Colombia was the incarnation of this mix of arguments and subterfuges. It was legitimized at home primarily by the need to cut flows of cocaine to the United States after the crack epidemic hit inner city communities across the country. While such policies have never been formally sanctioned by any UN body, Plan Colombia, like source country interventions elsewhere, in many ways gained international legitimacy from the ideological tenor of the global drug prohibition regime (see Bewley–Taylor 2001: 186).

After the Medellin and Cali drug syndicates were decapitated in the early 1990s and interdiction had proven largely ineffective, the attention of the war on drugs refocused on the main production areas of primary material. An all-out attack was staged on the coca economy concentrated in areas under control by the single largest remaining armed insurgency on the American continent, the leftist Revolutionary Armed Forces of Colombia (FARC). Huge amounts of military aid flowed into Colombia turning the country into the third largest recipient of US military aid after Israel and Egypt. Counter-drug battalions were trained, equipped with state-of-the art attack helicopters and sent into the Amazon jungle areas of Putumayo and Caquetá in the south. A chemical war against illicit crops was unleashed spraying until now up to 700,000 hectares of coca and opium poppy. From the start it was clear the objectives were mixed: defeat the last guerrilla movements on the continent, pacify the country for economic reasons, especially for the Colombian oil reserves, and diminish the flow of drugs to the United States. The ideology accompanying Plan Colombia consequently highlighted the latter because Congressional restrictions were in place for counter-insurgency, an obstacle that proved to be relatively easy to remove post-11 September.

Since 11 September 2001, increasingly and most explicitly so in the cases of Afghanistan and Colombia, the counter-drug and counter-terror rationales are being woven together. Mixing these agendas has multiple benefits for the United States. First, as mentioned above, the war on drugs was being questioned since operations aimed at the disruption of drug supply appeared to have achieved nothing of consequence. Redefining the aims of the drugs war thus re-legitimized a mission that had become seriously discredited as being expensive and unsuccessful. Now, as SouthCom commander General Craddock explained to the US Congress in 2005:

> Success in this mission area will not only stem the flow of illegal narcotics on US streets, but also deny a source of funding that terrorist groups may use to finance their operations. . . . We continue to employ our limited air-, sea-, and ground-based intelligence, surveillance, and reconnaissance (ISR) assets to detect, identify and monitor illicit activities, particularly terrorist groups, their support network, and the criminal elements that serve terrorist purposes. (Craddock 2005)

Therefore, he concludes, 'Southern Command is a good investment of American taxpayer's dollars and trust'.

Secondly, mixing the agendas facilitates the removal of post-Cold War restrictions on US military involvement in counter-insurgency imposed in the 1990s. On 2 August 2002, a legal provision regarding anti-terrorist emergency funds (HR 4775) allowed 'the Colombian government to use all past and present counter-drug aid – all the helicopters, weapons, brigades and other initiatives of the past several years – against the insurgents' (VIP 2003). While the United States had had to hide its strategic objectives behind the militarization of drug control efforts and the continuation of its military presence abroad, in the post-Cold War 1990s under the shaky pretext of the war on drugs, the 'narco-terrorist' argument seemed to provide a more sustainable ideology at the start of the new millennium.

Afghanistan

In Afghanistan, the Taliban regime had imposed in 2000–2001, its last year in power, an opium ban which had the most profound impact on global opium–heroin supply in modern history. Poppy cultivation in areas under their control dropped to virtually zero. As with many other authoritarian policies of the Taliban, the opium ban had dramatic consequences, one of the most severe of which was the sudden total breakdown of the informal credit system based on opium. Many indebted former poppy farmers, unable to live through the winter and defaulting on their seasonal loans, moved to Pakistan and Iran, or were forced to reschedule their payments – one of the direct causes behind the full rebound of poppy cultivation the following year – and sell land, livestock, and even their under age daughters. The short-lived Taliban drug-control 'success story' can enter history as one of the most blatant examples of a humanitarian crisis being consciously aggravated under the guidance of the international community who pressed the regime at the time to take adequate action against the growing opium economy.

After the US-led intervention and removal of the Taliban, poppy cultivation in Afghanistan reached record new levels, leading to heated debates within the reconstruction donor community. Many commentators labelled it as yet another example of US hypocrisy in its war on drugs. Indeed, quite a few examples of such hypocrisy have been amply documented elsewhere. While the United States has long championed the fight against drugs overseas, it has also frequently subordinated that fight to broader foreign policy goals. Back in the Vietnam war, covert operations were financed with heroin trafficking. The CIA-supported contras in Nicaragua were financed with large-scale cocaine smuggling with the Iran–Contra affair adding another dimension to this drugs-for-arms trade. Despite the anti-drugs rhetoric surrounding the military operation to oust Noriega, the fact of the matter was that the dictator had been on the CIA payroll since at least the early 1970s. In Afghanistan, the CIA actively encouraged Pakistan's military intelligence to facilitate heroin trade to arm the mujahideen in its fight against the occupying Soviet forces (see McCoy 1991; Scott and Marshall 1991). And indeed, initially, following the invasion, curbing the opium economy was not high on the US priority list. The more immediate military objectives to first defeat the Taliban regime, and later neutralize Taliban remnants, chasing Al Qaeda operatives and Osama bin Laden in particular, had led to tactical alliances with quite a few warlords heavily involved in the opium economy.

Still, that was only one of the reasons why the opium economy fully recovered from the blow of the Taliban ban; there were also social and economic ones. Hundreds of thousands of Afghans were caught in an unsustainable debt trap, opium prices had increased tenfold, and many refugees were returning to their homes where most had simply no other choice than to grow poppy again. Furthermore, it was not the United States, nor the United Nations, but Britain who was given the lead in international drug-control efforts in the country within the established framework for reconstruction. Britain, well aware of the total opium-dependence economically of at least ten per cent of the population, made for good reasons a conscious decision not to repeat the earlier drama. It opted for an approach in which repressive actions were aimed at the level of heroin-processing and trafficking, while the emphasis was put on creating alternative livelihoods for farmers with regard to poppy cultivation. A gradual and long-term process was envisioned that would not pull the opium-carpet away from underneath the reconstruction process at a time when the opium market was about the only functioning part of the Afghan economy, equivalent to 60 per cent of legal GDP.

Things changed by 2004 when record harvest figures and altered US priorities made patience run out. Then the Congressional Research Service noted:

> The failure of US and international counternarcotics efforts to significantly disrupt the Afghan opium trade or sever its links to warlordism and corruption since the fall of the Taliban has led some observers to warn that without redoubled multilateral action, Afghanistan may succumb to a state of lawlessness and reemerge as a sanctuary for terrorists. (Blanchard 2004)

Robert B. Charles, US Assistant Secretary of State for International Narcotics and Law Enforcement Affairs, set the tone for the revised US approach in his April 2004 testimony before a US Congress subcommittee hearing under the pointed title: 'Are the British Counternarcotics Efforts Going Wobbly?' Mr Charles made it clear that the issue of eradication was a point of disagreement with Britain. The opium economy was 'a cancer that spreads and undermines all we are otherwise achieving in the areas of democracy, stability, anti-terrorism and rule of law.' The British, he said, used 'targeting criteria, while designed with the best of intentions, may be overly restrictive. Criteria such as requiring alternative development to be in place and a preoccupation with avoiding any possibility of resistance may restrict our ability to collectively reach key eradication goals' (Charles 2004). He added that 'if there is heroin poppy there which needs to be eradicated, we shouldn't be picking and choosing, we shouldn't be delaying, we shouldn't be making it conditional, upon providing an instant and available additional income stream.' He acknowledged that for some farmers 'it is just survival, but what we have to do is make it crystal clear there is such a thing as a rule of law . . . the point being that our priority should not be, it seems to me, some kind of misplaced sympathy.'

During the summer of 2004, the Bush administration undertook a review of US operations in Afghanistan, concluding that a closer merging was required between the War on Terror and the War on Drugs. Immediately after the Bush re-election in early November, Mr Charles announced the start of 'something tantamount to a Plan Afghanistan, which has parallels to the Plan Colombia effort' (see also TNI 2005a). Afghan drugs 'fund bad people and bad things, and in particular, we know that they have funded some of the warlords, they fund everyday criminals, they fund extremists within that country and terrorists.' Now the United States needed to get the key players on board for a more aggressive approach; at least the Karzai government, Britain and the United Nations needed to shift away from their 'misplaced sympathy' based policy.

'In Afghanistan, drugs are now a clear and present danger', stated Antonio Maria Costa, Executive Director of UN Office on Drugs and Crime (UNODC) in November 2004. '[O]pium cultivation, which has spread like wildfire throughout the country, could ultimately incinerate everything – democracy, reconstruction and stability' (UNIS 2004). In a meeting one week earlier, Mr Charles, representing the biggest donor of UNODC, had told Mr Costa that US funding might be in jeopardy unless he would express clear support for an eradication strategy. Responding by letter the very next day, Mr Costa (2004) wrote: 'I am happy that large scale eradication is under consideration.' In December, President Hamid Karzai used even stronger words placing the drugs fight on top of his new government's priority agenda:

> Opium cultivation, heroin production is more dangerous than the invasion and the attack of the Soviets on our country, it is more dangerous than the factional fighting in Afghanistan, it is more dangerous than terrorism . . .. Just as our people fought a holy war against the Soviets, so we will wage jihad against poppies. (Graham 2004)

His Minister for Rural Reconstruction and Development (MRRD) Hanif Atmar backed him saying that 'Surgery is required, which will involve bloodshed and problems but only a shock-therapy against the opium economy can save the state-building endeavour.'[12] Finally, Bill Rammell, the British Foreign Office minister added when he announced the wider use of British troops in counter-narcotics operations: 'You need a stick as well as a carrot. The rules of engagement have changed' (Burke 2004).

It is only now, in 2006, that drug control efforts in Afghanistan appear to have become an effort to replicate the Taliban opium ban disaster. This could prove to be extremely damaging to the prospects of genuine state building, conflict resolution and prevention, economic recovery and the slow process of constructing legitimacy and popular trust by the Karzai administration.

Emerging Contradictions

Many cracks and contradictions have arisen around the changing role of drugs as a moral evil and a useful enemy within the ideology. In contrast to the United States' successful post-War proselytization embedding its zero-tolerance ideology firmly in the UN Conventions to the point that the treaty system became the embodiment of the quixotic dream of a drug-free world, the United States was never so successful in rallying global support for its militarized application in the

Andean and Central Asian regions. Europe as well as UN agencies largely maintained a 'cordon sanitaire' around the real 'war on drugs', keeping a distance from any direct involvement in the military aspects of Plan Colombia, much to the frustration of Washington.

Also, in the case of Afghanistan today, sharp divisions cut through the policy debates about how to engage the opium economy in the broader context of reconstruction and nation building. As Ashraf Ghani (2004), former Finance Minister (now Chancellor of Kabul University) put it, 'Today, many Afghans believe that it is not drugs, but an ill-conceived war on drugs that threatens their economy and nascent democracy.' Powerful multilateral entities such as the World Bank and the European Commission take an openly critical view of the US 'Plan Afghanistan' approach and its militarized forced eradication. Attempts by the United States to expand the mandate of NATO-led ISAF forces in the country to include an anti-drugs mission, also failed at the end of 2005. Only Britain, which already expanded the mandate of its 'Operation Freedom' forces, supported the US efforts within NATO. 'If you pull at the thread of counter-narcotics the wrong way, because of the sheer proportion of the gross domestic product wrapped up in this business, you should be careful of unintended consequences,' cautioned General James Jones, NATO Supreme Allied Commander for Europe (*Financial Times* 2005).

However, the ongoing merging of the drugs and terrorism agenda carries the risk of reducing the existing differences in approach, since the war on terror has become more and more a shared goal. Under the pressure of Washington's 'you're either with us or against us' approach to foreign relations, most European countries and UN agencies, in spite of sharp disagreement over Iraq, have sided with the United States on the broader anti-terror agenda. Merging drugs and terror may also have the effect of reaffirming adherence to the zero-tolerance ideology behind the global prohibitionist regime, whose moral roots have become widely and profoundly disputed.

Discourse in Distress

While this could be the case, the first years of the new millennium may enter history as the moment the world at large shifted away from drug control dogma to pragmatism. A US-style zero-tolerance attitude to illicit drug use is in many nations gradually being replaced by the decriminalization of drugs for personal use, a harm reduction discourse and a consequent review of domestic drug laws. This trend has for some time been particularly noticeable among many European Union member states, with other countries like Canada, Australia and Brazil also engaging with similar re-evaluation processes to varying degrees.

The HIV/AIDS crisis has played an important role in the shift towards the harm reduction approach. And this is now particularly relevant to Asia, the former Soviet Union and Eastern Europe. A humane and pragmatic response to injecting drug use is increasingly regarded as the only effective way to reverse the HIV/AIDS epidemic. Harm reduction measures that aim to reduce the sharing of contaminated needles among drug users, urge them to adopt safer injection or non-injection consumption patterns, offer them treatment to reduce or end their drug use, and promote safe sex practices, are now widely seen as essential in the fight against the spread of HIV/AIDS.

Asia, a continent where for decades strong allies were found for the US zero-tolerance ideology, is moving fast away from it. China started pilot needle exchange and methadone projects in 2000, but is now scaling up harm reduction services at high speed, opening about a hundred methadone treatment centres in the course of 2005 and aiming to have a thousand clinics operational within five years. In June 2005, the Chinese Health Ministry issued new guidelines in favour of harm reduction approaches and called on local communities around the country to promote needle exchange programmes and free condoms distribution. In predominantly Muslim countries such as Iran, Pakistan, Malaysia and Indonesia the pragmatic breakthrough has also become apparent. Iran has opened more than 20 methadone clinics over the past three years and established a National Harm Reduction Committee to coordinate fast implementation of country-wide drop-in centres, substitution treatment and distribution of clean injecting equipment, including in prisons. A new drug law is being drafted using harm reduction language and redefining drug users as patients rather than criminals. Also, in Indonesia a review of the highly repressive drug laws is currently in process and the National AIDS Commission has embraced a harm reduction approach. Malaysia started its first methadone treatment centre in 2005 and the Health Ministry has announced for 2006 needle exchange and free condom distribution among drug users.

Obviously, these advances are only one side of the picture. Meanwhile the war on drugs is still raging on in most Asian countries including extreme measures such as death penalties or extra-judicial killings of dealers, mass incarceration, extreme prison sentences for simple possession for personal use, etc. Human rights are violated on a daily basis on the continent in the name of the fight against drugs. Still, slowly but surely, the balance is shifting in favour of harm reduction, eroding the justification behind this ongoing repression of drug users.

Developments in Asia reflect a global trend, which prompted the Bush administration and Republican drug warriors in the US Congress to launch a counter-attack. The US government – the biggest donor of UNODC – threatened to cut funding to the agency unless UNODC abstained from any involvement in or expression of support for harm reduction, including needle exchange programmes (TNI 2005b). The US Congress issued a ban on the use of federal funds for needle exchange, endangering the continuation of various USAID-supported programmes in Asia. Opinion-leading newspapers condemned the US pressure in their editorials in strong wording. *The New York Times* on 26 February 2005 referred to 'a triumph of ideology over science, logic and compassion' and urged the Bush administration to 'call off their budding witch hunt' against needle exchange and 'allow the rest of the world to get on with saving millions of lives'.

A day later, *The Washington Post* under the title 'Deadly Ignorance', called on the US government 'to end this bullying flat-earthism'.

The US pressure became a highly tense issue at the 48th session of the UN Commission on Narcotic Drugs in March 2005 in Vienna, the UN body providing policy guidance to UNODC. Delegates from around the globe stood up to defend the overwhelming evidence that harm reduction measures are effective against the spread of HIV/AIDS. In a marked shift from previous years, the European Union presented a common position on this issue, and Latin American, African and Asian countries almost unanimously showed support for harm reduction programmes. The CND session thus became an impressive demonstration of changed attitudes around the world concerning harm reduction in the HIV/AIDS context. The US maintained its moral opposition, arguing that harm reduction practices allow for drug abuse to continue and that the only answer is to enforce abstinence (INI 2005c).

Conclusion: Cracks in the Vienna Consensus

In the case of its drugs-and-terror eradication approach in Afghanistan, as well as on the issue of harm reduction – the paradigmatic antidote to zero-tolerance – the United States felt it was losing ground and resorted to blunt funding pressure to keep at least the UN lead agency, UNODC, in line. Other UN agencies – WHO, UNAIDS, UNDP, FAO – regularly entering the UN drugs debate from a health and developmental perspective, however, have already left the moral path of zero-tolerance. Also, the International Federation of Red Cross and Red Crescent Societies have taken a firm position on this issue:

> Forcing people who use drugs further underground and into situations where transmission of HIV/AIDS is more likely, and denying them access to life-saving treatment and prevention services is creating a public health disaster. This happens even though the evidence from scientific and medical research on best practices and cost benefit analyses is overwhelmingly in favour of harm reduction programming. This includes needle exchange, drug substitution treatment and condom distribution as part of the response to HIV/AIDS. The message is clear. It is time to be guided by the light of science, not by the darkness of ignorance and fear. (Red Cross and Red Crescent 2003)

It is, therefore, crucial for the United States to maintain its grip on the Vienna-based core of the UN drug control system, which it has done so far with considerable success. Cracks in the 'Vienna consensus' are, however, widening and bullying efforts by the Bush administration to maintain its stranglehold are being met with growing resentment and opposition. Contradictions are on the rise between, on the one hand, those who believe in the possibility of a drug-free world and for those whom zero-tolerance towards illicit drugs can be the only answer, and, on the other hand, those who try to find the most pragmatic and humane ways to deal with the reality of continuing drug use and a supply market that has proven to be resistant to policy interventions.

In summary, one can observe a clear paradigm shift from zero-tolerance to pragmatism. The reducing numbers of zero-tolerance proponents, in view of a disappointing impact vis-à-vis the realization of their moralistic impulse to create a drug-free world, tend to become more aggressive in their methods, resorting to radical approaches to curb production (spraying crops, military eradication units, opium bans, etc.), merging the fight against drugs, crime and terror, and introducing radical measures to curb drug use, such as mass incarceration and random drug testing.

Meanwhile, the growing numbers of proponents of pragmatic approaches find their options limited, since the room for manoeuvre for alternative policies and experiments is limited by legal obstacles in national legislation and in international treaties, obstacles that are not easily removed. As a confidential memorandum to the INCB by UNODC legal experts made clear, in fact most harm reduction measures are acceptable under the conventions; and where pragmatic policies are on a tense legal footing with some articles of the conventions, the memo stated: 'It could even be argued that the drug control treaties, as they stand, have been rendered out of synch with reality' (UNIDCP 2002).

Indeed, the past few years have seen noteworthy statements regarding the necessity of revisiting the Conventions. Three extensive parliamentary enquiries in Jamaica, Canada and Britain have suggested diplomatic initiatives at the UN level. The Jamaican Ganja Commission (2001) concluded that proposed changes in their marijuana laws 'require diplomatic efforts to join ranks with a growing number of Parties who unilaterally are taking measures to ameliorate their own anti-marijuana practices with respect to possession and use, our aim being to get the international community appropriately to amend the Conventions.' The Canadian Senate Committee (2002) recommended that 'the Government of Canada inform the appropriate United Nations authorities that Canada is requesting an amendment to the conventions and treaties governing illegal drugs'. The House of Commons Home Affairs Select Committee (2002) in Britain in the same year stated that 'we believe the time has come for the international treaties to be reconsidered' and recommended that 'the Government initiates a discussion within the Commission on Narcotic Drugs of alternative ways – including the possibility of legalisation and regulation – to tackle the global drugs dilemma.' The Report concluded: 'If there is any single lesson from the experience of the last 30 years, it is that policies based wholly or mainly on enforcement are destined to fail.'

These recent appeals add to numerous calls made before, such as a European Parliament resolution in 1995. Adopted with an overwhelming majority, this moved to 'encourage discussion and analysis of the results of the policies in force as laid down by the relevant 1961, 1971 and 1988 UN Conventions so as to permit a possible revision of those conventions' (European Parliament 1995). It is also important to recall that the first of the United Nation's own World Drug Reports in 1997 noted that 'Laws – and even the international Conventions – are not written in stone; they can be changed when the democratic will of nations so wishes it' (UNIDCP 1997: 199). A first step in this direction has been taken in 2006 by the Bolivian government as president Evo Morales seeks to withdraw the coca leaf from the UN conventions (TNI 2006).

Changes to the UN treaty system will not come easy. The current constellation of US–UN tensions, a pragmatic drug policy discourse spreading over the world from Europe to the East up to the far ends of Asia, and political shifts in Latin America, however, do offer opportunities not seen before. As a result, the global projection of the prohibition doctrine may be weakened and the United Nation's role as an underlying legitimizing force for the militarized fight against drugs can be reduced. This would make it more and more difficult for the United States to 'abuse' legitimate global concerns over drug-related health problems to pursue other military and economic interests under the disguise of drug control.

It is likely that this would cause US authorities to increase their efforts to connect the issues of drugs and terror in order to legitimize continued military operations and presence in Latin America and Asia, particularly in oil rich areas as the current instability in the Middle East continues to maintain record oil prices. In its ongoing bullying of the international community to preserve the ideological principles behind the war on drugs, the United States, however, is gradually becoming as isolated and globally contested as it is in its war in Iraq and its disdain for multilateralism in general. The war on drugs proved useful in bridging an ideological gap between the Cold War and the war on terror in terms of justifying US wars, and it may still prove useful for some time in playing the 'narco-terrorist' card. Still, the fundamental principles behind it have eroded, a climate change in global drug-policy making is underway, and it has become an ideology in distress.

Notes

1 The Dutch were perhaps the first to implement the notion of user licenses. The government established opium monopoly in the late nineteenth century and began licensing addicts in the late 1910s, a system that only ended in 1944 (MacCoun and Reuter 2001: 234).

2 Also see Trebach (1982: 119–70) for a discussion of the Act and the debates surrounding interpretation of the legislation's original aims.

3 For a concise overview see Levine and Rainarman (2004).

4 For examples from Britain see Mott and Bean (1998: 38–39).

5 The 1924–1925 Geneva Conventions and the 1931 Limitation Convention.

6 The 1936 Illicit Trafficking Convention.

7 Christie and Bruun (1991; cited in Gerber and Jensen 2001). Also see Elvins (2003) for an excellent discussion of the relationship between anti-trafficking policies and the maintenance of state power within the European Union.

8 The United Nations has, in recent years, toned down rhetoric associated with drug control and largely dropped terms like 'war', 'evil' and 'scourge' from its vocabulary. Nonetheless, even without such emotive phraseology the Organization's image remains important for regime adherence. Also see Room (1999).

9 The author, who was an eyewitness of the events, was a UN officer (staff member of the Division of Narcotic Drugs) between 1967 and 1973, the author of a number of documents of the Commission on Narcotic Drugs and the Plenipotentiary Conference, as well as the joint secretary of the Technical Committee of the Plenipotentiary Conference.

[10] It has also been argued that many nations were willing to go along with the United States in the multilateral arena simply because they saw it as a way of avoiding unilateral action by the United States. See Green (1998: 36; cited in Boister 2000: 50).
[11] The author is an Air Force pilot flying AWACS missions between 1994–96.
[12] Interview with MRRD Minister Hanif Atmar, Kabul 16 February 2005.

References

Abbott, Colonel Michael (1988), 'The Army and the Drug War: Politics or National Security?', *Parameters*, December.

Andreas, Peter (1999), 'When Policies Collide: Market Reform, Market Prohibition, and the Narcotization of the Mexican Economy', in H. Richard Friman and Peter Andreas (eds), *The Illicit Global Economy and State Power* (Lanham MD: Rowman and Littlefield Publishers): 127–128.

Bayer, István (1989), *Development of the Convention on Psychotropic Substances, 1971*, unpublished manuscript, Budapest, Hungary.

Bennis, Phyllis (2000), *Calling the Shots: How Washington Dominates Today's UN* (New York: Olive Branch Press).

Bertram, Eva, Morris Blachman, Kenneth Sharpe and Peter Andreas (1996), *Drug War Politics: The Price of Denial* (Berkeley: University of California Press).

Bewley–Taylor, David (1999), 'The Cost of Containment: The Cold War and US International Drug Control at the UN, 1950–58', *Diplomacy and Statecraft*, Vol. 10, No. 1, March: 147–71.

——— (2001), *The United States and International Drug Control, 1909–1997* (New York: Continuum).

Blanchard, Christopher M. (2004), *Afghanistan: Narcotics and US Policy*, Congressional Research Service, CRS Report for Congress, 7 December.

Block, Alan A. (1989), 'European Drug Traffic and Traffickers between the Wars: The Policy of Suppression and its Consequences', *Journal of Social History*, Vol. 23.

Boister, Neil (2000), *Penal Aspects of the UN Drug Conventions* (The Hague: Kluwer Law International).

Bruun, Kettil, Lynn Pan and Ingemar Rexed (1975), *The Gentleman's Club: International Control of Drugs and Alcohol* (Chicago: University of Chicago Press).

Burke, Jason (2004), 'British troops wage war on Afghan drugs', *The Observer*, 5 December.

Canadian Senate Committee (2002), *Cannabis: Our Position for a Canadian Public Policy*, Report of the Senate Special Committee on Illegal Drugs, Final Report, September.

Charles, Robert B. (2004), *Afghanistan: Are the British Counternarcotics Efforts Going Wobbly?*, Assistant Secretary for International Narcotics and Law Enforcement Affairs, Testimony Before the House Committee on Government Reform Subcommittee on Criminal Justice, Drug Policy, and Human Resources, 1 April, Washington DC.

Christie, Nils and Kettil Bruun (2001), *Der Nuetzliche Feind: Die Drogenpolitik and ihre Nutzniesser* [*The Useful Enemy: Drug Policy and Its Beneficiaries*] (Bielefeld, Germany: AJZ Verlang).

CIP, Center for International Policy (2003), International Policy Report, *The 'War on Drugs' meets the 'War on Terrorism': The United States' involvement in Colombia climbs to the next level*, Washington DC, February.

Claude Jr., Inis L. (1994), 'Collective Legitimization as a Political Function of the United Nations', in Frederich Kratochwil and Edward D. Mansfield (eds), *International Organization: A Reader* (New York: Harper Collins); first published in *International Organization*, Vol. 20, 1966: 267–79.

Corcoran, Major Kimberly (1997), *DOD Involvement in the Counterdrug Effort: Contributions and Limitations,* Air Command and Staff College, AU/ACSC/0077/97-03, March.

Costa, Antonio M. (2004), Letter of 11 November, available at http://www.colombo-plan.org/www/images/pubs/pdf/unodcnov2004.pdf.

Craddock, General Bantz J. (2005), Posture statement of General Bantz J. Craddock, United States Army Commander, United States Southern Command before the 109th Congress House Armed Services Committee, 9 March.

De Ruyver, B., G. Vermeulen, T. Vander Beken, F. Vander Laenen and K. Geenens (2002), *Multidisciplinary Drug Policies and the UN Drug Treaties*, Institute for International Research on Criminal Policy, Ghent University (IRCP), Maklu, Antwerpen/Apeldoorn.

Dorn, N. and A. Jamieson (2000), *Room for Manoeuvre: Overview of Comparative Legal Research into National Drug Laws of France, Italy, Spain, the Netherlands and Sweden and Their Relation to Three International Drug Conventions*, Study of Drug Scope for The Independent Inquiry on the Misuse of Drugs Act 1971, London.

Elvins, Martin (2003), *Anti-Drugs Policies of the European Union: Transnational Decision-Making and the Politics of Expertise* (Basingstoke: Palgrave Macmillan).

Espectador, El (1999), 'La agenda secreta para Colombia', Bogotá, 4 June.

European Parliament (1995), A4-0136/95, *Resolution on the communication from the Commission to the Council and the European Parliament on a European Union action plan to combat drugs (1995–1999)*, (COM(94)0234 – C4-0107/94), Article 59, 15 June.

Financial Times, The (2005), 'Poppy Crackdown Could Alienate Warlords And Imperil Afghan Poll, Say US Generals', 3 January.

GAO (1993a), *Drug Control: Heavy Investment in Military Surveillance Not Paying Off*, US General Accounting Office, GAO/NSIAD-93-220, September.

——— (1993b), *Expanded Military Surveillance Not Justified by Measurable Goals or Results*, Statement of Louis J. Rodrigues, Director, Systems Development and Production Issues, National Security and International Affairs Division, GAO/T-NSIAD-94-14, 5 October.

——— (1999), *Assets DOD Contributes to Reducing the Illegal Drug Supply Have Declined*, US General Accounting Office, GAO/NSIAD-00-9, December.

Gerber, Jurg and Eric L. Jensen (2001), 'The Internationalization of US Policy on Illicit Drug Control', in Gerber and Jensen (eds), *Drug War American Style: The Internationalization of Failed Policy and Its Alternatives* (New York: Garland Publishing).

Ghani, Ashraf (2004), 'When democracy's greatest enemy is a flower', Op-Ed, *The New York Times*, 11 December.

Goffus, Major Tom (US Air Force) (1998), *Air Expeditionary Forces: Forward Base Access*, unclassified document, Naval War College, Newport, 13 February.

Graham, Stephen (2004), 'Karzai urges Afghans to give up lucrative opium trade, says Taliban profiting', Associated Press, 9 December.

Green, P. (1998), *Drugs, Trafficking and Criminal Policy* (Winchester: Waterside Press).

Gregg, Robert W. (1993), *About Face?: The United States and the United Nations* (Boulder: Lynne Rienner Publishers).

House of Commons Home Affairs Select Committee (2002), House of Commons Home Affairs Select Committee's Report, *The Government's Drugs Policy: Is it Working?*, United Kingdom, May.

Howard, Lieutenant Colonel Stephen P. (US Air Force) (2001), *The Military War on Drugs: Too Many Assets, Too Few Results*, Air University, April.

International Conference on Drug Abuse (1988), *Declaration of the International Conference on Drug Abuse and Illicit Trafficking and Comprehensive Multidisciplinary Outline on Future Activities in Drug Abuse Control* (New York: United Nations).

Jamaican Ganja Commission (2001), *A Report of the National Commission on Ganja to Rt. Hon. P.J. Patterson, Q.C., M.P. Prime Minister of Jamaica*, 7 August.

Robert Keohane (1984), *After Hegemony: Cooperation and Discord in the World Political Economy* (Princeton: Princeton University Press).

Krajewski, K. (1999), 'How flexible are the United Nations drug Conventions?', *International Journal of Drug Policy*, Vol. 10.

Levine, Harry G. (2002), 'The secret of world-wide drug prohibition; The varieties and uses of drug prohibition in the twentieth and twenty first century', *The Independent Review*, December.

——— (2003), 'Global Drug Prohibition: Its uses and crises', *International Journal of Drug Policy*, Vol. 14.

Levine, Harry G. and Craig Reinarman (2004), *Alcohol Prohibition and Drug Prohibition: Lessons From Alcohol Policy for Drug Policy* (Amsterdam: CEDRO).

Lippmann, Walter (1967), 'The Underworld as Servant', *Forum*, January and February 1931; excerpted in Gus Tyler (ed.), *Organized Crime in America* (Ann Arbor: University of Michigan Press): 58–69.
McAllister, William B. (2000), *Drug Diplomacy in the Twentieth Century: An International History* (London: Routledge).
MacCoun, Robert J. and Peter Reuter (2001), *Drug War Heresies: Learning from Other Vices, Times and Places* (Cambridge: Cambridge University Press).
McCoy, Alfred W. (1991), *The Politics of Heroin: CIA Complicity in the Global Drug Trade* (Westport CT: Lawrence Hill Books).
Mott, Joy and Philip Bean (1998), 'The Development of Drug Control in Britain', in Ross Coomber (ed.), *The Control of Drugs and Drug Users: Reason or Reaction?* (Amsterdam: Harwood Academic Publishers).
Musto, David F. (1999), *The American Disease: Origins of Narcotic Control* (New York: Oxford University Press).
Nadelmann, Ethan A. (1990), 'Global Prohibition Regimes: The Evolution of Norms in International Society', *International Organization*, Vol. 44, No. 4.
——— (1993), *Cops Across Borders: The Internationalization of US Criminal Law Enforcement* (University Park: Pennsylvania State University Press).
Red Cross and Red Crescent (2003), International Federation of Red Cross and Red Crescent Societies, *Spreading the Light of Science: Guidelines on Harm Reduction related to Injecting Drug Use*, http://www.ifrc.org/what/health/tools/harm_reduction.asp.
Room, Robin (1999), 'The Rhetoric of International Drug Control', *Substance Use and Misuse*, Vol. 34, No. 12, 1999: 1689–1707.
Scott, P. D. and Jonathan Marshall (1991), *Cocaine Politics: Drugs, Armies and the CIA in Central America* (Berkeley: University of California Press).
Sinha, J. (2001), *The History and Development of the Leading International Drug Control Conventions*, Report prepared for the Canadian Senate Special Committee on Illegal Drugs.
Spencer, Bill (Deputy Director, Washington Office on Latin America) (1998), 'Drug Certification', in *Foreign Policy in Focus*, Vol. 3, No. 24, Interhemispheric Resource Center (IRC) and the Institute for Policy Studies (IPS), Albuquerque, New Mexico, September.
Stewart, David P. (1990), 'Internationalizing the War on Drugs: The UN Convention Against Illicit Traffic in Narcotic Drugs and Psychotropic Substances', *Denver Journal of International Law Policy*, Vol. 18.
TNI, Transnational Institute (2005a), 'Plan Afghanistan', TNI Drug Policy Briefing 10, February.
——— (2005b), 'The United Nations and Harm Reduction', TNI Drug Policy Briefing 12, March, available at http://www.tni.org/drugs/
——— (2005c), 'The United Nations and Harm Reduction – Revisited: An Unauthorized Report on the Outcomes of the 48th CND Session', TNI Drug Policy Briefing 13, April.
——— (2006), 'Coca Yes, Cocaine No? Legal Options for the Coca Leaf', Drugs and Conflict Debate Paper 13, May.
Trebach, Arnold S. (1982), *The Heroin Solution* (New Haven: Yale University Press).
UN Conference for the Adoption of the Single Convention on Narcotic Drugs (1964), Vol. II (New York: UN Publications).
UNIDCP, United Nations International Drug Control Programme (1997), *World Drug Report* (Oxford: Oxford University Press).
——— (2002), E/INCB/2002/W.13/SS.5, *Flexibility of Treaty Provisions as regards Harm Reduction Approaches*, prepared by the UNIDCP Legal Affairs Section for the 75th INCB session, 30 September, http://www.tni.org/drugsreform-docs/un300902.pdf.
UNIS (2004), 'United Nations Drugs Office Reports Major Increase in Opium Cultivation in Afghanistan', Press Release, United Nations Information Service, UNIS/NAR/867, 18 November.
Walker III, William O. (1994), 'An analytical overview', in Raphael Perl (ed.), *Drugs and Foreign Policy: A Critical Review* (Boulder: Westview Press).

White House (1993), *Presidential Decision Directive for Counternarcotics* (PDD-14), 3 November.
——— (1995), *National Drug Control Strategy,* February.
Whitten, Major Daniel L. (US Air Force) (1999), *Perspective on the Military Involvement in the War on Drugs – Is there a better way?*, Maxwell Air Force Base, Alabama, Air University, AU/ACSC/227/1999-04, April.
Whynes, D.K. (1991), 'Drug Problems and Policies', in D.K. Whynes and P.T. Bean (eds), *Policing and Prescribing: The British System of Drug Control* (Basingstoke: Macmillan).
Woodiwiss, Michael (2003), 'Transnational Organized Crime: The Global Reach of an American Concept', in Adam Edwards and Peter Gill (eds), *Transnational Organised Crime: Perspectives on Global Security* (London: Routledge).
Woodiwiss, Michael and David Bewley–Taylor (2005), *The Global Fix: The Construction of a Global Enforcement Regime,* TNI Briefing Series No. 2005/3, TNI Crime and Globalisation Programme, Amsterdam, October.
Zirnite, Peter (1997), *Reluctant Recruits: The US Military and the War on Drugs,* Washington Office on Latin America and TNI, Washington DC, August.

Conclusion

Achin Vanaik

> We are entering a new American century, in which we will become still wealthier, culturally more lethal, and increasingly powerful. We will excite hatreds without precedent. . . . The de facto role of the US armed forces will be to keep the world safe for our economy and open to our cultural assault. To these ends we will do a fair amount of killing.
>
> Ralph Peters, former US Army Intelligence Officer, 2003

Every contributor to this volume has in his or her own way written about and criticized different dimensions and aspects of the US empire-building project as it has unfolded since the end of the Cold War. Not one of the authors here has any doubt that there *is* such a project. Indeed, they would argue that it is inconceivable that there could be any room for such doubt, though the project itself might carry different names and labels. Media pundits might call it 'making the world safe for democracy'. Academics schooled in international relations might call it providing 'hegemonic stability'. Economists might be inclined to say that the prosperity that today's globalization brings requires that 'globalization have a global leader'. There are, of course, other variations on this same theme. The hard US right, however, has the inestimable merit of calling a spade a spade. Yes, they say that after the end of the Cold War the United States is globally predominant and intends not only to stay that way, but to further entrench its position! Call it empire-building if you will or whatever else you want. Such behaviour is good for America and what is good for America is good for the world.

Such confident self-assertiveness, indeed self-righteousness, cannot, however, quite cover up an intellectual–political embarrassment of sorts for the less fervent citizens of the United States and the West. If the US role in the Cold War era was all about it 'defending the free world' and 'containing Communism', then why has the United States become more aggressive internationally after its end? Why is there now more, rather than less, talk about the 'American empire'? Wasn't 'Soviet expansionism' supposed to be the real danger to the world order? Wasn't the Soviet Union the real and the only empire-builder that had to be stopped? In the face of US imperial behaviour post-1991 and the collapse of the

Soviet Union, there would seem to be a limited number of possible explanations or responses.

The first response is to be so unaware or unconcerned about such behaviour as to effectively ignore or even deny it. This is something that unfortunately comes all too easily to very large sections of US society, as pointed out in the chapter on American Exceptionalism in this book. A second response, also quite popular, is to see this as an aberration from, or a rupture with, the US past. A third response, by no means incompatible with holding on to some version of the second, is to justify such post-Cold War behaviour as being for the global good. It is not just the hard US right or more traditional conservatives who make such a claim. It is to be found also among US liberals, even those who would declare themselves left-liberals.

The second response is an interesting one. For those critical of the 'turn', it is the emergence, nay pre-eminence, of neoconservative thinking in foreign policy in the administration of Bush Junior that best explains this. But this will not do. The rise of neocons to power may explain changes in the manner in which imperial purposes have been pursued or certain 'excesses' carried out, even certain policy changes and actions undertaken. But it cannot explain why such imperial behaviour predates it. The Clinton administration has too much to answer for – the military assaults on Sudan, Afghanistan, Bosnia–Herzegovina, Serbia and Haiti, while Bush Senior did not hesitate to attack Panama or rule out any serious search for a non-military resolution of the Iraq–Kuwait crisis of 1990–91, when this was very much on the cards. Besides which, throughout the period since the end of the Cold War (or even before it), bipartisan support (Democratic and Republican) for the US government's imperial–military behaviour abroad has been overwhelming in virtually all instances. Indeed, all the contributors to this volume would insist that the true answer to why there is an apparent shift from Cold War 'containment' and 'defence' to post-Cold War aggressiveness is that it is precisely only apparent. In actual fact, there is no such shift! Throughout the Cold War era and even before, the United States has behaved like an imperial power, reasons for which need to be properly understood. This issue about whether one can talk of a US imperialism and not just of its 'occasional imperial behaviour' will be taken up later. But a brief discussion at this point about putative neoconservative rupture may not be amiss.

The Neoconservatives: Rupture or Continuity?

The 'neoconservative rupture' in US foreign policy has a definite point of origin. It did not begin with Bush Junior's accession to power, nor even with the 11 September attacks and the assault on Afghanistan. It really began with the decision of the United States to carry out an invasion of Iraq in early 2003 and became ever sharper with the difficulties that the country as an occupying force has had to face since. The notion that Bush Junior's administration is different from previous ones is true. But the question is how different? Who exactly are the neocons? Is the foreign policy of Bush Junior sufficiently different to justify the claim that there is more of a rupture than a continuity? That avowed and self-declared neoconservatives like Francis Fukuyama have taken a distance from the current foreign policy of the Bush Junior government has further complicated matters, as much as the fact that Bush Junior, Donald Rumsfeld, Dick Cheney and Condoleezza Rice did not belong to the neocon intellectual camp (Fukuyama 2006). Furthermore, both traditional Republican conservatives and all shades of neoconservatives claim Ronald Reagan (as President) as their political mentor.

There is a good reason for this last claim. Fukuyama is surely correct when he points out that the original neoconservatives of the 1950s, 1960s and 1970s – a group of largely Jewish intellectuals such as Irving Kristol, Daniel Bell, Patrick Moynihan, Norman Podhoretz, Midge Dexter, Seymour Martin Lipset – developed and popularized key socio-political themes, which became from the 1980s onwards part of the common sense of a much wider grouping including a second generation of neoconservatives, traditional conservatives, New Democrats and others. Externally, this Reaganite common sense was a belief (in contrast to conventional realists) that the internal character of regimes did define the basic character of their foreign policies. The United States being a great democracy, therefore, had a responsibility to use its power for moral purposes, that is, to shape other countries and the world in its image. International law and international institutions like the United Nations were not capable of bringing about global security and justice, and should not be afforded undue legitimacy. Internally, this neoconservatism attacked the welfare state and the premises on which it was founded. It thus helped pave the way for the emergence of a neoliberalism whose basic tenets it had no problems in endorsing.

In so far as there is a distinction between the neocon 'cabal' of Wolfowitz, William Kristol, Robert Kagan, Charles Krauthammer and other neocons like Francis Fukuyama, it did not exist between those who supported and opposed the invasion of Iraq in 2003. Far too many people, including Fukuyama himself supported this idea. Indeed, Clinton stalwarts, both inside and outside the government, provided the strongest intellectual rationale for why Saddam Hussein had to be unseated in order to complete the 'unfinished business' left over from the 1991 assault.[1] Nor was the distinction to be found in some strategic shift from multilateralism to unilateralism. It was Madeleine Albright who said, under the Clinton presidency, that the United States was 'the indispensable nation' and declared 'multilateralism if we can, unilateralism if we must'. It was Anthony Lake, Clinton's first term National Security Advisor who, in 1993 at Johns Hopkins University, justified a post-Cold War aggressive stance in foreign policy in a speech titled 'From Containment to Enlargement'. The combination of multilateralism and unilateralism has been a constant feature of US foreign policy from 1945 onwards.

The most that can be said is that Bush Junior has accentuated the unilateralist posture so that what seems to most distinguish him from his predecessors is not so much his greater willingness to use military force as his greater willingness to make it a *declared* policy of his administration. After all, the collapse of the Soviet Union is obviously a much more important turning point in history than either 11 September or the 'rise of neoconservatives', and it is from that point on that we see a greater willingness by the United States to exercise its military power abroad. Another two lines of demarcation from others of the current Bush administration are said to be the 'Israelization of US foreign policy', which all the more strongly alienates the general public in that all-important zone of West Asia, where hearts and minds had to be won; and the inflation of the danger of terrorism. Terrorism is a technique or means of violence and one cannot properly wage a war against a technique or tactic. Declaring an unlimited war on terrorism not only greatly exaggerates the problem posed by the likes of Al Qaeda, but, in carrying it out, guarantees that the United States will promote greater global instability.

Such differences, real enough though they are, pale in comparison with the shared similarities of thought, attitudes and general foreign policy orientation between the current neocon 'cabal' and its critics, whether neoconservative, traditional conservative, realist or liberal internationalist. The United States, say the critics, is basically a moral force for good in the world and must exercise its power to protect US interests and serve global interests, but must do so, unlike the neocon cabal, with a measure of pragmatism, caution and legitimacy. This is ultimately an expression of basic agreement in respect of the strategic goals and purposes of US foreign policy behaviour between all disputants.

But the qualifying note introduced provides considerable room for disagreement about how exactly the US government should pursue these aims and objectives and thus for claims that there are significant doctrinal–ideological category distinctions.

Is Today's United States an Imperialist Power?

While the term 'imperial' is often used as a shorthand expression for 'imperialism', as is effectively the case throughout this volume, there is nevertheless a claim that there is a subtle difference between the two terms. To talk of imperialism is to imply an inescapable negativity. Imperialism exploits and oppresses. On the other hand, imperial powers, it is said, are comparatively strong powers that have the 'responsibilities' associated with being powerful, which they can then exercise judiciously or abuse. Imperialism, it is claimed, is bad, but imperial behaviour and even empires are not necessarily so; hence the current efforts to portray the historical balance sheet of the British empire as basically positive, and the existing US empire-building project as even benign. This empire project is clearly connected to the imperatives of neoliberalism, globalization and capitalism. To call the United States an imperialist power requires us not only to distinguish between these phenomena but to examine their interconnections.

Historically, the term imperialism has been understood as a political phenomenon involving political–military subordination, usually formal, of other countries and regions by the imperialist power in question. The motive may have been partly economic and undoubtedly involved economic transfers of wealth from the dominated regions to the 'centre'. Ideology, often religious, was also important for pacifying the conquered regions. But it was, above all else, a political–military phenomenon. It is only from the late nineteenth and the early twentieth century that a new and different understanding of imperialism emerges. This is of a *capitalist* imperialism whose driving forces are economic and profoundly different from the imperialisms of the pre-capitalist past. This new kind of imperialism retains a crucial political–military component. But because it is based on the evolving character of capitalism itself, it need not be an empire of formal colonies or permanent territorial conquest. It is an imperialism of changing political forms. The 500 odd years of capitalist development worldwide has therefore witnessed centuries of brutal territorial conquest, colonization and permanent appropriation, devastating wars between competing colonizers and would-be colonizers (the two World Wars of the twentieth century), as well as the end of formal colonization and the emergence of informal modes of political domination.

But what remains constant throughout these phases of capitalist imperialism is the economic exploitation of weaker and poorer nations by richer and stronger ones, rooted in the inescapable *unevenness* of capitalist development worldwide. This is not to deny the dynamism of capitalism as an economic system, nor the fact that it has brought unimaginable benefits to millions. But it is to insist that such prosperity does not apply to all peoples, nations and classes, and that there are always the two poles of wealth and impoverishment, and, therefore, an inequality and an exploitation that are structurally founded. Inequality is of two types – between classes within and across countries, and between the countries themselves. Capitalist imperialism is about maintaining such a structure of exploitation and inequality worldwide. There are imperialist and exploiting ruling classes, exercising their rule within a state, even as they extend their influence and their wealth and capital to many other states. Dominant classes in imperialist states exploit other countries through politically dominating and influencing the governments of those countries and through economic collaboration with their dominant classes. In so far as there are some 'spread effects' of such transfers of wealth and 'trickle-down' effects of cross-country collaborations, the lower classes of dominant countries benefit more than the lower classes of dominated countries.

The economic globalization that has been taking place over the last 30 years is a neoliberal globalization which is basically a form of class warfare making the already rich, both absolutely and relatively, richer than the already poor and working classes. Neoliberal globalization is the economic form taken by the current phase of capitalist imperialism. But to sustain neoliberalism globally requires more than economics. It necessarily involves the exercise of political, military and ideological–cultural power to keep the whole system going, including laying down and sustaining the norms and laws (still for the most part national) that can allow capital, capitalists and capitalism to flourish. And it is states that are here the crucial actors and regulators. They provide the legal, regulatory, institutional and infrastructural framework. They police capital–labour relations in favour of the former. They manage the macro-economy. They are the mediums (especially if they are electoral democracies) that provide the popular legitimacy for elite rule. Geopolitics and geo-economics are thus inescapably intertwined. An ever-expanding and globalizing economy requires a politically stable system of nation-states. It needs 'hegemonic stabilization' or a global coordinator which can either be a single imperialist power (the United States), or a more collective grouping of major imperialist powers to lay down the rules and norms for behaviour both for states and for the dominant classes that seek to operate through their respective states. This is all the more necessary because capitalism is also always about competition between capitals and between the states that support their 'own' capitals and classes, and this competition must not be allowed to get out of hand. Imperialist hegemony may be necessary but the unequal power distribution among imperialist countries is also a source of tension that must be controlled.

Geopolitics today is functional for the stabilization of a neoliberal form of geo-economics, but it is not *only* functional. Geopolitical rivalry also has a relatively independent dynamic. There are all kinds of other political, military, diplomatic, ideological, cultural, territorial conflicts and ambitions that complicate state-to-state relations, while empire-builders like the governing elite of today's United States do what they do for reasons that go beyond the cost-benefit calculations of the purely economic kind. It is perfectly true that capitalism must forever seek to expand or else die; that it must seek endless growth since that is the only way it can be endlessly profitable, and is its driving force. And as Hannah Arendt (1968: 23) pointed out long ago: 'A never-ending accumulation of property must be based on a never-ending accumulation of power. . . . The limitless process of capital accumulation needs the political structure of so "unlimited a Power" that it can protect growing property by constantly growing more powerful.' But in so far as empire is a long-term and general objective and cause, there are always some *general* purposes and reasons that also motivate the actions of empire-builders. The US invasion of Iraq is not just about oil, but like invasions elsewhere (Serbia) it is also about establishing the *credibility* of the United States as a world power and a means to ensure its global dominance. Precisely because even the United States does not have the capacity to militarily intervene everywhere, the message it must send across is that it can intervene anywhere at anytime, so that the threat itself will suffice anywhere, anytime, and it would not have to intervene!

On Global Inequality

Supporters of neoliberal globalization, and these would include the supporters of US empire-building, naturally deny that imperialism is a relevant category for describing the world of today. Neoliberalism is, after all, a rehashed version of older 'modernization theory' which stipulated that if all countries simply followed the right policies there would be a convergence of wealth and prosperity globally. Thus the issue of whether, on balance, global inequality has grown or declined in the last 30 years becomes a decisive indicator of whether one is at all justified in talking of a new neoliberal phase of capitalist imperialism.[2]

The annual World Development Reports (WDR) – the flagship publication of the World Bank – is an interesting place to start. Over the last decade, there has been a noticeable shift of emphasis in these Reports, away from the naked advocacy of neoliberal policies for governments that the World Bank itself did so much to usher in. Going well beyond the idea of markets as the 'ideal allocator', new themes have been taken up such as governance, health, education, and most recently in its WDR 2006, the issue of 'Equity and Development'. WDR 2006 says that inequality of incomes and wealth as well as other kinds of inequalities (social and cultural) are bad for development and even for growth. Fair enough, even though the Report says nothing about its more profound political implications.[3] Increasing commodification of health and education, growing inequalities of income and wealth and therefore of power, systematically undermine democracy and the basic principles of justice.

Let us take some accepted, indeed indisputable facts: (i) The combined wealth of the world's 3 richest people is greater than the total GDP of the 48 poorest countries. (ii) In 1960, the average income of the richest 20 per cent of the world's population was 30 times higher than that of the poorest 20 per cent. By 1995 this had become 82 times greater (UNDP Report 1998). (iii) In 1970, the gap between the per capita GDP of the richest country, the United States ($5070) and that of the poorest, Bangladesh ($57) was 88:1. In 2000, the gap between the richest, Luxembourg ($45,917) and the poorest, Guinea-Bissau ($161) was 267:1. (iv) A study of 77 countries (with 82 per cent of the world's population) showed that between the 1950s and the 1990s inequalities rose in 45 countries and fell in 16 countries.

Now surely all this indicates that inequality of income (which strongly determines the levels of consumption and accumulation of wealth) increased greatly in the neoliberal era, and that this must count as a severe indictment of the current economic model? Defenders of this model, however, from *The Economist* (26 June 2003) to Jagdish Bhagwati (2004) would insist, not at all. Even the World Bank which has done so much to promote and justify neoliberalism, is not about to throw in the towel despite its partial backtracking. Defenders have three responses. First, they can acknowledge that there has been an acceleration, or, at least, a steady and continuing increase in inequality, but claim that this is the necessary price to pay for overall greater prosperity. Understandably, this is not the kind of response that is likely to prove persuasive to others or comforting to the defenders.

The second response generally carries the most authority and is present in the WDR 2006 itself. It points out that since we only have country-wise statistics for income inequality, and leaving aside the comparability problems of such data (some countries use more reliable income data from tax records, others use more unreliable consumption data to make income estimates), such data cannot give us true estimates for global inequality. This we get only if we treat the world as one country and measure properly the distribution of income within it, which so far we have not been able to do. So the jury must remain out about whether global inequality has increased or decreased although inter-country inequalities have undeniably increased and inequalities within each country have varied, increasing and decreasing in different countries, even if there are more countries in the former category.

What do *The Economist* and Bhagwati say? The former acknowledges that the gap between the richest and the poorest segments of the world's population has been growing. But this particular journal far from harbouring any leftist attitudes, does not even entertain moderate centrist–liberal views of the Rawlsian kind that would be deeply appalled at this growing impoverishment of the already poorest, and see the phenomenon itself as a decisive indictment of the current form of economic globalization.[4] Instead, *The Economist* claims that the high and sustained growth rates of China, above all, (though the Indian performance also contributes) have pulled up the 'in-betweens' of hundreds of millions closer to the world average for annual incomes, and therefore have actually reduced global inequality! That is to say, the differences between average incomes in the richer and poorer parts of the world have lessened.

Bhagwati's response is equally interesting. In a book of over 300 pages he devotes less than two full pages to a sustained discussion of this issue of global inequality, only to claim first that since we only have country-wise data, cross-country comparisons are inherently misleading, and so there is 'just so much irrelevant data-mongering'. This more cautious initial judgement based on a recognition of a genuine statistical problem quickly gives way (without any serious survey, let alone analysis, of a vast literature on this subject) to a more ambitious conclusion that the 'evidence points in just the opposite direction'. Global inequality, according to Bhagwati, is decreasing in the neoliberal era.

Given the prevailing statistical complications, is there a way of reaching an informed and authoritative judgement about whether global inequality has risen or fallen? Yes, there is. According to the International Monetary Fund's own database we have the undisputed fact that if we divide the world into advanced countries on one hand and the rest of the world (including China and India) on the other, then we see that in 1980 the 18 per cent of the world's population that lived in the advanced countries had 71 per cent of the world's income. In 2000, the proportion of the world's population living in the advanced countries had come down to 16 per cent but they now shared among themselves 81 per cent of the world's income. So in 1980, 82 per cent got 29 per cent of the world's income cake, while in 2000, 84 per cent had to share out 19 per cent of the cake, albeit a bigger one. This means that contrary to the claim of *The Economist*, the average incomes in the two parts of the world have diverged – and not converged. In which case, individual incomes in these two parts of the world would also have to diverge. Nothing else is statistically possible even if there are difficulties in making *exact* measurements from existing country-wise data.

Moreover, in so far as neoliberals claim that the incomes of many people in the developing world have risen significantly, given that the average incomes in the two parts have diverged over the last 20 years, then clearly this category of 'richer people' in the developing world simply cannot be very big. Defenders of neoliberalism can either claim that it has *greatly* benefited some people or *widely* benefited people in the developing world but cannot claim both. If a group has become much richer then it cannot be that big. If it is big then it cannot have become that much richer. Thus, despite all problems of data comparison, the most informed and authoritative judgement that one can make is that global inequality of incomes, wealth and consumption have risen dramatically in the era of neoliberal economic globalization.

The United States as Global Hegemon

The United States is today militarily an unchallengeable power. It is the greatest imperialist power within the bloc of imperialist nations. Can it succeed in remaining the global hegemon for decades to come? This depends on how it is able to deal with three crucial problem areas. The first is its ability to handle inter-imperialist tensions, notably with Europe and Japan, and those that may accompany the rise of other powers, notably Russia, China and India. The second is how it copes, if at all it can, with its internal economic weaknesses. The third is how successful it will be in projecting a global face of benevolence. That is to say, how persuasive will be its claim that it is fighting for a wider transnational, even universally beneficial cause? How effective will the software of empire be in sustaining the kind of popular acceptance, active or passive, that in the longer term all empires rely upon and without which they cannot survive? Alternatively, can it prevent the emergence of the kind of popular resistance and opposition to its empire project that this book is, in fact, dedicated to arousing? For the United States, the first is, relatively speaking, for the time being at least, the easiest of the three problems. However, success in 'managing' inter-imperialist tensions and possible rivalries with rising powers is essentially contingent on how well in the longer term the United States is able to deal with the second and third problem areas.

To start with, we need to recognize that 1945 marks a major turning point in the history of inter-imperialist rivalries. After the end of the Second World War, not only was the United States by far the most dominant capitalist military power, and not only was there a new systemic challenge (a non-capitalist Soviet Union) that required greater unity and collaboration among all the major capitalist imperialist states old and new (the Atlantic Alliance and the US–Japan Security alliance), but a fundamental change in the character of the world capitalist economy began to take place. Before 1945, despite substantial inter-penetration of capital amongst the advanced industrialized countries, the major powers had their own spheres of economic influence and dominance and guarded these against the intrusion of others. In fact, Japan, Italy and Germany as later industrializing countries were seeking to establish their 'own' spheres of economic–political dominance in a world already carved up in this respect. US dominance was exercised informally in North America, much of Latin America and the Pacific region.

The 60 years and more since the end of the Second World War have seen so profound and deep an interpenetration of capital amongst the advanced countries, so deep an integration in terms of the flows of goods and services, that even if the United States was not so militarily dominant there really is no question any more of imperialist countries going to war against each other or against the superpower, the United States. This integration is regional – within the European Union, East Asia, North America – but also to a very considerable (even if lesser) degree, between the three regions. Serious tensions related to capitalist competition remain but the inter-imperialist rivalries have to be played out in an altogether more moderate and non-militarist register today. What about countries like Russia, India and, particularly, China? The very purpose of the neoliberal form of globalization is to establish, transnationally, much closer economic–structural linkages between the elites and middle classes. In this way, the elites and middle classes of rising powers would come to recognize that they have more in common with their counterparts in the advanced capitalist world than with their own 'nationals' lower down the class structure. Moreover, any attempt to establish a condominium of rising powers to seriously challenge the 'older' ones would not necessarily be beneficial to them.

The future of Sino–US relations will be determined essentially by the latter not the former. The last thing China wants for at least the next 20 years while it pursues rapid modernization–development is to have the United States treat it as a strategic enemy. The Chinese ruling elites believe they have too much to lose and hope that with the two economies getting more closely intertwined such an outcome can be avoided. But it is the US behaviour that will determine how this relationship unfolds. Within the ruling establishment of the United States there are those who see strategic opposition as almost certain, just as there are those who believe that this is avoidable and that economic and other factors can push the two to cooperate much more openly. Currently, US preparations seem to be going in both directions – to treat China as both a potential opponent and a potential friend. Taiwan, of course, remains a sticking point with its capacity to tilt the issue decisively in one way or the other and even force a military engagement. What the future holds for Sino–US relations cannot be confidently predicted.

To rule out the possibility of inter-imperialist or inter-state or inter-ruling class rivalries (among major powers) assuming a military form does not mean that they cannot take severe economic and political forms. It is conceivable that Europe, Japan and some of the emerging powers could challenge the United States. True, this is still in the realm of speculation for this would require the emergence of certain pre-conditions such as a serious crisis of the global economy beyond the problems it faces today; and a stronger political resistance to the US empire-project by peoples and nations much beyond that existing at the moment. But the portents for the United States, especially after its invasion of Iraq in 2003, cannot be comforting to its empire-builders. It is simply not enough that it is the single most powerful country in the world militarily, economically and technologically. That is to say, if the United States does not just want to be the globally supreme power but also a globally hegemonic power then the ruling elites of other powerful countries must be prepared to accept and support the *leadership* of the global hegemon for a prolonged period of time. And this they would do for two positive reasons.

First, if they stand to benefit materially from such leadership. In the 'golden age', Europe and Japan grew faster than the United States. Their elites and masses in relative terms prospered more than their US counterparts, however much Americans might have prospered. Not only did this promote greater inter-elite sympathies with the United States, but because European and Japanese elites had the economic wherewithal to build and sustain strong and stable welfare states benefiting the rest of their populations, it made it easier for the institutions of civil society of these countries and ordinary people to endorse the pro-US orientation of their governments. But now, the fact that the period of neoliberal globalization is one of slower global growth, as compared to the golden age, it means a fiercer competition to get adequate shares of the overall pie. There is less to parcel out among claimants, be these economic sectors, geographical regions or social classes. The welfare state is under assault as never before. Poverty and inequality are considerably greater than they were in the golden age. It is no wonder then that a certain unease is growing, even among US allies about how the US government is behaving globally.

Second, the hegemon 'leads' because it is admired and therefore persuades. It is able to do so because it can plausibly present a model of society – a vision of what life can be – that can inspire countless others and is seen as worth emulating in important respects. For a whole historical period, the United States was seen by millions as both the main guarantor and a key representative of capitalist prosperity and democracy. The reality of US brutality abroad was softened by the relative strengths of its system at home in comparison to its main rival, the Soviet Union whose external behaviour was far from unblemished, even if nowhere near as tarnished as that of the United States. And as a backward and authoritarian upholder of an alternative vision of socialist prosperity and freedom, the Soviet Union clearly suffered by comparison, even as its very existence forced its Western opponents to adopt a more humanized 'social democratic' form of capitalism. Ironically, the collapse of the Soviet Union has also left the United States more naked and exposed. Capitalism of today is a much more mean and miserly one than that existing during the historically brief interregnum of the golden age. It is a capitalism gone rampant creating unacceptable extremes of poverty and inequality and threatening the environment as never before. The democracy that the United States can claim to represent is more shallow and constricted at home, and its foreign policy is as self-serving and brutal as it has always been, if not more so. The 'vision' it now upholds is much less persuasive.

Recognition of the declining capabilities of the United States to be a global hegemon finds expression, especially in Europe, in the rising clamour that the United States must behave more multilaterally and with greater respect for international institutions, laws and norms. The ruling classes of Europe and Japan have, of course, never in the last 60 years distinguished themselves as honourable and consistent defenders of moral principles in world affairs. Otherwise they would never have been the more or less faithful allies of US foreign policy they were and still are. But what the Europeans are implicitly suggesting is that now that the Soviet Union has collapsed and China no longer a systemic or ideological rival, it is time that the world be guided by a more collective hegemon. This would leave the United States as *primus inter pares* but locked in an institutionalized collaborative structure of discussion, decision-making and action with major European powers. It is this new collective hegemon instead of the United States aspiring to be the single hegemon that would have to take on the responsibility of maintaining 'world order'.

This is not, however, likely to come about, nor would it work. Whatever the dilemmas the United States faces as a candidate for providing 'hegemonic stability' it is still superior to Europe or others in its claim to make for a more collective form as an alternative. If Europe is to succeed in getting the United States to accept being part of a collective hegemon, then it must have the relative power behind it so as to persuade the United States. However, it does not have such power. It is only economically that Europe can claim to seriously challenge the United States and that only in the form of the European Union as a collective economic zone. But the European Union is not a unified economic zone in the same way as the United States is. Politically, it is far more of a federation of nation-states than a single supra-state, and the competition between capitals within the European Union is reinforced by nationality differences. Nor for some time to come, if at all, is the Euro likely to have the same status as the dollar, as *the* international currency. In the financialized neoliberal world economic order of today it is Wall Street and its junior helpmate London, not Frankfurt or Tokyo that is the main hub. On all other fronts – military, technological, political, cultural – Europe is no real match for the United States even in current travail.

The advantages possessed by the United States in comparison to Europe as a global defender of capitalists and capitalism, and as policeman of the system of nation-states, can be simply stated. The United States is the *largest* single advanced capitalist state in the world. It possesses immense natural resources. It has a huge population which scores over the more populated EU zone by being nourished by high levels of immigration and is much younger than that of Europe. It is the *strongest* capitalist state not just militarily but also technologically. It pays particular attention to Research and Development and invests heavily in it. If, in 1981, the United States spent almost as much on R&D as Japan,

Germany, Italy, Britain, Canada and France, in 2000, it spent more than these other six countries together. Between 1981–2000, as compared to the 20 years before that (1960–80), the US share of global high-tech production – aerospace, pharmaceuticals, computers and office machinery, communication equipment, scientific instruments – remained roughly the same at 32 per cent of world production. The German share halved to 5 per cent, Japan's share fell by a third to 13 per cent, while China's rose from 1 to 9 per cent and South Korea from 1 to 7 per cent. In the six areas of frontier technology – personal computers, gene splicing, high temperature superconductivity, neural networks, communications satellites and magnetic resonance imaging – Europe is a serious challenger only in the last (Therborn 1995: 264).

The United States is far more *politically unified* than the European Union, and can therefore act on a world scale with a speed and authority not available to the latter. It is the *safest* capitalist state being blessed geographically as an island continent, and socio-politically by having a capital–labour relationship that is more strongly institutionalized in favour of the former than in any other democracy anywhere in the world, let alone in Europe. The tweedledum-tweedledee of political alternation between the Democrats and the Republicans is but one aspect of this overwhelming institutionalist bias. Where would the global rich most want to park at least some of their wealth if long-term safety of their assets was an important consideration? Finally, the United States is the *purest* of all capitalist states. Not possessing the social and cultural density of the European countries it has no history of other kinds of societies or the 'mixture' of values, beliefs, attitudes and traditions that they have. Pre-capitalist societies characteristically had as the other side of the privileges held by their elite, the duties and obligations of those very elites to subordinate populations. These traditions of a longstanding pre-capitalist past could, therefore, historically found more collective commitments and responsibilities of rulers to ruled, even in capitalist modernity. US modernity is thus the shallowest of all historical modernities and the most individualist and least collectivist in spirit. This very shallowness coupled with its immigrant character, makes its forms of mass and popular culture, from films to TV serials to dance and music, relatively the most easily assimilable and most likely to be imitated in other societies. Whether they be its particular forms of capitalist organization such as joint stock companies, Taylorism, Fordism, accountancy norms, etc. or its cultural products, the very 'purity' of its capitalism makes them modular and transportable in a way that other capitalisms cannot emulate.[5]

None of these properties in any way guarantee that the United States will succeed in its efforts to become an enduring global hegemon. But it does suggest that the chances of it being replaced by some collective hegemon are remote. In short, a collapse and repudiation of the US global empire project will not so much allow for a more collective alternative of coordinated elite rule to come about that can somehow 'rectify' its failures, but rather it can open the way for another possibility – the emergence of a non-hegemonic, altogether more humane and worthwhile project of global cooperation. The fall of the US empire, then, could be the fall of the last empire project of modernity! This would be 'an end of history' of a kind rather different from what Francis Fukuyama had in mind.

The Catch-22 of the US Economy

The necessary but not sufficient condition for the US empire project to succeed is that it retain a strong economy globally. So how strong is the US economy in the global context? Walden Bello in his chapter has already provided a powerful argument and a warning in this respect. The jottings here are, therefore, of a supplementary order.

The era of neoliberal globalization in certain respects strengthened the US economically vis-à-vis Japan and Europe that had outpaced it in earlier decades. The United States had slightly higher average growth rates, lower unemployment and higher productivity per worker, though not higher productivity per hour, compared to key European rivals. But the issue here is also what has happened to its absolute economic power given the absolute character of its political ambition globally? Because due to neoliberal globalization the United States has gained in relative terms, it has every interest in sustaining this as the economic form of imperialism in this period. But this imperialism has only delayed or somewhat staved off a growing weakness of the US economy caused by the very openness of the neoliberal form of globalization. It is a kind of Catch-22 situation. The United States has to sustain the very process, which in part benefits it, but also in another sense undermines it.

The position of the US economy in the global economy is, in certain respects, relative to other advanced capitalist countries, strong. Its non-financial transnational corporations (TNCs) are expanding their control. US financial institutions are becoming more powerful than ever in the world. The US is sucking in huge amounts of capital from abroad. US foreign direct investment (FDI) is now 20 per cent of all investment made by US investors at home and abroad. Not only has this FDI by the United States grown steadily over the decades since 1945, but as a result of this cumulative growth, the profits today generated by such FDI are now over 50 per cent of the profits generated by US companies/investors at home. Total financial income generated from abroad is now over 100 per cent of domestic profits. It was around 10 per cent in 1948, rising to 45 per cent in 1978. If we compare US investment abroad to those investing in the United States, we can see how important economic expansion abroad is for the United States, that is, why it must continue to behave imperialistically. FDI, as a proportion of total US investment abroad, is 50 per cent, while this is only 20 per cent for foreigners investing in the United States. The ratio of FDI to financial investment abroad is much higher for the United States than is the ratio for foreigners investing within the country. This is important because FDI gives control over productive units in a way that much of financial activity does not. The average rate of return on US investments abroad is considerably higher than the average rate of return obtained by foreigners investing in the United States. In both cases, there was an increase in this rate of return after 1980 compared to the period before that. For US investors abroad it jumped from 6.2 to 9.3 per cent in the two periods, while for foreigners the figures were much lower, rising from 1.8 per cent to only 4.5 per cent in the respective periods. That is to say, US investment abroad is more efficient than the investment by foreigners in the United States.

Imperialist countries export capital and goods abroad on a big scale which the United States certainly does. Imperialist countries also import goods and capital on a big scale which, once again, the United States certainly does. What spoils the relatively rosy picture portrayed in the above paragraph about the US position in the world economy is that when we look at the absolute or *total* figures we find that inflows into the country exceed the outflows from it, and have been so for some time. In 2003, US financial holdings abroad amounted to 30 per cent of its net domestic product (NDP). But foreign holdings in the United States amounted to 36 per cent of its NDP.[6] The US economy lives beyond its means and has so far been able to get away with this in a way that no other country could possibly have. But for how long can this go on? The United States imports more than it exports and has to become a net borrower of capital thereby allowing foreigners more and more control over its assets, productive and financial, even though its own control over foreign assets is substantial and growing, albeit relatively more slowly. The United States has a miserably low and declining savings rate. Interestingly, even though inequalities are growing in the country – the rich becoming richer – this is not leading to a higher savings rate. This is simply not a situation that can carry on indefinitely. We do not know when the day of reckoning for the United States would come, but come it will.

In the Name of Democracy

Any would-be global hegemon, it has been argued, must be able to present itself as the main harbinger of some immensely desirable vision for others. That vision must have both a negative and a positive dimension. It must be presented as a counter to some kind of global threat or enemy, and it must also be infused with a moral appeal related to notions of justice and progress. In the post-Cold War era what could this be for US empire-builders? One possible appeal – the 'promise' of globalization (even if it is considered inevitable) – does not make the grade. Despite the tidal waves of argument and rhetoric in its favour, from ruling classes and their ideological servitors and from a global mass media, it does not sufficiently convince. The promise is so clearly unfulfilled for too many, the reality too starkly depressing. Globalization may be, as Zbigniew Brzezinski (2005: 141) points out, 'the natural doctrine of global hegemony'. But its claim to virtue rests on it being able to prove its success in eliminating poverty and reducing inequality – the twin faces of the 'global enemy' of mass backwardness and suffering. As such globalization is simply too strongly contested. Indeed, neoliberal globalization cannot regard poverty and inequality as enemies when they are, in fact, its associates. What it fears, though it might not speak out its name loud too often, is the instability and upheaval that the continuation of such poverty and inequality might arouse against the existing order and its greatest beneficiaries.

Though the Global War on Terrorism (GWOT) is currently the most frequently and widely used rationale for organizing the empire project, it too lacks the necessary qualities that a potentially hegemonizing discourse must have. Yes, it does postulate a global enemy – terrorist groups and their leaders – who must be countered. But that postulation is itself embarrassingly selective and hypocritical. For terrorism is a technique used not just by non-state actors but also by the US government, and by too many of its states-allies – a reality that the United States would wish to ignore or hide, but which is far too obvious to so many for it to be used with sufficient success. What is more, the easy slippage of GWOT into a demonization of Islam is a guarantee that this particular cause cannot persuade in key parts of the world. Nor does GWOT express a positive vision of a new, more just and humane world order that can inspire loyalty to any empire project carried out in its name. What the 11 September attacks did was to fracture the United States' sense of invulnerability, and its launching of GWOT is in part the expression of an impossible, indeed dangerous, attempt to reclaim that invulnerability at all costs – costs to be paid by the innocent citizens of other countries if need be. This is a particularist and obsessive vision of how the United States should behave globally, and cannot be the basis for securing hegemonic acceptance.

There remains, then, just one potential candidate for constructing an effective hegemonic discourse that can best serve the needs of empire. The enemy to be fought against is 'global instability' or disorder, and the way to do so is by 'spreading democracy'. For this will kill two birds with one stone. It will overcome instability, thus laying the foundations for progress everywhere. And it is a wonderful moral–political argument in its own right. So, even as the GWOT and the other ideological banners discussed in this book remain in place to serve empire's interests, as well as for other reasons, if the empire project is to sustain itself, then the discourse of 'global democratization' must also grow. The justifications for *forcible* forms of carrying out 'humanitarian interventions', and for externally enforced regime changes, all in the name of democracy are going to be around for a long time to come. All the more reason therefore to end this volume with a further look at the theme that has already been lucidly explored by Mariano Aguirre and Phyllis Bennis. The aim is to drive some more nails, as it were, into the coffin that houses this 'democratic' justification for unacceptable military behaviour.

The establishment of a basic set of human rights has been a product of modern history. It is now accepted that these are universally applicable to all human beings and derive their sanction from the fact that human beings are moral beings, and that simply by the virtue of being human all individuals are owed such rights. In this respect, human rights must from now on be seen as transhistorical and transnational. Since nation-states are historically contingent phenomena, the rights of nations such as national self-determination cannot, in principle, override such universal human rights. We do have an obligation to intervene across national boundaries to promote human rights. This much is not really in dispute as a normative attitude, principle or injunction. It allows for all kinds of external initiatives – diplomatic, cultural, humanitarian, etc. – to correct wrongs and to promote justice. But the real point of dispute is not the legitimacy or morality of such kinds of intervention, but whether forcible military intervention from outside the country in question to secure human rights or prevent human rights violations is justifiable?

There are three positions in this regard. The greatest act of global political emancipation of the last half of the twentieth century was decolonization, and the institutionalization of the formal principle of the equality of all nations, and therefore of the right of national self-determination or national sovereignty as the supreme legal principle of the international political order. If not always in practice, then at least within law, this was and is a crucial form of protection for the weaker and newly emerging countries vis-à-vis the more powerful countries. Existing international law in this respect, particularly the UN Charter formally accepted by all states who are UN members, represents a major gain for global peace, security and justice. Those who are now advocating military intervention in the name of human rights would not dispute that this is a violation of international law, but would insist that it is nevertheless morally justified. Those who would defend existing laws against such interventions have powerful arguments on their side: (a) It is naïve and false to believe that the main motivation for powerful states to intervene elsewhere is for humanitarian reasons. (b) Sovereignty is supreme and citizens are the exclusive responsibility of their state and their state is entirely their business. (c) The exceptions provided in the UN Charter – namely, 'the right to self-defence' and the authorization of the Security Council to militarily rectify a 'breach' of international peace as a last resort measure – must not be extended. To do so by making the correction of human rights another 'exception' is to ensure that there will be more abuses in the name of this exception. (d) There will always be a selective application of the principle of forcible humanitarian intervention. Therefore, there will always be inconsistency in the execution of this policy. (f) There is no consensus between the states of the world on what should be the principles justifying forcible humanitarian intervention. The level of order and justice currently involved in the principle of non-intervention, that exists already legally, is far better than the disorder and injustices that might result from accepting periodic violation of the non-interventionist principle in the name of human rights.

Among those who have defended the various interventions, in whole or in part, carried out by the United States since the end of the Cold War, there are those who have sought to make a normative case for their position, which is the second position. They have argued: (a) Morality must trump legality and moral considerations demand intervention no matter what the legal position is internationally. (b) Whatever be the motives of interveners, they say, it is outcomes that are more important according to them, and if the intervention ends the human rights violations then this is what is most important. Since there are both short-term outcomes and long-term ones, the first can justify external military intervention to end a crisis; the second can justify longer occupation and even regime change. The judgement of how long the occupation must last, will rest, of course, on the judgement of the intervener.

The third position is closer to the first than to the second. But it does allow for military intervention in the name of human rights under very specific conditions, and are by their nature much rarer in their occurrence and, therefore, of little comfort to those who advocate US imperial behaviour in the name of democracy. This third position bases itself on the normative principle of respecting the freedom of peoples. It is morally not just legally founded. This view recognizes and respects the fact that we live in a world where different nations are constituted by different peoples. It therefore insists that we must respect the right of peoples to overthrow their *own* tyrants! That though we may oppose colonialism or apartheid or authoritarian dictatorships and provide help from the outside in myriad ways, including material forms of support to a just cause (even arms supplies), to those fighting such evils, we are not justified in carrying out external military interventions to overthrow the Shah of Iran or the White South African apartheid regime or British colonial rule in a particular colony. In brief, we are not entitled to substitute ourselves for the oppressed peoples in question (who may also be ethnic minorities opposing majority oppression), for to do so would be to deny them their agency, and their freedom to fight against their own tyrant. That is to say, the suffering people have a right to claim our support, but they themselves must be respected as the primary agents in shaping their future.

In normative terms then, there are only two qualifications to this injunction which can call for external military interventions. First, if one side in a civil war or conflict calls for and gets external military help on its side, then the other side can be entitled to do the same. This happened, for example, in Angola in 1975 when a left–nationalist guerrilla force, the MPLA or Movement for the Liberation of Angola, a leading force in the struggle against Portuguese colonial rule, came to power after the departure of Portuguese colonial rule. Precisely because it was a left–nationalist regime, UNITA the guerrilla insurgency force ranged against it, was supported by the United States and the apartheid regime of South Africa. UNITA asked for and got White South African troops to militarily intervene on its behalf in order to try and overthrow the MPLA government. Then at the request of the MPLA, Cuban troops were invited to come fight for the national government against the South Africans and UNITA. The latter were decisively defeated.

The second qualification is even more important. To respect the right of a people to overthrow their own tyrant is to presume that the people can, in the first place, exist. That is to say, their very survival as a people is not at stake. If their very existence as a people is at stake then, regardless of the motives, military intervention is called for. Mass expulsion of a people does not qualify as a justification for such intervention as people retain their agency to struggle for justice even in exile. In the last three decades there have been three such occasions when the existence of a people was at stake. In 1975, East Timor suffered a massacre by the Indonesian troops, determined to hold on to East Timor, though its native population was waging a just struggle for national liberation. One-third of the people of East Timor were massacred once the United States had given the go ahead (Kissinger left Jakarta a day before the military campaign was launched by Indonesia in January 1975), to one of its most faithful allies. There was, in fact, no intervention to save the East Timorese. Another example when such intervention was called for (Aguirre refers to this in his essay) took place in Rwanda in 1993, when a majority of the Tutsi people were massacred. Again, neither the United States nor any European power had any interest in intervening to prevent this slaughter since Rwanda, unlike the Balkans, had no strategic–political value for the West. Finally, there is the Vietnamese invasion of Kampuchea in 1979 to put an end to the execrable Pol Pot regime that decimated more than half the population of Kampuchea. Whatever the motives behind the Vietnamese action, it was an outcome devoutly to be wished for. But both the Chinese and the US governments, for political–strategic reasons, bitterly opposed the Vietnamese action and in fact continued to support, militarily and politically, the remnants of Pol Pot's troops in exile or underground.

According to the moral standard embodied in this third position, all the US military interventions in the 1990s – in the Balkans, West and Central Asia, Central America, the Caribbean – were unjustified. There is also a need to set up a truly impartial and international force, not beholden to or acting on behalf of any power or concert of powers and capable of intervening to maintain international peace and security. Many had hoped, rightly or wrongly, that the United Nations could set going in this direction. But the conditions under which even such a force as the United Nations could militarily intervene would have to remain restricted. We are, of course, far from securing such a force. But the whole point of this discussion about normative principles is that what the US empire-builders have done in the name of humanitarian intervention must not be allowed to cloak itself in the garb of moral rectitude and integrity.

Not in Our Name

Baron von Clausewitz, in his famous work, *On War*, gave his verdict on the question that had dogged many a military and political thinker – should one speak about war as an art or a science? Clausewitz declared that war was more like commerce! What he meant by this was that fighting in war was like cash transactions in business and trade. Most economic transactions do not involve cash since ledger transfers and other forms of financial activity perform the same function. But ultimately the whole system rests on the actuality of cash payments and the assurance that this is indeed the case. Similarly, most international politics is not about war, but winning wars is, in the final analysis, the truly decisive element in the field of international politics. Many a military and political thinker today would still regard this as an irrefutable truth.

But however true this might have been during Clausewitz's time and for the most of the nineteenth century, as a supposed axiom of international politics it has been found increasingly wanting from the beginning of the twentieth century onwards. The reason for this is not difficult to grasp. It is the emergence of mass politics with the entry of huge numbers of ordinary people (and not rulers or nobles, upper classes or elites), into the arena of political life that has changed everything. Mass approval, that is, mass legitimacy has become the inescapable background condition of contemporary politics. Its importance waxes and wanes at different times and in different contexts but it is a fact that can neither be ignored nor neglected.

Political struggle, now more than ever, is not primarily a contest of arms or of economic strength. It is, above all, about the imposition of the will of one side on the other, where one's military and economic strengths are among the means to bring about this imposition. But what happens when the will of the militarily and economically weaker side is no longer that of a small ruling coterie but the will of huge numbers of people? What happens when that shared 'mass will' becomes so determined as not to give up, no matter how weak 'materially' that side is relative to its opponent? What does the other side do when that determination rests on an unshakeable belief in the moral righteousness and justice of its cause for which people are prepared to make the most extraordinary and sustained sacrifices? It means that, as in the cases of decolonization, the defeat of the United States in Vietnam, of the Soviet Union in Afghanistan, the collapse of the apartheid regime in South Africa, and of the Soviet Union itself, the issue of mass legitimacy has become paramount. A so-called soft power ultimately acts more decisively than the hard power of immense military and economic might.

We live in a world where in that coupling of force and consent that comprises 'hegemony', the dimension of consent for the hegemonizer has become increasingly important as a general rule, and, in particular cases, absolutely decisive.[7] In the past, all empires and empire-builders have had to organize consent at least from local and other elites if they hoped to stabilize their rule. Today's empire-builders have to organize such consent more seriously, more deeply, more widely and more determinedly than ever before. Since the end of the Cold War and into the first decade of the new millennium, this is the challenge that the United States and its current empire-building project face, and it is a challenge that one believes and hopes it will fail to meet. This is why its empire project will, in historical terms, be short-lived unlike the empires of the past that rose, plateaued and declined over centuries rather than decades, precisely because the mass of ordinary working people were at such far remove from the political life of their times.

One of our greatest modern historians, Eric Hobsbawm (2002: 413–14), now in the twilight of his years, had this to say in his recent autobiography:

> Living for over eighty years of the twentieth century has been a natural lesson in the mutability of political power, empires and institutions. I have seen the total disappearance of the European empires, not least the greatest of all, the British Empire, never larger and more powerful than in my childhood, when it pioneered the strategy of keeping order in places like Kurdistan and Afghanistan by aerial bombardment. I have seen great world powers relegated to the minor divisions, the end of a German Empire that expected to last a thousand years, and of a revolutionary power that expected to last for ever. I am unlikely to see the end of the "American century", but it is a safe bet that some readers of this book will.

But the fact that the US empire project will ultimately fail is not in itself that much a source of solace as one might assume. The longer it does last and the longer its empire-builders persist, the more damage the project will do to the world. What is more, the damage it wreaks may be so great that the tasks of reconstructing a far better world will be made that much more difficult. In fact, the tasks of envisioning and fighting to construct a better world – an 'alter-globalization' as many now call it – is inseparable from the struggle to tilt the balance against the United States' hegemonic ambitions, to dismantle its empire project. And the struggle to defeat its empire project is inseparable from the struggle against dominant classes in one's own countries, prepared to accommodate, in greater or lesser ways, to that project depending on how the wind blows. How that wind blows, however, will be determined ultimately by what ordinary people worldwide think and feel and ultimately how they might behave. Will they provide or deny the mass legitimacy that the empire-builders crave? There is, then, a particular responsibility for ordinary US citizens located in the heart of empire to oppose what the government and its supporting elites are doing in their name. This is the kind of 'leadership from below' that is needed and that will rally around it many, many millions throughout the world.

Nelson Mandela was once asked as to when he realized his struggle against apartheid was going to succeed? His answer was, 'when we realized that we had captured the moral imagination of enough people'. He did not say 'all the people', nor did he even say 'a majority of the people'. He simply said 'enough' people. There is a lesson here for all of us. What ordinary people, for example, the readers of this book, think, feel and behave matters a great deal. The US empire project will also collapse when its opponents have captured the moral imagination of enough people. It is this belief that has inspired the Transnational Institute to put together this volume as its way of contributing to the achievement of that goal.

Notes

[1] See Bobbit (2002). The supposed 'bible' of the neocons – the Project for a New American Century (PNAC) – has a number of signatories and a large number of supporters who come from outside this 'neocon cabal'. Other intellectuals who rallied to the flag on Iraq were Paul Berman, Michael Ignatieff and ex-leftist Christopher Hitchens.

[2] See the excellent collection of essays, especially the chapter by Freeman in Freeman and Kagarlitsky (2004). The discussion that follows owes much to Freeman's chapter.

[3] These are highlighted by the renowned scholar, Brian Barry (2005).

[4] The American, John Rawls could lay legitimate claim to being the most famous and frequently cited political philosopher of the twentieth century. He is best known for his classic work *A Theory of Justice* (1971) where he laid down his two principles of justice, the second one being that socio-economic inequalities could only be justified if in conditions of equal opportunity to all offices, they could be shown to favour the most disadvantaged. For all the huge impact that his theory had in US academia, it had no effect whatsoever on government policy.

[5] Perry Anderson (2002), founding editor of the *New Left Review* had this to say in his article 'Force and Consent':

'. . . the coordination problem can be satisfactorily resolved only by the existence of a superordinate power, capable of imposing discipline on the system as a whole, in the common interest of all parties. Such imposition cannot be a product of brute force. It must correspond to a genuine capacity of persuasion, ideally a form of leadership that can offer the most advanced model of production and culture of its day, as target of imitation for all others. That is the definition of hegemony, as a general unification of the field of capital. But at the same time, a hegemon must, can only, be a particular state: as such, inevitably possessed of a differential history and set of national peculiarities that distinguish it from all others. . . . By definition . . . a hegemon will possess features that cannot be shared by others, since it is precisely those that lift it above the ruck of its rivals. But at the same time, its role requires it to be as close to a generalizable, that is, reproducible model as practicable. Squaring this circle is, of course, in the end impossible, which is why there is an inherent coefficient of friction in any hegemonic order. Structurally, a discrepancy is built into the harmony whose function it is to install.'

Anderson also points out the structural differences of Western Europe from the United States that ensure unease in their relationship: 'In Western Europe on the other hand, virtually all the terms of the American equation are reversed. Nation-states are small or medium in size, easily besieged or invaded: populations go back to Neolithic times; social and cultural structures are saturated with traces of pre-capitalist origin; the balance of forces is less disadvantageous for labour; by and large, religion is a played-out force. Consequently, the centre of gravity of European political systems is to the left of the American, more socially protective and welfarist, even under governments of the right. In the relations between Europe and the US, there is thus abundant material for all kinds of friction, even combustion.'

What could be said of the cultural–ideational attraction of the United States outside Europe? Anderson does point out that it is least in West Asia both among elites and masses, which clearly makes the US effort to establish its hegemony in this region more difficult. But what he has not registered is that for the elites and middle classes of China and India, two rising powers, it is not Europe but the United States that provides the crucial point of reference for the kind of modernity they should strive for.

[6] These and other statistics obtained from Duminel and Levy (2001) and US National Income and Product Accounts (2004).

[7] There are two senses in which the term 'hegemony' is used. In one case it is taken as a synonym for the organization of consent; in the other, as above, it is taken to comprise the domains of both force and consent.

References

Anderson, Perry (2002), 'Force and Consent', *New Left Review*, Vol. 17, September–October.

Arendt, Hannah (1968), *Imperialism* (New York: Harcourt, Brace, Jovanovich).

Barry, Brian (2005), *Why Social Justice Matters* (Cambridge: Polity Press).

Bhagwati, Jagdish (2004), *In Defense of Globalization* (New Delhi: Oxford University Press).

Bobbit, Philip (2002), *The Shield of Achilles: War, Peace and the Course of History* (New York: Alfred Knopf).

Brzezinski, Zbigniew (2005), *The Choice: Global Domination or Global Leadership* (New York: Basic Books).
Duminel, G. and D. Levy (2001), 'Costs and Benefits of Neoliberalism, A Class Analysis', *Review of International Political Economy*, Vol. 8, No. 4.
Freeman, A. and B. Kagarlitsky (eds) (2004), *The Politics of Empire: Globalization in Crisis* (London: Pluto Press and the Transnational Institute).
Fukuyama, Francis (2006), *America at the Crossroads: Democracy, Power and the Neoconservative Legacy* (New Haven: Yale University Press).
Hobsbawm, Eric (2002), *Interesting Times: A Twentieth-Century Life* (London: Allen Lane).
National Income and Product Accounts (2004), Bureau of Economic Analysis, US Department of Commerce.
Therborn, G. (1995), *European Modernity and Beyond: The Trajectory of European Societies 1945–2000* (London: Sage Publications).

Contributors

MARIANO AGUIRRE is the Director of Spanish International Relations Foundation (FRIDE), and a Fellow of the Transnational Institute. He is the author of *La Ideología Neoimperial: La Crisis de EEUU con Irak* (2003).

TARIQ ALI is an independent writer, playwright and filmmaker based in London, and a member of the editorial board of *New Left Review*. His latest books include *The Clash of Fundamentalisms* (2003), *Bush in Babylon* (2003) and *Rough Music* (2006).

WALDEN BELLO is Director of Focus on the Global South; a Programme Board member of the International Centre for Trade and Sustainable Development, Geneva; and Fellow of the Transnational Institute. He is the author of *Dilemmas of Domination: The Unmaking of the American Empire* (2005).

PHYLLIS BENNIS is Fellow of the Institute for Policy Studies, Washington DC. She is also a Fellow of the Transnational Institute. Her latest book is *Challenging Empire: How People, Governments and the UN Defy US Power* (2006).

DAVID BEWLEY-TAYLOR is Professor of American Foreign Policy at the University of Wales Swansea, United Kingdom. His latest book is *The United States and International Drug Control: 1909–1997* (2001).

SUSAN GEORGE is Vice President of ATTAC France, and Chair of the Planning Board of the Transnational Institute. Her recent books include *Another World is Possible If...* (2004) and *Nous, Peuple d'Europe* (2005).

MARTIN JELSMA is Coordinator of the Transnational Institute Drugs & Democracy Programme, a Fellow of the Transnational Institute and author of *Trouble in the Triangle: Opium and Conflict in Burma* (2005).

MIKE MARQUSEE is an independent journalist and writer based in London. His latest books include *Redemption Song: Muhammed Ali and the Spirit of the Sixties* (1999) and *Chimes of Freedom: The Politics of Bob Dylan* (2003).

ZIA MIAN is a physicist by training and expert on nuclear disarmament issues. He is currently Lecturer in Public and International Affairs at the Woodrow Wilson School, Princeton University. He is co-editor of *Out of the Nuclear Shadow* (2001).

DAVID SOGGE is an independent consultant to NGOs on development aid and aid policy and a specialist on southern Africa. He is also a Fellow of the Transnational Institute. He has written *Give & Take: What's the Matter with Foreign Aid?* (2002).

ACHIN VANAIK is Professor of International Relations and Global Politics at the Political Science Department of the University of Delhi. He is a Fellow of the Transnational Institute and has edited *Globalization and South Asia: Multidimensional Perspectives* (2004).

Index